TRANSFORMING VISIONS:
Feminist Critiques in
Communication Studies

THE HAMPTON PRESS COMMUNICATION SERIES

Feminist Studies
Lana Rakow, supervisory editor

Transforming Visions: Feminist Critiques in Communication Studies
  Sheryl Perlmutter Bowen and Nancy Wyatt (eds.)

Forthcoming

Women's Friendships Across Cultures
  Mary McCollough

TRANSFORMING VISIONS:
Feminist Critiques in Communication Studies

edited by

Sheryl Perlmutter Bowen
Villanova University

Nancy Wyatt
Penn State-Delaware County Campus

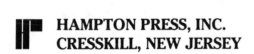 HAMPTON PRESS, INC.
CRESSKILL, NEW JERSEY

Printed in the United States of America

Library of Congress Cataloging-in-Publication Data

Transforming visions: feminist critiques in communication studies, edited by Sheryl P. Bowen and Nancy Wyatt.
p.   cm.—(The Hampton Press communication series. Feminist studies)
Includes bibliographical references and index.
ISBN 1-881303-06-3 (cloth).—ISBN 1-881303-07-1 (paper)
1. Communication—Research. 2. Communication—Sex differences.
3. Feminist theory. I. Bowen, Sheryl P. (Sheryl Perlmutter)
II. Wyatt, Nancy. III. Series.
P91.3.T74 1992
302.2'082—dc20

92-38173
CIP

Hampton Press, Inc.
23 Broadway
Cresskill, NJ 07626

Table of Contents

Preface   vii
Acknowledgments   xi

Visions of Synthesis, Visions of Critique
    Sheryl Perlmutter Bowen and Nancy Wyatt   1

Enlarging Conceptual Boundaries: A Critique of
Research in Interpersonal Communication
    Julia Wood   19

Organizing and Relating: Feminist Critique of
Small Group Communication
    Nancy Wyatt   51

Performing Differences: Feminism and
Performance Studies
    Kristin M. Langellier, Kathryn Carter,
    and Darlene Hantzis   87

New Voices in Organizational Communication:
A Feminist Commentary and Critique
    Marlene G. Fine   125

Aristotle and Arimneste ("Nicanor's Mother"):
Theatre Studies and Feminism
    Patti P. Gillespie   167

Opposites in an Oppositional Practice:
Rhetorical Criticism and Feminism
    Celeste Michelle Condit   205

Feminist Critique of Mass Communication Research
    Cynthia M. Lont   231

Enlarging Conceptual Boundaries: A Critique of Research
in Intercultural Communication
    Alberto Gonzalez and Tarla Rai Peterson   249

Author Index   279
Subject Index   291

Preface

The chapters in this volume incorporate the work of many more scholars and collaborators than could be represented in a single slim volume. This collective effort had its beginnings partly in a small conference organized at Penn State University in 1984 by Julia T. Wood and Gerald M. Phillips. At this initial conference, participants addressed issues of gender and communication research. The conference was carefully crafted to be interactive, and the participants focused on defining issues and clarifying perspectives. The participants sought to create a collaborative climate in which questions could be explored and definitions and concepts could evolve with supportive criticism of colleagues from a variety of disciplines. At that conference, the participants decided not to organize formally, but to maintain a flexible structure in keeping with the feminist stance described by Gilligan (1982). Not surprisingly, most of the participants at this initial conference were women. Most of the participants of this annual floating conference are still women. The conference was held again at Penn State University for several years. The specific impetus for this book came from the conference held at the Delaware County Campus of Penn State University, where the participants suggested that we summarize our discussions in a book.

Participating in this conference over the years has been an invigorating and exhilarating experience. Each year the conference takes on a new focus and form and includes different people, as the planners build on past experience to envision new goals and directions. Unlike many more formal conferences, dialogue is often informal and passionate as perspectives clash, shatter, and arise again from their own shards. But careful attention to process, which is the focus of this conference, counters the centrifugal force of this whirlwind of conversation/discussion/argument that characterizes each session. Our thanks to the many participants who have contributed to the creation of this book.

A second impetus for this volume developed from the critical work carried on by members of the Women's Caucus of the Speech Communication Association. Panels critiquing traditional speech communication research elicited disagreements, rebuttals, and more panels as dialogue developed within the formal structure of annual conventions. The same passion and commitment so evident in the gender and communication research conference has characterized this interaction. The articles and position papers written for these panels informed the work of the authors of the chapters in this volume, in particular, articles published in special issues of *Women's Studies in Communication*, Volume 11, 1988, and *Journal of Communication Inquiry*, Volume 11, 1987. We are proud to have been a part of this process, which created in 1990 a new Division of Feminist and Women Studies within the Speech Communication Association. Clearly feminist scholarship is proving vital to the discipline and is beginning to receive official recognition. We hope that this volume will prove to be another part of the important process of bringing feminist insights into our discipline.

Editing a volume like this one has been a challenging task. The very task of envisioning the book has entailed a number of important philosophical and practical decisions. We began also with the goal of incorporating our feminist principles into the process of writing and editing this book, as well as into the content of the chapters. That meant that we all had to collaborate on the whole book, and that meant that we had to come to some agreement on goals and definitions, or we had to agree to disagree. In the end we did both. We began with a group of authors who contributed chapter proposals in their areas of speech communication. Supported by editors Brenda Dervin and Barbara Bernstein, we all met at the 1989 SCA convention to work out a focus and a modus operandi. At that meeting, we worked out many of the philosophical, strategic, and practical details of creating this book.

Feminism advocates interdisciplinary study by breaking down artificial barriers between areas of scholarship. We had to decide whether to live up to our principles by spanning boundaries and creating new areas for communication study based on feminist perspectives or whether we should limit ourselves in this initial effort to the critique of traditional areas of study within the relatively amorphous discipline called speech communication. Meeting as a group of authors, we decided that our primary goal was to reach the widest possible audience and that goal could be achieved most easily by working within familiar areas of scholarship, providing critiques and correctives to the traditional scholarship that has historically excluded women's and minority concerns and perspectives. By detailing the distortions within traditional areas of our discipline, we could position ourselves to argue for new definitions and new connections among the disparate areas of our discipline.

We all began with a common outline in three parts: (a) summary and critique of the traditional literature in our respective areas, (b) summary and critique of the feminist research and theory in that area, and (c) suggestions for further research or theory that seemed called for by a feminist perspective. When our first drafts were completed, we all read every chapter and provided comments and criticisms to one another for improvements. This procedure proved to be extremely helpful, not only because we learned a great deal about areas in speech communication with which we were not previously familiar, but also because we found that our own expertise had something to contribute to other areas of our discipline. Each chapter also went through the traditional review process by outside readers, both feminist and nonfeminist. At the 1990 SCA convention, the authors all met again briefly to choose a title and renew our commitment to the project and to the process.

We envision this volume as an introduction to feminist theory and practice for our colleagues and the graduate students who will become our colleagues in future years. Most of us have had to learn our feminism from other disciplines or through individual study. Very few courses in speech communication incorporate either feminist readings or feminist principles or practices. We hope to change that by providing a volume that can be used as supplementary reading for any course in speech communication—graduate or undergraduate. Our volume can also provide an introduction to feminism and feminist critique of our discipline for scholars who are still asking, "What do those feminists want?"

USING THIS TEXT

We chose the title for this volume with care. *Transforming Visions* is a small but ambitious effort to recast our collective vision of the speech communication discipline in light of important social, political, and economic changes affecting our universities, our nation, and the world. The next century, now only a few years away, will see our world, the nation-states that now comprise that world, and the social institutions that comprise the nation-states radically altered. Universities and disciplines within those universities will not be immune to these changes. As scholars we cannot proceed with business as usual while the world outside is in radical transition. The authors of the chapters in this book offer new visions of the possibilities open to our discipline as we participate in some of the exciting social transformations now affecting our universities as well as other social institutions.

There are nine chapters in this book. Following this chapter, eight chapters critique traditional content areas of communication studies. Deciding exactly how to place the chapters was a difficult decision. One of the most fascinating and frustrating aspects of our discipline is that you never know exactly where departments will be placed within a university. Communication studies incorporate both humanistic studies and the social sciences. Sometimes we call ourselves art and sometimes science. The fact that we cross these lines ourselves makes it doubly difficult to categorize and classify our own work. We finally decided to arrange these chapters by their context, from smallest to largest. After an introductory essay, the next three chapters proceed from interpersonal to small group to organizational communication. Following are chapters on theater, rhetoric, and mass communication. Intercultural communication, the focus of the last chapter, is perhaps the most recent to gain a stronghold in the field, and the authors provide caveats regarding the inclusion of culture to scholars working in any area of communication studies.

While each essay focuses on a specific area of specialization within communication studies, we urge readers not to read selectively. Resist the impulse to listen only to familiar voices or to read only in the areas with which you are already knowledgeable. Each chapter complements every other chapter, and no single chapter is exhaustive. The power of the feminist critique is most evident in its application across the artificial boundaries of our subdisciplinary specialties. Each scholar presents a slightly different definition and application of feminist critique, and the harmony of these various perspectives is both complementary and illuminating. Unfortunately, we do not have chapters from every special area within communication studies. We do not, for example, have chapters from health communication, political communication, instructional communication, human communication technologies, nonverbal communication, and many other areas. We hope that our book will inspire other scholars to apply similar critiques to other areas in communication studies, and in the process, to discover new and revolutionary ways of viewing communication research and theory in those areas.

We invite you to step outside your traditional academic garb and stance to view our discipline through a different set of lenses. What you read may intrigue or infuriate you, may liberate or dismay you. We hope that you will in any case be interested enough to read the whole volume and to respond as you feel appropriate either personally or in some other form to the ideas we present in this volume.

REFERENCE

Gilligan, C. (1982). *In a different voice: Psychological theory and women's development.* Cambridge, MA: Harvard University Press.

Acknowledgments

We would like to thank the many scholars whose names are not on the chapters but who helped considerably in a variety of ways to create and refine the ideas presented in this book. Our special thanks to Barbara Bate, Oscar G. Brockett, James Chesebro, Gladys Crane, Caren J. Deming, Brenda Dervin, Dennis S. Gouran, Lee Jenkins, Lynne Kelly, Beverly W. Long, Paula Michal-Johnson, Robert Shuter, and Mary S. Strine for thoughtful manuscript reviews. Brenda Dervin and Lana Rakow provided valuable contact between publisher and discipline. We are honored to continue our working relationship with Barbara Bernstein, who has provided unflagging support for this project since its inception. There are surely others whose names we have left out who have made their marks on our thinking, writing, and developing. To all of you, we express our gratitude.

Chapter 1

Visions of Synthesis, Visions of Critique

Sheryl Perlmutter Bowen
Villanova University
Villanova, PA

Nancy Wyatt
Delaware County Campus
Penn State University
Media, PA

In his book *Seeing Voices: A Journey Into the World of the Deaf*, Oliver Sacks (1989) describes his discovery of the completely visual American Sign Language and how it illuminated his own taken-for-granted understanding of oral and verbal language. "It is all too easy," he says, "to take language, one's own language, for granted—one may need to encounter another language, or rather another *mode* of language, in order to be astonished, to be pushed into wonder, again" (p. ix). In our own discipline, we often take for granted our own understandings of communication and of speech, going about our business as usual in our classrooms, conferences, and committees. In this volume, we hope to offer readers a new perspective on our ordinary understanding of communication—a new perspective from an alternative point of view. We don't have anything as radical as a completely new form of language. What we do have is a different vocabulary and a fresh way of looking at the phenomena that we deal with, both as scholars and as ordinary people, every day of our lives. We hope that readers will come away with a new perspective on communication studies, with new questions and with a renewed appreciation for the complexity and sophistication of the ordinary communication processes we study.

1

One of the most important developments currently in progress is the inclusion of women and minorities as important and increasingly activist elements in the social, political, and economic arenas. We invite readers to explore the possibilities opened up to our discipline with the inclusion of women and minorities in our research and theory. The essays in this volume offer new accounts of the roots of our discipline and how that discipline has grown and prospered, as well as how it has been pruned and shaped by specific social and political agendas. Our authors offer insights and suggestions on ways in which communication studies scholars can contribute significantly to shaping the discipline to meet the challenges that will be inevitable in the 21st century.

In this volume we present a feminist analysis and critique of communication studies. While feminism has had various and important effects on many other areas in the humanities and social sciences, its impact in our own area is less clear. In this volume, scholars from a variety of specialty areas within communication studies have done that for us. They have stepped outside the traditional knowledge base of their areas to provide summaries and critiques of their respective areas from a feminist perspective. Each scholar has discovered discrepancies, distortions, and lacunae within traditional scholarship resulting from the absences of women and minorities in theorizing and in the research process. By applying a feminist perspective, the authors of the essays in this volume have suggested new research foci that will invite innovative insight into the communication processes that will be useful to us during the social changes that will take place in the future.

GENERALIZATIONS ABOUT FEMINISM

There is no single definition of "feminism," or "feminist" precisely because it is the nature of "feminism" and "feminist" thought and inquiry to resist definitive statements. Feminism is essentially an oppositional practice within a structure and context that is sometimes more and sometimes less inimical to its existence. Despite the difficulties in defining just one mode of feminism or feminist thought, there are a number of statements that may ease the understanding of what is generally meant by feminism. The following statements are meant to provide an introductory-level summary of feminist thinking and research, capturing the flavors of the feminist scholars writing in this volume and in others. As many have discussed, feminism is concerned with a variety of social, personal, economic, professional, philosophical, and political questions.

Feminism is concerned with women's lives. Feminism seeks to take women from the margins of society and of scholarly attention and to center them and their concerns as the focus of study and theory. To this end some feminists work to document women's absence from theory and practice and to recover women's history and contributions to society and to scholarship. In their chapter in this volume, Gonzalez and Peterson (Chapter 9) have called this process "excavating women's voices from their tombs." Feminist scholars are exploring the lacks, the losses, the lacunae, and the silences where women have been ignored or oppressed and where we might otherwise expect their presence and voices to have had an effect. Some feminists seek to [re]discover and document female authorities and thinkers from the past; some study the attitudes and practices that have suppressed or marginalized and continue to suppress and marginalize women and women's thought and work.

In the same way that scientists after 1895 began to see x-rays where they had not seen them before (Kuhn, 1970), the feminist perspective has generated the study of phenomena reflecting sexual politics that had not been previously studied. For example, rape, spouse abuse, sexuality, childbirth, housework, incest, sexual harassment, pornography, and prostitution are all now studied by social scientists. Other examples of newly studied topics include the gendered nature of language, environmental policy, technology, body language, everyday talk, and advertisements (Nielsen, 1990).

Feminism is concerned with theories about humans. Some feminists are involved in analyzing models of human behavior and the extent to which those models do or do not reflect women's experiences, insights, values, attitudes, and knowledge. Feminists are concerned with the analysis of taken-for-granted knowledge about humans and question the basis of assumptions about the nature of human nature. Some feminists take as their work the analysis of the social construction of meaning, particularly in the analysis of concepts such as "masculinity" and "femininity." Feminists study the ways in which gender as a concept is socially and symbolically constructed, as well as the ways in which human social institutions are gendered. Some feminists struggle with the definition of gender, with the processes of gendering, and with the effect of gendering on human behavior and social institutions.

Feminism is concerned with issues of social practice. Specifically, feminists focus on the differences between women and men in wealth, power, access, work, and opportunity. Feminism is concerned with the economic, political, and legal difficulties women face and with all such forms of oppression. Feminism is activist, seeking to change or eliminate oppressive practices. Feminist research partakes in this activism, undertaking research in order to empower women and other oppressed minorities. Some feminists seek redistribution of wealth and resources, and some feminists seek reform of the whole social, legal, and economic system. In particular, feminism is concerned with empowering women and other oppressed minorities to generate and promulgate knowledge, since knowledge is an important source of power. The social change sought by feminists extends beyond women to all other oppressed groups, including ethnic minorities, children, old people, the differently abled, and so on. While some feminists emphasize the connection among women, and some emphasize the differences, both are agreed on the importance of fighting oppression against women wherever they find it. Feminism is revolutionary.

Feminism is concerned with the nature of knowledge. Feminists seek to place women at the center of the generation of knowledge by empowering women to name and own their experiences. Feminists consider all humans to be capable of generating knowledge about themselves and their own experience; all humans are active agents and constructors of meanings. Having experienced "objectivity" as subjects of research, many feminists argue that women's double consciousness—knowing both their own subjective world and the description of that world generated by mainstream scholars—enables them to be particularly sensitive to and cognizant of the complexity of human experience within a particular society and culture. The act of naming is an act of power; feminism is particularly concerned with language and the relationship between language and reality. Feminism uses the analysis of sexist, racist, classist, and other forms of oppressive language as a method by which to analyze the ideological underpinnings of social structures and forms and their effect on the humans who create and inhabit those forms.

Feminism is concerned with the ways in which knowledge is generated and legitimated. Feminists are overtly self-reflexive, accounting for personal experience in their selection or construction of research questions as well as in the political goals and methodology of their research. The personal is the political, and the professional concern is also the personal concern. Feminists analyze and critique research methodologies to develop or adapt ones that are amenable to their research goals and consistent with their philosophies. Feminists seek to bring diverse methodologies to the study of complex reality. Interdisciplinary and cross-disciplinary connections are very evident in the work of most feminists, as are connections between the academy and the community. Feminists are concerned with connecting the theoretical with the practical, the personal with the academic, and feminist with traditional knowledge. Feminists are particularly concerned with finding the right questions to ask; they connect their research questions to questions about appropriate and legitimate research goals, methods, and the uses to which the knowledge will be put. Some feminists work within traditional forms, while others challenge those forms. Again, this diversity is generally seen as a strength and the dialogue among scholars as useful to the community as well as to scholarship.

Feminism is concerned with the "canon" of traditional knowledge. Feminists question the standards by which knowledge is judged to be legitimate or not. Categories such as "public" and "private" come under suspicious analysis, and the definition of what is considered "rational" or "logical" is equally suspect. Feminists concern themselves with the construction and maintenance of privilege in any form, particularly the privilege of naming, defining, and judging. Feminists argue for the inclusion of many truths and for a variety of perspectives, for empowering the voices of previously oppressed minorities in deciding what is and is not considered to be true or valuable. Within the academy, feminists challenge the definitions of what is and is not scholarship, arguing for broader and more inclusive definitions and categories. Feminists study the ways and the extent to which ideas and language are gendered and the effects of such gendering on people's everyday lives.

The essays in this volume question the canon by offering reinterpretations of previously unexplored phenomena. Langellier, Carter, and Hantzis (Chapter 4) urge reconceptualization of oral interpretation into performance studies, broadening the canon and shifting the focus from emphasis on the voice to emphasis on the body. Wood (Chapter 2) urges another look at the model of exchange presumed in mainstream interpersonal communication theory and a broadening of study to include more than heterosexual romantic relationships. Wyatt (Chapter 3) explicates a number of questions that were left unasked in previous research. Fine (Chapter 5) recommends empowering members of organizations by including them in the design and interpretation of organizational communication studies.

Feminism is concerned with process and with connection. In studying women and women's lives, feminists often share a fundamental identity with the participants in their research. Such identity is seen as a strength, not a drawback, to the research process, as feminists also seek to empower the participants in their research to name their own experiences and to share in the research design and process. Studying connections and relationships is a very complex undertaking, entailing careful attention to assumptions and methods. Recognizing their personal connections to their professional research, feminists struggle with the concepts of objectivity and subjectivity and with the political and practical implications of these definitions to their work. Feminists seek to explicate their own political, epistemological, and methodological commitments as well as to describe and critique traditional scholarship. Feminists struggle with concepts of diversity and plurality, with competing voices, and with alternative interpretations of reality. Ethical concerns play a very important part in feminist inquiry and theorizing.

In general, these are the concerns the reader will find reflected in the essays in this volume. Each chapter will reflect some of these concerns; probably no chapter reflects them all. We consider it a strength of the volume that our authors disagree among themselves about the definition and nature of feminism and of feminist research and inquiry. Each author's position will illustrate for readers one possible perspective on feminism and on communication scholarship. We do not claim that the views of our authors represent the final word on a feminist analysis or critique of any areas represented in this volume. Other scholars might have written different chapters, and we welcome disagreement and discussion. The main aim of this book is to generate discourse on the nature and practice of the study of communication, and we solicit responses from all scholars who find our views exciting, illuminating, controversial, or even possibly offensive.

Having so far summarized a set of principles which loosely define a feminist perspective, we now turn to addressing the relative impact of feminism on the academic environment and on communication studies.

COMMUNICATION STUDIES, FEMINISM, AND THE ACADEMY

In developing this volume, we contextualized feminist theory and research from our own discipline within a more general framework of academe. The task was formidable for several reasons. Within our own discipline, communication studies cross over the traditional division between humanities and social sciences. But, as we learned in working on this book, to be well read in all areas of communication studies is nearly impossible. To complicate our task, we found that the boundaries of communication scholarship overlap and interface not only within areas of our own discipline, but also within related disciplines. The development of feminist theory and research in communication studies parallels or follows the development of feminist thought in many other academic disciplines. Far from seeing these connections as a weakness, or feminist communication studies as derivative, we see this cross-disciplinary fertilization as entirely in keeping with the philosophical commitment of feminism to interdisciplinary studies. In *The Impact of Feminist Research in the Academy*, Farnham (1987) documented feminist contributions to anthropology, history, religious studies, psychology, biology, economics, political science, English, and sociology.

Nielsen (1990) has argued that feminist scholarship represents a "paradigm shift" (à la Kuhn, 1970), an explanatory framework she uses to discuss the many reinterpretations, reconstructions, and reanalyses of existing data from new feminist perspectives. Anomalous findings sparked by the inclusion of women's lives and experiences forced new theories and explanations, as in Kelly-Gadol's work on the Renaissance in history (1976), Gilligan's work in psychology on moral development (1982), or Johnson's work on the language of women (1983). We have also seen resistance and conversion to this shift in communication studies, as discussed by such authors as Goodall (1990) and Pearce and Cronen (1980). Finally, studies which include gender as a significant focus are increasingly becoming "normalized" in communication studies. This has not happened rapidly, but there are signs that it is occurring

As scholarship changes and evolves, we find ourselves working in the midst of continual revisions and redefinitions, both of content areas and of cognitive domains. Disciplinary boundaries within the academy and within our own field have become closer to administrative categories than conceptual delineations, and we have found it difficult to state with any degree of certainty that any single perspective characterizes communication studies. Needless to say, we have found that defining a "feminist perspective" for communication studies has proven equally elusive.

Feminism has been used as a general framework of thought, as well as a more specific platform or agenda for change (Hirsch & Keller, 1990). As each author in this volume has pointed out, feminism holds various meanings for different people—scholars and nonscholars alike. Our authors have defined "feminism" for their specific essays, and the definitions have varied widely. The single element that seems to unite most definitions of feminism is the conviction that feminist critique and theory is driven by a recognition of women's subordination in many personal and professional spheres. Feminists are concerned with the ways in which women live in, know, act in, and experience the world; interests that have not been represented in traditional, "malestream" academe. The authors in this volume have also argued that change is imperative, although some authors have advocated a more explicitly radical program than others. For all the scholars who have contributed directly or indirectly to this project, a feminist transformation is imperative for the growth and legitimacy of communication studies. Feminism focuses on process, not product, so it is the connections and relationships among ideas that constitute our focus. Feminists, then, are not necessarily seeking truth so much as they are seeking to continue the dialogue.

THE CONTINUED PRESENCE OF FEMINISM IN COMMUNICATION STUDIES

Foss and Foss (1989) also link their review of feminist studies of communication to new paradigm research. Feminist scholarship has been showcased at specialized conferences such as the Conference on Research on Gender in Communication and at conferences sponsored by the Organization for the Study of Communication, Language, and Gender (OSCLG). OSCLG has recently aligned itself with the journal *Women and Language*, which has been another outlet for feminist research. Regional associations have groups that include feminist work. The Western Speech Communication Association includes the Organization for Research on Women and Communication (ORWAC) and publishes *Women's Studies in Communication*. In the Eastern Communication Association, however, women's studies are included within a broader division named "Minority Voices." The Speech Communication Association has long had a Women's Caucus, which advocated for women within the organization and sponsored conference programs of feminist and women's studies. At the 1990 SCA convention, a new division of Feminist and Women Studies was created to sponsor scholarly work, while the Women's Caucus remains as a political group acting on behalf of women's interests within the organization. The Feminist Scholarship Interest Group in the International Communication Association is very active. Outlets for feminist work are growing, and perusal of any speech communication convention program will reveal that feminist scholarship is programmed regularly, not only within women's and feminist interest groups, but also throughout the other divisions and interest groups in the various professional organizations.

While we can document considerable feminist activity at conferences and conventions, the audience for such research remains localized among scholars who are friendly and receptive to feminist interests. In such arenas, we are, so to speak, preaching to the choir. Communication scholars have edited several excellent volumes which contain feminist theoretical and research essays (e.g., Bate & Taylor, 1988; Carter & Spitzack, 1989; Lont & Friedley, 1989). Yet, dialogue within the larger community of communication scholars has been notably lacking. One important barrier that has hampered the dialogue between feminist and nonfeminist scholars in our field has been the limited number of feminist studies appearing in the mainstream communication journals. Feminist work in this arena is not entirely lacking. In the *Quarterly Journal of Speech*, Spitzack and Carter (1987) invited attention to women in communication studies by borrowing McIntosh's (1983) framework of phases for curriculum revision. Foss and Foss (1983) similarly reviewed the literature on women in communication (also see their essay in Carter & Spitzak, 1989). While eschewing the label "feminist," Dervin argued for "The Potential Contribution of Feminist Scholarship to the Field of Communication" in the *Journal of Communication* (Autumn 1987). Both *Women's Studies in Communication* (vol. 11, 1987) and *The Journal of Communication*

Inquiry (vol. 11, 1988) published special issues on gender and feminist studies. *Critical Studies in Mass Communication* devoted a recent issue to gender and empowerment (vol. 7(3), 1990), and *The Southern Communication Journal* Winter 1992 issue contained only articles on feminist criticism. Still, on the whole, feminist scholarship has been scant in major communication journals.

Many of the insights and critiques made in these articles and in the chapters in this volume have also been made by other scholars who do not call themselves feminist. We also like to think of this volume as informed by and contributing to a dialogue that includes critical voices from such sources as the annual *Communication Yearbook* series, as well as individual volumes that appear regularly. Several authors have referred to chapters in Benson's (1985) *Speech Communication in the Twentieth Century*. A more recent volume, *Speech Communication: Essays to Commemorate the 75th Anniversary of The Speech Communication Association* (Phillips & Wood, 1990), has several articles that make arguments similar to ones the reader will find in this volume. The authors in this volume will lead you to more such references, where mainstream scholars have voiced concerns similar to the ones expressed by feminist critics.

One problem in bringing feminist perspectives to the field of communication studies has been the relative absence of feminist scholarship in the classroom in both undergraduate and graduate programs. Most of the feminist scholars in speech communication have not learned their feminism in their own disciplines. Rather, they have gone outside speech communication to other disciplines or to women's studies programs to develop their feminist perspectives. While gender and communication courses have become more common, those courses are not necessarily taught from a feminist perspective. Too often such courses and the texts for them retain a traditional focus that does not encourage the kind of critical analysis espoused by feminist scholars. Young scholars interested in feminism and in women's issues are still cautioned against such scholarship as possibly being detrimental to their careers. Graduate students or new scholars in the field may feel constrained by the "either/or" choice of traditional study or feminist study. This is an unfortunate state of affairs and one which has prompted the design of this volume.

An additional pressing problem within the feminist community of scholars in communication studies has been how to reconcile the variety of perspectives calling themselves "feminist." Shall we remain pluralistic or shall we attempt to forge a more coherent definition of "feminism"? There are good arguments on both sides. Some scholars (e.g., Harding, 1986) have argued that pluralism is valuable and that feminists should work toward keeping the categories unstable. Only a complex variety of perspectives can begin to describe the realities that constitute our various experiences and the diversity of social forms. Since reality is complex, the foci and methods of study should reflect that complexity. Other scholars (e.g., Steeves, 1987) have cautioned against the lure of pluralism. A more coherent definition of feminist study, they argue, would encourage greater academic rigor and criticism and would allow for more a powerful political presence within the academy.

In this volume, we have opted for plurality. We have encouraged the authors to define feminism for their own chapters in order to illustrate for our readers as wide a variety of feminist perspectives as possible. We hope in this way also to demonstrate the dynamic nature of feminist theorizing and the emphasis on dialogue and discovery that is a vital part of feminist scholarship. As the chapters in this volume illustrate, feminists within communication studies have found themselves in varying positions regarding the masculinist and androcentric biases inherent in their areas. The politics of the subdisciplines and the range of acceptable theoretical perspectives have also differed among areas. In interpersonal communication, for example, there has been relatively little influence from feminist scholarship; almost no theoretical description of nonwhite or homosexual relationships exists, and little attention has been devoted to other than middle-class subjects. Interpersonal communication is fundamentally conservative in its metaphors and theoretical concepts. On the other hand, feminism has had a various and important presence in theater, where it has existed side by side with traditional practices. Feminist oppositional dialogue, Condit (Chapter 7) argues, fits nicely within the context of the dialogic nature of rhetorical studies. In general, we note that the humanities have been more hospitable to feminist perspectives than have the social sciences.

We believe that communication studies need all of these scholars working on the important issues of gender, class, and race as they affect human communication. Feminists from a variety of perspectives can contribute to communication study by expanding previous conceptions and theories. Feminists can continue to explore applied communication contexts, particularly pedagogy and health communication among them. Feminists can also contribute to communication studies by providing alternatives to traditional methodologies. By checking existing research goals and practices to insure that they fit with women's experiences, and by developing goals and practices that are compatible with women's experiences, feminist scholars can insure that the people we study are empowered by our study instead of oppressed or treated exclusively as subjects for our theorizing.

The research process, from conception to publication, is political and should be acknowledged as such. Women are still subordinate in many spheres, including academe, and we must address that subordination in order to rectify past errors. We must begin to correct the myth that research is linear and routine by acknowledging that it is fluid and that unpredictable things often happen in the research process (McGrath, Martin, & Kulka, 1982). We need to emphasize the interactive nature of research with human beings in order to take account of the complexity of not only the phenomena we are studying, but also of the research process itself. Feminist scholars have struggled and continue to struggle with just these issues. Feminist perspectives offer one avenue toward the realization of a study of social behavior that can encompass the complexity of our human nature.

VARIETIES OF FEMINISM USED BY VOLUME AUTHORS

Given the plurality of feminisms, instead of a definition, in this section we will present a catalog of feminisms and feminist thought drawn from all the chapters in this volume. In each of the chapters the reader will find some of these aspects of a feminist perspective, but they will also undoubtedly notice that many times the items in the catalog of feminist thought seem to contradict one another. For example, some feminists seek the inclusion of women within existing social structures and practices, while others seek the radical revision of existing social structures. Some feminists insist on gender as the basic social category that subsumes other social categories such as race and class, while other feminists insist that the very concept of gender is culturally embedded in those other categories. These points of view coexist and inform each other in a dialogue. Feminists do not see these differences as a weakness, but as a strength. Given that reality almost infinitely complex, how can we expect theory and inquiry to be otherwise?

Steeves (1987) has identified three positions as characterizing feminist scholarship in speech, media, and literary studies in the United States: liberal, radical, and socialist. Steeves explains that these feminist theoretical perspectives can be differentiated by their perceived locus for change. For radical feminists the locus for change lies in "biological manipulations and/or political separatism" (p. 96). Liberal feminists look to individual behavior and/or social psychological factors for change. Marxist and socialist feminists identify revolutionary sociocultural and economic events affecting social psychological conditions and individuals as necessary in order to bring about change. Steeves explains that each branch of feminism makes different assumptions about the role of the media and the function of communication in society. While there may be some disagreement concerning the labels, we have loosely characterized the authors' work in this volume as belonging to one of these three feminist positions.

Liberal feminism, according to Steeves, has had the most influence on feminism in the United States. Much of the research influenced by liberal feminism is based on assumptions about equal opportunity in achieving individual rational mental development, and focuses on the roles and images of women in literature and mass media. Some liberal feminist media research extends the analysis to the examination of how particular perceptions of reality are cultivated through media depiction of women and children. In communication studies, liberal feminists have compared women's speech to men's speech, often identifying styles conceptually as masculine, feminine, or androgynous. Most of the gender and communication textbooks fit squarely within this framework. Some of these texts by authors as well known as Pearson (1985) and Stewart, Cooper, and Friedley (1986) do not even mention feminism (Wood, 1991).

Marxist and socialist feminists address class oppression under capitalism as a fundamental factor in women's oppression and argue that race, class, sexual preference, and cultural background are important factors in a feminist analysis (Steeves, 1987). Some socialist feminists have attempted to reformulate psychoanalytic theory in explaining gender inequity. In the United States, some literary and film studies have incorporated socialist criticism. Most of the Marxist-influenced feminist research on the media has been carried out by British cultural studies scholars.

Steeves found little systematic research in communication studies which incorporates a radical perspective. This perspective often focuses on such highly controversial issues as pornography, and generally advocates the need for a separate feminist press. Radical feminists attempt to cultivate writing and speaking styles as separate and independent of men's styles, and exclusively study women's communication, including the communication of black and/or lesbian women. Steeves' definition may, however, be too stringent for some who consider their proposals for alternative study of gender and communication to be radically different from existent approaches.

The commitment to a particular definition or approach to feminism is undoubtedly the result of a complex mix of personal and professional experiences and concerns. In turn, the act of articulating or advocating a particular definition of feminism has important consequences in both professional and personal terms. Indeed, each type of feminism is characterized by some diversity in application. We look on this pluralism as a strength of the feminist perspective, as it allows a wide variety of insights and interpretations into the complex phenomena we include under the umbrella term "communication."

Within the loosely defined community of feminist communication scholars, we can identify two general groups: speech communication scholars interested in issues of gender, and women's studies scholars interested in communication. Each group's primary philosophical affiliation has influenced not only the kinds of research questions they pursue, but also the way in which they orient themselves toward research and toward the academy. The women's studies scholars seem willing to dismiss patriarchal restrictions on their research, and to move on to address different issues and to develop new theories and innovative research methods. We could expect more radical and socialist/Marxist research from these scholars. Speech communication scholars, in general, seem to prefer to work within their more traditional framework. As we have found, liberal feminism seems to predominate among these scholars.

Steeves is optimistic, as we are, that each of these feminist perspectives in communication studies will provide important additional perspectives in communication research and theory. We have attempted to categorize the various perspectives of the scholars who have contributed to this volume within this framework of liberal, radical, and socialist/Marxist feminisms. Jaggar (1983) and others have identified additional feminist categories, but we opted to narrow the field to three for the purposes of this volume. It proved difficult to put any of the essays into a single camp since the categories are necessarily abstract and idealized. Some of the authors specifically identify the liberal and radical contributions in their work, but for others we have had to infer their frameworks.

None of the authors in this volume espouses a radical feminist perspective, although some of the authors point to radical feminist critiques within their areas of communication scholarship. For example, both Gillespie in her chapter (Chapter 6) on theater and Langellier, Carter, and Hantzis in their chapter (Chapter 4) on performance note radical feminist scholarship in performance theory. Lont (Chapter 8) also describes attention to women's media as an example of a radical feminist research program.

The liberal feminist perspective is most clearly characterized in Condit's chapter (Chapter 7) on rhetorical theory. Condit is also perhaps the most optimistic of all the authors about the acceptability of feminist research in mainstream communication studies. She writes, "Rhetorical criticism is incorporating progressive feminism with relatively little hostility" (p. 208). She suggests that the gendering of rhetoric as a practice has provided a feminized alternative to male violence, despite the historical emphasis on rhetoric as an art appropriate for the public, male-dominated sphere. Condit offers a critique of rhetorical theory and criticism which fundamentally focuses on two points: the use of sexist language and the masculinist bias of the rhetorical canons. Condit calls for a "gynandrous" world in which women and men both employ ranges of the qualities we have mistakenly labeled either "feminine" or "masculine." She opposes the radical suggestions of other feminist critics, calling separatism "suicidal."

Wood's (Chapter 2) focus is very close to Condit's. While Condit says that feminist studies should be viewed broadly as "efforts that seek to increase our understanding of women's lives, their interests, and the social structures that gender human beings" (p. 208), Wood is interested in "exploring the nature and extent to which women and women's ways of knowing, acting, and experiencing are included and represented in research on interpersonal communication" (p. 20). Wood critiques exchange theory and the developmental models which have been commonly used to study interpersonal communication. However, Wood moves toward the socialist feminist position by suggesting that fundamental and structural changes are necessary to incorporate women's experiences into both the research process and the research questions. She calls for attention to collaborative knowing, daily talk, and self-concept as important and previously ignored areas of study. Wood calls for greater attention to reasons for initiating and ending relationships, as well as for greater attention to relationships other than the dyadic, heterosexual relationships usually studied in interpersonal communication. She also suggests studying the values for women and men in membership in informal social groups, and the motives for and dynamics of relationship in volunteer organizations. She argues that "interpersonal communication is an area of scholarship and pedagogy ideally situated to identify and act to alter oppressive, exploitative, and abusive practices in personal relationships" (p. 41).

Wyatt (small group communication), Langellier, Carter, and Hantzis (performance theory), Lont (mass communication), Fine (organizational communication), and Gonzalez and Peterson (intercultural communication) fit the definition of a socialist feminist perspective in that they see questions of gender inextricably tied to those of race and class, and in that they call for social change.

Wyatt (Chapter 3) conducts her feminist critique of small group communication from a perspective in which "gender, class, and race constitute major bases for social organization" (p. 51). She points out that small group research has historically left out the concerns of women in emphasizing work groups within organizations over volunteer and community groups. Too often researchers have not taken any notice of the gender, race, or class of their subjects. Wyatt envisions a feminist research program that would go beyond providing knowledge for its own sake or for the sake of increasing performance within an organizational structure. "Our research [should] be undertaken with the goal of empowering the people we study, not getting them to work harder for someone else" (p. 80).

Lont's (Chapter 8) critique of mass communication research has included more research influenced by feminist theory than some of the other areas of communication studies. Lont reports and critiques the liberal feminist research on mass media, as well as the historical narrative approach which looks at women as processors of media. In her view, which she identifies as a "feminist cultural approach," research should be "activist in nature, acknowledging that representations of women (and men) cannot change unless the structures of patriarchal economic and social relationships also change" (p. 241). Such a position places Lont within the socialist feminist perspective.

Gillespie (Chapter 6) documents the influence of feminism in theory and criticism of drama. Theater, like media studies, has had a feminist presence for some time. Tracing the evolution of feminist perspectives in theater, Gillespie reports that current feminist theory in theater has begun to consider "how ideology (especially that connected with gender) was embedded in texts and performances, how spectators were positioned to accept such ideologies unquestioningly, how feminists might best come to accept texts and performances in order to subvert them, and how performances might contribute to the disruption of such ideologies" (p. 31). She notes that examining the past in theater keeps males at the center of focus of criticism and suggests a number of productive research directions for feminist theater scholars.

Gonzalez and Peterson (Chapter 9) speak directly to the issue of ethnocentrism which is mentioned by many of the other authors in this volume. They remind us that the interconnections among such concepts as age, gender, race, and class may not be the same in all cultures. They argue that culture must be considered along with gender and class in efforts to theorize about communication. They echo Johnson's (1989) proposal for examining women's culture as a co-culture, existing parallel to men's (or dominant) culture. Gonzalez and Peterson see promising links between feminist perspectives and intercultural communication studies in the future.

Fine (Chapter 5) comes close to representing a radical viewpoint; however, we characterize her perspective as socialist feminist, since she argues not for separation but for transformation of existing organizational structures. Her interest as a feminist researcher is to "seek to understand how gender is socially and symbolically constructed within organizations and how organizations themselves are gendered" (p. 129). Fine reports that feminist researchers have studied problems central to women's experiences in organizations, such as sexual harassment, discrimination in hiring and promotion, family care policies, and inflexible work structures. Feminist researchers have also sought to identify the ways in which women define such work-related concepts as work, success, and supervision, as well as how women make decisions, supervise subordinates, and communicate with other organizational members. According to Fine, feminist research should address "women's problematics," which she defines as "the relationship between organizational structures and gender enactments" by "uncovering the ways that organizational ideologies, including hierarchy and bureaucracy, and modes of discourse silence oppress women and other powerless members of organizations" (p. 29). Fine proposes a "synalitic" methodology that would go beyond positivistic research to embrace subjective knowledge and replace the usual male-oriented definitions of concepts relevant to the understanding of organizations and organizational research.

Langellier, Carter, and Hantzis (Chapter 4) offer the most radical critique in this volume. After an extensive analysis of the masculinist and androcentric biases in theory, interpretation, and performance in their area of study, they conclude that feminist models cannot just be tacked on to extant theoretical models. Placing women in the center of inquiry and creating methods of reading that empower women requires asking sociopolitical and sexual-political questions about performance, performer, text, and audience. Langellier, Carter, and Hantzis conclude that although, so far, feminist study has been marginalized in the area of oral interpretation and performance studies, feminist scholarship offers extraordinarily rich resources for social change. It is this emphasis on social change as the object of research that leads us to categorize this chapter as radical in its perspective.

Regardless of the authors' feminist stance, these chapters extend the discussion of synthesis and critique in the communication discipline. Readers should want to learn from these authors, and then to ask questions, to develop new studies, in short, to continue the dialogue of feminism and communication studies.

REFERENCES

Bate, B., & Taylor, A. (Eds.). (1988). *Women communicating: Studies of women's talk.* Norwood, NJ: Ablex

Benson, T.W. (Ed.). (1985). *Speech communication in the twentieth century.* Carbondale: Southern Illinois University Press.

Carter, K., & Spitzack, C. (Eds.). (1989). *Doing research on women's communication: Perspectives on theory and method.* Norwood, NJ: Ablex.

Critical Studies in Mass Communication, 7(3), 1990.

Dervin, B. (1987). The potential contribution of feminist scholarship to the field of communication. *Journal of Communication, 37*(4), 107-120.

Farnham, C. (Ed.). (1987). *The impact of feminist research in the academy.* Bloomington: Indiana University Press.

Foss, K.A., & Foss, S.K. (1983). *The status of research on women and com-*

munication. Communication Quarterly, *31*, 195-204.

Foss, K.A., & Foss, S.K. (1989). Incorporating the feminist perspective in communication scholarship: A research commentary. In K. Carter & C. Spitzack (Eds.), *Doing research on women's communication: Perspectives on theory and method* (pp. 65-91). Norwood, NJ: Ablex.

Gilligan, C. (1982). *In a different voice: Psychological theory and women's development.* Cambridge, MA: Harvard University Press.

Goodall, H.L., Jr. (1990). A cultural inquiry concerning the ontological and epistemic dimensions of self, other and context in communication scholarship. In G.M. Phillips & J.T. Wood (Eds.), *Speech communication: Essays to commemorate the 75th anniversary of the Speech Communication Association.* Carbondale: Southern Illinois University Press.

Harding, S. (1986). *The science question in feminism.* Ithaca: Cornell University Press.

Hirsch, M., & Keller, E.F. (Eds.). (1990). *Conflicts in feminism.* New York: Routledge.

Jaggar, A.M. (1983). *Feminist politics and human nature.* Sussex, England: Harvester Press.

Johnson, F.L. (1989). Women's culture and communication: An analytical perspective. In C. Lont & C. Friedley (Eds.), *Beyond boundaries: Sex and gender diversity in communication* (pp. 301-316). Fairfax, VA: George Mason University Press.

Johnson, F.L. (1983). Political and pedagogical implications of attitudes towards women's language. *Communication Education, 31,* 133-138.

Kelly-Gadol, J. (1976). The social relation of the sexes: Methodological implications of women's history. *Signs, 1,* 809-823.

Journal of Communication Inquiry, 11, 1988.

Kuhn, T.S. (1970). *The structure of scientific revolutions* (2nd ed.). Chicago: University of Chicago Press.

Lont, C.M., & Friedley, S.A. (Eds.). (1989). *Beyond boundaries: Sex and gender diversity in communication.* Fairfax, VA: George Mason University Press.

McGrath, J.E., Martin, J., & Kulka, R.A. (1982). *Judgment calls in research.* Beverly Hills, CA: Sage.

McIntosh, P. (1983). *Interactive phases of curricular re-vision: A feminist perspective* (Working paper #124). Wellsley College Center for Research on Women. (Reprinted in B. Spanier, A. Bloom, & D. Boroviak (Eds.), *Toward a balanced curriculum.* Cambridge: Schenckman, 1984.)

Nielsen, J.M. (1990). *Feminist research methods: Exemplary readings in the social sciences.* Boulder, CO: Westview Press.

Pearce, W.B., & Cronen, V.E. (1980). *Communication, action and meaning: The creation of social realities.* New York: Preager.

Pearson, J.C. (1985). *Gender and communication.* Dubuque, IA: Wm. C. Brown. (2nd ed. w/ L.H. Turner & W. Todd-Mancillas, 1991).

Phillips, G. M., & Wood, J. T. (Eds.). (1990). *Speech communication: Essays to commemorate the 75th anniversay of the Speech Communication Association.* Carbondale: Southern Illinois University Press.

Sacks, O. (1989). *Seeing voices: A journey into the world of the deaf.* Berkeley, CA: University of California Press.

Southern Communication Journal, 57(2), 1992.

Spitzack, C., & Carter, K. (1987). Women in communication studies: A typology for revision. *Quarterly Journal of Speech, 73,* 401-423.

Steeves, H.L. (1987). Feminist theories and media studies. *Critical Studies in Mass Communication, 4,* 95-135.

Stewart, L., Cooper, P.J., & Friedley, S.A. (1986). *Communication between the sexes: Sex differences and sex role stereotypes.* Scottsdale, AZ: Gorsuch Scarisbrick. (2nd ed. also with A. Stewart, 1990).

Women's Studies in Communication, 11, 1987.

Wood, J.T. (1991). Politics, gender, & communication: A review of contemporary texts. *Communication Education, 40,* 116-123.

Chapter 2

Enlarging Conceptual Boundaries: A Critique of Research in Interpersonal Communication

Julia T. Wood
University of North Carolina
Chapel Hill, NC

Interpersonal communication is a rapidly growing area marked by prolific and diverse research. The impressive body of scholarship in this area is especially noteworthy given the relatively brief span of years in which interpersonal communication has gained salience as an area of scholarship and pedagogy.

The expansive character of this area is evident not only by the increasing number of courses, books, and articles, but also by the immediate success of a new journal devoted exclusively to it. In 1984, stating that research on interpersonal relationships had grown to exceed the resources of existing publication fora, *The Journal of Social and Personal Research* was launched to "publish work on all aspects of social and personal relationships by workers from any discipline" (Duck, Locke, McCall, Fitzpatrick, & Coyne, 1984, p. 1).

Considerable critical reflection has accompanied the quickly accumulating research on interpersonal communication. In addition to articles that evaluate specific selected foci of study, several recent major volumes have included broad critical assessments of interpersonal communication research (Bochner, 1984; Hewes, Roloff, Planalp, & Seibold, 1989; Rawlins, 1985). While each of these evaluative essays has offered valuable perspectives on interpersonal communication scholarship, the judgments rendered and—even more fundamentally—the questions posed and criteria invoked to evaluate research reflect conventional and conserv-

19

ative understandings of the research process and its products. That is to say, the essays rely on taken-for-granted assumptions that have long been entrenched in academic research. Within the framework of those assumptions the critiques have been useful.

The established frameworks for producing, understanding, and evaluating research, however, are themselves open to question. By stepping outside of accepted views and practices of research, it is possible to see a body of scholarship in new, often enlightening, ways. From an outside vantage point a critic may identify questions that have been ignored and assumptions whose influence on scholarship has not been adequately considered.

This chapter offers such a critique. Feminism, including its ideology, philosophy, and theory, informs my critical stance and moves it outside of conventional orientations to scholarship. While feminism reflects a complex and diverse intellectual tradition, its central concern is the inclusion and valuing of women, in society as well as in scholarship. Thus, this chapter—as a feminist critique—is especially interested in exploring the nature and extent to which women and women's ways of knowing, acting, and experiencing are included and represented in research on interpersonal communication. By intentionally adopting this partial focus I will be able to provide concentrated attention to the status of women in interpersonal communication scholarship and, by extension, to the integrity of the area itself which claims to be concerned with human, that is, male and female, interpersonal phenomena.

Three sections comprise this critique. First, I examine major trends in extant research on interpersonal communication in order to identify and comment upon the foci, methods, and assumptions that currently prevail. Next, I review specifically feminist research in interpersonal communication to discover whether it offers substantive insights and methodological approaches capable of transforming mainstream research. Finally, drawing on the first two sections, I suggest directions for future research that would be more inclusive and would reflect an enlarged understanding of human relationships and the communication that constitutes them.

CONTEMPORARY RESEARCH ON INTERPERSONAL COMMUNICATION

In the past seven years at least three broad assessments of research in interpersonal communication have been published (Bochner, 1984; Hewes et al., 1989; Rawlins, 1985). Another such comprehensive review would be duplicative and is not my goal here.

Instead, I wish to focus on four emphases in existing research on interpersonal communication. Two concern theoretical matters and two focus on methodological issues. First, I discuss exchange theory, which has achieved status as a theoretical orientation in the area. Second, I consider the pronounced emphasis on developmental views of relationships. The third emphasis I explore is methodological conventions that limit the relevance of research to a specific population: white, middle-class, heterosexual, educated, and somewhat liberal Americans. Finally, I examine the variable analytic approach that still dominates research; specifically, I discuss its tendency to reduce gender to a mere variable, a move that distorts gender's primacy as a fundamental constituent of human experience.

Social Exchange as the Primary Theoretical Orientation

Social exchange theory maintains that fundamental to all relationships is the principle of justice, which holds that there should be a balance between what one invests and what one receives from a relationship; that is, reciprocity is a primary consideration for partners in a relationship. This idea, basic to the various versions of exchange theory, represents the focus of the theory that enjoys a privileged place in interpersonal communication scholarship.

Reflective of the privileged status exchange theory enjoys are three widely used and cited textbooks by Knapp (1978), Miller and Steinberg (1975), and Roloff (1981) which rely on the reward/cost ratio of exchange theory as the explanatory principle of interpersonal communication. Equally influential have been writings from outside speech communication, notably those of Altman and Taylor (1973), Levinger and Snoek (1972), and Brehm (1985), all of which adhere to strict exchange theory. In addition, a spate of articles endorsing exchange theory have appeared in *The Journal of Social and Personal Relationships*, the premier publication in interpersonal communication (Argyle & Henderson, 1984; Cline, 1989; Lund, 1985; Michaels, Acock, & Edwards, 1986; O'Connell, 1984; Utne, Hatfield, Traupmann, & Greenberger, 1984). While a number of these publications voice some reservations about exchange theory and/or seek to qualify its tenets, they nonetheless indicate the prominence of exchange theory in explanations of interpersonal behavior.

Despite—or perhaps because of—its prominence, questions should be raised about the appropriateness of exchange as a—much less the—theoretical focus of research on interpersonal communication. One strong critical voice has come from Bochner, whose own commitments to a systems view of interpersonal relationships are not compatible with exchange theory. Less than convinced that exchange theory offers a viable explanation of relationships, Bochner noted (1984):

> For those writers willing to associate themselves with that most merce-
> nary metaphor of justice, economic exchange, social behavior is no
> different from any other marketplace transaction. The main rule in
> social interaction . . . is to make sure that profits are at least equal to
> losses. (p. 555)

Offering an extensive critique of social exchange, Bochner argues it is tau-
tological, fails to provide an adequate explanation of developmental
dynamics in relationships, and attempts to reduce the irreducible by viewing the interactive communication process within a fixed, individualistic,
and causal framework (pp. 578-579).

   In addition to sharing Bochner's reservations, I have two other
criticisms of social exchange as a theory of interpersonal relationships and
the communication within them. First, while exchange may explain both
marketplace and some social relationships, there is reason to doubt its per-
tinence to intimate or close relationships, for example, those between
friends, lovers, parents and children, siblings, and spouses. Intimacy differs
in important respects from other relationships. For instance, intimate relationships typically assume a long-term future and some personal commitment that transcends particular qualities, incidents, and so forth that
accrue from association. These differences seem ones that directly challenge the relevance of a theory based on a principle of strict exchange and
a computation of rewards and costs. More than speculation, this point is
supported by some convincing research which indicates that, indeed, intimacy may not be amenable to exchange explanations. A decade ago
McDonald (1981) reported that exchange principles are routinely violated
if trust and commitment exist between social actors. More recently, Clark,
Quellette, Powell, and Milberg (1987) found reciprocity actually led to
dissatisfaction in communal relationships such as families and romantic
bonds. O'Connell (1984) demonstrated that imbalances of exchange are
tolerated without resentment in relationships marked by trust and long-
term commitment. Finally, Lund (1985) reported that love and rewards are
less predictive of relationship continuity than are investment and commitment.

   These findings cast substantial doubt on the appropriateness of
exchange as a complete or even primary way of explaining behavior in
intimate relationships. Given this finding, we should have textbooks on
intimacy that make use of alternative theoretical explanations or, at the
very least, that do not rely exclusively on exchange. Before this can come
about, however, there must be research that seriously explores alternative
theoretical frameworks for close relationships.

   A second criticism of exchange is that it reflects a set of values
and assumptions that largely exclude feminine interests. The instrumental
and individually centered criteria for evaluating relationships that

exchange insists upon—equity, reciprocity, and positive outcomes—seem inconsistent with what we know of feminine (and often, but not necessarily, women's) values and relationship orientations. Some feminist theorists (Bernard, 1971; Jaquette, 1984), in fact, argue that the language of self-interest with its utilitarian overtones is incompatible with the interpersonal reality learned by most women in a gender-conscious social order. Diamond and Hartsock (1981), for example, reject concepts of interests altogether and propose needs as a concept more appropriate to women's ways of experiencing and acting within interpersonal relationships. This proposal recognizes (as exchange theory does not) the reproductive labor of intimacy (i.e., that occurring in the private sphere: nurturing, homemaking, caretaking), and (again, as exchange does not) it accords value to reproductive activities.

Gilligan's early research (1982), as well as related work by Belenky, Clinchy, Goldberger, and Tarule (1986), Wood (1986; in press), Miller (1986), and Schaef (1981) indicate that women tend not to think of relationships in terms of equity, fairness of outcomes, or individuals' rewards and costs. Decidedly, more empirically characteristic of women is a stance that emphasizes "showing care." The caring orientation would predictably be most pronounced in caring and caretaking relationships (e.g., parent-child, taking care of an elderly parent or in-law) where women disproportionately situate themselves. Given these research findings, we would expect needs, not rights, to be the focus of women's thought about and actions in relationships (see Petchesky, 1980, 1983), and we would expect maintaining a connection to be a more primary goal than achieving a positive balance sheet. Foci such as showing care, responding to needs, and sustaining connections have no place in exchange theory. They are irrelevant to the preeminent theory of interpersonal phenomena. Thus, exchange theory excludes what recent research suggests many women learn as the "appropriate" ways to define themselves and their attitudes and actions in relationship to others.

An exchange framework has potential both to suppress and to distort women's interpersonal experiences. By not including concepts such as care and needs, it suppresses, that is, neglects what may be central in how women typically learn to perceive and communicate within relationships. Further, the concepts that are emphasized within exchange theory are ones that potentially distort and misrepresent many women's experiences by forcing them into conceptual categories that are alien to ways in which many women have learned to think and feel about interpersonal relationships (Spender, 1980).

But Exchange Works. Criticisms of exchange can easily be dismissed by arguing that, in fact, exchange does "work;" that is, it describes how many relationships, including ones in which women participate, operate. One reader of an early draft of this chapter responded with the comment that "I use it in my classes and students do understand and agree with exchange as the basis of many, if not all, of their relationships." I cannot refute this response; I actually agree with it—as far as it goes. Yet, in two ways I do find it wholly inadequate as a "defense" of exchange as the principle theory by which we describe and explain human sociation.

First, to admit the utility of exchange theory is not to accept it as the only way of understanding or being in relationships. Further, admitting utility certainly does not imply that exchange orientations are an ideal toward which humans should aspire in close relationships. Instead, scholars interested in interpersonal communication should seek to discover the possibilities inherent in human intimacy—the range of diverse orientations to an enactment of closeness with others in sundry circumstances. This openness to possibilities is precluded when a scholarly community privileges any single theory. To do so is to close off our own questioning about alternative explanations so fully that the dogma of theory blinds us to recognizing multiplicities in experience. My argument for enlarging our vision is not original. It is highly reminiscent of Marcuse's (1964) critique of the established order's inability to conceive of the dialectical existence of alternatives. This inability leads, he believes, to "the immediate identification of reason and fact, truth and established truth, essence and existence" (p. 85).

A second way in which the "but it works" response is inadequate lies in its limited recognition of how practice is constrained by particular social and cultural beliefs and, especially, by the hegemony of a given culture. It should surprise no one that exchange as a way of being in relationships thrives in western culture where many voices and visions of human relationships have been systematically suppressed or made peripheral to "the real business" of the culture. Just as members of any culture learn its language and customs, so too do they learn its typical and implicitly approved orientations toward relationships. Exchange flourishes in America (and elsewhere) because it is suited to relations in the public sphere, which has been privileged, and because it is consistent with values and preferred interpersonal modes of those who hold power in our society—white males. It reflects an interpersonal code based on rights, fairness, and independence which is empirically more associated with white males than other groups, and which was, in fact, developed predominantly by white males. This code, however, neither reflects nor explains a range of relationships in the private sphere. For instance, exchange does not fit well with caretaking activities, such as raising children or taking care of elderly parents or in-laws. In such relationships there is seldom any expected, immediate payoff for investments of time, energy, attention, love, and concern; there is certainly not usually an expectation of a reciprocal return. Thus, the explanatory power of exchange theory appears limited to a particular type of relationship, rather than to all interpersonal bonds.

The prominence of exchange theory seems to represent another effort to universalize masculine experiences and ways of relating into a (mis)representation of all human relationships. Simultaneously, exchange theory reflects and perpetuates a culturally entrenched hierarchy that prioritizes the public sphere and productive labor over the private sphere and reproductive labor. By extension, it accords differential and higher value to the particular ways of relating that are most prominent in the public sphere.

Interpersonal Communication as Developmental

Clearly one of the most pronounced foci in contemporary interpersonal communication scholarship is relational evolution. Initiated by Altman and Taylor's germinal work (1973) in psychology, developmental conceptions of relationships debuted in the field of Speech Communication with publication of two texts by Knapp (1978) and Phillips and Wood (1983). Substantial interest in the developmental nature of relationships is reflected in a growing body of scholarship (Baxter, 1982, 1984; Berger & Calabrese, 1975; Wood, 1982). The essential claim of the developmental trend is that relationships are not static entities, but rather develop over time and should be studied and understood in terms of their dynamic, developing character. Thus, researchers have sought to create models that describe typical relational development, to determine the kinds of communication characteristic of sundry stages, and to identify the ways in which various communicative strategies predispose particular relational trajectories.

That relationships develop over time is hardly arguable. Beyond this truism, however, what is the value of scholarship on relational evolution? Answering that question requires us to carefully examine the assumptions inherent in developmental conceptions of interpersonal communication.

First, consider the basic assumption of developmental models: Interpersonal relationships develop in a generally sequential manner toward a peak or goal, bonding, and then may deteriorate, again in a generally sequential manner. Once we recognize this as the central assumption inherent in developmental models, several questions seem appropriate. We might first note that the model is almost exclusively derived from a base of data that reflects the courtship and relationship norms of one particular group—white, heterosexual, middle-class Americans. Other demographic groups do not necessarily proceed through the stages depicted in prevalent models. Arranged marriages, still practiced in some cultures, certainly do not conform to the model favored in Speech Communication research. It is also questionable whether minority groups adhere to the sequence in the models—I say "questionable" because the bulk of research is based on white respondents, so we are handicapped by a dearth of data that might allow us to understand patterns (if any exist) of other groups. We know little about romantic relationships between Asians, Hispanics, Afro-Americans, and mixed-race couples; researchers have accorded virtually no attention to courtship practices of the elderly; and scholarship on gay and lesbian partnerships remains embarrassingly sparce.

Unfortunately, the limitations inherent in the empirical base of developmental theories has not dampened the inclination to universalize data from young, heterosexual, white college students. Thus, the empirical base of the developmental view is not inclusive; it is narrowly restricted to a select and atypical segment of the population.

A second question about the value of developmental models arises when we consider the emphasis placed on the bonding stage of relationships, that point at which a couple commits to a relationship. Bonding is the clear goal of most models of development—it is the objective toward which communication is supposed to aspire. The accuracy of this model and, thus, its value are, however, questionable. Defining bonding as the titular stage of interpersonal relationships is not consistent with empirical reality, since only a marked minority of relationships launched ever eventuate in a bonded commitment. The vast majority of human sociations plateau at less intense levels or dissipate entirely due to logistical problems and/or a lack of interest from one or both participants.

It is also the case that developmental theories which have been advanced to date imply a hierarchy among the stages in relational evolution in which certain stages (e.g., bonding) are represented, however undeliberately, as somehow "better," "more successful," or "more advanced." Missing is a nonhierarchical understanding of process, one that recognizes change is not necessarily toward better or worse, but only and always toward difference. This processual understanding would naturally value diversity and respect the multiplicity of ways in which individuals may develop their particular relationships.

Further questions may be posed regarding the advisability of championing bonding as the goal toward which persons should aim. Many bonded relationships are not healthy for one or both participants in which case encouraging continuation seems imprudent. To emphasize bonding as the height of interpersonal ambition adds to already substantial pressures to pair, to find, and to keep a mate. Finally, the concept of bonding is one that must be criticized for its restrictiveness. As viewed by prominent theorists such as Knapp (1978), it refers to the public commitment between heterosexual romantic partners. Such a definition privileges one particular type of commitment—heterosexual marriage. By implication, it excludes other major interpersonal relationships including enduring gay and lesbian bonds, committed cohabitation between romantic partners, and deep personal friendships between same- or opposite-sex partners, not to mention cross-generational bonds. Friendships are consistently reported to be a mainstay in women's lives (Rubin, 1985), but they are neglected by the developmental perspective as currently conceptualized. Existing developmental models, perhaps inadvertently, ignore vital, enduring forms and dimensions of human interpersonal experiences.

A feminist critical stance also leads to criticism of the developmental models' emphasis on outcomes and its corresponding neglect of process. As articulated so far, developmental views of relationships focus on outcomes, notably bonding, and also on termination. Little scholarly attention has yet been given to relational processes, especially communication (for an exception see Wood, 1982). Existing research has done little to illuminate *how* relationships actually operate or to study the integrity (or lack thereof) of processes by which relationships are built, sustained, and—in some cases—dismembered.

Scholarly emphasis on outcomes tells us little about how intimate partners experience the growth, joy, and personal changes that occur from involvement in the processes of interpersonal relationships. Thus, we know relatively little about how relationship partners participate in each other's development, nurture or handicap their relational cultures (Phillips & Wood, 1983; Wood, 1982), invest themselves in a bond, and so forth.

By emphasizing outcomes and neglecting processes, the corpus of existing research leaves us knowing considerably more about what tends to happen (in probabilistic terms) in some limited kinds of close relationships than about how those outcomes are brought into being and what they mean to those intimates who are involved.

From the standpoint of a feminist criticism, the neglect of processes is imprudent. From it we do not—cannot—understand in fundamental ways what relationships are. Research informed by feminist understandings (Harding, 1986; Keller, 1985; Schaef, 1981) would surely inquire centrally into the ongoing processes by which relationships develop, thrive or falter, and dissolve, and into what those processes mean to intimate partners. As any weaver, artist, gardener, or involved parent knows, the final product of one's efforts is not the only, or even primary, measure of the value and meaning of an investment. A person's engagement in the doing of something is in itself a matter of intrinsic integrity.

Before concluding this critical review of the developmental conception of relationships, I wish to note one further issue. The models and the goals inherent in them clearly place value on committing to relationships. In fact, there is a decided bias toward the diminution of the individual in subordination to the relationship. The language used by scholars implies the appropriateness and naturalness of a loss of self within commitment. For instance, Knapp (1978) uses the phrase "self surrender" to describe the process of becoming committed to another and giving oneself up to "we-ness." I have two reservations regarding unqualified encouragement of "we-ness." One arises from established knowledge about dynamics in intimacy; the other pertains to the implications of emphasizing we-ness, particularly for women.

Work in psychology and psychoanalysis (Scarf, 1987) is unequivocal in noting the constant interplay of two basic human needs in intimacy: autonomy and connection. Both are normal human requirements and it is the interplay of the two that creates complexity and often clashing expectations between intimate partners. Yet, discussions of relational development emphasize only one of these two forces: connection. The need for, nature of, and normalcy of the sister dynamic, autonomy, is largely neglected. Disproportionate and unbalanced emphasis on connection implies that while connection is a natural need and goal in intimacy, autonomy is not. The role of autonomy is at best dimly recognized and little incorporated into theoretical conceptions of how relationships do operate and into subsequent inferences about how they should operate.

The underrepresentation of autonomy is especially a problem for women, who empirically comprise the majority of the audience for textbooks and advisories on interpersonal communication that are derived from research. Historically, women have not been encouraged to recognize and develop themselves as autonomous persons. Instead, cultural expectations and norms have socialized women to see themselves in relation to others, particularly men, and to subordinate their identities, needs, aspirations, and preferences to others. Given this situation, theoretical models and foci that emphasize seeking connection and that neglect the importance of balancing connection with maintaining autonomy threaten to compound socialization practices that have historically oppressed women and restricted their autonomous definition and development.

The Conservative Bias of Interpersonal Research

A third major theme in scholarship on interpersonal communication is its conservative bias. By this I mean that methodological convention and convenience have resulted in a corpus of research that focuses on the normative behavior of people who represent a privileged, nonmajority segment of the population—white, middle-class, educated people. It is difficult to find studies that have anyone other than college undergraduates as participants. Equally difficult is finding research that includes representative numbers of non-white participants. Society as a whole, of course, is not primarily white and student; the majority of people engaged in relationships is not white students. Yet, the vast bulk of research is conducted on white students and thus it does not—cannot—accurately represent the population as a whole. Consequently, what we know of relationships is highly limited to a small and privileged sample, one that cannot represent the humans it purports to describe and study. This problem with the internal validity of research is obvious and has been the subject of several critical essays (Miller, 1979; Wood, 1983), although no substantial change has been forthcoming.

Yet, lack of internal validity is not the only issue entailed in recognizing the methodological bias in contemporary research on interpersonal communication. An important concomitant of the essentially conservative bias is that it does not criticize or challenge the established social structure and the rules, roles, and relational forms comprising it. By studying patterns of white middle-class relationship formation, commitment, and decline, we contribute to a false perception of these as normative and correct.In doing that we further marginalize all forms of relationships that do not conform to the established standard, regardless of how atypical they actually are of the majority of people. Needed are studies of a range of classes, races, ages, and ethnicities. Such research could be instrumental in one of the established functions of scholarship—constituting a critical voice that can challenge current social forms and practices which privilege some at the cost of others. Research on minority groups and alternative relationship forms could usefully enlarge our awareness of alternatives to status quo standards, legitimize options that have been muted in our culture, and expand our understanding of human nature as well as our vision of the possibilities of human relationships.

The Variable-Analytic Tradition and the Status of Gender

Cirksena (1987) has pointed out that "communication research has an historical basis in quantitative, positivist orientations stemming from its applied and administrative roots in social psychological studies" (p. 19). This tradition is exemplified in the variable-analytic model of research in which variables are analyzed to determine what causes and/or is caused by certain communication behaviors. Variable-analytic research, as the label implies, proceeds by defining variables for study. Whatever is to be examined is regarded as a variable, that is, a phenomenon whose strength, degree, or character varies contingent on other phenomena, and is considered alongside other variables selected for analysis. The methodological assumptions entailed within this model include the possibility and necessity of separating the researcher (knower) from subjects (known), the objectivity of quantitative and experimental methods, and the research goals of prediction and control. This model, including its accompanying assumptions, still dominates research in interpersonal communication.

In recent years the variable-analytic model of research has come under increasing attack from postmodern and feminist scholars. Central to this criticism is the rejection of the assumptions that undergird the model. Critics, including Bleier (1986), Harding (1986), and Keller (1985), claim that the knower and known are not independent and cannot be separated in the research process. The knower/researcher is inevitably connected with the known/participants in research by the nature of what is being studied and by their complementary roles in that pursuit. Recognizing separation of knower and known as false upsets the second assumption of variable analysis, since connection between a researcher and participants renders objectivity impossible. Instead, the research process in its entirety is recognized as necessarily subjective, reflecting personal values, biases, and interpretive inclinations. In short, research is recognized as a social enterprise. Critics also question the goals of variable analysis, arguing that prediction and control reflect an undesirable hierarchy in which the researcher elevates him/herself over participants in order to dominate and direct them. As alternative goals, critics suggest that understanding and liberation are worthy pursuits of scholars.

Summarizing an alternative model for research, Cirksena (1987) writes that knowledge is "process and interaction" in which the researcher and participants collaboratively generate understandings (p. 20). Rose (1986) insists on the importance of experiential and subjective knowledge as their complexity and diversity render them more complete and accurate than the information gained from reductionistic research.

Research that seeks understanding through interaction between researcher and participants is incompatible with the variable-analytic tradition's insistence on separating phenomena into distinct, discrete units, a practice that fractures the complex nature of reality and thereby falsifies the nature of what is studied. Interactive research also rejects the assumption that all phenomena can be reduced to variables without distorting their inherent quality. In particular, gender is not accurately regarded as a mere variable, one among a host of characteristics to be included in a formula for determining behavior.

Within the variable-analytic tradition both sex and gender (Bate, 1988) have been studied, often without recognizing the critical distinction between the two concepts. During the past decade, in fact, sex has been routinely included in many studies of interpersonal communication. Researchers often include women, incorporate sex or psychological sex as a variable, and/or append "women's issues" to the research agenda. The manner in which these issues are represented in research, however, implies that biological sex is isomorphous with socially learned gender ideals (Bate, 1988).

Not surprisingly, the ways in which sex has been included in contemporary research designs has not satisfied many scholars who argue it creates misrepresentation in two important ways. First, treating sex or even gender as a variable represents it as only an individual quality, such as green eyes or I.Q. This definition of sex ignores the larger fact that gender, that is, cultural beliefs and teaching about what biological sex means, is a property of social structures, beliefs, and practices. As such it permeates and defines all aspects of human interaction in ways that geography and occupation, for instance, do not. Second, it is wholly insufficient to simply add sex or gender into the collection of variables under study, according it the same status as variables such as geographical location and profession. Gender is far more fundamental to human nature than the majority of variables studied and feminists have demonstrated this. It is a basic and major aspect of human identity and culture. As such, it is central to understanding how humans think, act, communicate, and interpret within particular social structures. Gender is not an incidental variable such as geographic location, nor is it a relatively mutable aspect such as age, occupation, or marital status. Rather, with race and class, gender is a primary and enduring constituent of personal identity, and it is so because of the ways in which it is defined, valued, and generally contextualized within a given society. The fundamental character of gender cannot be captured within the variable-analytic framework, which reduces it to the same status as a host of other, less-profound variables included for study. Such a reductionist view of gender is inevitably distorted.

Therefore from a feminist critical perspective, existing research on interpersonal communication is inadequate, because it ignores, distorts, or misrepresents both sexes and the nature of feminine interests. The existing corpus reflects two theoretical and methodological emphases which do not recognize the socially constructed nature of gender, and which, therefore, do not value either both sexes or both genders. Exchange theory is the premiere theoretical orientation for scholarship. Its reductive and mechanistic orientation, along with its privileging of androcentric criteria for evaluating relationships, comprise serious challenges to its appropriateness as a primary way to conceive human relationships and the communication within them.

A second emphasis characteristic of contemporary research on interpersonal communication is a focus on the developmental nature of relationships. That relationships develop over time is both obvious and inarguable. If developmental views are to produce substantive knowledge about interpersonal dynamics, then research must expand to include participants other than white, middle-class, heterosexual college students and must give appropriately proportionate attention to autonomy and connection as legitimate interpersonal goals.

As previewed above, a third quality of existing research and theory is its nearly exclusive grounding in data gathered from people in relatively privileged levels of Western society. The overwhelming reliance on participants atypical of the broader population restricts the generalizability of findings from our research. It further establishes false norms and ideals of relationship patterns and processes—norms and ideals uninformed by and unresponsive to major segments of the population whose relationships may differ from what research suggests is normative.

A final theme in contemporary research is its continued allegiance to the variable-analytic model of inquiry, despite severe and sustained criticism of the assumptions and limits inherent in it. Problems with the variable analytic model include its insistence on separating knowers/researchers from known/subjects, its belief in objectivity and neutrality, and its goals of prediction and control. Variable analysis is particularly ill-equipped to study gender appropriately since the model demands reducing gender to a mere variable, thus distorting its fundamental character as a pervasive and primary dimension of both individual and social experience.

To summarize this section, it seems reasonable to conclude that contemporary research on interpersonal communication, while impressive in sheer amount, has not developed concepts, theories, and methods that are able to represent the breadth of interpersonal forms, styles, and activities characteristic of the range of human sexes, gender, races, classes, ages, and ethnicities. In the next section I consider some emergent work from feminist scholars who attempt to address some of the problems identified in extant research on interpersonal communication.

FEMINIST SCHOLARSHIP IN INTERPERSONAL COMMUNICATION

Despite a significant lack of interest from many mainstream publication fora (Foss & Foss, 1988), feminist scholars have generated an impressive amount of research in the last decade. Rather than classifying this work, however, I again opt to focus on themes that recur in and define the emerging corpus of feminist scholarship on interpersonal communication. Two themes occupy my attention. First, I consider the feminist emphasis on the fundamental character of gender, previewed in the previous section. Then, I discuss feminist efforts to revalorize women's knowledge, communication, and experiences.

Gender as Fundamental

Initially, feminist scholars sought to add women to accounts of history, art, politics, social life, and so on, to recognize women's contributions to society; and to document misogynist and sexist practices that oppress women (Harding, 1986, p. 30). These necessary first efforts proved insufficient, because they were based on an impoverished understanding of the centrality of gender as a fact of individual and social life. As feminist scholars realized the restrictiveness of this view, their goal expanded to revisions of the research process itself. Essential to the feminist project is the reconstruction of the methodology of communication research to recognize gender as a basic analytic category that is so centrally definitive of humans that it influences all of their experiences and actions. According to Harding (1986), "gender is a fundamental category within which meaning and value are assigned to everything in the world, a way of organizing human social relations" (p. 57).

Elaborating the importance of gender, Warren (1988) explains that

> gender and age are among the most basic categories of the social fabric; . . ., Living within a society presupposes a gendered interaction, a gendered conversation, and a gendered interpretation. Just as all knowledge—even language itself—is political. . ., all knowledge is gendered. (p. 10).

For interpersonal communication research, the implications of this view are major. If all interaction is gendered and if interpretation of that interaction is also gendered, then gender cannot be properly understood as merely one among many variables. Instead, it must be recognized as underlying and permeating all of our communicative behavior as well as all of the research process. A gendered view of social life, in short, demands a gendered view of social science, a point well documented by Keller (1985) and Harding (1986) in their extensive analyses of the sexist biases in social science as routinely practiced.

Redefining the conceptual domain of interpersonal communication to include gender as a basic analytic category cannot be accomplished within the variable-analytic framework. Its limit is to include sex as a variable, reducing it to one of many variable influences on behavior. Stepping outside of the variable-analytic tradition, feminist scholars propose a reformulation of categories of thought in ways that allow for an understanding of communication in terms of gender. This requires developing gender-focused models in research that can systematically account for women's experiences as generated within a set of social relationships defined by gender.

One heuristic model of such research was provided by Gilligan (1982), who based her analysis of women's moral reasoning on the then-radical assumption that one's sex was primary in accounting for how one understood and responded to moral situations. This is far different from including sex as a variable in studies of moral reasoning. That study had already been done. It led to the conclusion that women's moral development is stunted; a finding based on measuring women according to a model which totally excluded their experiences. By contrast, Gilligan assumed that thought is gendered, and this assumption made her sensitive to the distinctive moral voice of women. Her work exemplifies a gender-focused model for research. In my own research (Wood, 1986 in press) I have used Gilligan's theory to inform a gender-focused analysis of communication between intimates during times of crisis. This approach allowed me to notice and appreciate the fundamentally different ways in which women and men define what constitutes relationship crises and the ways they respond to them and to understand the connection between those differences and the socialization of the sexes. In short, I came to realize that defining and responding to intimate crises are gendered processes.

Other work illustrating the power of gender-focused models comes from Hall and Langellier (1988), whose study of mother-daughter storytelling revealed communicative patterns and goals that reflect women's roles and socialization that have been either ignored or misrepresented in studies that assume a universal standard of storytelling, based on male strategies and applied to women and men alike. Another excellent example is Spitzack's (1988) study, "Body Talk: The Politics of Weight Loss," which is premised on an understanding of the ways in which contemporary Western culture socializes women to feel about their bodies and themselves. In gathering and interpreting women's talk about weight, Spitzack understood from the outset that weight is a gendered issue—its meaning is assigned by the culture and has become primary in many women's views of themselves. Had Spitzack not recognized the gendered nature of weight as an issue in women's lives, her understanding and interpretation of women's talk would have been less insightful. Each of these examples demonstrates the significance of research grounded in the recognition of gender as a basic analytic category.

(Re)valorizing Research

Yet, feminist scholarship aims for more than inclusion of women in established, that is, androcentric, contexts that have historically been the focus of research. It aims for even more than recognition of gender as a basic analytic category. Feminist scholarship's goal is not to assimilate women into existing conceptual and theoretical schemes, but to change the very nature of the research process (French, 1985, p. 443). Central to feminist scholarship is the goal of valuing women and women's ways of thinking, acting, knowing, and being—ways that may be outside of what has been conventionally recognized and studied.

The revalorizing emphasis in feminist research has significant implications for how we conceive and conduct research in interpersonal communication. First, it means that feminine values must be fully incorporated into how we think about interpersonal relationships and interpersonal communication. Inclinations to respond, nurture, empower, and build connections have been shown to be associated with women's moral orientation, yet they have not achieved notable salience in scholarly inquiry. Because the bulk of research has not focused on the presence or absence of these qualities in relationships, we know little about them; because we know little, they remain obscured; because they are obscured, women's ways of experiencing relationships are silenced, hidden, unacknowledged (Spender, 1980).

Let's consider how incorporating feminine principles into interpersonal communication scholarship might affect what we study and how we study it. To take one example, studies of relationship health would not be confined to the usual measures of satisfaction, defined in terms of reciprocity, equity, and so forth. Instead of, or in addition to, these measures of satisfaction, analysis informed by feminist scholarship would inquire into relational dimensions demonstrated to be important to women. Feeling connected, responsiveness (instead of initiative), caring (instead of fairness from the exchange model), and empowerment of others (in contrast to power balance, which has been amply studied) are concepts that suggest themselves as key measures of relational health when that is conceived in a manner that includes women's priorities and preferences.

Women's ways of knowing have also received scant attention in the interpersonal communication literature. According to Belenky et al.'s (1986) landmark study, women's ways of knowing include being voiceless and passive receivers of knowledge. While we may not wish to celebrate these particular ways of knowing and what they imply about the self that knows, we do need to acknowledge that they operate in women's lives and to conduct research that helps us understand them more fully, particularly as we think about powerless individuals—women in abusive relationships, victims of rape and incest, and so on, who are likely to employ these ways of knowing. If we are to reach any accurate understanding of how abusive and exploitative relationships are sustained and how they might be altered or ended, we must understand how the participants perceive themselves, abuses, and their relationships.

Collaborative knowing, another epistemological position identified by Belenky et al. (1986), also seems a mode preferred by women. Further, Hall and Langellier's (1988) work suggests collaboration is a favored conversational mode among women as they tell stories. This view of communication is not represented in the prevailing models of interaction. These models define talk in terms of control and assume interaction is a talk stage in which one person is in control, that talk is fairly monologic and sequential, and that talk is desirable because it is a primary base of power.

An alternative model of interaction is offered by Nelson (1988). She reports women's talk functions to include not exclude, to encourage cooperation rather than competition among interactants, and to create an interactive, shared conversation instead of a monologic, sequential one. It seems reasonable to assume this kind of talk might occur in interpersonal relationships not just between women, but also between women and men, and possibly between men in some situations. To value collaborative communication means to study it. This requires us to name it and then incorporate it into our research models so that we can study how it operates in relationships and what kinds of understandings, feelings, and communicative patterns it generates.

Another focus of research that would reflect valuing of women's ways is the daily talk between partners in relationships. To date, most research focuses on *significant* talk or event talk—communication that deals with some issue defined by prevailing research models as important. Reflection on our experiences in relationships, however, quickly indicates that the vast majority of communication is not about big events or issues. Rather, it is about what contemporary research paradigms define as small matters, nuances of thought, daily activities and feelings, and so forth. These comprise the bulk of interaction in any ongoing, significant relationship, and they have been reported to be of greater interest and importance to women than men (Bate, 1988).

Existing research has largely ignored daily talk in favor of event talk, so we know more about how couples handle occasional crises and periodic decision making than about how they coordinate routine activities and alert each other to transient feelings, moods, and thoughts. Daily talk has not been studied, probably because it lies outside of the androcentric emphasis on "significant" events, so evident in models of conversation and storytelling (Hall & Langellier, 1988). If we value women and their ways of communicating, then daily talk should assume greater salience in our research, following the initiatives of Nelson (1988) and Hall and Langellier (1988). Further, in studying daily talk researchers should not limit themselves to talk between spouses or romantic partners. Equally important in understanding the range of interpersonal relationships that exist is investigating the kinds of talk that comprise and sustain parent-child bonds, friendships, and co-worker relationships.

The final area I consider in (re)valorizing research is topics of talk. Some pioneering work by Spitzack (1988) as well as Hall and Langellier (1988) suggests a major topic of talk among women is food—its preparation, nutritional values, taste, and temptation for dieters. People, especially family and friends, are another major topic of talk among women (Bate, 1988; Hall & Langellier, 1988; Rubin, 1985). Gilligan's (1982) work suggests caring and caretaking and maintaining connections among people are primary concerns of women, ones we would expect to see reflected in talk. Scholarly focus on these kinds of topics is essential if we are to value and fully include women in scholarship.

Still in its nascent stage, feminist scholarship has already demonstrated its ability to change and enrich contemporary research on interpersonal communication. The feminist insistence on the primacy of gender as an analytic category has led to new understandings of moral reasoning, crisis communication, storytelling, and weight loss, to name but a few areas of study. These findings merely hint at the possibilities for expanding knowledge that emanate from fully including women in the ways in which scholars conceive research topics and practices.

Feminist scholarship has also pointed the way toward studying previously neglected aspects of interpersonal communication—ones predominantly used and/or valued by women. Attending to communicative activities such as responding, demonstrating care, and empowering others increases our understanding of the scope of interpersonal communication and the diversity of preferences and patterns used by communicators.

While feminist scholarship is still clearly a minority, it has produced work that indicates to us the possibilities of expanded conceptions of interpersonal relationships and communication that are possible when women's concerns, priorities, and preferences are recognized, valued, and included.

To more fully realize the ways in which feminist thought might change and enhance scholarship on interpersonal communication, I move now to suggest some provocative directions for future feminist research.

CHARTING FUTURE DIRECTIONS FOR FEMINIST SCHOLARSHIP IN INTERPERSONAL COMMUNICATION

In the first two sections of this chapter I reviewed major themes in the extant research on interpersonal communication as well as emergent ones from feminist scholars. What remains now is to inquire into the future of our work, specifically the desired future and how we might achieve it. Two issues command my attention in this section. First, I want to add my voice to a number of others who have called for greater inclusiveness in scholarship. In the years ahead feminists should lead the way in insisting on research that is more sensitive to and inclusive of a range of races, classes, ethnicities, and so on. Second, I identify change as a primary goal of feminist scholarship and consider how well we have met that goal to date as well as how we might address it more vitally in future work.

Inclusive Scholarship

As a philosophical, political, and intellectual movement, feminism has consistently been dedicated to its inclusion as both a goal and an ongoing process. Broadly defined, inclusion has focused on including women and their interests in the institutions and practices of society.

Within the more specific context of the academy, the goal of inclusion has entailed not only enlarging women's presence, that is, hiring, tenuring, and promoting them as well as appointing them to committees, but also revising theories to recognize women's participation, contributions, and interests in all fields of study. Thus, revisionist accounts of history give attention to how women assisted in war efforts as well as to building American society; inclusive theories of political science entail explanations of gender-based interests in social policies (Jones & Jonasdottir, 1988); and revisionist approaches to anthropology provide theories that include identification and explanation of female primates' aggressive and sexual initiatives (Haraway, 1986). Developing theories that represent women's activities, interests, and modes of experience has been and remains a primary objective of academic feminism. Within the field of Speech Communication, voiced commitment to the goal of inclusiveness has thus far outstripped actual development of inclusive theories and research practices. In two significant ways, development of inclusive theories has been constrained in interpersonal communication. The first impediment to truly inclusive theorizing of interpersonal communication was the subject of Spitzack and Carter's (1987) exhaustive survey of the ways in which women's communication has been distorted, demeaned, or marginalized within the discipline of Speech Communication. After demonstrating that women and their experiences have not been adequately represented, Spitzack and Carter called for research and theory that "requires not only an understanding of women within the parameters of communication studies, but includes analysis of gender as an organizing force in social interaction" (p. 419).

Despite Spitzack and Carter's persuasive arguments, however, there has not been a groundswell of redirected scholarship consistent with their recommendations. To the that extent women are included in communication studies, it is almost invariably the "add women and stir solution" against which Spitzack and Carter cautioned (1987, pp. 418-419). Serious reconceptualizations of the ways in which research is conducted and theory is built have been written, but their impact on the field as a whole has been minimal since they have not appeared in the primary, mainstream publication fora. One clear priority for future scholarship, then, is a redoubling of efforts to develop truly inclusive theories that gain a hearing in influential publications. Achieving this objective is essential for feminist scholarship and for the intellectual vigor and integrity of interpersonal communication.

A second impediment to the development of truly inclusive theories of interpersonal communication is rooted in a somewhat narrow view of inclusion as referring to women only. Because feminism is a movement for women's value and rights, its obvious and immediate concern is naturally the inclusion of women in social and political life as well as in academic enterprises. Yet, as a philosophical stance, feminism argues for the intrinsic importance of inclusion, not merely for its specific application to women. Feminism opposes oppression, exclusion, and domination as inherently unworthy, unacceptable practices, regardless of those on whom they are imposed. This implies an understanding of inclusion with interests beyond women. If inclusion is intrinsically right, then research and theory must stretch to include a range of persons outside of white, middle-class, heterosexual college students who have been the standard participants in academic research. Theories must account for the interests and experiences of people of different ages, colors, ethnicities, sexual preferences, educational levels, and classes. We have made embarrassingly little progress in achieving this goal.

As I argued previously, conventional research practices allow nearly exclusive reliance on white, middle-class, heterosexual college students as the source of data from which theories are constructed. The resulting theories can only reflect the interests, experiences, and values of that narrow group. Necessarily excluded are the experiences of all those who are older, employed full time, less educated, and so on. Pragmatically, they also largely exclude those who are of color, rural, and socially more conservative. Thus, exclusion is a pervasive problem in academic work, one that is encouraged by the convenience of college students for research and by the pressures to publish prolifically. These reasons do not, however, comprise an adequate justification for continued reliance on a narrow and noninclusive group of participants for research and the construction of theories about interpersonal communication.

On this issue, feminist scholars in communication have not been as active as our ideals might impel us to be. In fact, Stanback (1988) claims that

> 'liberal' or 'bourgeois feminism,' the dominant feminist intellectual and political perspective in the United States is inappropriate to the study of black women because it is neither systemic nor inclusive. . . . Liberal feminism represents white middle-class women's success in universalizing their experiences of womanhood. (p. 29)

It is impossible to refute Stanback's charge by pointing to a significant corpus of work—feminist or otherwise—that includes people of color in proportionate numbers. We simply haven't conducted such research in substantial amounts. There are other systematic exclusions that mark interpersonal communication scholarship and limit its value. We have not included gays and lesbians in many studies of communication in romantic relationships, although their numbers are increasing and they engage in relationships potentially as enduring and meaningful as those of heterosexuals. We have not studied older, that is, over 23, people's patterns of courtship, intimacy, daily interaction, and problem solving. The list of those excluded from the thrust of interpersonal communication research and theory could continue to unfortunate lengths. I need not provide such exhaustive enumeration, however, to demonstrate that our scholarship practices exclusion in a manner both routine and substantial. This leads to identifying a major priority for the future as more inclusive scholarship, which includes, but is not limited to women.

The Goal of Change

Feminism focuses on social, political, and personal change—improvement in the lives of women and in the nature, assumptions, and practices of society. Feminist scholarship embraces the goal of change. Consciously departing from the traditional research goals (the viability of which has been questioned by many including Bleier, 1986) of neutrality and objectivity, feminist scholarship is deliberately, explicitly, and avowedly political: It aims to promote change, specifically to promote the betterment of women's lives, and generally to reduce the oppressive structures characteristic of patriarchical culture. Scholars such as Campbell (1988), Condit (1988), Fine (1988), Rakow (1987), and Wood (1988) all highlight change, particularly political and social change, as central to feminist scholarship.

I join other feminist scholars in affirming change in the structure of society as a primary goal of our work, as I have previously stated (1988). Yet, aligning ourselves with change is insufficient. The abstract goal of change must be translated into specific foci and routinely evaluated in terms of the extent to which desired changes are being generated. In the discussion that follows I specify some particular changes in interpersonal communication scholarship that feminist researchers are well positioned to foment. I then turn my attention to assessing our success in bringing about sought changes.

Foci of change. "The personal is political." That rallying slogan of the second-wave feminist movement serves as a basic directive for some important substantive changes feminist scholars can instigate in the area of interpersonal communication. The political issues of feminism grow out of personal, material conditions of life, and the aims of feminism are to change those aspects of personal life that are oppressive.

Interpersonal communication is an area of scholarship and pedagogy ideally situated to identify and alter oppressive, exploitative, and abusive practices in personal relationships. Three particular foci for research suggest themselves. First, we should study enduring primary relationships between adults, including marriage, cohabitation, and gay and lesbian bonds. In conducting such research, it is advisable for us to stretch beyond those kinds of relationships that comprise the conventional foci of research, that is, ones that are fairly balanced and satisfying to participants. We need to inquire into primary bonds that entail violence, oppression, and abuse. As we learn about the conditions that foster and/or allow harmful relationships and the experiences of participants in them, we may be empowered to identify correctives at personal and social/legislative levels. Equally important, knowledge about oppressive relationships may enable those who participate in them to change their situations or their actions, thus advancing the feminist goal of empowering the powerless.

A second valuable focus for future research on interpersonal communication is community and social relationships. By doing research here we name as important such understudied and undervalued relationships as friendships, informal social groups, and ties among volunteers in civic and service organizations. We need to know more than we presently do about the motives for engaging in and ending friendships, the values women and men experience from membership in informal social groups, and the motives for and dynamics of relationships in volunteer organizations. What does each of these relationships provide to those who participate? What does each require of them? How does each reflect and create a sense of self for involved individuals? To what extent does an understanding of these relationships require a gender-based analysis of interests and inclinations?

A third focus I suggest for our research is self-concept and self-definition. The topic itself is, of course, not new; indeed, self-concept has long been a mainstay in literature on interpersonal communication. What I am calling for, however, is reconceptualizing self-concept as a necessarily and thoroughly gendered concept. The explanations that apply to the development, maintenance, and change of males' self-concepts may not pertain, in part or in whole, to females' senses of self. Based on the provocative work of Gilligan (1982), Belenky et. al. (1986), and Miller (1986), there is strong reason to suspect women's sense of self has bases, dimensions, and implications distinct from those of men. Thus, it seems appropriate to suspend current theories and findings, suspecting that they reflect universalizing of white male norms and experiences to all humans. Existing research indicates it might be prudent to return to a basic investigation of what comprises self-concept and how it develops in each sex. From this we might gain a much needed increased understanding of how each sex defines self and what contributes to the process and outcomes of those definitions. Knowing how men and women define themselves could enable us as scholars and educators to address the dynamics of human development in ways that might enhance each sex's self-esteem and both sexes' understanding of human diversity.

Developing research approaches and theories of interpersonal phenomena that are gender-based should command central attention for feminist scholarship in the years ahead. Increased and improved understanding of primary, social, therapeutic, and civic relationships and of self-definition are also important foci for future research, because they appropriately expand the boundaries of interpersonal communication as an area of inquiry.

The symbolic focus. As we enlarge our understanding of what comprises interpersonal communication, I hope that we will not lose sense of its center. Elsewhere (Wood, 1988) I have argued we should pursue committed study of communication in its broad sense, understood to include the entire symbolic order that constitutes society and individuals within it. Language constitutes individual identity, including gender. Yet, too often communication itself has been a peripheral or subordinate focus in studies of interpersonal communication. I regard it as of enduring and central importance to our work as feminists and as scholars of interpersonal communication. As I argued earlier (1988), "If we believe that symbolic activities are means of oppression, means of resistance, and means of lifting veils of mystification, then nothing could be more central to feminist scholarship in general than serious, committed study of communicative assumptions and practices" (p. 26). Hence, as we pursue research, including perhaps some of the topics I've identified in this chapter, I encourage direct and systematic focus on symbolic interaction as a primary means through which gender is constructed and enacted in human relationships. ·

Assessing change. Scholars, including feminist scholars, need to pause periodically to assess what changes their work has occasioned and, when appropriate, to redirect their efforts to achieve greater impact. In this final section, I assess feminist scholars' efforts to create change in three areas: creating a scholarly community, pedagogy, and transforming the academy.

The changes brought about by feminist scholars are most heartening in one arena. They should feel substantial pride in the extent to which they've changed themselves and each other both personally and professionally. Many, perhaps the majority, of active feminist scholars received little or no formal training in feminist thought. Feminist theory, along with courses in women's studies and gender and communication, were virtually nonexistent when many of the now-established feminist scholars were students. Rather than allowing the lack of ready training to impede their interests, feminist scholars became self-educated through their own reading, thinking, and—quite significantly—communication with each other. There is a vital feminist community within Speech Communication, one created and sustained by our own efforts and one that fuels our continued work. Prima facie evidence of the vitality of this community is the increasing number of programs sponsored by the Women's Caucus at SCA conventions, the success of *Women's Studies in Communication*, the continuing existence of the National Conference on Gender and Communication Research, begun in 1984, and the expanding network of feminist scholars who work formally and informally to advance scholarship and women's presence in the discipline. Such a community did not exist, except as a goal, 15 years ago, and it is a major change and achievement.

A second arena in which significant change is evident is pedagogy. The current generation of feminist scholars has created courses at a range of educational levels that present information on gender issues and that more often than not entail at least an implicit feminist philosophy. Frequently, gaining acceptance for these courses required doing battle on campuses where feminist and gender topics were politically somewhere between controversial and unwelcome. That such courses now exist, enroll healthy numbers of students, and have solid textbooks to accompany them (Bate, 1988; Pearson, 1985; Stewart, Cooper, & Friedley, 1986) is an inarguable measure of change—structural change in the academy and what it defines as education.

Moreover, through teaching, feminist scholars have changed the lives of many, many students. At the very least they have introduced students to information about some of the bases, dynamics, and consequences of living in a gendered social world. In some cases—a substantial number I suspect—the impact has been deeper, affecting how students understand their society and themselves. Teaching grounded in feminist scholarship is able to show them alternative ways of experiencing personal and social action and to suggest to them alternative visions of how society and personal relationships might be structured.

The full impact of teaching is probably far greater than what I've indicated. The change cannot be precisely gauged for two reasons. First, much of the teachers' influence is long term, and educational institutions do a poor job of assessing that. Second, a significant portion of the impact of teaching is indirect, affecting people who never appear in classrooms taught by feminist scholars. As students change through the content and processes in their classes, they affect their acquaintances and intimates, who in turn affect theirs in a process that magnifies the impact of teaching far beyond those who are actually instructed.

Acceptance in the academy. Assessing impact in one other area is less gratifying. One recalcitrant force favoring the status quo is the academy as a whole. Feminist scholarship is not yet widely accepted, nor yet taken seriously in many quarters of academe. While the body of feminist research has grown dramatically in the past decade, the audience for it has not enlarged correspondingly. To an unfortunate extent, feminist research is read and used primarily by feminists. How many mainstream, nonfeminist scholars subscribe to *Women's Studies in Communication*? How many will order and use this book? The answers to such questions are not satisfying. Farnham (1987) is unqualified in her opinion that books and articles in most academic fields seldom pay attention to feminist theories and research. Thus, while the number of feminist scholars and feminist publications has expanded, the position they occupy within the academy has not altered substantially. Feminist research remains too peripheral, still ghettoized in academic institutions.

Repeating an issue discussed earlier, it is important to realize that the great majority of feminist scholarship does not appear where it will enjoy wide readership. Instead, it appears in feminist or women's studies journals, in special issues of more established journals, or in edited feminist works. All of these options marginalize feminist scholarship by marking it off from the intellectual currents that define and influence the field as a whole.

The marginal status of feminist scholarship is an entrenched and major barrier to the goal of producing significant changes in theory and methods of inquiry (Foss & Foss, 1988). It reflects a deeply seated, vociferously denied, and virtually impenetrable bias within the field. Established scholars function as gatekeepers who control what is published through their service on editorial boards and as reviewers for publishing houses.

No doubt every feminist scholar has several accounts of rejections based on uninformed or blatantly sexist reviews. Even if we assume a measure of vested interest in interpreting bases of rejection, there appears to be a systematic and broad lack of receptivity to feminist work. It is reasonable to suspect feminist scholarship, no matter how well conducted, is inherently unacceptable to many in positions that influence what is published. This bias constitutes a formidable barrier to a wider recognition of feminist thought and a wider influence on scholarship in communication.

Frankly, I have no ready plan for surmounting this problem. I've participated in several formal discussions of it and countless informal ones, and the recurrent conclusion is that this is a Catch 22 issue: To publish, feminist scholars find it necessary to accommodate to conventional methods and theories, and doing that at the least dilutes and often dismembers a feminist focus of research (Foss & Foss, 1988).

Perhaps the one suggestion I can offer is political action as that might lead to gradual erosion of the barrier. Feminists can exercise some influence in the selection of gatekeepers who are not hostile to feminist scholarship through block voting for officers in our organizations, lobbying for journal editors, and lobbying elected editors for associate editors who are receptive to feminist research topics and practices. We can also use the positions we have to raise general awareness of feminist research. For instance, many feminist scholars read for journals, convention programs, and publishing houses. As we review submissions, we can make it a practice to routinely recommend authors consult and then incorporate relevant feminist research into their work. By doing this, we introduce other scholars to feminist research of which they are often wholly unaware, and we increase the visibility of feminist thought within the discipline as a whole. Simultaneously, we may also gradually erode the bias against feminist scholarship and facilitate its movement toward the center of the field.

CONCLUSION

This chapter argues that the central concepts, theories, and methods of interpersonal communication are not value free. The bulk of existing work reflects a host of androcentric assumptions and systematic exclusion of a range of persons making up contemporary society. The emerging body of feminist research offers expanded conceptions of what comprises interpersonal communication and how we might inquire into it. Moreover, feminist scholars have made a convincing case for the need not just to include women in research, but to develop gender-based theories that recognize the pivotal, pervasive nature of gender as constituting individuals, relationships, and society.

In the relatively brief time during which feminist scholarship has been a significant intellectual force, it has brought about many changes. While it remains too marginalized to have major impact on mainstream interpersonal communication scholarship, its value and visibility are increasing. Perhaps an appropriate closing for this chapter is a question, one intended to provoke both imagination and action: What would be the result of a concerted effort to develop interpersonal communication theories which account for gender-based interests, self-definitions, and interpersonal orientations?

REFERENCES

Altman, I., & Taylor, D. (1973). *Social penetration: The development of interpersonal relationships.* New York: Holt, Rinehart, & Winston.

Argyle, M., & Henderson, M. (1984). The rules of friendship. *Journal of Social and Personal Relationships, 1,* 211-237.

Bate, B. (1988). *Communication and the sexes.* New York: Harper and Row.

Baxter, L. (1982). Strategies for ending relationships: Two studies. Western *Journal of Speech Communication, 46,* 223-41.

Baxter, L. (1984). Trajectories of relationship disengagement. Journal of Social and Personal Relationships, 1, 29-48.

Belenky, M., Clinchy, B., Goldberger, N., & Tarule, J. (1986). *Women's ways of knowing: The development of self, voice, and mind.* New York: Basic Books.

Berger, C., & Calabrese, R. (1975). Some explorations in initial interaction: Toward a developmental theory of interpersonal communication. *Human Communication Research, 1,* 99-112.

Bernard, J. (1971). *Women and the public interest: An essay on policy and protest.* Chicago: Aldine/Atherton.

Bleier, R. (Ed.). (1986). Introduction. In R. Bleier (Ed.), *Feminist approaches to science* (pp. 1-17). New York: Pergamon.

Bochner, A. (1984). The functions of human communication in interpersonal bonding. In C. Arnold & J. Bowers (Eds.), *Handbook of rhetorical and communication theory* (pp. 544-621). Boston, MA: Allyn and Bacon.

Brehm, S. (1985). *Intimate relationships.* New York: Random House.

Campbell, K. (1988). What really distinguishes and/or ought to distinguish feminist scholarship in communication studies? *Women's Studies in Communication, 11,* 4-5.

Cirksena, K. (1987). Politics and difference: Radical feminist epistemological premises for communication studies. *Journal of Communication Inquiry, 11,* 19-28.

Clark, M.S., Quellette, R., Powell, M. C., and Milberg, S. (1987). Recipient's mood, relationship type, and helping. *Journal of Personality and Social Psychology, 53,* 93-103.

Cline, R. (1989). The politics of intimacy: Costs and benefits determining disclosure intimacy in male-female dyads. *Journal of Social and Personal Relationships, 6,* 5-20.

Collective Editors. (1987). Feminist studies and feminist theory in communication. *Journal of Communication Inquiry, 11,* 19-28.

Condit, C. (1988). What makes our scholarship feminist? A radical liberal view. *Women's Studies in Communication, 11,* 6-8.

Diamond, I., & Hartsock, N. (1981). Beyond interests in politics: A comment on Virginia Sapiro's "When are interests interesting?" *American Political Science Review, 75,* 717-23.

Duck, S., Locke, A., McCall, G., Fitzpatrick, M.A., & Coyne, J. (1984).

Social and personal relationships: A joint editorial. *Journal of Social and Personal Relationships, 1,* 1-10.

Farnham, C. (Ed.). (1987). *The impact of feminist research in the academy.* Bloomington, IN: Indiana University Press.

Fine, M. (1988). What makes it feminist? *Women's Studies in Communication, 11,* 17-19.

Foss, S., & Foss, K. (1988). What distinguishes feminist scholarship in communication studies? *Women's Studies in Communication, 11,* 9-11.

French, M. (1985). *Beyond power: On women, men, and morals.* New York: Summit.

Gilligan, C. (1982). *In a different voice: Psychological theory and women's development.* Cambridge, MA: Harvard University Press.

Hall, D., & Langellier, K. (1988). Storytelling strategies in mother-daughter communication. In B. Bate & A. Taylor (Eds.), *Women communicating: Studies of women's talk* (pp. 107-126). Norwood, NJ: Ablex Publishing Corporation.

Haraway, D. (1986). Primatology is politics by other means. In R. Bleier, (Ed.), *Feminist approaches to science* (pp. 77-119). New York: Pergamon.

Harding, S. (1986). *The science question in feminism.* New York: Cornell University Press.

Hewes, D., Roloff, M., Planalp, S., & Seibold, D. (1989). Interpersonal communication research: What should we know? In G. Phillips & J. Wood (Eds.), *Speech communication: Essays to commemorate the 75th anniversary of the Speech Communication Association* (pp. 130-180). Carbondale, IL: Southern Illinois University Press.

Jaquette, J. (1984). Power as ideology: A feminist analysis. In J. S. Stiehm, (Ed.), *Women's views of the political world of men* (pp. 7-29). Dobbs Ferry, NY: Transnational Press.

Jones, K., & Jonasdottir, A. (Eds.). (1988). *The political interests of gender.* Beverly Hills, CA: Sage.

Keller, E. (1985). *Reflections on gender and science.* New Haven, CT: Yale University Press.

Knapp, M. (1978). *Social intercourse: From greeting to goodbye.* Boston: Allyn and Bacon.

Levinger, G. & Snoek, J. (1972). *Attraction in relationship: A new look at interpersonal attraction.* Morristown, NJ: General Learning Press.

Lund, M. (1985). The development of investment and commitment scales for predicting continuity of personal relationships. *Journal of Social and Personal Relationships, 2,* 3-23.

Marcuse, H. (1964). *One dimensional man.* Boston: Beacon Press.

McDonald, G. (1981). Structural exchange and marital interaction. *Journal of Marriage and the Family, 43,* 825-39.

Michaels, J., Acock, A., & Edwards, J. (1986). Social exchange and equity determinants of relational commitment. *Journal of Social and Personal Relationships, 3,* 161-176.

Miller, G. (1979). On rediscovering the apple: Some issues in evaluating the social significance of communication research. *Central States Speech Journal, 30,* 14-24.

Miller, G., & Steinberg, M. (1975). *Between people: A new analysis of interpersonal communication.* Palo Alto, CA: Science Research Associates.

Miller, J. (1986). *Toward a new psychology of women* (2nd ed.). Boston: Beacon.

Nelson, M. (1988). Women's ways: Interactive patterns in predominantly female research teams. In B. Bate & A. Taylor (Eds.), *Women communicating: Studies of women's talk* (pp. 199-232). Norwood, NJ: Ablex Publishing Corporation.

O'Connell, L. (1984). An exploration of exchange in three social relationships: Kinship, friendship, and the marketplace. *Journal of Social and Personal Relationships, 1,* 333-346.

Pearson, J. (1985). *Gender and communication.* Dubuque, IA: Wm. C. Brown, Co.

Petchesky, R. (1980). Reproductive freedom: Beyond a woman's right to choose. *Signs, 5,* 661-85.

Petchesky, R. (1983). *Abortion and women's choice.* New York: Longman.

Phillips, G., & Wood, J. (1983). *Communication and human relationships: The study of interpersonal communication.* New York: Macmillan.

Rakow, L. (1987). Looking to the future: Five questions for gender research. *Women's Studies in Communication, 10,* 79-86.

Rawlins, W. (1985). Stalking interpersonal communication effectiveness: Social, individual, or situational integration? In T. Benson (Ed.), *Speech communication in the 20th century* (pp. 109-129). Carbondale, IL: Southern Illinois University Press.

Roloff, M. (1981). *Interpersonal communication: The social exchange approach.* Beverly Hills, CA: Sage.

Rose, H. (1986). Beyond masculinist realities: A feminist epistemology for the sciences. In R. Bleier (Ed.), *Feminist approaches to science* (pp. 57-76). New York: Pergamon.

Rubin, L. (1985). *Just friends: The role of friendship in our lives.* New York: Harper & Row.

Scarf, M. (1987). *Intimate partners.* New York: Random House.

Schaef, A. (1981). *Women's reality: An emerging female system in white male society.* Minneapolis. MN: Winston.

Spender, D. (1980). *Man made language.* London: Routledge & Kegan Paul, Ltd.

Spitzack, C. (1988). Body talk: The politics of weight loss and female identity. In B. Bate & A. Taylor (Eds.), *Women communicating: Studies of women's talk* (pp. 51-74). Norwood, NJ: Ablex Publishing Corporation.

Spitzack, C., & Carter, K. (1987). Women in communication studies: A typology for revision. *Quarterly Journal of Speech, 73,* 401-23.

Stanback, M. (1988). What makes scholarship about black women and communication feminist scholarship? *Women's Studies in*

Communication, 11, 28-31.
Stewart, L., Cooper, P., & Friedley, S. (1986). *Communication between the sexes: Sex differences and sex role stereotypes.* Scottsdale, AZ: Gorsuch Scarisbrick.
Utne, M., Hatfield, E., Traupmann, J., & Greenberger, D. (1984). Equity, marital satisfaction, and stability. *Journal of Social and Personal Relationships, 1,* 323-332.
Warren, C. (1988). *Gender issues in field research.* Beverly Hills, CA: Sage.
Wood, J. (1982). Communication and relational culture: Bases for the study of human communication. *Communication Quarterly, 30,* 75-84.
Wood, J. (1983). Research and the social world: Honoring the connections. *Communication Quarterly, 32,* 3-8.
Wood, J. (1986). Different voices in relationship crises: An extension of Gilligan's theory. *American Behavioral Scientist, 29,* 273-301.
Wood, J. (1988). Feminist scholarship in communication: Consensus, diversity and conversation among researchers. *Women's Studies in Communication, 11,* 22-27.
Wood, J. (in press). Gender and relationship crises: Contrasting reasons, responses and relational orientations. In J. Ringer (Ed.), *Gayspeak II.*

Chapter 3

Organizing and Relating: Feminist Critique of Small Group Communication

Nancy Wyatt
Delaware County Campus
Penn State University
Media, PA

INTRODUCTION

In this chapter I look at small group communication research through a feminist lens. To define a feminist viewpoint for this chapter is not to define a feminist viewpoint for all time, for all feminists, or for all subjects. It is not even to define what a feminist viewpoint *should* mean for this topic. The purpose of this chapter, as of all chapters in this volume, is to generate discussion and to encourage alternative ways of approaching communication research. To borrow an image from Virginia Woolf, I have thrown my line into the water and brought out the ideas that clung to my line.

The feminist perspective in this chapter—my fishing line—is spun from two basic feminist precepts. The first precept derives from the observation that gender, class, and race constitute major bases for social organization. The experiences of people of different genders, classes, and races vary widely within our culture, and probably within all cultures. As the experiences of persons of different genders, races, and classes vary, we might expect their communication styles and practices to differ. To what extent has our communication research acknowledged and reflected these potentially relevant differences? In this chapter I use gender as the almost exclusive focus for my observations for several reasons. For one thing, most studies of small group communication in our discipline have dealt with white, middle-class people and institutions. This fact makes any comparisons on the basis of race and class problematic. Additionally, my own knowledge and experience are similarly limited. The pragmatic limitation of space in this volume precludes an extensive treatment of race and class. In future discussions, race and class should command increased attention from all communication researchers, myself included.

The second feminist principle informing my viewpoint in this chapter is the observation that a power differential exists between women and men, with women's perspectives and experiences consistently subordinated to those of men. To the extent that women of different classes, races, and ethnicities have anything in common, they experience subordination to men as a basic fact of their existence.

Defining these two precepts operationally, I approach the critique of small group communication research with two specific questions: To what extent has communication research in small groups taken into account the race, class, or gender of the subjects in the design of the study or in the generalization of the findings? To what extent has feminist theory informed the choice of research questions or the design of the study? In exploring these questions, I found it useful to review the history of the study of communication in small groups, to examine the theoretical perspectives generated by this research in our discipline, and to report on extant studies of women's communication or feminist studies of communication to date. I conclude with some suggested directions for the study of communication in small groups for the future.

HISTORY OF SMALL GROUP COMMUNICATION RESEARCH

There are two distinct strands in the study of small group communication derived from different traditions and focused on different goals. Much early writing on small group communication was pedagogic, grounded in rhetorical theory and aimed at teaching students how to participate more effectively in democratic group discussion. Not until the late 1960s did research into communication processes in small groups begin to appear in speech journals (Gouran, 1985). Since pedagogy is not a theme in this volume, I will concentrate my critique on the second strand—research on communication in small groups conducted by communication scholars and published in communication journals.

Research on small group dynamics dates approximately from the late 1930s, when a number of very practical concerns with leadership and productivity helped to shape the field. Research on how small groups served as a socializing influence on individuals and on how individuals influenced one another within small groups was initiated in both nonacademic and academic centers. Small groups proved to be an indirect but more manageable way of studying larger social groups (Swanson, 1953), as well as a way to understand individual psychology (Asch, 1951, 1955, 1956). Additionally, study of small groups began to be undertaken as an end in itself (Zander, 1979).

Many early studies of small group dynamics were carried out by social psychologists whose research interests and methodologies have strongly influenced our own field (Gouran, 1988). The funding sources for this early research shaped research goals and designs, limiting interest in small group dynamics to a relatively narrow context. Consequently, many important small group contexts and functions were ignored, and those omissions have influenced theory construction. The attitude that privileges research on small groups in the work context is exemplified by the comment in a recent review article on small group research that, "Work on special kinds of small groups (e.g., therapy groups, families, children's groups) is typically excluded because of its limited generalizability" (Levine & Moreland, 1990, p. 586). It is not at all clear why work on therapy groups is less generalizable than work on military units, but it is clear that funding is more likely to be available for the latter than for the former.

Early group dynamics studies were funded by the Office of Naval Research (ONR) in collaboration with a number of civilian organizations. Macmillan and Page (1963) described how the research project originated:

> The research . . . was undertaken by the Office of Naval Research in response to requests by Naval officers who had learned something of social science research during the war years and immediately thereafter, and who believed that research in human relations could produce results which were applicable to and necessary in over-all military operations. (p. 267)

The problems faced by the Navy were those common to the armed services in general: wastage of time through AWOLs, deserters, men who would not fight, and training failures. The goal of the research was to turn out "men who can perform at a high degree of competence" (Macmillan & Page, 1963, p. 268). Civilian organizations faced similar personnel problems. Under the direction of the ONR, large-scale, long-range research projects were undertaken in the Navy, as well as in a variety of civilian organizations, and experimental studies were carried out in university settings.[1]

Thus, the research contexts and subjects for these early studies were almost exclusively male, and the purpose for studying small groups was to improve performance from the point of view of management, who were funding the research.[2] This concentration on one type of group behavior was duly noted in a summary of conference proceedings by Darley (1963b), who wrote:

> The groups used in the research studies were either created by the experimenters or were chosen from work groups. These groups are, in a sense, involuntary groups . . . . There are many groups in our society based on voluntary participation . . . . Such groups may present a different order of phenomena for study and may have a substantial influence on social change. *Yet they do not attract our experimental interest, apparently. Nor have we turned our attention to groups of children.* (p. 259; emphasis added,)

Voluntary community groups probably did not attract the attention of researchers because there were no sponsors who would benefit financially from funding such studies. Research funds expended by corporations and by the armed forces were considered an investment in human resources; these institutions expected to recoup their money in increased productivity of their workers. One explanation for this development can be found in economic theory, specifically in the definition of "labor." Economists defined the labor of men in factories or in the military as "productive" labor, since it yielded a product that could be sold or that could be used by the organization in attaining its goals.

The work done in the voluntary community organizations that were not studied has been defined by economists as "reproductive" labor, labor that reproduces the social order and maintains the connections within the social fabric but does not create a product that can be traded or sold. Not coincidentally, most reproductive labor is done by women, people of color, and people of lower social classes. Reproductive labor or "women's work"—largely unpaid and not producing goods or services that could be sold—was never valued equally with productive labor and was consequently seldom considered an appropriate topic for study.[3] This is not to say that work done by women was never studied; when women were working at "productive" tasks, their labor became the legitimate focus of research. But without adequate funding, researchers interested in studying types of small groups other than task groups would have found themselves severely handicapped by a lack of adequate resources. As a consequence, most studies focused narrowly on male-dominated, white, middle-class group behavior.

Evidently the reproductive work of women, people of color, and people of lower social classes genuinely was invisible to the early group dynamics researchers as well as to the sponsors. While noting the absence of studies on children, Darley (1963b) neglected to comment on the absence of women and women's groups from the research. But as a result of the narrow focus of these early research efforts, theory developed and advanced as theory of human behavior in small groups was for the most part theory of male behavior in small groups of men. At least the basis for its development was empirical work based almost exclusively on the behavior of particular classes of men in a select set of circumstances.

In spite of criticism by Mead (1963), that research findings should be situated within a specific cultural framework, the social psychologists who designed these studies apparently did not realize that they were studying a very select portion of human behavior in small groups.[4] In an introduction to the research study, Darley (1963a) noted the lack of historians or anthropologists as members of the research teams. Lacking the perspectives of historians and anthropologists, the researchers' work was situated ahistorically and aculturally; important metatheoretical issues were, therefore, never addressed. Researchers did not question the basic categories of research, the means of analysis, or the goals of the research studies. The study of small group dynamics was carried out as though all small groups throughout history and across classes and cultures were isomorphic. Not only was the research selective, and therefore unrepresentative, but the researchers themselves seemed unaware of that fact. In a recent review article in *Studies in Symbolic Interaction,* Couch, Katovich, and Miller (1987) remarked that early group researchers ignored the social context of the laboratory settings in which their research was carried out. Their criticism was quite harsh:

> This is a surprising feature of laboratory research by sociologists. Of all people sociologists should be reflective about social contexts. Their failure to use the laboratory in a reflective manner stems, in part, from an overriding concern with displaying their scientific (it might more accurately be called scientistic) mantle than with displaying their sociological tradition or imagination. The obvious shortcoming of this approach is that in our own everyday life, failure to pay attention to our surroundings is defined as a form of lunacy—autism. (p. 170)

Early small group communication research in our own field inherited this narrow focus as well as the apparent blindness to the historical and cultural implications of focusing on a highly selective segment of human behavior in groups. As Gouran (1988) pointed out, speech communication scholars took social psychology as their model and dealt primarily with personal and contextual variables in decision-making groups in studies that were "largely derivative rather than originative" (p. 2).

In his summary of research on small groups, McGrath (1984) identified three large and relatively separate bodies of work within the study of group dynamics: (a) the social influence school, or the study of groups as vehicles for delivering social influence; (b) the interaction process school, or groups as a structure for patterning social interaction; and (c) the task performance school, or groups as task performance systems. Although the discipline of speech communication has paid some attention to the interaction process in groups, most research in small group communication has focused on task performance. Communication scholars have identified variables that correlate with one another or with outcomes as a way of discovering how to improve decision making and problem solving by making these procedures more rational and presumably more effective. This focus is entirely consistent with our discipline's early roots in speech pedagogy, but hardly good theory building.

In choosing to study primarily task groups, the speech communication field has helped to perpetuate the unrecognized white, middle-class, male bias of the early group dynamics work. The task groups or committees studied by small group communication researchers were largely drawn from college classrooms or from committees within organizations. Both of these contexts historically have been male-dominated, white, and middle class; even when the groups were not composed exclusively of males, the contexts in which the groups operated were dominated by white, middle-class males and by their norms and values.

Most small group communication studies have been carried out in communication classes in colleges[5]. While we might like to think that college classrooms are gender-neutral, that is not the case. Hall and Sandler's (1982) report, "The Classroom Climate: A Chilly One for Women?" produced by the Project on the Status and Education of Women for the Association of American Colleges, documented many ways in which women's contributions and participation are routinely excluded or devalued in college classrooms. This report illustrated how social interactions and women's performance in the classroom are affected by sexist biases of both male and female instructors, as well as male students. Hence, the studies of small group communication in the classroom are also studies of small group behavior in predominantly male contexts, even when the groups include female students. It goes almost without saying that American college students are also predominantly white and middle class. As a matter of fact, most of the classroom studies do not report the gender, age, or ethnicity of the subjects. Small group communication researchers seem as blind to historical and cultural differences as the early group dynamics researchers.

Researchers studying communication in small groups have consistently focused their research on two dimensions of group behavior that

they treat as more or less separate: task performance and group maintenance (Fisher, 1979). Rosenfeld (1973) referred to task functions as those
functions that "provide rewards to members by virtue of the group's ability
to operate in its given environment," and maintenance functions as those
that "provide compensations to insure that each member is kept above his
[sic] Comparison Level for Alternatives" (p. 21). Napier and Gershenfeld
(1973) distinguished between task roles that help the group "select and
define the common goals and work toward solution of those goals," and
group maintenance roles that focus on the personal relations among members in a group (p. 145). Fisher (1973) defined task dimensions as "the
relationship between group members and the work they are to perform,"
and social dimensions as "the relationship of group members with each
other—how they feel toward each other and about their membership in
the group" (p. 92). Feminists would point out that this division is based on
a male perspective of separation of work and social relationships.

Feminist critiques of traditional sociology have noted that the definition of work and its conceptual separation from leisure is based on the
structure of men's lives in which work is separate from home or social life
(Oakley, 1974). Oakley claimed that the neglect of housework as a topic
of study is grounded in three axioms:

1. Women belong in the family, while men belong `at work';
2. Therefore men work, while women do not work;
3. Therefore housework is not a form of work (p. 25).

Exploring the concept of work, Oakley pointed out that the functionalist
theory in sociology operates specifically to deny the status of housework
as work. She described the functionalist definition of work as follows:

> According to functionalist theorists, the role of `task leader' in the fam-
> ily involves `instrumental' activities such as decision-making, earning
> money, and `manipulating the external environment'; the role of
> `sociometric star' carries `expressive' duties such as the expression of
> emotional warmth and the integration of internal family relationships.
> Men perform an instrumental role, women an expressive one. (pp. 27-
> 28)

This description is strikingly similar to much theorizing about the roles of
task and social maintenance functions in communication in small groups.
It is surely not surprising then that support, therapy, and consciousness-
raising groups, which take the development and maintenance of relationships as the main task of the group, have been studied very little. The work

that is done in such groups, besides contributing little to the gross national product, is not generally defined as "work." At least, this appears to be the presumption underlying this neglect.

In summary, for a variety of reasons, small group communication researchers have studied almost exclusively white, middle-class, male behaviors in small groups within white, middle-class, male contexts. Consequently, theory development has been biased by this narrow focus. For example, the division of group activities into task and social mainte- nance categories reflects a male perspective on the nature of work. By including the study of women in women's groups, as well as the study of people of other races, ethnicities, and classes in their own contexts, we will be able to broaden our definitions of small group communication to create theories more nearly representative of human communicative behavior in small groups.

TRADITIONAL SMALL GROUP COMMUNICATION THEORY

Three major approaches have characterized the study of small groups in speech communication: the functional approach, structuration, and sym- bolic convergence. To what extent do these theoretical perspectives reflect, or could they reflect, women's experiences and values? Have they been informed by feminist theory? The following sections address these questions.

The Functional Approach

The functional approach focuses on the study of decision making and problem solving in small ad hoc task groups. The main tenet of the func- tional approach is that certain critical decision-making functions must be performed for a group to reach a high-quality decision (Gouran & Hirokawa, 1983). The functional research approach attempts to account for the quality of decisions made in small task groups by identifying specif- ic functions that promote or impede decision making (Cragan & Wright, 1988). To illustrate how this functional approach is applied, I refer to a study by Hirokawa (1983) as typical of the functional research effort.

Hirokawa (1983) hypothesized five task-achievement functions necessary to achieve high-quality decisions: (a) the group must establish a set of operating procedures; (b) the group must understand and analyze the problem; (c) the group must generate alternative solutions to solving the problem; (d) the group must develop a specific set of criteria for evalu- ating the worth of a given alternative solution; and (e) the group must evaluate each alternative solution before choosing a final decision or solution (p. 67). These task functions as described by Hirokawa constitute a propositional formal discourse associated with literate and male communication styles (Presnell, 1989). The communication necessary to accomplish task functions described as task related by Hirokawa is lineal and hierarchical in nature, reliant only on intratextual cues for its interpretive context, and topically relevant when extracted from its original context. In other words, when a transcript of discourse is generated from the group discussion, the statements must stand alone and make sense to a reader who was not present during the discussion.

By valuing exclusively a particular type of discourse—linear, propositional, and task-oriented—the functional approach to the study of small group communication excludes and devalues other types of discourse described as common among many people, including women and people from predominantly oral cultures. The exclusive emphasis of this approach on a particular type of discourse as relevant to the quality of a decision also obscures the relevance of context to the judgment of the quality of the decision. The question, "High quality to whom and for what purpose?" is never asked or answered. The choice of the problem for solution may also be problematic with this type of research. In relying on external sources for criteria for "correct" solutions, the researchers have confined themselves to specific types of problems which may call for particular types of discourse for their solution. Citing Favreau (1977), who argued that most research on problem solving tasks has been limited to areas in which men do well, such as mathematical and spatial relationships, Jenkins and Kramer (1978) argued that there is little or no research on problem solution in interpersonal contexts, where women's linguistic and relationship skills might be more relevant. "The spheres of linguistic and inter-personal communication abilities," they wrote, "are not seen as problem solving areas, although every inter-personal communication situation could be seen in a problem-solution format" (p. 78).

In the functional approach to small group decision making, the definition of high-quality decisions is not made problematic in the research design. Most functional researchers appear to assume that the quality of a decision can be measured either by reference to a "correct" decision or solution to the problem, or by agreement by a panel of external judges. That is, the quality of the decision has to be clear to judges who were not present during the discussion; the standards for such judgments require a type of discourse that is lineal and propositional, and not dependent on extratextual cues for its interpretation. Circular reasoning characterizes this approach to research. The functional approach posits a type of literate propositional discourse as necessary to high-quality decisions, while the recognition and judgment of high-quality decisions is itself dependent on the participants' having used just that style of discourse.

Some studies of women's communication suggest that the talk among women does not necessarily take the form of literate propositional discourse. Women's discourse has been described as episodic and non-hierarchical in structure, relying on extratextual and nonverbal cues for its interpretive context (Clinchy, 1987; Jones, 1980; Kalcik, 1975; Presnell, 1989; Roach, 1985; Yocum, 1971). Instead of applying logical inference to determine correct moral choices, women determine a moral response situationally by seeking to minimize harm to all persons within the social context (Gilligan, 1982). Baird (1976) reported a study that found men to be more interested in winning and women more interested in a fair outcome (p. 188). Women's decision making involves exploring the consequences of possible actions to each person involved in the situation (Belenky, Clinchy, Goldberger, & Tarule, 1986).

Judging the quality of decisions made through episodic and conversational discourse, with emphasis on contextual and nonverbal cues for interpretation, would require familiarity with the group's discussion; evaluations of such decisions by a panel of outside judges would not be an appropriate way to evaluate their quality since the decisions themselves would not necessarily be understandable outside the context of the decision-making process. Lacking a set of hierarchical propositional criteria against which to judge the quality of such decisions, judges might conclude that the decisions were inadequate if not unintelligible. Thus, women's discourse in decision making would be as unlikely to meet the standards for adequacy in this model as women's discourse was in the descriptions of moral decision making formulated by Kohlberg (1981). By equating task-relevant communication with literate propositional discourse, and by making the judgment of the quality of the decision dependent on its incorporation of such low-context propositional discourse, this approach has effectively excluded from consideration forms of task-relevant communication or decision making most often associated with women's communication styles.

I am not proposing to substitute one method of judging the quality of a decision for another, or even to compare the relative merits of either method. There are occasions when linear, propositional discourse is absolutely appropriate and necessary to the process of decision making as well as to the evaluation of such decisions. Deliberations in law making and in court decisions are examples of such occasions. On the other hand, to equate task-relevant communication *solely* with low-context propositional discourse unnecessarily limits the ability of researchers to describe and evaluate group decision making in general. Such an equation further carries the risk of misconstruing decision-making communication patterns appropriate in other contexts.

A second assumption made by the functional approach is that communication can be unequivocally categorized as relevant to the task or not. Task-relevant communication is defined by its form and by its topic. In the study reported by Hirokawa (1983), coders categorized 1,903 functional utterances, basing their decisions "*not* on their perceptions of the *intent* of the speaker . . . but rather, on their perception of how the utterance appeared to function in the course of the discussion" (p. 68; emphasis in the original text). This assumption again reflects an understanding of decision making as a procedure based on low-context propositional discourse, since the function of any utterance must be apparent to an external judge in order to be correctly categorized. Comments not specifically addressed to the topics defined in the model as task relevant would not be construed as contributing to the decision-making process, and thus would be judged irrelevant.

Alternative styles of discourse described above as typical of women—reliant on context cues for interpretation and characterized by episodic and nonhierarchical structure—would not be recognized as task relevant in this model. Women's communication has been described as focusing on maintenance of relationships, avoiding overt conflict, and promoting social unity and cohesion. Belenky et al. (1986) described "connected learning" as a style of learning and knowing preferred by women. Connected knowing is a process of empathy or an attempt to "share the experience that has led the person to form the idea" (p. 113). Women attempting to make a decision might share personal stories related to the topic at hand as a way of understanding one another's experiences in order to evaluate the possible consequences of a proposed action to people who would be affected by the decision. These stories would serve both to establish close relationships among the group members and to enable them to move toward a decision on the problem. In such a model of communication, the distinction between social maintenance and task-relevant communication breaks down; the distinction is difficult if not impossible to make.

Thus, both the form and content of women's communication may lie outside the parameters of the functional model of small group communication. While this approach may be relevant to a small number of task groups that function in the public sphere, the model will not suffice to describe all decision making in all small group contexts.

The Structurational Approach

In 1983, Poole reported that small groups do not necessarily follow a unitary model of decision making as described in much of the traditional research (e.g., Hirokawa), and he developed a multiple sequence model of small group decision making. "Multiple sequence theories," Poole wrote, "explain decision processes as a function of contingency variables that lead groups to take various decision paths" (p. 207). Poole, Seibold, and McPhee (1986) postulated that the key problem pervading small group research is the lack of a theoretically encompassing approach to small group dynamics. In pursuit of a theory of small group decision making that could account for both process and content as well as stability and change, Poole, et al. turned to a macrosociology theory called structuration (Giddens, 1976, 1979) and adapted structuration theory to the study of small group dynamics and decision making.

Structurational theory describes how group systems, defined as regularized relationships between individuals and groups, are generated by rules and resources within groups. Rules are propositions that indicate how something should be done, while resources are materials, possessions, or attributes of group members. As described by Poole, Seibold, and McPhee (1985), structuration represents a complex and flexible framework for studying a variety of behaviors in small group contexts. Applying structurational theory to a group would require a variety of forms of data, including researcher observations and accounts from group members. Poole et al. stipulated that the process of interpretation of data would require an interaction among these forms of data to elucidate the various levels and forms of group interaction. In this abstract form, there seems to be no reason why such a theoretical perspective should not be able to explicate women's experiences and values in small groups.

However, a feminist critique of structuration theory reveals that the theory is grounded in a study of formal institutions that are both sexist and hostile to women. Giddens's theory (1976) hypothesized three elements of structure involved in social interaction. The first, communication or signification, is drawn from the study of language. The second, power or domination, is drawn from the study of political economy. The third element, morality or legitimization, is drawn from the study of religion, ethics, and law. All of these institutions have actively participated in the subordination and devaluation of women (Coote & Gill, 1974; Gilligan, 1982; Oakley, 1974; Spender, 1980; Waring, 1988). Giddens had no choice but to study sexist institutions; at the macro level of social analysis there are no alternative institutional structures. But it remains to be seen whether a theory thus derived can explicate the lives and experiences of women in women's groups.

In applying structuration theory to small group dynamics, Poole et al. (1986) retained the sexist underpinnings of structuration theory in several ways. In their analysis of small group decision making, Poole et al. adopted Giddens' three elements of interaction, interpreting them as (a) members' expression of preferences (communication), (b) argumentation as a means of advancing and modifying decision premises (power), and (c) strategic tactics members employ to win assent for their proposals (norms) (pp. 84-85). As conceptualized by Poole et al., decision making involves a choice premised on a series of literate propositional statements which compete for acceptance by group members. I have already established that this model may not adequately describe women's decision-making processes.

Additionally, Poole et al. did not question Giddens' conflation of power with dominance, a particularly male definition of power. Poole et al. (1986) defined power as "the capacity to alter a course of events by intervening" (p. 79). An alternative feminist interpretation of power would encompass all three elements of interaction, requiring a different definition of those elements. "The true representation of power," wrote Heilbrun (1988), "is not of a big man beating a smaller man or a woman. Power is the ability to take one's place in whatever discourse is essential to action and the right to have one's part matter" (p. 18). In this definition of the concept, power is not a unidirectional force exerted by an agent on others, but a dynamic relationship among group members implying both a willingness to share one's ideas and an openness to consider the ideas of others.

Aries (1976) found that groups made up of all women tended to shift leadership rather than having a fixed dominance, and Jenkins and Kramer (1978) reported the development of a concept of "rotating leadership" adopted by feminist action groups and collectives. In a study of a women's craft guild, I found the same system of sharing leadership responsibilities among the members (Wyatt, 1988). In these cases, power becomes defined as a kind of shared responsibility instead of as a force exerted on some group members by other group members. Incorporating this definition of power into the structurational theory would require a reconceptualization of the elements of interaction.

Additionally, there is some evidence that women and men differ in the strategies they use to achieve their goals. Stoll and McFarlane (1973) found that while men excelled at games in which competition was rewarded, women excelled at games in which cooperation was rewarded. Aries (1976) reported that men in all men's groups established a sense of comraderie through story telling, while women developed a sense of intimacy through self-revelation.

Communication within women's consciousness raising groups illustrates a very different set of strategies leading toward a goal of mutual education and support. In such groups the members avoid confrontation by taking turns speaking, a process which also creates a "leaderless" group structure. Members' satisfaction is the measure of group success, and emotion and personal experience are highly valued as contributions to the group discussion. Speech strategies of filling in (leaving phrases and sentences unfinished for another speaker to complete), tieing together (providing explicit transitions to new subjects), and serializing (several speakers collaborate to complete a story) were common in the consciousness-raising groups (Jenkins & Kramer, 1978). So the possibility exists that the strategies used by women may not be recognized or acknowledged as strategies, if the definition for strategy incorporated into structuration theory reflects sexist practices of groups at the macro level of analysis.

Although structuration incorporates a number of sexist assumptions, this perspective has two important advantages for the study of women's communication in small groups: (a) structuration recognizes the relevance and importance of reproduction of the social order; and (b) structuration requires coordination of the perspectives of both researchers and subjects for data interpretation.

Unlike the functional approach, structurational theory recognizes reproduction of the social order as important work. Social structures, like language, are produced and reproduced by the behaviors of group members. The structurational perspective does not privilege some actions over others, at least in theory. Foregrounding the importance of the production and reproduction of specific social practices focuses on the kinds of interactions most often associated with women's communication: maintenance of relationships, avoiding overt conflict, and promoting social unity and cohesion. Understanding decision making as a process requires attention not only to formal propositional statements, but also and especially to communication more often adopted by women's ways of knowing and learning, such as shared stories or episodic development of stories, as well as to extracontextual cues such as nonverbal communication.

Structurational theory differs from traditional social scientific theories in employing dialectical explanations, a mode of explanation that combines causal and interpretive frameworks (Poole et al., 1985). This requirement necessitates linking researchers' and subjects' perspectives on the small group process. In other words, explaining what goes on in a small group requires not only description by an observer, but also accounts from the participants in the group. Furthermore, study of a group must take place over time so that the development of structurational elements can be examined. With these methods of study, participants in the research have the opportunity to offer explanations and interpretations of their own communicative behaviors. Participants could explain their processes of idea development and provide accounts of the nonverbal cues or other extratextual cues that modify the meaning of verbal statements.

Although structurational theory as presently constituted incorporates a number of sexist elements, there seems to be no intrinsic reason why the framework could not be adapted usefully to the study of women's communication within women's groups. By identifying elements of structure appropriate to women's definitions of power, morality, and language in place of the male definitions proposed by Poole et al., we should be able to describe and analyze how women organize and make decisions in small groups. The necessity within this theoretical perspective for consultation with participants in order to interpret data and the importance of long-term study are also valuable elements of this framework for the study of women's small group communication.

Symbolic Convergence

Bormann (1972, 1986) developed symbolic convergence theory from the study of communication in small groups, so this theory is particularly appropriate for such study. In contrast to the functional approach, which aims to describe and evaluate specific types of interaction/outcome relationships, Bormann (1986) called convergence theory a general theory that can account for broad classes of events. Symbolic convergence theory has three parts: (a) the discovery and arrangement of recurring communicative forms and patterns that indicate the evolution and presence of shared group consciousness; (b) the description of the dynamic tendencies within communication systems that explain why group consciousness arises, continues, declines, and disappears; and (c) the effects that it has in terms of meaning, motives, and communication within the group (Bormann, 1986, pp. 220-221). Group consciousness arises when members of a group share a group fantasy, defined as "the creative and imaginative shared interpretation of events that fulfills a group psychological or rhetorical need" (p. 221).

Researchers can identify and study group fantasy themes by collecting samples of group interaction through written or electronic records of the communication or by using individual or focus group interviews or pencil and paper tests (Bormann, 1986). From these data, researchers reconstruct a description of the dramatic elements of fantasy shared by group members in the form of puns or other word play, double entendres, figures of speech, analogies, anecdotes, allegories, fables, or narratives (Bormann, 1986, p. 224). The psychological process of participating in a fantasy theme drama includes emotional identification with one or more of the characters in the drama or of empathy with such characters. In sharing a group fantasy, group members jointly experience the same emotions and develop narratives that make sense of their common experiences and common fate in the group.

Symbolic convergence theory was developed from the study of classroom groups, which may account for Bormann's (1986) identification of the elements of narrative as good and bad characters in a sequence of interrelated incidents (p. 225). A university classroom is quintessentially a male-dominated and literate environment, where women's ways of knowing and learning are not highly valued (Belenky et al., 1986; Hall & Sandler, 1982). Bormann's description of narrative as having a beginning-middle-end development closely resembles the narrative form associated with literate environments and with men's communicative style (Presnell, 1989).

In contrast, women's narratives have been described as nonlinear, using "kernel stories" which might or might not be elaborated by a single speaker or by a series of speakers (Jones, 1980; Kalcik, 1975; Roach, 1985). Kernel stories are defined as brief references to the subject, the central action, or an important piece of dialogue from a longer story, in other words, as a potential story. "Kernel stories," Kalcik reported, "may be developed by adding exposition and detail or adding nonnarrative elements such as a rationale for telling the story; an apology; an analysis of the characters, events, or theme; or an emotional response to the story" (1975, p. 7). Kernel stories are shaped to fit the situation and may appear alone or in a series. Using Bormann's description of narrative, a researcher might not recognize this form of narrative often used by women, which features an episodic development elaborating a theme from different points of view rather than story development toward a climax (Presnell, 1989, p. 126). If symbolic convergence theory were applied to discourse without concurrent interpretation by both researchers and group participants, the necessity to recognize narrative elements out of context might impose a literate/male bias on data interpretation.

To illustrate the application of symbolic convergence theory to a specific instance, I refer to a case study by Bormann, Pratt, and Putnam (1978) that poses questions of women's leadership and participation in small group decision making. Bormann et al. used fantasy theme analysis to interpret the interaction of students in small groups in a semester-long organizational simulation exercise. Their extensive case history documented the emergence of women as leaders in the developing organization. Women constituted the majority of students in this class and ended up occupying all positions of leadership. Bormann et al. characterized the women's leadership in the resulting organization as follows:

> In the absence of authorized formal leadership, the females conducted the routine functions of GDI [the organization] through a complex informal network of interpersonal contacts. (p. 155)

This explanation for how and why women emerged as leaders in the orga-

nization was based on an interpretation of sexual fantasies including cas-
tration and homosexuality initiated by the male group members who did
not achieve leadership. Bormann et al. accounted for the lack of formal .
structure by noting that the male members of the groups refused to legitimize the female leadership with their support, implying that the women
organized in this fashion by default instead of by design. But an alternative
interpretation could posit that the women preferred a informal, nonhierarchical network of interpersonal contacts as a modus operandi (Belenky et
al., 1986; Gilligan, 1982; Jenkins & Kramer, 1978; Wyatt, 1988). The
women might have created such a structure because they preferred that
way of organizing.

The possibility also exists that the women's fantasies were not recognized as such, because they did not fit the researchers' definitions of
narrative. If the women's shared fantasies took a high-context, episodic
form, they might not have been immediately recognizable by observers or
researchers who were not involved in the interaction. The men in the
groups may not have recognized the elements of shared female fantasies,
and thus may not have responded to the women's stories, which would
have left them unable to participate within a system with which they were
not familiar.

Bormann (1986) warned that some evidence of shared fantasies
might be furnished by "cryptic allusions to common ground" (p. 227),
which could include symbolic cues such as words, phrases, slogans, or
nonverbal signs or gestures. Perhaps Bormann was referring to elements
defined by Kalcik (1975) as "kernel stories." Close attention to such subtle
cues and an interactive process of data interpretation would perhaps provide indications of women's storytelling as well as the more commonly
understood male narrative forms.

Symbolic convergence theory has several advantages to
researchers interested in studying communication within women's groups.
The theory can be used to explore a variety of small groups, not just decision-making task groups. The general character of this theory allows for
the exploration of consciousness-raising groups as well as other voluntary
groups that take as their purpose the production and reproduction of the
social fabric. The themes of the shared fantasies emerge from the interaction of the group, so the methodology imposes a minimum of preconceived notions on the collection and interpretation of data. Finally, the
methodology associated with this theoretical perspective is flexible and
allows for interactive interpretation by researchers and participants within
the small group. While Bormann does not stipulate a cooperative interpretation of the research data, such a procedure would seem to be compatible with the theoretical perspective.

Analysis of the three most important theoretical perspectives commonly used to investigate small group communication reveals that the functional approach offered little possibility for describing and interpreting women's communication patterns. Structuration offered a more complex and flexible theoretical perspective in which to study communication, and it could be adapted to the study of women's small group communication if we could discover the basic structural elements of oral forms of discourse often associated with women's communication. Symbolic convergence theory is a general theory that holds promise for the investigation of women's communication if interpretation of the data can be focused on identifying elements of women's as well as men's fantasy themes, and if the interpretation of the data is informed by the group participants as well as by researchers' perceptions.

STUDIES OF WOMEN'S COMMUNICATION

The amount of research on communication in small groups within our discipline palls in comparison with the amount of research into small group dynamics carried out in sociology, social psychology, management, and related fields. In a recent review article, Levine and Moreland (1990) listed 431 studies from 59 different journals and books as representative of work done since 1980 on group dynamics. They found the field quite vigorous but badly fragmented, noting that many people who study small groups publish in different journals and do not read one another's literature. Of the 431 citations in their representative, rather than exhaustive, analysis, they cited one article published in *Human Communication Research* (Hirokawa, 1983) and one article published in the *Quarterly Journal of Speech* (Poole et al., 1985). These two were the only works from our discipline cited in this review; they represented respectively the functional and structurational approaches to the study of small group dynamics.

Study of women, sex, and gender in small groups is similarly carried out largely outside our own field. In a recent review of the literature on leadership and gender, Shimanoff and Jenkins (in press) cited 102 articles from 26 journals. Of these 102 articles, 8 articles (7.8%) were published in communication journals, while the rest appeared in sociology, social psychology, or management journals. Shimanoff and Jenkins have summarized findings from these articles, noting that the studies were carried out almost exclusively with white, middle-class groups. They reported on leadership behaviors of women and men in groups, the effectiveness of women and men as leaders, the effects of sex-role stereotypes on the perception of women and men as leaders, and the role of group dynamics in defining leadership in small groups. Shimanoff and Jenkins ended with recommendations for eliminating sexist assumptions and stereotypes in small groups in order to increase leadership effectiveness, and to increase the possibility that more competent women will become leaders. Not surprisingly, Shimanoff and Jenkins found that both women and men can be effective leaders, but that men are more often perceived to be leaders than are women. Even when the behaviors of women and men as leaders are identical, men are perceived more positively than women. A number of stereotypes lead to the perception of women as less able or more negative than men.

Pearson (1985) summarized research on differences which exist in communication between women and men in small group interaction and differences in their leadership behavior. Citing research conducted in the 1960s Pearson reported that men tend to initiate more verbal activity than do women and to be more informative, objective, and goal-oriented. Women were reported to be more opinionated than men and more likely to withdraw from unpleasant interactions. Research indicates that women are sometimes perceived to be less competent in problem solving or decision making.

The question of the relative competitiveness and cooperativeness of women and men has generated considerable research; this literature seems relevant to the study of behavior in small groups. Pearson again cited research from the 1970s indicating women are more cooperative than men and more willing to share resources. Researchers have claimed that men play to win, while women play to avoid losing and that women are more interested in a fair outcome than in winning (1985, p. 317).

Conflict and its resolution have direct implications for behavior in small groups, and some research from the 1960s and 1970s indicate that women and men differ in how they engage in both. Pearson (1985) reported that men are more likely to engage in aggression or in deception and deceit than are women; women are more likely to use socially acceptable behavior to resolve conflict.

One of the problems in using reviews such as those by Pearson (1985) and Shimanoff and Jenkins (in press) to examine the topic of gender and communication within the context of small groups is that the reviews tend to cite research studies uncritically, regardless of the context of the research. For example, studies cited to support the different behaviors of women and men in situations of conflict and conflict resolution quoted by Pearson (1985) included an unpublished article by Gordon and Cohn (1961) entitled, "The Effects of Affiliation Drive Arousal on Aggression in Doll Interviews" and a book by Lefkowitz, Eron, Walder, and Huesmann (1977), *Growing Up to be Violent: A Longitudinal Study of the Development of Aggression.* The review gave these sources equal weight. A number of articles cited by Shimanoff and Jenkins (in press) are studies of dyads or tryads, and an argument could be made that such studies do not accurately represent the behavior of women and men in larger groups (Edelsky, 1981). Articles from 30 years ago are given equal credence with more recent publications, although an argument might be made that social changes have rendered the validity of these reports questionable. The possibility clearly exists that by citing such studies without critically examining their assumptions and methodologies, we are contributing to the stereotypes that are a confounding factor in much of the research on women's and men's attitudes and behaviors in small groups. We should not be surprised to find, for example, that a number of researchers report that in general, males appear to possess masculine characteristics consistent with the instrumental or task-oriented behaviors expected of a male leader (e.g., independent, aggressive, analytical, competitive, self-disciplined, objective, and task-oriented), while females are said to display expressive or relational behaviors when serving as a leader (e.g., dependent, passive, nonaggressive, sensitive, subjective, and people-oriented) (Pearson, 1985, p. 322).

Bradley (1980) researched the effect of gender stereotypes on the evaluation of women and men as group members. In a study of student interaction using confederates, she demonstrated that "highly competent women succeeded in exerting influence and in eliciting reasonable, less dominant, and less hostile treatment" from other group members, although she also noted that such highly competent women were not well liked by the males in the groups (p. 110).

To review the literature on women's and men's communication within small groups would take up too much space in this chapter and would probably bore readers. Several good reviews have already been cited (Baird, 1976; Cragan & Wright, 1988; Gouran, 1985; Shimanoff & Jenkins, in press). Instead, I propose to take a single topic and show how different researchers working from a variety of perspectives have handled that topic. I illustrate how an approach consistent with a feminist perspective will bring to light new definitions, new findings, and new questions.

An important topic in the investigation of women's and men's communication in groups concerns interruptions or simultaneous talk. Early on, the study of interruptions was framed as a question of social dominance; interruptions were seen as taking the speaking turn away from someone else, and in that way serving as a domination strategy. Men were generally found to dominate women in these studies. Willis and Williams (1976) found that:

> Men are much more likely to talk simultaneously when women are speaking than when men are speaking but the reverse is not true for women. Although women were observed to agree with men more

often than they disagreed with them, men were observed to disagree with women over four times more often than they agreed with them. (p. 1070)

Willis and Williams concluded that "patterns of simultaneous talking may prove to be a useful index of dominance" (p. 1070). Zimmerman and West (1975) found that males were responsible for 96% of the interruptions in the male-female conversations they studied. Other researchers also report that men interrupt more than women (Eakins & Eakins, 1978; Natale, Entin, & Jaffe, 1979). In general, interruptions were interpreted in terms of their function in the communication process, with people who interrupt others seen as socially dominant over people who are interrupted, and who presumably are thereby silenced.

As it turns out there is disagreement not only on the interpretation of research results, but even on what actually happens in the interaction. Kraemer and Jacklin (1979) and Dindia (1987) have asserted that these findings are artificial artifacts of faulty statistical analysis. In a study using the statistical method devised by Kraemer and Jacklin, Dindia found that both men and women interrupted opposite-sex partners more than they interrupted same-sex partners (p. 362). Taking a different perspective, Kennedy and Camden (1983) disputed the assertion that interruptions function as dysfunctional, dominant communicative acts. Studying interactions among graduate students, these researchers concluded that "interruptions appeared to function as healthy functional communicative acts" (p. 55). They noted that nearly half of the interruptions confirmed the speaker, while the remaining interruptions were disagreements with or rejections of the speaker. Kennedy and Camden concluded that, "Interruptions are dysfunctional by definition only, not necessarily by function" (p. 55).

Most of these research studies on interruptions were carried out using dyads in contrived and formal settings, with the researchers using variables that were designated a priori. The roles of women and men in the communicative interaction were conceptualized in an almost mechanistic way (Edelsky, 1981). Researchers functioned as observers who set up the communicative interactions, chose the levels of analysis, created and applied the coding schemes for analysis, and interpreted the results unilaterally. It is not unusual for conversational analysis researchers to hire people to transcribe the recorded dialogue.

In contrast to these practices, Edelsky (1981) conducted a conversational analysis of a series of committee meetings in which she was herself a participant. Her study embodies many aspects of feminist theory and criticism. In her study, Edelsky functioned both as participant and as observer, using one perspective to enrich her understanding of the other. She used a form of "connected knowing" (Belenky et al., 1986) in applying an intuitive, empathic approach to transcription and interpretation of the data, in addition to the traditional analytic approach (which she found to be inadequate). She placed her interpretation of the interaction within the context, even to the point of refusing to aggregate the data of the five meetings on the grounds that each was very different from the others. She paid careful attention to process both in the interactions she was studying and to the process of doing the research. Her report of her research study is reflective and nonauthoritative; she illustrates her journey through the process with examples and stories, moving easily from report to reflection and back. She described her research study as a "fishing expedition," which I thought was a happy coincidence with my own characterization of this chapter.

Edelsky found that the concept "turn" was inaccurate in describing the communicative interactions she was studying. She explained that conversation has been theoretically constituted as speaking "one-at-a-time," but that characterization may be an artifact of the research methodology or of a certain type of interaction studied. Instead of comparing women and men speaking in turn and drawing conclusions from those comparisons, Edelsky found that she had to find a different way to describe and categorize the interactions she had observed. She distinguished "turn," which she defined as "on-the-record speaking behind which lies an intention to convey a message that is both referential and functional" (p. 403) from "floor," which she defined as "the acknowledged what's-going-on within a psychological time/space" (p. 405). Using these concepts, Edelsky found that it is possible to take a turn without having the floor, and that someone can have the floor without speaking. If there is nothing going on in a group, she found, there may be no floor.

Edelsky distinguished and described two different kinds of floors which she nominated F1 and F2. F1 is developed when people speak one-at-a-time, while F2 is developed collaboratively among many speakers. She found that there were at least twice as many F1s in most meetings, and that each F1 episode was considerably longer than most F2 episodes. F1 episodes consisted of individuals sequentially reporting or analyzing, while F2 episodes consisted of many persons idea-building simultaneously. F2 episodes were characterized by "deep overlaps" during which several persons talked simultaneously with their communication serving the same function and having similar content.

After she had described these two phenomena, Edelsky was able to analyze the relative participation of men and women in each. She found that in F1s the men held forth, took longer turns (though not more turns), and dominated the floor by talking more. In F2s women didn't talk more, but men talked less, occasionally even less than the women. In F1 episodes men's turns were 1 1/4 to nearly 4 times longer than women's turns (about 31.87 words per turn for men and 8.58 words per turn for women), but in F2 episodes both women's and men's turns averaged about 6.5 words. In F2 episodes women joked, argued, directed, and solicited responses more and men less, exactly the reverse for F1s. Edelsky concluded that women are trained not to assert themselves in situations characterized by monologues, single-party control, and hierarchical interaction where floors are won or lost. In more informal, cooperative ventures women felt safe in displaying a fuller range of language ability. Edelsky pointed out that the traditional understanding of conversation is framed in a metaphor of competition in which someone controls or dominates, and where it is possible to win or lose. That characterization was found to be inadequate to describe some of the interactions she studied.

Fisher (1985) wrote that our ignorance of leadership in groups far outweighs our knowledge. In regard to gender, he noted that the gender or sex role of leaders has been found to have a significant main effect on member perceptions (of leadership) (Greene, Morrison, & Tischler, 1981), an effect swamped by behavioral variables (for example, Alderton & Jurma, 1980), and no discernible effect at all (for example, Eskilson & Wiley, 1976). The last word on women and leadership seems to be that nobody knows.

Fisher proposed the study of leader-as-medium as potentially more useful in describing leadership in all of its complexities than previous approaches. Instead of trying to simplify leadership into its component roles and to identify the roles or the proportion of roles that inhere in leadership, Fisher proposed that we begin with the notion that leadership functions as a mediator between events or group actions and the final conclusion or actions by the group in terms of performance outcomes (p. 183). The functions or qualities necessary to become a leader and to maintain leadership are quite different, and so wide experience and flexibility in behavior would characterize an effective leader. The leader-as-medium concept poses leadership as a series of parallel social relationships (p. 190). Posed in this general way, such an approach would seem to be amenable to the study of women in groups and to bypass the focus on stereotypical male/female roles that has plagued previous studies of gender and communication in small groups.

To summarize, the study of women in small groups has largely treated gender, usually confounded with biological sex, as a variable among other variables and has compared women's communicative behavior, styles, and attitudes with men's. The comparison has often assumed polarity, asking how women are different from men and what the consequences of those differences are. But gender is not a variable; gender is basic to all forms of human experience. Gender forms a basic category of analysis, and to conduct research from a feminist perspective is to recreate the research process (Foss & Foss, 1989).

FEMINIST STUDIES IN SMALL GROUP COMMUNICATION

A survey of titles in *Women's Studies in Communication* from 1983 to 1988 showed considerable research in a variety of contexts, but only one article dealt with small group communication. In 1987, Wieder-Hatfield investigated differences in self-reports of leadership behavior between women and men. A search of the social science literature outside our own field revealed a number of studies of women in small groups and studies that were feminist in conception, but none of those studies dealt directly with communication.

Three of the 13 chapters in *Women Communicating: Studies of Women's Talk* (Bate & Taylor, 1988) described communication in small groups of women: "Shared Leadership in the Weavers Guild" (Wyatt, 1988), "Jock Talk: Cooperation and Competition within a University Women's Basketball Team" (Booth-Butterfield & Booth-Butterfield, 1988), and "Women's Ways: Interactive Patterns in Predominantly Female Research Teams" (Nelson, 1988).

My study of decision making in a craft guild in a small community (Wyatt, 1988) combined individual interviews, participant observation, and an examination of guild documents to describe a negotiated process of leadership. I found two types of leaders in the group: opinion leaders and organizers. The opinion leaders articulated different visions of the group's purpose and direction, while the organizers were different people each year, sharing the duties and responsibilities of the guild in the manner described by Jenkins and Kramer (1978) for feminist action groups. The group's activities varied as the influence of the opinion leaders waxed or waned, but the opinion leaders were very careful not to create division among group members. No status differences were associated with either of these leadership roles; indeed, power and status were not relevant concepts for group members. Individual members carefully orchestrated their behavior in a nonhierarchical pattern to maintain a balance of influence and responsibility so that each member could meet her own goals in the group, thereby ensuring the group's continued existence.

Booth-Butterfield and Booth-Butterfield (1988) investigated the themes of cooperation and competition within a women's athletic team. Using a combination of focused group interview, a Likert-type questionnaire, and individual interviews, the authors described how the coach and team members carefully managed their communication patterns and topics to coordinate their efforts and avoid intrateam competition. The authors concluded that team members avoided the possible role strain inherent in the differing societal expectations for "women" and "athletes" by forming their own subculture within the team. In this subculture, competition and cooperation were not gender-linked, but appropriate or inappropriate as defined by the team. The women on the team managed their communicative behavior to create a social space within which cooperation led to team unity, and individual competition was avoided or suppressed by carefully focusing such communication and behavior toward other teams.

Nelson (1988) described the communication of five successive teacher-research teams in a university writing center. Nelson's account drew from a variety of sources including: (a) research reports and other writing done for the tutor-training courses; (b) audiotapes of classes, staff meetings, and research sessions; and (c) interviews with team members. Nelson illustrated how the teams she worked with created a collegial workplace within the usual hierarchical academic structure. Team members created laterally organized groups in which analysis and decision making were collaborative, offering each other emotional support as well as constructive criticism. Nelson concluded that "women's ways" are not exclusively female, since the males who were on the teams quickly learned those ways.

Outside the discipline of speech communication, researchers have described similar patterns of organizing and communicating within women's consciousness raising groups (Jenkins & Kramer, 1978; Kalcik, 1975), a quilting bee (Roach, 1985), and a family reunion (Yocum, 1971).

The communication patterns within the groups described above differ in significant ways from patterns described in traditional small group communication research. Teamwork and leadership take on different meanings in the context of women's interactions. Equally interesting were the forms of the research reports themselves; the reports included many details of the context and references to individuals. The participants in the research were not "subjects," and the researchers did not claim to be reporting "objective reality." The researchers carefully described their research purposes, their relationships to the group members, and their own subjectivities as these factors might have influenced the conduct of the study or the interpretation of the results.

PROPOSALS FOR FEMINIST RESEARCH

This chapter has offered a feminist critique of scholarship in small group communication. Two basic precepts of feminism have informed my critique. First, a feminist critique posits that gender, class, and race form basic organizing principles of social organization. Within a single culture the experience of women and men can be strikingly different; studies of social institutions or practices that do not account for the different experiences of male and female persons cannot be complete or representative.

Second, a feminist critique attempts to account for the observed power differential between the genders and for the routine subordination of women and their perspectives within the culture. A feminist stance toward scholarship in speech communication can shed new light on our routine assumptions and practices, casting some into the shade and highlighting others. The result is not unlike a stage set when the lights change from blue to yellow, with different aspects of the set then highlighted. While the furniture and actors remain the same, a new vision of the play emerges.

In the foregoing sections of this chapter I established that traditional academic scholarship on small group communication has to varying degrees ignored or devalued women's roles and experiences in small groups. The question now arises: What should we do to remedy these inequities? What practices can we adopt that will honor women's roles and value their perspectives and experiences both in small groups and in the scholarship that addresses communication in small groups?

The following discussion of the new shapes and textures feminist research in small group communication might take has been informed by the thoughtful comments of many scholars. Two important sources were journal issues that addressed feminism in communication research: *Women's Studies in Communication*, Volume 11, 1988, and the *Journal of Communication Inquiry*, Volume 11, 1987. Discussions with feminist scholars and researchers at meetings and conventions have also influenced this chapter. Comments and suggestions from my coauthors in this volume have sharpened and expanded my analysis. Drawing from elements of these feminist critiques and theory, as well as from previous critiques of mainstream small group communication research, I offer three directions for future research. We must study groups of women and minorities in their own contexts. We must reexamine our research goals and assumptions for evidence of bias, and look to feminist theory for new directions. Finally, since feminism is a political movement, we must work in our research as well as in our teaching for a revaluation of women's experience, work, and ways of knowing in the scholarly world as well as in the community.

Our first task will be to locate and begin to study groups that have not been studied previously, either because access to them was difficult for researchers, or because they were not thought important enough for serious academic attention. We will have to study more groups of women in women's contexts, and by extension other groups including people of color and people of different social classes in their own contexts. In the past we have concentrated our research efforts on studying what was convenient, as opposed to what needed to be studied. That is, we have studied small group communication using the material most readily available—students in our small group and organizational communication classes. This observation is not news, but it becomes particularly important when we realize just how narrow that focus is. Excluded from these studies are community groups that exist and work over long periods of time, groups of people with less than college degrees (which are most of the people in the United States), people who work in voluntary organizations, and many work groups in business and industrial settings. We cannot claim to have developed a theory of human communication behavior in small groups when we have studied so unrepresentative a sample of small groups.

Not only is the sample that we studied unrepresentative in terms of the kinds of groups studied, but it is also unrepresentative in terms of the contexts in which the small groups are nested. The university setting is and has always been dominated by males in the administration, in the professoriate, and in the student body. For most of their existence universities have actively excluded women, people of color, and people of lower social classes, either by setting quotas or by setting the entrance standards selectively. The ratio of females to males in the student body has now shifted, but the rest of the university has not made the same shift. Women in the academy often find themselves in hostile territory, their ideas, values, and contributions unappreciated if not overtly rejected. We are unlikely to discover how women and other minorities organize themselves and work in groups if we study only those examples that occur in the artificial setting of the university.

Universities are places where literacy is at a premium, and literate discourse is the *lingua franca*. Our studies have assumed literate modes of critical thinking as the basis for discourse, and our methodologies are not designed to recognize the oral forms of discourse that characterize much of the talk of people outside the academy. Yet, those oral forms of discourse prevail in most of the small groups operating within our society today. As educators we try to instill literate communication skills, but as researchers we must be able to recognize, understand, and appreciate alternative forms of discourse.

Where will we find these groups to study? I began this chapter by sitting down to inventory the places where such groups of women could be found and I discovered that I had no idea where to look. The work of women has been made invisible by the definitions of both economists and sociologists, and I have been so thoroughly trained in traditional academic lore that even as a woman I was at a loss for where to begin. Perhaps our first step should be to look around and inventory what kinds of groups are currently operating in our communities. We should figure out how groups contribute to the social welfare of the communities and organizations in which we live and begin to develop some new taxonomies of group types. We need to know what there is before we begin making assumptions about what is important to study. While teaching a small group communication theory course to adult students, I found myself embarrassed by our narrow focus. Older students politely but firmly pointed out to me that most of the groups in which they worked were not represented in our studies, indicating that the ad hoc committees we focused on may not be so relevant as we assumed.

We can begin by looking at places where women have traditionally functioned in the community. In voluntary associations women run thrift shops and many community services, such as those for elderly people. Women run daycare centers and self-help organizations and services, both profit and nonprofit. Women raise funds for charities. Women organize school activities and raise money for schools through parent-teacher organizations. Women work in art alliances and small theaters and other cultural organizations. Women own and run small businesses. Women are the nurses and service workers within larger organizations. Wherever groups contribute to the reproduction of the social fabric, we will find the work of women, people of color, and people of lower social classes. Once we enter this world, I am sure that we will find a wealth of research opportunities lying to hand.

Concurrent with studying different types of groups, we will have to examine the assumptions behind our research goals and methods for inherent bias and develop new ways of researching that take account of lived experience on the terms of the people who are living that experience. Small group communication researchers initially took their cues from social psychologists who were paid by the armed forces and by corporations to find ways of getting more work out of their employees. The biases implicit in this task have spilled over into our own work and have colored our research goals, assumptions, and methods. We have focused on decision making and problem solving to the exclusion of other, equally important, elements of group process. We have accepted without critique the artificial split between task and social maintenance made by sociologists, valuing one above the other.

Small group communication researchers have been moving toward more complex theories and more participatory research methods, but these new directions sometimes unwittingly have incorporated sexist assumptions. We must carefully analyze our taken-for-granted knowledge to find where sexism, classism, and racism may lurk. Language, as many scholars have pointed out, is not the raiment for our thoughts; it is the very fabric of our thoughts themselves. We must examine the language we use to describe how people in small groups think, talk, and act so that we do not perpetuate the mistakes of the past.

For instance, the concept of leadership has been intimately tied to the notion of power, with power defined as influence over the actions of others. But as Wood (1988) has pointed out, Kanter (1977) and Kramarae, Schultz, and O'Barr (1984) have challenged this identification of leadership with power and suggested an alternative concept of empowerment, which proceeds by collaboration toward mutual goals and within a win-win orientation. Heilbrun's (1988) definition of power as "the ability to take one's place in whatever discourse is essential to action and the right to have one's part matter" (p. 18) seems more appropriate to the study of both leadership and small group communication. If we approach the study of small group communication with this focus on collaboration and cooperation, with an understanding and appreciation for empathic ways of understanding one another, and with an appreciation for the time-consuming, complex, and delicate work of establishing and maintaining connections among group members, we might begin to develop a new and exciting body of scholarship.

I have already pointed out how the methods we use may not be well designed to capture the ways of knowing and learning that are most often used by women. We will need new ways of listening to discover and document the oral discourse patterns and collaborative strategies for sharing experience used most often by women. The standard stance of observing groups and reporting our observations may not be well designed to take account of complex interactions that depend on highly contextual cues for their interpretation. We will have to design methods of collaborative investigation to begin to understand women's groups. Presnell (1989) pointed out the ways in which standard interviewing techniques may not be appropriate to the study of women's communication. By looking to feminist theories we will be able to design new ways of listening to and valuing the voices of women.

Collaborative research is not unknown to social science. In his account of research with street gangs, Whyte (1984) described how his contacts with and observations of the gangs he studied were facilitated by a gang member who was eager to have an accurate account of his social group reported to the larger world. Ethnographers and anthropologists regularly establish working relationships with the people they study. If we achieve understanding of others by our connections with them, then the process by which we achieve those insights can itself become an important source of knowledge. Psychoanalysts have described countertransference as the understanding gained from interaction between the participants in a psychoanalytic relationship. We can use such insights in our own research efforts. In her "Appendix on Methods" to *The Court of Last Resort: Mental Illness and the Law*, Warren (1982) described some of the knowledge she gained from her studies of how people are involuntarily committed to mental hospitals through the court system and explained why that knowledge did not become part of her formal findings. The knowledge did, however, influence the findings and the form in which they were presented. If we make such ways of knowing and such knowledge a formal part of our study, we can increase our understanding of others, of the research process, and of ourselves as persons and as researchers. We must work toward establishing such research methodologies as useful and legitimate in the study of communication. In our research we must train ourselves not only to look and observe, but also to listen and understand.

The third direction indicated by a feminist perspective is a commitment to political change, so that our research will be undertaken with the goal of empowering the people we study, not getting them to work harder for someone else. Feminism posits the personal as the political, and until very recently women's lives have been largely excluded from the public forum. But the status quo is also a political position, and defense of the status quo is also a form of political action. Merely to describe the subordination of women or any other social group without attempting to remedy the situation would constitute tacit, if not overt, complicity in the process of subordination.

We can act to remedy social, economic, and political inequities in several ways. We can work within the academy for the reformulation of ways of knowing to include women's as well as men's experience and to incorporate women's values and experiences into our knowledge base (Foss & Foss, 1988). As part of this effort we can work to bring feminist studies into the mainstream publication of scholarship. We can work to bring our scholarship into the classroom, thereby influencing future generations to understand, appreciate, and value the complex social skills necessary for the reproduction of the social structure. We can work within the women's community to bring recognition and respect to the activities and values of women who are reproducing the social order. We can bring increased respect among women as well as men for women's ways of knowing and for women's work.

In this final section, I suggested ways in which we can begin to formulate a feminist perspective in the study of communication within small groups. Such a perspective includes two important elements: (a) the recognition and valuation of women's ways of knowing and organizing; and (b) advocacy for legitimization of those ways in both public and private, academic and political forums. In this effort, we seek not to overthrow previous scholarship, but to elaborate and extend it. The research efforts and findings of the past that incorporated sexist, and possibly racist and classist, assumptions and methods have not been wrong, just narrow. By advocating a comprehensive and ongoing critique and extension of the study of small group communication, we seek to bring the study of communication into a deeper understanding of the human condition.

NOTES TO CHAPTER 3

1. Social science research was funded by the Navy in cooperation with a number of civilian companies that faced personnel problems similar to those of the armed forces. These companies, along with the military services, were also the research laboratories in which the social scientists studied their subjects. In an interim report from the United States Navy's Conference of its Human Relations Advisory Panel and Research Contractors at Dearborn, Michigan, in September 1950, Guetzkow (1963) described research from a variety of sites including an insurance company, a public utility, an automobile manufacturing company, a tractor manufacturing company, and a group of railroad workers. Studies were carried out at the Naval Air Training Command, in the Office of Naval Research, in Naval ROTC classes, and in Naval submarines. Sanford (1963) interviewed people in Philadelphia about leadership. Harris (1963) studied a tuberculosis sanitorium. Mead (1963) reported on an anthropological research project. Laboratory experiments were also carried out at universities, mainly Ohio State University and the University of Michigan.

2. In the late 1940s and early 1950s, universities still had quotas for women students, who did not make up a significant proportion of the student body. The professoriate was also almost exclusively male. Although the 1948 Women's Armed Services Integration Act, P.L. 625, established career opportunities for women in the armed forces, the Act restricted the number of women in the armed services to 2% of the total number of military personnel. The studies of group behavior carried out in the Navy, therefore, were studies of men in exclusively male contexts. Few of the work groups in the civilian organizations described in these studies contained females. If female work groups were the focus of research, as they were in the Harwood Manufacturing Corporation studies done by Coch and French (1948), the women worked within a male-dominated, hierarchically organized and strictly controlled context. Women and minorities who were in the work force at that time had little or no opportunity to shape the group context in which they worked, because they did not occupy supervisory or managerial positions.

3. For a discussion of the definitions of "productive" versus "reproductive" labor, and the implications of these definitions for social science research as well as for women's lives, see Waring (1988), *If Women Counted: A New Feminist Economics*.

4. Darley (1963b) noted: "Several times during the meeting, Dr. Mead faced us with the importance of viewing our findings in a reference frame that is characteristic of the anthropologist—a viewpoint which we as psychologists admittedly understand insufficiently well" (p. 261).

5. In their critique of small group research, Jenkins and Kramer

(1978) wrote, "Typically the small group in academic research is composed of from 2 to 20 members usually drawn from a white middle class
university setting and brought together under laboratory conditions, often
for only one session. There are many social scientists who would question
whether these are groups at all. Perhaps we are looking at encounters
between aggregates of strangers" (p. 77). Jenkins and Kramer went on to
question the focus on concrete outcomes as opposed to patterns of communication as well as the mechanistic and rule-based models for communication used by most communication researchers.

REFERENCES

Alderton, S.M., & Jurma, W.E. (1980). Genderless/gender-related task
    leader communication and group satisfaction: A test of two theses.
    Southern Speech Communication Journal, 46, 48-53.
Aries, E.J. (1976). Interaction patterns and themes of male, female, and
    mixed groups. *Small Group Behavior, 7,* 7-18.
Asch, S. (1951). Effects of group pressure upon the modification and dis-
    tortion of judgment. In H. Guetzkow (Ed.), *Groups, leadership, and
    men* (pp. 177-190). Pittsburgh, PA: Carnegie Press.
Asch, S. (1955). Opinions and social pressure. *Scientific American, 193,*
    31-35.
Asch, S. (1956). Studies of independence and conformity: I. A minority of
    one against a unanimous majority, *Psychological Monographs, 70,*
    (9, whole no. 416).
Baird, J.E., Jr. (1976). Sex differences in group communication: A review of
    relevant research. *Quarterly Journal of Speech, 62,* 179-192.
Bate, B., & Taylor, A. (Eds.). (1988). *Women communicating: Studies of
    women's talk.* Norwood, NJ: Ablex Publishing.
Belenky, M.F., Clinchy, B. Mcv., Goldberger, N.R., & Tarule, J.M. (1986).
    *Women's ways of knowing: The development of self, voice, and
    mind.* New York: Basic Books.
Booth-Butterfield, M., & Booth-Butterfield, S. (1988). Jock talk:
    Cooperation and competition within a university women's basketball
    team. In B. Bate & A. Taylor (Eds.), *Women communicating: Studies
    of women's talk* (pp. 177-199). Norwood, NJ: Ablex Publishing.
Bormann, E.G. (1986). Symbolic convergence theory and communication
    in group decision-making. In R.Y. Hirokawa & M.S. Poole (Eds.),
    Communication and group decision-making (pp. 219-236). Beverly
    Hills, CA: Sage Publications.
Bormann, E.G. (1972). Fantasy and rhetorical vision: The rhetorical criti-
    cism of social reality. *Quarterly Journal of Speech, 58,* 396-407.
Bormann, E.G., Pratt, J., & Putnam, L. (1978). Power, authority, and sex:
    Male response to female leadership. *Communication Monographs,
    45,* 119-155.

Bradley, P.H. (1980). Sex, competence and opinion derivation: An expectations states approach. *Communication Monographs, 47*, 101-110.

Clinchy, B.McV. (1987). Silencing women students. In L.E. Edmundson, J.P. Saunders, & E.S. Silber (Eds.), *Women's voices* (pp. 39-45). Littleton, MA: Copley Publishing.

Coch, L., & French, J. R. P., Jr. (1948). Overcoming resistance to change. *Human Relations, 1*, 512-532.

Coote, A., & Gill, T. (1974). *Women's rights: A practical guide.* Hammondsworth; Penguin Books.

Couch, C. J., Katovich, M. A., & Miller, D. (1987). The sorrowful tale of small groups research. *Studies in Symbolic Interaction, 8*, 158-180.

Cragan, J.F., & Wright, D.W. (1988, November). *Small group communication research of the 1980s: A synthesis and critique.* Paper presented at the Speech Communication Association Annual Convention, New Orleans, LA.

Darley, J.G. (1963). Five years of social science research: Retrospect and prospect. In H. Guetzkow (Ed.), *Groups, leadership and men: Research in human relations* (pp. 3-15). New York: Russell & Russell.

Darley, J.G. (1963). An overview of the conference and its controversies. In H. Guetzkow (Ed.), *Groups, leadership and men: Research in human relations* (pp. 257-266). New York: Russell & Russell.

Dindia, K. (1987). The effects of sex of subject and sex of partner on interruptions. *Human Communication Research, 13*(3), 345-371.

Eakins, B., & Eakins, R.G. (1978). *Sex differences in human communication.* Boston: Houghton-Mifflin.

Edelsky, C. (1981). Who's got the floor? *Language and Society, 10*, 383-421.

Eskilson, A., & Wiley, M.G. (1976). Sex composition and leadership in small groups. *Sociometry, 39*, 183-194.

Favreau, O.E. (1977). Sex bias in psychological research. *Canadian Psychological Review (Psychologie Canadienne), 18*, 56-65.

Fisher, B.A. (1973). *Small group decision-making: Communication and the group process.* New York: McGraw-Hill.

Fisher, B.A. (1979). Content and relationship dimensions of communication in decision-making groups. *Communication Quarterly, 27*, 3-11.

Fisher, B.A. (1985). Leadership as medium: Treating complexity in group communication research. *Small Group Behavior, 16*(2), 167-196.

Foss, S.K., & Foss, K.A. (1988). What distinguishes feminist scholarship in communication studies? *Women's Studies in Communication, 11*(1), 9-11.

Foss, K.A., & Foss, S.K. (1989). Incorporating the feminist perspective in communication scholarship: A research commentary. In K. Carter & C. Spitzack (Eds.), *Doing research on women's communication: Perspectives on theory and method* (pp. 65-94.) Norwood, NJ: Ablex Publishing.

Giddens, A. (1979). *Central problems in social theory: Action, structure and contradiction in social analysis.* Berkeley: University of

California Press.

Giddens, A. (1976). *New rules of sociological method.* New York: Basic Books.

Gilligan, C. (1982). *In a different voice: Psychological theory and women's development.* Cambridge, MA: Harvard University Press.

Gordon, J., & Cohn, F. (1961). *The effects of affiliation drive arousal on aggression in doll interviews.* Unpublished manuscript.

Gouran, D.S. (1985). The paradigm of unfulfilled promise: A critical examination of the history of research on small groups in speech communication. In T.W. Benson (Ed.), *Speech communication in the twentieth century* (pp. 90-108). Carbondale, IL: Southern Illinois University Press.

Gouran, D.S. (1988, November). *Current status and future expectations of small group communication research: Decision making.* Paper presented at the Western Speech Communication Association Convention, San Diego, CA.

Gouran, D.S., & Hirokawa, R.Y. (1983). The role of communication in decision-making groups: A functional perspective. In M.S. Mander (Ed.), *Communications in transitions: Issues and debates in current research* (pp. 168-185). New York: Praeger.

Greene, L.R., Morrison, T.L., & Tischler, N.C. (1981). Gender and authority: Effects on perceptions of small group coleaders. *Small Group Behavior, 12,* 401-414.

Guetzkow, H. (Ed.). (1963). *Groups, leadership and men: Research in human relations.* New York: Russell & Russell.

Hall, R.M., & Sandler, B.R. (1982). *The classroom climate: A chilly one for women?* Washington, DC: Association of American Colleges.

Harris, D.H. (1963). Social and psychological factors in the rehabilitation of the tuberculous. In H. Guetzkow (Ed.), *Groups, leadership, and men: Research in human relations* (pp. 218-233). New York: Russell & Russell.

Heilbrun, C.G. (1988). *Writing a woman's life.* New York: Ballantine Books.

Hirokawa, R.Y. (1983). Group communication and problem-solving effectiveness II: An exploratory investigation of procedural functions. *Western Journal of Speech Communication, 47,* 59-74.

Jenkins, L., & Kramer, C. (1978). Small group process: Learning from women. *Women's Studies International Quarterly, 3,* 67-84.

Jones, D.J. (1980). Gossip: Notes on women's oral culture. *Women's Studies International Quarterly, 3,* 193-198.

Kalcik, S. (1975). "...Like Ann's gynecologist or the time I was almost raped." In C.R. Farrer (Ed.), *Women and folklore* (pp. 3-11). Austin and London: University of Texas Press.

Kanter, R.M. (1977). *Men and women of the corporation.* New York: Basic Books.

Kennedy, C.W., & Camden, C.T. (1983). A new look at interruptions. *Western Journal of Speech Communication, 47,* 45-58.

Kohlberg, L. (1981). *The philosophy of moral development.* New York: Harper & Row.

Kraemer, H.C., & Jacklin, C.N. (1979). Statistical analysis of dyadic social behavior. *Psychological Bulletin, 86,* 217-224.

Kramarae, C., Schultz, M., & O'Barr, W.M. (Eds.). (1984). *Language and power.* Beverly Hills, CA: Sage.

Lefkowitz, M., Eron, L. D., Walder, L. O., & Huesmann, L. R. (1977). *Growing up to be violent: A longitudinal study of the development of aggression.* New York: Pergamon Press.

Levine, J.M., & Moreland, R.L. (1990). Progress in small group research. *Annual Review of Psychology, 41,* 585-634.

Macmillan, J.W., & Page, H.E. (1963). Making military application of human relations research. In H. Guetzkow (Ed.), *Groups, leadership and men: Research in human relations* (pp. 267-274). New York: Russell & Russell.

McGrath, J.E. (1984). *Groups: Interaction and performance.* Englewood Cliffs, NJ: Prentice-Hall.

Mead, M. (1963). Columbia University research in contemporary cultures. In H. Guetzkow (Ed.), *Groups, leadership and men: Research in human relations* (pp. 106-118). New York: Russell & Russell.

Napier, R., & Gershenfeld, M.K. (1973). *Groups: Theory and experiences.* Boston: Houghton-Mifflin.

Natale, M., Entin, E., & Jaffe, J. (1979). Vocal interruptions in dyadic communication as a function of speech and social anxiety. *Journal of Personality and Social Psychology, 45,* 700-705.

Nelson, M.W. (1988). Women's ways: Interactive patterns in predominantly female research teams. In B. Bate & A. Taylor (Eds.), *Women communicating: Studies of women's talk* (pp. 199-233). Norwood, NJ: Ablex Publishing.

Oakley, A. (1974). *The sociology of housework.* New York: Pantheon Books.

Pearson, J.C. (1985). *Gender and communication.* Dubuque, IA: Wm. C. Brown, Publishers.

Poole, M.S. (1983). Decision development in small groups II: A study of multiple sequences in decision making. *Communication Monographs, 50,* 206-232.

Poole, M.S., Seibold, D.R., & McPhee, R.D. (1985). Group decision-making as a structurational process. *Quarterly Journal of Speech, 71,* 74-102.

Poole, M.S., Seibold, D.R., & McPhee, R.D. (1986). A structurational approach to theory-building in group decision-making research. In R.Y. Hirokawa & M.S. Poole (Eds.), *Communication and group decision making* (pp. 237-264). Beverly Hills, CA: Sage.

Presnell, M. (1989). Narrative gender differences: Orality and literacy. In K. Carter & C. Spitzack (Eds.), *Doing research on women's communication: Perspectives on theory and method* (pp. 118-136). Norwood, NJ: Ablex Publishing.

Roach, S. (1985). The kinship quilt: An ethnographic semiotic analysis of a quilting bee. In R.A. Jordan & S.J. Kalcik (Eds.), *Women's folklore, women's culture* (pp. 56-62). Philadelphia: University of Pennsylvania Press.

Rosenfeld, L.B. (1973). *Human interaction in the small group setting.* Columbus, OH: Charles E. Merrill.

Sanford, F.H. (1963). Leadership identification and acceptance. In H. Guetzkow (Ed.), *Groups, leadership and men: Research in human relations* (pp. 158-176). New York: Russell & Russell.

Shimanoff, S. B., & Jenkins, M. M. (in press). Leadership and gender: Challenging assumptions and recognizing resources. In R. S. Cathcart & L. A. Samovar (Eds.), *Small group communication: A reader.* Dubuque, IA: Wm. C. Brown.

Spender, D. (1980). *Man made language.* London: Routledge and Kegan Paul.

Stoll, C.S., & McFarlane, P.T. (1973). Sex differences in game strategy. In C. Stasz Stoll (Ed.), *Sexism: Scientific debates* (pp. 622-657). Reading, MA: Addison-Wesley.

Swanson, G. (1953). A preliminary laboratory study of the acting crowd. *American Sociological Review, 18,* 522-532.

Waring, M. (1988). *If women counted: A new feminist economics.* San Francisco: Harper Row.

Warren, C.A.B. (1982). *The court of last resort: Mental illness and the law.* Chicago and London: The University of Chicago Press.

Whyte, W. (1984). *Learning from the field.* Beverly Hills, CA: Sage.

Wieder-Hatfield, D. (1988). Differences in self-reported leadership behavior as a function of biological sex and psychological gender. *Women's Studies in Communication, 10*(1), 1-14.

Willis, F.N., & Williams, S.J. (1976). Simultaneous talking in conversation and sex of speakers. *Perceptual and Motor Skills, 43,* 1067-1070.

Wood, J.T. (1988). Feminist scholarship in communication: Consensus, diversity, and conversation among researchers. *Women's Studies in Communication, 11,* 22-27.

Wyatt, N. (1988). Shared leadership in the weavers guild. In B. Bate & A. Taylor (Eds.), *Women communicating: Studies of women's talk* (pp. 147-177). Norwood, NJ: Ablex Publishing.

Yocum, M.R. (1971). Woman to woman: Fieldwork and the private sphere. In E.A. Jordan & S.J. Kalcik, (Eds.), *Woman's folklore, women's culture* (pp. 45-53). Philadelphia: University of Pennsylvania Press.

Zander, A. (1979). The study of group behavior during four decades. *Journal of Applied Behavior Science, 15,* 272-282.

Zimmerman, D., & West, C. (1975). Sex roles, interruptions and silences in conversation. In B. Thorne & N. Henley (Eds.), *Language and sex: Difference and dominance* (pp. 105-129). Rowley, MA: Newbury House.

Chapter 4

Performing Differences:
Feminism and Performance Studies

Kristin M. Langellier
University of Maine
Orono, ME

Kathryn Carter
University of Nebraska
Lincoln, NE

Darlene Hantzis
Indiana State University
Terre Haute, IN

We begin with a most obvious fact: In interpretation and performance studies we embody texts in communication with audiences.[1] Somewhat less obvious, "doing literature" and performing do not just invite an analysis of gender but require such an analysis. For as we read and write and perform and direct, we participate in a social discourse with profound and political consequences for what it means to be a woman or a man in our culture and society. All meanings contest, reaffirm, or leave intact existing gender relations. These meanings for gender are everywhere constituted, including which texts are read or not read, how texts are analyzed and performed, and which interpretations are privileged and which are suppressed.

The historical and continuing presence of women and women's texts in oral interpretation and performance studies attests to the visibility and influence of women's scholarship. We assume that teachers and scholars of oral interpretation are interested in gender issues but have, as yet, little systematic guidance and analysis on how to incorporate feminist scholarship into performance theory and practices. For, in comparison to

the blossoming of feminist criticism in related disciplines, especially literature and film, feminist critique in our field is quite sparse, nascent, and just
emerging, or "marginalized within the marginalized." By the latter we
mean the tendency to marginalize performance studies within communication studies coupled with the muting of feminist critique within performance studies. For example, with perhaps one exception, Spitzack and
Carter's (1987) paradigmatic essay on women in communication studies
does not cite performance studies research. In recent reviews of performance studies, feminist criticism is neither named nor discussed, although
its influence is intimated under the rubric of "performance in social contexts" (e.g., Capo, 1983a; Langellier, 1986; Pelias & VanOosting, 1987;
Strine, Long, & HopKins, 1990; Taft-Kaufman, 1985). The inauguration of
the first journal devoted particularly to oral interpretation and performance
studies, *Literature in Performance* (later renamed *Text and Performance
Quarterly*) marked an increased visibility of women's texts and performances as well as women's scholarship: Women author approximately
one-half of the articles and book reviews, and they staff approximately
one-half of the editorial board. But even with this powerful presence, feminist criticism is seldom cited and discussed. As such, its impact on the theory and practice of performance remains to be ascertained.[2]

The situation of feminist analysis in oral interpretation and performance is thus cause for both celebration and critique. In describing the
place of feminist analysis in interpretation and performance studies, we
wish to avoid two extremes of response to the present situation: on the one
hand, the celebratory response that nothing more need be done because
women have already been mainstreamed into performance studies; on the
other hand, the critique of a women's silence so complete that there has
been no feminist presence—indeed, feminist criticism and performances
exist, although much of this activity is unpublished performance and
therefore difficult to access and assess.[3] Our response is to undertake a
feminist critique that does not just include women as objects of analysis,
that is, performance by, about, and on women, but that also advocates a
performance theory and practice for women (Duelli-Klein, 1983). We
argue with Spitzack and Carter (1987) that the visibility of women does
not guarantee empowerment for women unless the analysis and performance of women's texts serve to challenge and complicate the theory and
practices of performance. Without such challenges to dominant assumptions about performance, the insights gained by feminist scholars are easily
placed back into the preestablished frameworks that have distorted and
marginalized women's performance in the past.

Performance for women requires that performance be conceptualized not only as an aesthetic act, but also as a political act in the interest
of women in their racial, ethnic, class, and other social diversities. The

feminist analysis here takes three directions: first, a critique of the masculinist bias that informs the interpretation and performance tradition, particularly of neutralizing concepts which accommodate women but continue to mask the politics of sexual and other social differences; second, a documentation and discussion of feminist work extant in the field; and third, an outline of some future directions for feminist analyses of performance studies, what we call "performing differences." As we conduct our feminist critique, we acknowledge that there are many feminisms (Case, 1990; Donovan, 1987), although our discussion minimizes their differences in order to present a variety of feminist concerns for interpretation and performance studies.

THE CLASSROOM PERFORMANCE TRADITION

The classroom has traditionally been the setting for interpretation and performance. Our intent in saying this is not to privilege the classroom so much as to establish the discursive context within which performance studies take place, a context which, as Strine et al. (1990) point out, is responsive to supporting cultural climates, both academic and professional, as they generate and maintain particular performance activities. For obvious reasons, we shall be concerned with structural and institutionalized sexism, but also with racism and classism, as a prevailing context and climate for performance activities. Tracing research in performance studies from the 1950s to the 1970s, Strine et al. identify a tradition in which oral interpretation is defined as a unique and invaluable method of literary study focusing on literary genres and figures. Interpretation theory integrated the principles of New Criticism and dramatism as an approach to textual analysis. Interpretation practice supplemented conventional textual analysis with an emphasis on the humanizing values inherent in oral interpretation, particularly as they were elaborated by Bacon (1966). The authors conclude that the "the common presuppositions here were that literary texts are repositories of enduring insight and value, and that latent meanings and values embedded within literary texts become manifest and most fully accessible when experienced holistically through the act of performance" (Strine et al., 1990, p. 182).

Moreover, these humanistic assumptions about literary texts and meanings persist in the pedagogical practices of the present classroom. Weedon (1987) describes how the persistence of the humanistic perspective on literary texts participates in the hegemony of liberal humanist discourse, discourse which can serve to guarantee and justify existing social and gender relations. As the basis for the political demands of equal opportunity and self-determination, liberal humanist discourse assumes that each man or woman possesses a unique human essence, usually rationality, which is the source of self-knowledge and knowledge about the world. But the assumption of a rational individual masks the contradictory experiences assured by institutionalized sexism, racism, and classism. According to Weedon, "The structural and institutional oppression of women disappears behind the belief that I as a rational sovereign subject freely choose my way of life on the basis of my rational consciousness which gives me knowledge of the world, then I am not oppressed" (p. 84). Adopted uncritically, a humanistic perspective reinforces rather than challenges existing social structure, and maintains rather than subverts gender, class, and race hierarchies. In this section we trace ways in which the liberal-humanistic classroom tradition functions to include women's voices but to mute feminist critique of the conceptual framework of performance.

The Performance Canon

We use the term "performance canon" here as an analog to the literary canon, or "great works," legitimated throughout academic history in university curricula, in publishing literature and textbooks, in literary criticism and reviews, and in awarding literary prizes. In the classroom, the performance canon as "great performances" is daily fleshed out in basic and advanced interpretation courses by way of anthologies and interpretation textbooks, which include literary selections to illustrate pedagogical concepts and to perform for assignments. But significantly, the literary canon and performance canon are not identical. The response to the demands of oral performance and diverse students, including women and minorities, has resulted in a performance canon more democratic and egalitarian than the dominant, androcentric literary canon which privileges white male texts. Interpretation textbooks continue to respond to demands since the 1970s to include more diverse literary selections. It is possible, for example, to analyze how subsequent editions of textbooks have moved gradually in the direction of gender-balancing as well as adding racial, ethnic, national, and class diversity in their literary selections, although we cannot assume that institutionalized sexism, racism, and classism have been erased.

Other academic performances, such as in university theaters, at festivals, or at speech communication conventions, attest to the inclusion of women, for example, the performance of literature on or about women written by male authors (e.g., Gray, 1983; Lee, 1980) and literature by and about women (e.g., Martin, 1987; Miller, 1988; Park-Fuller, 1983). Of special significance is the recent expansion of the performance canon to include verbal art and ethnographic materials (Carlin, 1986;

Conquergood, 1985; Fine & Speer, 1977; Speer, 1985) and conversation analysis (Stucky, 1988). Jenkins (1987) and Langellier and Peterson (1992), for example, describe women's personal narratives as new texts and performance forms.

Undoubtedly, many more performances by and about women have been presented, but documenting the inclusion and empowerment of women in classroom and other academic performances presents some special difficulties. First is the simple problem of knowing what has been done because performances seldom leave a publication record. In this regard, interpretation and performance studies share with women's culture the constraints of a largely oral tradition: in the absence of a cultural record, usually written, the creativity, research, intellectual contributions, and plain hard work of women's scholarship may remain quite invisible, and, as significantly, devalued according to the standards of the more publicly legitimated genres, such as publication in academic journals. Moreover, when analyses of women's texts and performances are published, more specific reference to women and feminist criticism would highlight these contributions. For example, the significance of expanding the performance canon to women's texts in the oral tradition could be situated within the particular constraints of women and Third World cultures, that is, within the fact that the large majority of the world's illiterate are women, and within the fact that the majority of women's writing has been considered to be outside the literary canon (Hoffman & Culley, 1985).

Liberal-Humanist Discourse and the Concept of Embodiment

To count all the performances by and about women would tell a positive story about the inclusion of women in performance studies, but such a story would still be partial. As Spitzack and Carter (1987) assert, "although female visibility and diversity may contribute to a knowledge of women's communication, the suggestion that mere presence or strength in numbers signals understanding may be overly optimistic" (p. 401). The inclusion of women in the performance canon cannot guarantee women's empowerment if the dominant assumptive bases of performance theory and practice remain unchallenged. Performance for women must not only include women, but also question androcentric codes and concepts of performance. As feminist critics have repeatedly pointed out, the position of dominant culture is clothed in the neutrality of concepts such as humanism and universality. Weedon (1987, p. 140) clarifies how human values and universal truths claim to transcend political ("special") interests and to speak for all people as an ungendered, unclassed, nonracially specific whole. Interpretation and performance studies also participate in this liberal humanist discourse by virtue of theoretical constructs and practices that assume the rational individual as the source of knowledge about self and the world without problematizing the institutional and structural context of power relations, including gender, race, and class.

Feminist literary critics have argued since the early 1970s that women learn to read as men, to reflect male interests, concerns, and perspectives within the conflation that male is universal or definitively human. Recently, performance studies scholars have joined this dialogue. Nudd (1991) asks, "Is there a sex in this text?" by analyzing how undergraduate interpretation students have learned to read Katharine Anne Porter's short story "Rope." "Rope" narrates a gender-balanced battle of the sexes with "wonderful ambiguity." Because the argument between the husband and wife is written without quotation marks, the reader must decide not only who is speaking or thinking, but also the speaker's tone and motivation. In student essays analyzing the story, Nudd locates a pattern of interpretation in half of the readings which empathize almost totally with the male character. Nor were the results substantially different by gender: Both women and men read the gender-balanced text from a male perspective. Nudd specifies two particular interpretive strategies that result in these androcentric readings: one, the automatic and unconscious tendency to resolve ambiguities in the text from the interests and perspectives of the male character; and, second, the tendency of students to omit or distort incidents in the story which portray the male character less favorably (often simultaneously blaming the female character for the same incidents). As Nudd notes, androcentric reading cannot be completely explained by the greater predominance of literature by men in the literary and performance canons. Reading strategies intersect with other discursive strategies—in the case of these students, particularly with mass media images—which inform the gender politics of capitalist patriarchy.

Nudd's analysis suggests the significance of examining learned modes of interpretation for understanding androcentric practices in performance. In a similar effort, Langellier (1983, 1988) examined the construct of embodiment in performance theory for its gendered assumptions and implications. Within oral interpretation theory, embodiment refers to the act, described variously as experiential, dramatic, or rhetorical, wherein a reader gains access to literature through performance (Bacon, 1966; Geiger, 1952, 1967; Sloan, 1962, 1966). The individual performer who embodies a poem in the performative act is the source of knowledge about literature and the self. As the source of truth and human values, the concept of embodiment privileges the body-act of the performer "doing a poem" over the body-fact of the performer in the interpretive experience. The body-act of performance neutralizes the body-fact of the performer's sex (race, class), so that, in the interest of truth and human nature, gender becomes a marginal or nonissue in performance.

In theory, the concept of body-act as gender-neutral should not discriminate against women. Yet, it is important to distinguish between the conviction that gender should not make a difference in performance and the reality that it does, for a closer look at patterns of gender performance reveals the muting of women's voices. In fact, the body-fact of performers never completely disappears in performance practices. First is the mundane observation that female readers routinely and unself-consciously embody texts by and about men, whereas male readers less frequently read literature by and about women. Put another way, both women and men unreflectively read masculine voices, but it is women who more often read feminine voices. When a male reader does perform women's voices, the performance is often marked as deviant in some way, for example, by a disclaimer by the performer, a reference to the comic or burlesque effect by the audience, or alternately, the special challenge to avoid the stereotyping the performance presents. Significantly, no such marking accompanies a female's reading of a masculine text because it is normative. This asymmetrical pattern of gender performance by women and men has one and the same consequence: the greater visibility and audibility of masculine voices, which both women and men perform, and the lesser visibility and audibility of women's voices, which men, if not also women, are restricted from performing because they are "special interests" rather than human, that is, male, experience.

This asymmetrical pattern, or double standard, is notable for the normalcy, even "naturalness," that makes it almost unnoticeable—therein lies its power. Structural and institutional sexism disappear behind the concept of embodiment because it is lodged in the individual performer, male or female, whose body-act transcends sexual difference for human nature. Body-fact addresses sex as an attribute of the individual, but obscures gender as the social and cultural system of power relations in which performance is situated. Body-act privileges male voices and interests and masks its gender politics; it purports to be gender-neutral when it cannot be because body facts—who reads which voices—continue to assert themselves. Despite the neutrality promised by the concept of embodiment, the androcentric, male norm is assumed and women's voices are muted and marginalized. The consequences for performing as a woman are this: Either a woman as reader divides herself against herself by denying her own body-fact and reading as a human, that is, a man; or she is defined as a marginal (female) voice within the dominant patriarchal paradigm. So long as interpretation conceives literature as the repository of human values, most fully manifested in the neutral body-act of performance rather than in a conceptualization of differences, women can be included in performance practice, but feminist critique cannot displace the neutralizing constructs of liberal humanist theory.

Cross-gender Performance

Further implications for a feminist critique of performance emerge from a recent Forum in *Literature in Performance* (Smith, 1988) which examined the phenomenon of "cross-gender performance." Commentary on gender and performance dates from the 1960s, but we note that such a forum was unlikely before the feminist challenge, although the editorial introduction carries no references to feminist theory or practice. The historical fact that in Greek, Shakespearean, and Kabuki drama all roles were played by men is drawn without the accompanying feminist statement that women were excluded from public performance. The decades of Expression, Interpretation, and Performance Studies, when women read literature by and about men, similarly go without comment. Within the long history of male-as-norm, what does becomes noteworthy is men reading women's texts, and indeed, the essays clearly reflect a general concern with men's experiences and responses while eschewing what reading as men has meant for generations of women. Here, the feminist exercise of role reversals is instructive: Can we imagine, for example, a convention program or symposium devoted to "The Female Interpreter of Male Literature" (Colson, 1988)? Then we must ask, why not? To fail to do so would suggest that cross-gender performance benefits women more than men because women have centuries of learning to read like men, whereas the opposite (men reading like women) case is neither true nor likely. What remains obscured in the focus on men is the fact that women have been encouraged, until recently, to read as men. Thus, the androcentric basis of interpretation and performance studies is again revealed; even a concept for embodiment which explicitly problematizes gender risks masking the politics of sexual difference.

What forces constrain reading as a woman and the performance of women's voices? As noted above, the forum's discussion explicitly or implicitly assumed the case for males performing women's voices to be more problematic and more challenging than women performing men's voices. Shields (1988) and Colson (1988) note the risks of stereotyping, particularly how men can convey "femininity without effeminacy" (p. 118). Nudd (1988, p. 124) notes that male readings of female texts often result in boring performances or "bad drag acts." Langellier (1983, pp. 48-49) suggests that performance is grounded not only on male-as-norm but also heterosexual-as-norm, thereby maintaining "compulsory heterosexuality" and muting homosexual existence. In this way, analyses of gender and performance suggest the fruitful collaboration possible between feminism and performance studies. Significantly, sex as an attribute of the individual is replaced by gender as a social construction informed and constrained by sexism, homophobia, and misogyny, all of which share a devaluing, fear, and hatred for what is feminine in men as well as women (Pharr, 1988). Gender as a constructed system rather than a biological fact has a further implication: Gender belongs to a social system of power relations and a cultural system of meanings rather than to individual authors, personae, or readers (Peterson, 1988). To analyze gender is to analyze the meanings of masculinity and femininity in a particular culture and the social consequences of these sexual differences.

Finally, the dialogue on cross-gender performance is notable for the innovative classroom practices it suggests. Performance projects are described in Langellier (1988) and Nudd (1991), and scholars have begun to empirically examine cross-gender performance in the classroom (Shields & Arneson, 1989). In addition, Merrill (1988, 1989) complicates cross-gender performance with other social differences, especially race and ethnicity. She describes an approach to Chamber Theatre which situates students within a matrix of social relations and sexual codes that interrogate the discursive construction of meanings. Once an individual performer embodies a third-person narrator, for example, the narrative position can no longer be perceived to be "neutral" and separate from the human agency which views and presents the world in a particular way. "The audience member to interpretive performance perceives narrative as emanating from a specific source with a given gender, culture, ethnicity, value system, and sexual preference, all of which help constitute her/his point of view" (1989, p. 5). This approach to "performing differences" makes explicit the social and discursive context for gender and other differences. It also suggests that performance studies teachers ought to be as concerned with developing social responsibility in the classroom as we are with developing authentic voices and individual performers' skills (Peterson, 1988).

Expanding the number of texts by women available for performance, examining patterns of cross-gender performance, and proposing pedagogical approaches by which to explore social differences suggest that gender assumes a place of some importance in the oral interpretation classroom. But we must acknowledge that making gender a central or thematic concern, rather than an optional or occasional activity, remains quite rare in both more traditional oral interpretation programs and newer performance studies. As we have seen, the liberal-humanist assumptions about performance, which include women as participants in interpretation, often fail to challenge neutralizing constructs, such as embodiment, which mask the gender politics that privilege male texts and androcentric reading perspectives. To the extent that the performance adheres to the view of literature as the repository of universal, human values most fully realized in the body-act of the individual rational performer, the embodiment of literature continues to mean to read like a man who transcends the Otherness of Woman. The attempt to be gender-neutral, however well intentioned, denies the difference that gender and other social inequities make in the world—differences in wealth, work, power, access, and opportunity as well as in the production of culture. Rothenberg (1989) states that "a colorblind social policy in a racist society, a gender-neutral policy in a sexist society, simply guarantee that both racism and sexism will be strengthened and perpetuated instead of eradicated" (p. 18).

As has become increasingly clear, a feminist analysis of gender and performance challenges the traditional classroom to develop a theory and practice of social embodiment with accompanying concepts that can embrace the social facts of gender, race and ethnicity, and class differences. Such an effort is already underway in performance studies. We continue our examination of gender by examining the research tradition in interpretation and performance studies, particularly the changing history of literary criticism as it reflects feminist concerns with "reading as a woman."

FEMINIST LITERARY CRITICISM AND READING AS A WOMAN

Feminist scholars have produced a rich body of research on literature, interpretation, and performance. However, even poststructuralist criticism, which expresses the most interest in the body politic and sexual differences, has not, as Meese (1986, p. 83) observes, "produced many readings that address the power relationships expressive of sexual, heterosexual, racial, and class oppressions . . . most French and American male deconstructors evidence no more interest in women's texts than their predecessors or colleagues of other critical persuasions." Moreover, "most male-authored histories of modern criticism . . . condemn the apolitical nature of modern criticism and issue a ringing call for a worldly, secular, oppositional critical practice, ignoring all the while the socially-based feminist criticism going on for fifteen years right under the author's nose" (Showalter, 1984, pp. 30-31).

The fact is that while we see more and more articles on the new theories about the nature of literature, interpretation, and performance, recent scholarship most often presents us with "the new ideas of newly interesting men—Derrida, Foucault, Lacan, for instance—just as if no significant feminist transformations had taken place" (Gilbert, 1985, p. 37). Three symposia published in *Literature in Performance*, one on "Poststructuralism and Performance" (1983), one on "Performance and Critical Theory" (1988), and one on "Aesthetics and Anti-aesthetics of

Postmodern Performance," illustrate a similar tendency in performance studies. Feminist criticism has so far had little impact on our scholars' analyses of literary texts, whether we turn to New Criticism and dramatism or to reader-response criticisms, including those influenced by poststructuralist and postmodern thought.

New Criticism, Dramatism, and "Genderless" Texts

In part, scholars in interpretation studies have seldom analyzed texts by men or women writers from a feminist perspective because of the strong legacy of New Criticism on performance theory and practice. New Critics argued that literature must be analyzed as separate from social, historical, and cultural contexts. Poetry could not be understood by examining social institutions such as race, class, or gender nor by focusing on authorial intent or readers' responses. Rather, a poem's meaning, according to the New Critics, could only be grasped by engaging in a close intrinsic reading of the poem's verbal structure. For the New Critics, "the author's intentions in writing . . . were of no relevance to the interpretation of his or her texts. Neither were the emotional responses of particular readers to be confused with the poem's meaning: the poem meant what it meant, regardless of the poet's intentions or the subjective feelings the reader derived from it" (Eagleton, 1983, p. 48).

The New Critics focused on the intrinsic analysis of autonomous texts in order to emphasize the formal and aesthetic functions of literature. Wresting the poem from authors and readers, and locating meaning within the poem, affords literary critics the opportunity to argue that objective criteria determine which texts enter and remain in the great literature canon, which critical methods are best suited for analyzing the text, and which interpretations of texts are most valid. As Smith (1983) notes, critics explain that certain texts endure because of their transcendence and universality. She states, "the tendency . . . has been to explain the constancies . . . by the inherent qualities of the objects/or some set of presumed human universals" (p. 15). The inherent characteristics of truly great literature both transcend and illuminate human qualities universal to all.

By emphasizing the text itself and its transcendent, universal qualities, New Critics effectively dehistoricize literature, authors, readers, and critics. Disengaging texts from their social, political, and gendered contexts would appear to admit into the literary canon works by anyone, regardless of the writer's gender, race, or class. That is, if the poem meets the criteria of transcendence or universality, then it could certainly become a "masterpiece" or "classic." But as feminist scholars (and other critical theorists) repeatedly reveal, theories as to what becomes great literature are androcentric (the "masters") as well as class-marked (the "classics") (Case, 1988). Criteria about universal, human qualities, espoused as gender-neutral, are, in fact, those qualities typically associated with white, middle-class men.

Interpretation scholars, influenced by New Criticism, focused on the performance of the literary text as an object of study. Scholarship tended to be text-centered; however, the performance of literature was seen as the most effective means for realizing the text. Thus, while oral interpretation theory was influenced by New Critical tenets, the actual performance of literature added a dimension neglected in literary theory and criticism. Oral interpretation adapted New Criticism to suit its own needs. In particular, dramatistic perspectives were seen as valuable means for analyzing, responding to, and performing literature.

One of the most important concepts gleaned from New Criticism, according to Taft-Kaufman (1985, p. 162), was the claim "that poetry was a dramatic utterance." This concept supported the claim by oral interpretation teachers that performance, as the embodiment of the work's dramatic action, was one of the best ways to study and experience literature. Viewing literary works as dramatic action and experience required a model for analyzing the drama contained therein. Don Geiger's dramatistic version of Burke's pentad provided such a model.[4] The reader/performer, according to Geiger (1952, p. 189), can best study the action within the poem by answering the questions: "Who is performing what action or thought or feeling or deed? Where and when is it being performed? How is it being performed? Why is it being performed? How do these components relate and influence each other?" These questions formed the basis for the dramatistic scholarship and pedagogy in the field of oral interpretation. As Taft-Kaufman (1985, p. 163) observed, Geiger's "legacy to interpretation includes an emphasis on close textual analysis, the irreducibility of a poem, literature as a form of knowledge, and literature as dramatic experience."

Oral interpretation, influenced by New Criticism and dramatism, employed the formal and aesthetic standards of the intrinsic criteria of the "text itself" for the selection and evaluation of performances for their "truth" to the text. But to suggest that interpretation completely accepted the aesthetic and intrinsic criteria would be unfair. Perhaps because actual readers perform literature for actual audiences, interpretation never fully abandoned rhetorical and extrinsic considerations. Sloan (1962, 1966; Maclay & Stone, 1972), for example, pointed out that while intrinsic or text-centered analysis is important, extrinsic rhetorical analyses can be beneficial in performing literature because in some literature the literary speaker's purpose is to persuade or influence. In these cases, rhetorical analyses and biographical studies can illuminate the means by which such speakers accomplish their goals. Two Forum issues in *Literature in*

Performance, one on performances for authors (Dailey, 1985) and one on extrinsic criticism (Dailey, 1983), also illustrate oral interpretation's interests beyond intrinsic criticism.

Dramatism adapted New Criticism to the needs of oral interpretation so that a performer accomplishing a performance analysis could ask about sex as an individual attribute of literary authors and speakers as well as performers and audiences. But such an analysis remains limited because it cannot yet analyze gender as a system of power relations socially and historically structuring literature and performance. By the 1970s, however, interpretation scholars asserted with literary critics that performance theory and practices needed to be reconsidered within social, historical, and political contexts. Chester Long, for example, argues that "social values are intimately connected with performance, affecting both the choice of literature and the performance style" (in Taft-Kaufman, 1985, p. 173). Capo (1983a) further documents the field's interest in interpretation and social contexts. In her summary of oral interpretation projects that serve political functions, she observes that "practitioners have used solo and group performance to illuminate social issues, spur citizen awareness, and provoke public discussion" (p. 452). In addition, she identifies the historical tendency of interpretation theorists to see performance and literary structure in formal, rather than sociopolitical terms. Hence, some oral interpretation scholars recognized the limitations of New Criticism and dramatism, anticipating the critiques of feminism, critical theory, and the struggles against racism. But this recognition did not yet result in analyses of gender and patriarchy as an institutional context for interpretation. Even when interpretation turned to reader and reader-response criticism, the question "what if the reader is a woman?" was rarely raised.

Reader-response Criticisms and Reading Like a Man

While interpretation scholars explored performance in social contexts, literary critics of various persuasions began to examine the social networks of interpretation. Both turned to the relationship between texts and readers and the ways in which criticisms are value-laden. Tompkins (1980, p. ix) explains that "Reader-response critics would argue that a poem cannot be understood apart from its results. Its effects . . . are essential to any accurate description of its meaning, since that meaning has no effective existence outside of its realization in the mind of the reader." Similarly, interpretation scholars had already begun to describe the reader/performer as one who co-writes, co-produces, and co-creates literature (Kleinau & Isbell, 1977, p. 148).

Reader-response criticism does much to rehistoricize and repoliticize both the analysis and performance of literature and the reading subject. While there are a variety of reader-response or audience-oriented critical theories, ranging from more conservative text-centered studies to more radical reader-centered research, a gradual trend emerges wherein attention shifts from the text to the interaction between text and reader. Contemporary reader-response critics focus on the reader's experience of the text and argue that literature resides in both an aesthetic and sociopolitical realm. Further, such theorists contend that neither literature nor literary criticism are value-neutral (Tompkins, 1980, p. xxv).

Although contemporary reader-response criticism repoliticizes literature and literary criticism, many reader-response scholars do not consider sexual politics. That is, the majority of reader-response critics take for granted a white male reader, and thus limit their accounts to the white male reading experience. If, as reader-response critics (including many other critical approaches, such as Marxist and New Historicist) argue, reading and interpretation are value-laden, then gender is certainly one of the factors informing and constraining the reading experience and interpretations of that experience. Given its political stance that there is no such thing as a value-neutral interpretation, then "reader response critics cannot take refuge in the objectivity of the text, or even in the idea that a gender-neutral criticism is possible. Today they can continue to ignore the implications of feminist criticism only at the cost of incoherence or intellectual dishonesty" (Schweickart, 1986, pp. 38-39).

Feminist Theories of Reading

Feminist theories of reading provide a necessary critique or alternative to accounts of the reading experience. Feminist models of reading cannot, however, be simply added or tacked on to extant reader-response theories. Accounting for gender, race, and class radically alters the framework of reader-response scholarship. That is, posing such questions as "What if the reader is a woman?" (Showalter, 1985), or "What if the reader is a lesbian?" (Kennard, 1986; Zimmerman, 1985), or "What if the reader is a black woman?" (McDowell, 1985; Smith, 1985), challenges existing descriptions of the reading process.

Schweickart (1986, p. 39) proposes a feminist theory of reading which accounts for both gender and politics, issues ignored in most reader-response criticism. Schweickart states:

> The feminist story will have at least two chapters: one concerned with feminist readings of male texts, and another with feminist readings of female texts. In addition, in this story, gender will have a prominent role as the locus of political struggle . . . Finally, it will identify litera-

ture—the activities of reading and writing—as an important arena of political struggle, a crucial component of the project of interpreting the world in order to change it.

As can be seen by Schweickart's model, a feminist perspective on reading does not simply add women writers and readers to the body of discourse. Such an addition would simply change the object of research from men to women, leaving intact the critic's stance and critical methods. Instead, a feminist perspective requires that reader-response models must be defined for women: placing women in the center of inquiry and creating methods of reading that empower women as readers of both male and female texts.

Some recent scholarship has applied feminist criticism to literary texts for performance. Examples which contribute to the analysis of women writers and texts include Capo's (1987) study of Anne Sexton's early poetry; Taylor's (1990) examination of Grace Paley's women-centered language and storytelling; Greeley's (1989) look at playwright Martha Boesing; and Leibman's (1988) analysis of film noir. Focusing on the adaptation of narrative for performance, Nudd (1986) examines gender-biased and feminist dramatizations of *Jane Eyre* for how they support or undermine the romance plot. Sullivan (1988) also analyzes narrativity, this time in Spanish Honor plays, by applying a Kristevan feminist analysis which provides insights not only into sexist but also racist interpretations of this genre. Also connecting sexism with racism and classism, Madison (1988) calls for more literature on women of color.

To take one example, Strine (1989) shows how a feminist revision can contribute to interpretation scholarship in the area of voice. Using Bakhtin's dialogic theory, she defines voice as the material expression of self and its involvement in a world of social interactions and values. By examining how Adrienne Rich's voice asks women's questions, she locates such feminist strategies as assuming the authority of experience, using an open poetic form, and emphasizing self-enactment as ways that Rich reorders values in women's interest. Moreover, Strine asserts that Rich's reappropriation and transformation of poetry exposes the politics of genre which silence women's voices. Significantly, efforts such as this begin the task of explicating the real, historical, social relations of gendered texts, adaptations, and performances, a direction in which we encourage more research.

But we add to this encouragement of feminist analysis a series of concerns particular to interpretation and performance scholarship if we are not simply to add women's texts to the performance canon but to challenge and complicate traditional frameworks of performance. As has become clear in the discussion of embodiment in the first section and of reading in New Criticism, dramatism, and male-oriented reader response criticisms above, women readers traditionally "are expected to identify with a masculine experience and perspective which is identified as the human one" (Showalter, 1971, p. 856). Given their training in a predominantly male literary canon, and reading predominantly male scholarship about the canon, "woman can read and have read, as men" (Culler, 1982, p. 49). The first need in oral interpretation is to develop research and pedagogical strategies that enable both women and men to read as women.[5]

If men read women's texts and take women's stories (here we refer to both fictional stories and feminist stories of reading) as valid, credible, and significant, then male authors and readers are displaced from the center of universal experience and can no longer speak of male texts and male scholarship as those works which exhibit truly objective, universal qualities. Further, male authors, readers, and critics shift from their usual role as spectators of women to the role of spectacle. According to Flynn and Schweickart (1986, p. xix), "For men, reading women's stories means confronting themselves reflected in the eyes of women—they must endure the gaze of the other." In other words, for men, "reading as a woman" means deconstructing the privilege of male gender, as well as race and class. Similarly, reading as a woman calls women, especially white, middle-class women, to scrutinize their privileges of race, class, sexual preference, and so on.

For all interpretation scholars, "reading as a woman" suggests the need to ask sociopolitical and sexual political questions about performance, performer, text, and audience. For example, we might ask with regard to gender: Who is silenced and who is privileged by the performance and analysis of particular texts, by our research questions, by our critical methods and research methodologies? What community does the performance and research address and whom does it exclude? What are our starting assumptions and taken-for-granted beliefs about the nature and function of interpretation and performance? Who is privileged by these assumptions and beliefs?

The recent focus on performance as a social process enables scholars to address the preceding questions about the nature and function of performance. Langellier (1983) analyzes male and female readers performing the same poems, including audience responses to the performances. She states that "attention to context requires an acknowledgment that sexuality informs interpretation and that literary discourse participates in power relations that place specific constraints upon interpretive choices" (p. 48). Capo (1983a) points out that interpretation practitioners have worked with "minority," "powerless," and "voice-less" groups, such as women, the elderly, the handicapped, and the imprisoned, in order to empower those excluded by "traditional" standards of literary and performance theories. Such emerging perspectives not only include women as authors, directors and performers, and as the audience of performance, but also begin the process of challenging the androcentric framework that underpins performance studies. Thus, for example, a feminist perspective "may lead one to question the assumed centrality of the study of written texts given that so many women worldwide are illiterate and can author or transmit only oral texts" (Rice-Sayre, 1986, p. 247).

In addition to questioning the androcentricity of the canon, a feminist perspective requires a questioning as to whether critical methods are androcentric. That is, as scholars, we must ask ourselves if our scholarship exhibits "dependence on male masters and male theoretical texts" (Showalter, 1984, p. 37). Traditional scholarship in interpretation has relied heavily on scholars such as Bacon, Geiger, and Sloan; the recent turn to reader response and other theorists depends greatly on Booth, Iser, Fish, Bleich, Barthes, Eco, Derrida, Foucault, Lacan, Turner, Geertz, Bauman, Benjamin, and Bakhtin. Feminist critics such as Fetterly, Kolodny, Gilbert, Gubar, Rich, Showalter, Meese, Moi, Schweickart, Smith, Modleski, de Lauretis, Jacobus, Dolan, Case, Spivak, Kristeva, Irigaray, and Cixous, to name just a few, are used far less often in performance studies. Interpretation scholars need to ask if we are using male critical models to analyze women's texts, even though feminist critics have developed and are using sophisticated critical analyses of these very same authors. Schweickart's (1986) analysis contrasting Booth's and Rich's reading of Emily Dickinson, for example, is very instructive on this issue. Why, we ask, are the male masters of reader response and deconstruction more appealing than the women masters of the same critical persuasions?

Finally, as feminist performance scholars, we must ask ourselves if we are satisfied to be simply added on to or included in a plethora of critical choices. As Owens (1983, p. 62) points out, "the feminist voice is usually regarded as one among many, its insistence on difference as testimony to the pluralism of the times." In performance studies, Pelias and VanOosting (1987, p. 221) note that there is "an inclusionary impulse toward performers and audiences and a noncanonical attitude towards texts. To make such a claim questions the assumed authority of literary and artistic `experts.'" On the one hand, this shift appears to open a space and a place for feminism in our discipline. Indeed, such an emphasis affords feminists the opportunity to contribute to the ongoing debate regarding the future of the discipline.

On the other hand, inclusion, as one of many voices, is suspect. Arguments in support of pluralism usually imply an adherence to the liberal humanist tolerance for all critical methods. But as the study of the classroom performance tradition reveals, liberal-humanist discourse masks social differences, and in so doing, participates in their perpetuation. Spivak argues that pluralism is grounded in "an ideology of free enterprise at work:" pluralism implies that the individual (teacher, scholar, performer) has "the right and ability to choose from among any number of viable alternatives" (in Modleski, 1986, p. 122). But this is not quite the case. In fact, pluralism hides oppression by its taken-for-granted assumption that all have the freedom to choose. "Pluralism is the method employed by the central authorities to neutralize opposition by seeming to accept it" (Spivak, quoted in Meese, 1986, p. 141). Pluralism leads to a tolerant acceptance of feminism—there is a space and a place for it—without the attempt or responsibility to actually incorporate feminist analysis into our performance and scholarship (see Gordon, 1986, pp. 26-28).

But feminist criticism is not simply another method for literary or interpretation scholarship. Rich (1986, p. 86) notes that feminist criticism is a "politically motivated act of looking at literature, both by men and by women, in terms of sexual politics." Further, she states,

> I would not define as feminist literary criticism simply the writing by a woman about other women's books without consciousness of the political context of women's writing; or by an author who perceives herself as merely participating in some female "alternative reading" in a liberal supermarket of the intellect . . . . and I would like to invoke a definition of feminist criticism which implies continuous and conscious accountability to the lives of women. (p. 88).

Whereas we applaud interpretation scholars "questioning the assumed authority of 'experts'," given that those experts most often exclude women from the literary canon, most often use male-biased critical methods, and most often ignore feminist scholarship, we do not think feminists can afford to relinquish our voices of expertise along with the rest. As Modleski (1986, p. 127) observes, "Since when have women been granted the power of interpretation or our readings accorded the status of interpretive truth by the male critical establishment?"

Given the series of concerns regarding the space and place of feminist analysis in the interpretation discipline, we can hear the cry, "What do feminists want?" We want to point out the rather unique opportunity and responsibility that we in interpretation and performance studies have to raise issues of gender (of race, ethnicity, class, age, ableism, and sexual orientation) because every performance of actual readers and audience is unavoidably gendered and socially marked. Any scholarship that ignores these facts of social embodiment is partial and critically flawed. Gender is not simply another attribute of the individual (author, performer, audience) that can be ignored or included as one other variable in research on texts and performances. Rather "gender is both something we do and something we think with, both a set of social practices and a system of cultural meanings" (Rakow, 1986, p. 21).

Gender, race, and class are socially constructed positions in discourse, and these positions are inscribed in our language, our literature, our performances, and our research. In the next section, we advance our discussion of gender and feminism by turning from textual criticism to performance theory, and from readers' voices to performers' bodies. At the same time, we renegotiate a place for feminism in performance theory by tracing some directions for future research.

FUTURE DIRECTIONS IN FEMINIST PERFORMANCE THEORY

The recent move from interpretation of literature or oral interpretation to performance studies as the organizing identity of the field makes a significant statement about the theoretical understanding of performance.[6] Central to the direction of performance studies is the recognition of the social and political situation of performance. Conquergood (1985, p. 2) asserts that "performance does not proceed in ideological innocence or axiological purity." Pelias and VanOosting (1987) note that performance studies describes a practice that is inclusionary, noncanonical, personal, participative, and contextual. Feminist analyses, which recognize and confront the political in numerous forms of human action, have a significant place in determining the parameters and directions of performance studies.

Performance studies may be seen as emerging from or joining with the field of cultural studies. A 1989 conference entitled "Cultural Studies and Performance" offered cultural studies as a "rich conceptual framework" for performance scholarship. The conceptual grounding of cultural studies/performance studies suggests a potentially rich role for feminist theories. The feminist interest group that assembled during the 1989 conference remains active in articulating the need for and nature of feminist research and publication as performance studies continue to develop.[7]

Although the apparent emergence of an energetic feminist voice in performance studies compels celebration, we recognize that strategies of resistance and cooptation potentially place that voice at risk of being muted. Performance studies is not free of the move, evidenced elsewhere in communication studies (see this volume), to reduce a feminist voice to "a total absence or to an unthreatening, anorexic presence" (Modleski, 1986, p. 4). The tendency to marginalize feminism in classroom practice and textual analysis has been discussed earlier in this chapter. As will be noted, such marginalizing strategies also respond to the emergence of feminist scholarship in performance studies.

The minimal presence of a feminist voice in performance studies is particularly disturbing when we consider the special position performance potentially occupies with respect to some feminist theories. Modleski (1986) claims a performative dimension to feminist theory which seeks "to bring into being new meanings and new subjectivities . . . to be doing something beyond restating already existent ideas and views" (p. 14). Feminist theorists have long considered the presence of a performative aspect in the construction of sex roles (Butler, 1990; de Beauvoir, 1952/1949). Indeed, as we "do" our gender, there is a sense that we are engaged in performance, in performing masculinity and performing femininity as cultural productions. Perhaps most significantly, some primary theoretical questions that arise with (or are intensified by) the move to performance studies suggest a mutually enriching dialogue with feminist theories. Contemporary concerns about performance research, performance theory, representation and the body, and subject relations animate recent discourse in performance studies and specify its intersections with feminist theories.

Feminism and Performance Research

Traditional concepts of scholarship limit the practice of performance research. Scholars in the field are often occupied by producing performances; however, productions are not afforded value equivalent to traditional research projects and publications. While encouraging more "traditional" research in performance, scholars also argue that performance must be understood to function as epistemic, critical, and heuristic research (HopKins & Long, 1981). Performance studies continue to call for recognition of performance as scholarship and for an expansion of the modes of publication (Strine et al., 1990). In addition, the inclusion of nontraditional, noncanonical texts in performance studies compels the design and validation of alternate research methodologies, for example, ethnography, conversation analysis, and empirical phenomenology.

Feminist theorists also politicize the concern about alternate research methods, arguing that the rules that define publishable scholarship are grounded in patriarchal conceptions about the nature of knowledge. Feminist communication scholars challenge the norms of appropriate research questions, methods, and interpretations (Carter & Spitzack, 1989; Rakow, 1986). According to feminist critiques of traditional methodologies, research itself is a culturally situated discursive performance governed by patriarchal assumptions and interests. Notably, performance scholars share several concerns with feminist scholars, for example, the privileging of written over oral texts and of universal over personal texts, the objectification of the research subject, and the role of researcher as "expert." The similarly marginal positions of feminist and performance scholarship suggest their shared interest in reconceptualizing what counts as valid research.

The Need for Feminist Performance Theory

The call for new conceptualizations of research within the paradigm of performance studies accompanies a call for the continued articulation of theory addressing the political context of performance. Attention to the political context of performance critiques those approaches to interpretation which view the text and the performance of the text as art and which understand art as autonomous—outside of society, outside of ideology. The contextualization and politicization of performance, whether seen to precipitate or accompany the move to performance studies, calls for a theoretical understanding of the nature and acts of cultural performance. Citing the works of Clifford Geertz and Victor Turner, Conquergood (1984) identifies performance as a definitively human action in which cultural meanings are simultaneously constructed and construed. The scrutiny of performance itself seeks to understand its relationship to the establishment, maintenance, and change of cultural values (e.g., Bowman, 1988; Capo, 1983b; Pollock, 1988; Strine, 1983).

Conceptualizing performance as an explanatory theory of human action compels performance studies to investigate a broad spectrum of equally valid "performances"—from daily life rituals to traditionally defined spectacles—all of which are understood to be constitutive of identity. This conceptualization of performance also contributes to theory building and reveals ways in which the concerns of performance theory and feminist theory converge. For example, performance studies posits the "self" as continually constructed in acts of performance rather than as a pregiven, fixed, or finished identity. In the social context of performance, every interpretation (performance) of a text (self) constructs the reader (performer) even as reader (performer) constructs every interpretation (performance).

Feminist theorists also argue that the "self" is a performed cultural construct—with the stipulation that the self is a perpetually gendered construct (Dolan, 1988). Butler (1990) asserts that the performance of gender carries significant cultural value and meaning signified by punitive consequences, "if you don't do your gender right" (p. 326). Marranca (1987) urges that performance scholars "need to comprehend in a deeply political and social way how a society promotes and rewards socially acceptable roles" (p. 24). Gender is not the only facet of identity subject to cultural regulation; contemporary feminist scholarship addresses the perpetual and simultaneous presence of gender, color, ethnicity, class, sexuality, ability, and other aspects in the regulated performance (construction) of the "self." Much recent feminist theory posits identity as sexual and performance as a means to explain and examine sexual identity. In addition, the feminist concern for the production of social change calls for a theoretical articulation of performance as a site and agency of social change—a performance theory of resistance and revolution shared by Marxist and critical theory, although the promise of this common project is largely unrealized as yet in performance studies.

Representation and the Body

Although links with cultural studies and ethnographic theories and practice partially define performance studies, roots in western philosophical conceptualizations of art as representation inhere in the emerging discipline. The conceptualization of representation has been and continues to be identified as a central concern of interpretation and performance studies (Fuoss, Hantzis, & Hill, 1990; Hamera, 1990; Peterson, 1983). For example, discussions of the "presentational" style of group performance in interpretation (Kleinau & McHughes, 1980) describes it as always already a re-presentation. Peterson (1983) analyzes how interpretation as "speaking a reading of writing" calls attention to performance as a representation of a representation of a representation. The call to reintegrate the art of interpretation into society in ways that do not simply replicate, but rather oppose, the current order of oppression suggests in another way the conjunction of representation, performance, and feminist theory. Similarly, feminist performance scholars identify the significance of representation: "Issues of representation continue to constitute a major theoretical and practical problem for feminist performance" (Reinelt, 1987, p. 48).

Feminist performance theory challenges representation at the site of the body on which and through which identity is performed. The role of the body in oral interpretation theory and practice has often been disputed. However, dominant arguments in interpretation theory privilege the voice (orality) over the body in performance; such arguments also have worked to bracket the body in practice. The concern for reading and textual criticism delineated in the second section of this chapter also may be seen to demonstrate a privileging of voice over body in interpretation.[8] Emerging work in performance studies resituates the body in performance practice and indicates the potential articulation of a theory of the performative body. Performance studies scholars examine, for example, ritual, habitual masking and costuming, objectifying gestures, and other constitutive actions seen to construct identity through bodily inscriptions (Conquergood, 1984, 1990; Drewal, 1987, 1990; Hamera, 1989). Feminist theories extend such analyses of the body in their examination of the daily inscriptions of gender, color, ethnicity, age, ability, and sexuality on the bodies we live as and live with.

French feminist Irigaray (1985a, 1985b), among others, argues that the body is best understood as a regulated cultural construct and the primary site of difference(s); she further asserts that the traditional apparatus of representation acts as one agent of regulation. Owens (1983) also questions the function of representation in the process of producing cultural meanings and assigning cultural values. Specifically, Owens considers the position of anatomical differences and corporeal styles in the representation of a nude man and a nude woman on a NASA emblem, a representation in which the man's hand is raised in greeting.

Feminist theories challenge the possibility of any authentic representation of "Woman" within a system that regulates and punishes according to gender-marked prescriptions of identity. Feminist scholars advocate various means of "jamming" the machinery of representation to expose its regulatory mechanisms. French feminist conceptions of l'ecriture feminine join notions of "writing /or speaking through the body." Such practices function as rewritings and reevaluations through recognition of the status of the body as inscribed (regulated) cultural performance (Butler, 1990; Hantzis, 1987; Hill, 1988). Considering the work of Trinh T. Minh-Ha, Hamera (1990) concludes that Minh-Ha "defines `writing the body' as a `way of making theory in gender, of making of theory a politics of everyday life, thereby re-writing the ethnic female subject as site of difference'" (p. 238).

Traditional representational mechanisms seek to contain the body in/by performances of/on the body. However, if the body is understood not as a "natural" entity but as a linguistic and cultural category, the performed body may be deconstructed to reveal gaps, resistances, and spaces for change: "Bodily excesses" are released. Bodily excess reveals the potential for removal of the body from the patriarchal containments of representation, even as it reveals that containment. Irigaray's "excess" echoes feminist performance scholars' arguments for a performance theory that denies the containment of the body maintained by the traditional representational apparatus (Dolan, 1988; Fuoss et al, 1990; Pace, 1988).

Recent feminist performance theories continue to lead the discussion of representation to a consideration of the body. Hutcheon (1989) observes that feminism zeros "in on the representation of and reference to [the] body and its subject positions" (p. 142). The fact of the body and its potential for ideological inscription (what Butler calls the "surface politics of the body") are critical to the generation of performance theory and practice which does not limit itself to an analysis of speaking and the voice. Such a focus moves toward a performance and politics of the everyday voice and body. In this way, we are compelled to consider socially mandated estrangements of individuals from their bodies. For example, Marranca (1987) offers an example of daily "surface politics" when she suggests that the "Baby M" case constitutes judicial performance criticism: "The question is, who can best enact the role of parent? Here again the issue is that of representation" (p. 24). The questions raised by the Baby M case are, not incidentally, questions about the cultural regulation of the body. The analysis of the traditional representational apparatus features the politics of difference and grounds the conceptualization of subjectivity in a self-other relationship. Trinh (1989) joins feminist challenges to representation with critiques of subjectivity in her recognition that "we don't have bodies, we are body" (p. 34). Feminist theorists assert that the body serves as the primary site of difference; and the politics of difference organize the conceptualization of representation and subjectivity.

The Concept of the Subject: Multiplying Differences in Performance

Feminist critiques of subjectivity implicate the meaning and value of living daily as a woman or man, in a woman's or man's body, as gender intersects with all other aspects of identity (e.g., the meaning of living as a lesbian or heterosexual woman of color; abled or differently abled; wealthy, working class, or poor). de Lauretis (1986) asserts the need for an investigation into the complex relation between sociality and subjectivity. According to de Lauretis, such an investigation is aided by a rearticulation of the feminist adage, "the personal is political," in which the terms are not conflated, but rather sustain a tensive, reciprocal relationship. Modleski (1986) argues that our task as theorists is to articulate the conditions and forms for another conception of the social subject and thus to venture into the highly risky business of redefining aesthetic and formal knowledge.

A similar concern with subject relations in performance repeatedly appears in interpretation scholarship. Bacon's (1980) reiteration that interpretation requires a development of a "sense of the Other" situates this concern at the center of contemporary theory and practice. A sense of the Other suggests the importance of the relationship between the performer and the text, and the relationship between the performer(ance) and the audience. Text and audience stand in vulnerable positions of Otherness to the performer-Self who assumes the responsibility of protecting the integrity of the text from violation by the performer. The conceptualization of the performer-text/audience relationship in terms of the Self-Other ratio sponsors a discussion among performance scholars of the ethics and morality of performance, and complements assertions of the emotive and persuasive power of performance.

Performance studies scholars have recently begun to reconsider the concept of the Self-Other relationship. Poststructuralist theory and postmodern frameworks problematize traditional discourse on subject relations by challenging the authority ascribed to the performer, the notion of an objectively available "text," and the passive vulnerability of the audience (Carter, 1989; Hamera, 1986). Conquergood's (1984, 1985) "dialogical model" of performance, for example, addresses the particular subject relations constructed in ethnographic research as the positioning of Self and Other. According to Conquergood, dialogical performance is the method by which the Other moves from an inferior, vulnerable position to a position of mutuality with the Self. Conquergood echoes Clifford Geertz with the assertion that through dialogic performance the deeply different can be deeply known without becoming any less different. Other performance studies scholars are exploring Bakhtin's "dialogic theory" as an approach to the multiple voices in texts. Studies of multivocality and "dialogic performance" by Park-Fuller (1986) on Tillie Olsen, by HopKins (1989) on Flannery O'Connor, and by Strine (1989) on Adrienne Rich contribute to the effort to revalue differences and reconfigure Self-Other ratios.

Although the scholarship focusing on the reconceptualization of subject relations locates what is perhaps the most significant intersection of feminist theory and performance studies, it has unfortunately proceeded with little attention to the quite massive feminist work available on the subject. Even when the particular goal of performance theory is to account for differences rather than to relegate identification, the voice of the most everyday and historically defined Otherness—Woman—is too often muted. The formative role of feminist research in performance theory may be nowhere more significant than in the discussion of the Self-Other relationship and its reconceptualizations.

Indeed, the recognition of the need to interrogate and reconceptualize subjectivity arguably defines the project of contemporary feminist theory. Feminist theory aims to reveal the ideological apparatus and power relations that inscribe the role of the Other to difference, simultaneously assigning a negative value to difference while reifying and valorizing the dominant Self. Feminists locate the apparatus of patriarchy within the larger oppressive apparatus of Western culture itself, specifically in the dualist oppositions—of which gender (men/women) is only one example—which hierarchialize differences. The revelation of the inscription of Self and Other as power relations that perpetuate the given social hierarchy leads feminists to propose varying remedies. Some feminist theorists argue similarly with Conquergood: Self-Other relations must be equalized. However, other feminist theorists pursue the possibility of alternative models of subjectivity that dismantle the Self-Other ratio and constitute discursive concepts of "self" and "other."

Feminist theorists who view subjectivity as a discursive construct grounded in a patriarchal hierarchy argue that no consequential alteration of the Self and Other is possible because the very concept "subject" rests on the oppositional and unequal relation of Self and Other. Butler (1990) writes:

> It is precisely the construct of the subject that necessitates relations of hierarchy, exclusion, and domination. In a word, there is no subject [self] without an Other . . . . What may appear to be an equality of terms (here is the relevance of deconstruction for a critique of liberalism and for issues of gender) is in fact always a hierarchal relationship. (p. 326)

Jones (1985) similarly specifies how the gendered Self-Other hierarchical relationship functions to oppress women: "`I am the unified, self-controlled center of the universe,' man (white, European, ruling-class) has claimed. `The rest of the world, which I define as the Other, has meaning only in relation to me, as man/father, possessor of the phallus'" (p. 362). Thus, it is the notion of the unified self/subject—the "myth of the `I'"—that grounds patriarchy and the politics of difference.

Conquergood (1985, p. 35) suggests that performance potentially liquifies "us" and "them" into a "we;" feminist theorists counter that, given our discursive apparatus, the "we" inevitably functions to co-opt and condescend to the Other. Feminist theorists challenge the notion that the "I" (self) can choose to be more respectful of the "you" (other), to bring the other into a more equal relationship with the self; in this situation the desired equality (even the recognition of the presence of the other) remains a function of the inscribed authority of the self.

Irigaray writes of the need for a "true we." Mindful, however, of social and linguistic traps, she employs the construction "you/I" to express her challenge and reconfiguration of the subject. Trinh (1989) also posits an alternate subject and delineates the difficulties of such manipulations at the level of language:

> Not one, not two either. "I" is, therefore, not a unified subject, a fixed identity, or that solid mass covered with layers of superficialities one has gradually to peel off before one can see its true face. "I" is, itself, infinite layers. Its complexity can hardly be conveyed through such typographic conventions as I, i, or I/i. (p. 94)

Trinh's work echoes feminist theorists who argue for a resituation and multiplication of the sites of difference. Rather than maintaining difference as that which is external or alien (you, them, other), feminist theory proposes a notion of multiple sites of difference that confound the dualistic (illusory) boundaries of external/internal. The concept of multiplicity participates in the deconstruction of the unitary, univocal Self privileged in traditional subject relations, while at the same time problematizing the power relations of gender, race, ethnicity, and class. Multiplicity dismantles or radically displaces traditional, historical, oppositional categories of identity. Reinelt (1987, p. 41) recognizes a controversial consequence of such multiplicity, which "means giving up the 'feminine' as a privileged identity and acknowledging the possibility of multiple nuance and combinations of genders which may eventually bring down the whole historical construction man/woman."[9]

Performance scholars consider that performance puts the unified subject at risk. The application of Bakhtin's concepts of polyglossia and heteroglossia offer promising challenges to a unified self/subject, but we urge that they be accompanied by feminist analysis of gendered texts, readings, and concepts. Feminist interpretations and critiques of Bakhtin's dialogic theory (see Lundberg, 1989; Strine, 1989) assume particular importance in this regard. In addition, some performance scholars argue that difference and resistance are voiced in performance and should be recognized and encouraged (Carter, 1989; Langellier, 1989; Maclean, 1987; Merrill, 1989). Moreover, difference also may be understood as nonoppositional when it is accessed as/in performance, which confounds the dualism of "within/without" (Hantzis, 1988). Performance practice that employs deliberate multiplication of performance voices—cross-gender, cross-color, cross-ethnicity, cross-class—suggest the multiplicity of the subject and obviate the essentializing implied by the Self-Other relationship. Feminist performance scholars argue that such deliberate multiplication reveals performance as "performing differences" and exposes the myth of the single-voiced "I." The voicing of "others" with the voice of "self" sponsors a consciousness of the inherent otherness (differences) within self. Such a process necessarily warns against the notion that a self ever gives voice to an actual other. Rather, the emerging understanding is that of a multiple self. Butler (1990) argues that "the multiplicity and discontinuity of the signified rebels against the univocity of the sign" (p. 326).

The intersection of feminist and performance theories returns to the notion of "performing gender" that opened this third section. Butler's work sketches the potential of radical feminist revisions of performance theory. When gender is considered as a cultural performance, and cultural performance is revealed to be gendered, we encounter the discontinuity of gender and sex themselves. Butler observes instances of "gender performance" (performance of gender) in social (not necessarily theatrical) arenas. In particular, Butler examines the performative construction of butch/femme identities and drag queens. She posits that these examples of "gender parody" expose the ideological connection between any body and its discursive signification. Indeed, she proposes that:

> Gender parody reveals that the original identity after which gender fashions itself is itself an imitation without an origin. To be more precise, it is a production which in effect, that is, in its effects, postures an imitation. This perpetual displacement constitutes a fluidity of identities that suggests an openness to resignification and recontextualization, and it deprives hegemonic culture and its critics of the claim to essentialist accounts of gender identity. (p. 326)

Butler's work challenges the Western representational apparatus through a feminist critique of subjectivity. The acknowledgment of an irrecoverable origin significantly exposes the impossibility of authentic representation and, consequently, challenges the authenticity of subject constructs. Butler's articulation of the epistemological function of performance as feminist methodology reaffirms the potential for a revolutionary critique of subjectivity through feminist performance studies.

The conceptualization of all human action as performative—and the focus on the performative—positions performance studies scholars at the dialogic intersection of several theoretical discourses. Feminist performance scholars move among daily gestures and traditional spectacles to a delineation of the performative construction of subjects that deliberately interrogates the regulation and relation of identity. As Butler's analysis suggests, feminist performance can work to reveal the discontinuities of identity—aspects traditionally viewed and regulated as continuous. Butler focuses particularly on revealing the discontinuity of sex, gender, and sexuality; she argues that the notion of continuity among these aspects erases differences and functions as part of the regulation and punishment of gender performances. The discontinuities of sex, gender, and sexuality (as well as other aspects of identity) generate excess and shatter the illusion of the unified subject.

The exploration of performance as a site of difference, and of "performing gender" as a cultural production, is just beginning. The potential of this exploration is the possibility of a feminist theory of performance that does not privilege identification over difference; that multiplies and complicates difference rather then essentializing it (whether in the Other or the Self); and that locates human creativity in the play and display of differences. The development of a specifically feminist performance theory and practice deserves a place within the new parameters and directions of performance studies.

CONCLUSION

A feminist critique of interpretation and performance studies tells a story of both the inclusion of women and the marginalization of the feminist voice. Women are marginalized first by the liberal-humanist discourse which neutralizes sexual differences; next by the critical theories that assume a male reader and ignore feminist contributions; and finally, by some recent performance studies scholarship which accommodates the concerns of feminist scholarship but seldom results in analyses of gender as cultural critique, cultural performance, or cultural production. Even when women are included in the classroom, textual criticism, or performance studies scholarship, too often the social and political context of performance— sexism, patriarchy, and power—are omitted from discussion.

At the same time that our feminist analysis exposes the gender politics of the discipline, it politicizes the classroom, the performance canon, textual criticism, research methodologies, and performance theory. A feminist analysis has the potential to reshape knowledge on several current issues in the field, among them, authority and experience, access and privilege, identification and difference, embodiment and representation, and subject relations. Furthermore, feminist scholarship produces new performance texts and forms, new ways of reading, and new views on the nature and act of performance. We suggest, for example, that the classroom is a site of gendered performance which raises issues of social responsibility as well as aesthetic enjoyment and evaluation. We argue that both women and men need to learn to "read as a woman," and that a theory of performance must address the gendered body as well as the reader's voice. We outline some directions in the development of a feminist performance theory that views interpretation as the site of "performing differences"—sexual, racial, ethnic, and class—where differences are multiplied and complicated rather than essentialized, opposed to a male norm, or reduced to a single voice.

A feminist analysis of the classroom, textual criticism, and the nature and act of performance significantly converges with other formative areas of performance theory, research, and practice. In setting new directions in performance studies, women cannot be considered merely a "topic," a "problem," or even an "option" that can be attended to or ignored. Performing gender is a way of defining reality, of thinking, of interpreting and performing texts, and of living our lives no matter what our pedagogical orientation, our critical perspective, or our political persuasion.

NOTES TO CHAPTER 4

1. Although conventional theater and feminist theater may be considered within performance studies, we exclude them from our discussion because they are covered elsewhere in this volume.

2. As this chapter went to press, an article on feminist criticism by K. E. Capo and D. Hantzis was published for a special issue of *Text and Performance Quarterly*.

3. Feminism is frequently seen as a politically biased viewpoint, whereas other perspectives are considered to be value-neutral, or at least less political than feminism. We accept and declare our politics, but we reject the possibility of an "objective" position. Rather than choosing between "biased" and "objective," we believe the choice is between identifying and masking politics. Nor do we accept that scholarship devoted to at least half of the world's population—and far more than one-half of the Interpretation Division of the Speech Communication Association—represents a "special interest."

4. It is beyond the scope of this essay to fully explain dramatistic perspectives, Geiger's theories, and their influence on oral interpretation. For further discussion, see Taft-Kaufman (1985) and Gudas (1983).

5. Some feminist critics argue that men can learn to read women's texts, that they only lack the critical skills which can be taught and learned. Other feminists argue that "It is not that men can't read women's texts; it is, rather, that they won't" (Flynn & Schweickart, 1986, p. xviii). Similarly, Modleski (1986) argues that "women have been forced to find ways to enjoy or pretend to enjoy even the most virulently misogynist texts" (p. 123). Men, however, given their position of social and institutional power, do not need or have to read, enjoy, or even pretend to enjoy texts by women.

6. The Interpretation Division of the Speech Communication Association voted at the 1989 convention to begin procedures for an official name change to Performance Studies. Some other groups (regional divisions, university programs) have effected or are contemplating similar changes.

7. The 1989 summer conference seminars examined "New Empirical Approaches," "Marxist/Post-structuralist Approaches," and "Ethnographic Approaches" in addition to "Feminist Approaches." But we discourage the privileging and reifying of these four approaches for at least two reasons: first, because other approaches are both possible and actual; and second, because the titles represent arbitrary divisions among overlapping perspectives. Indeed, we encourage dialogue on women and feminism within every perspective. The development of feminist performance studies has primarily focused on theatrical arenas. See, for example, Case (1988,

1990), Dolan (1988), and Hart (1989).

8. The privileging of voice over body in interpretation may reflect the historical phonocentric orientation of the speech communication discipline.

9. Many feminists, particularly those influenced by poststructuralist theory, recognize the false ontology of "the feminine" or Woman as essential, unified, or universal categories. However, they also argue for a strategic, operational essentialism in order to advance a feminist program in the interests of women in their diversity. In a related discussion, bell hooks (1984) notes with suspicion how the theoretical objections to representation, the body, and the whole project of the subject appear at the same time that "marginal" persons—particularly women of color and lesbians—come into view.

REFERENCES

Aesthetics and anti-aesthetics of postmodern performance: Pina Bausch's *Tanztheatre* [Symposium].(1989). *Text and Performance Quarterly, 9*, 97-124.

Bacon, W.A. (1966). *The art of interpretation.* New York: Holt, Rinehart, & Winston.

Bacon, W.A. (1980). An aesthetics of performance. *Literature in Performance, 1*, 1-10.

Bowman, M. (1988). Cultural critique as performance: The example of Benjamin. *Literature in Performance, 8*, 4-11.

Butler, J. (1990). *Gender trouble: Feminism and the subversion of identity.* New York: Routledge.

Capo, K.E. (1983a). From academic to socio-political uses of performances. In D.W. Thompson (Ed.), *Performance of literature in historical perspectives* (pp. 437-457). Lanham, MD: University Press of America.

Capo, K.E. (1983b). Performance of literature as social dialect. *Literature in Performance, 4*(1), 31-36.

Capo, K.E. (1987, November). *"I have been her kind:" Anne Sexton's communal voice.* Paper presented at the Speech Communication Association Convention, Boston, MA.

Capo, K.E., & Hantzis, D. M. (1991). (En)Gendered (and endangered) subjects: Writing, reading, performing, and theorizing feminist criticism. *Text and Performance Quarterly, 11*(3), 249-266.

Carlin, P.S. (1986). Performance of verbal art: Expanding conceptual and curricular territory. In T. Colson (Ed.), *Renewal and revision: The future of interpretation* (pp. 116-131). Denton, TX: NB Omega.

Carter, K. (1989). Response: Residing on the line in between, or how not to resolve performative tensions. *Text and Performance Quarterly, 9*,

119-124.

Carter, K., & Spitzack, C. (Eds.). (1989). *Doing research on women's communication: Perspectives on theory and method.* Norwood, NJ: Ablex.

Case, S. (1988). *Feminism and theatre.* New York: Methuen.

Case, S. (1990). *Performing feminisms: Feminist critical theory and theatre.* Baltimore: Johns Hopkins University Press.

Colson, T. (1988). [Forum: Cross-gender performance]. *Literature in Performance, 8,* 118-119.

Conquergood, D. (1984). Performance and dialogical understanding: In quest of the other. In J.L. Palmer (Ed.), *Communication and performance* (pp. 30-37). Tempe, AZ: Arizona State University Press.

Conquergood, D. (1985). Performing as a moral act: Ethical dimensions of the ethnography of performance. *Literature in Performance, 5,* 1-13.

Conquergood, D. (1990, November). *Textual practices and discursive displacements.* Paper presented at the Speech Communication Association Convention, Chicago, IL.

Culler, J. (1982). *On deconstruction: Theory and criticism after structuralism.* Ithaca, NY: Cornell University Press.

Dailey, S.J. (Ed.). (1983). [Forum: Extrinsic Analysis]. *Literature in Performance, 4,* 114-122.

Dailey, S.J. (Ed.). (1985). [Forum: Performing for the author]. *Literature in Performance, 5,* 87-104.

de Beauvoir, S. (1952). *The second sex* (H.M. Parshley, Trans.). New York: Alfred A. Knopf. (Original work published 1949)

de Lauretis, T. (Ed.). (1986). *Feminist studies/critical studies.* Bloomington: Indiana University.

Dolan, J. (1988). *The female spectator as critic.* Ann Arbor: UMI Research.

Donovan, J. (1987). *Feminist theory.* New York: Ungar.

Drewal, M.T. (1987). From Rocky's Rockettes to Liberace: The politics of representation in the heart of corporate capitalism. *Journal of American Culture, 10,* 69-82.

Drewal, M.T. (1990). (Inter)text, performance, and African humanities. *Text and Performance Quarterly, 10,* 72-79.

Duelli-Klein, R. (1983). How to do what we want to do: Thoughts about feminist methodology. In G. Bowles & R. Duelli Klein (Eds.), *Theories of women's studies* (pp. 88-104). London: Routledge & Kegan Paul.

Eagleton, T. (1983). *Literary theory: An introduction.* Minneapolis, MN: University of Minnesota Press.

Fine, E.C., & Speer, J.H. (1977). A new look at performance. *Communication Monographs, 44,* 374-389.

Flynn, E.A., & Schweickart, P.P. (Eds.). (1986). *Gender and reading: Essays on readers, texts, and contexts.* Baltimore, MD: Johns Hopkins University Press.

Fuoss, K., Hantzis, D.M., & Hill, R. (1990, November). *Hysteria (un)chained: Argument, dialogue, and pre/ab/sent voices, or perform-*

ing babbling texts [Performance and unpublished scholarship]. Paper presented at the Speech Communication Association Convention, Chicago, IL.

Geiger, D. (1952). A 'dramatic' approach to interpretative analysis. *Quarterly Journal of Speech, 38,* 189-194.

Geiger, D. (1967). *The sound, sense, and performance of literature.* Chicago: Scott, Foresman.

Gilbert, S.M. (1985). What do feminist critics want? A postcard from the volcano. In E. Showalter (Ed.), *The new feminist criticism* (pp. 29-45). New York: Pantheon.

Gordon, L. (1986). What's new in women's history. In T. de Lauretis (Ed.), *Feminist studies/critical studies* (pp. 20-30). Bloomington, IN: Indiana University.

Gray, P.H. (Director). (1983, October). *Hedda Tesman based on a play by Henrik Ibsen* [Performance]. Presented at the University of Texas.

Greeley, L. (1989). Martha Boesing: Playwright of performance. *Text and Performance Quarterly, 9,* 207-215.

Gudas, F. (1983). Dramatism and modern theories of interpretation. In D.W. Thompson (Ed.), *Performance of literature in historical perspectives* (pp. 589-627). Lanham, MD: University Press of America.

Hamera, J. (1986). Postmodern performance, postmodern criticism. *Literature in Performance, 7,* 13-20.

Hamera, J. (1989). On reading, writing, and speaking the politics of (self-) re-presentation [Review essay]. *Text and Performance Quarterly, 10,* 235-247.

Hamera, J. (1990). Silence that reflects: Butoh, Ma, and a cross-cultural gaze. *Text and Performance Quarterly, 10,* 53-60.

Hantzis, D. (1987, November). *Speaking silence: The feminine reappropriation of discourse.* Paper represented at the convention of the Speech Communication Association, Boston, MA.

Hantzis, D. (1988, November). *Absence and excess: Situating the female subject.* Paper presented at the convention of the Speech Communication Association, New Orleans, LA.

Hart, L. (Ed.). (1989). *Making a spectacle: Feminist essays on contemporary women's theatre.* Ann Arbor: University of Michigan Press.

Hill, R.T. (1988, November). *L'ecriture feminine: Alternative texts, alternative performances.* Paper presented at the Speech Communication Association Convention, New Orleans, LA.

Hoffman, L., & Culley, M. (Eds.). (1985). *Women's personal narratives: Essays in criticism and pedagogy.* New York: MLA.

hooks, b. (1984). *Feminist theory: From margin to center.* Boston: South End.

HopKins, M.F. (1989). The rhetoric of heteroglossia in Flannery O'Connor's Wise Blood. *Quarterly Journal of Speech, 75,* 198-211.

HopKins, M.F., & Long, B.W. (1981). Performing as knowing and knowing as performing. *Central States Speech Journal, 32,* 236-242.

Hutcheon, L. (1989). *The politics of postmodernism.* London: Routledge.

Irigaray, L. (1985a). *Speculum of the other woman* (G.G. Gill, Trans.). New York: Cornell University.

Irigaray, L. (1985b). *This sex which is not one* (C. Porter, Trans.). New York: Cornell University Press.

Jenkins, M. (1987, November). *Performing life stories: Passions and pitfalls.* Paper presented at the Speech Communication Association Convention, Boston, MA.

Jones, A.R. (1985). Writing the body: Toward an understanding of l'ecriture feminine. In E. Showalter (Ed.), *The new feminist criticism* (pp. 361-378). New York: Pantheon.

Kennard, J.E. (1986). Ourself behind ourself: A theory for lesbian readers. In E.A. Flynn & P.P. Schweickart (Eds.), *Gender and reading: Essays on readers, texts, and contexts* (pp. 63-82). Baltimore, MD: Johns Hopkins University Press.

Kleinau, M., & Isbell, T. (1977). Roland Barthes and the co-creation of the text. In E.M. Doyle (Ed.), *Studies in interpretation II* (pp. 139-156). Amsterdam: Rodopi N. V.

Kleinau, M., & McHughes, J. (1980). *Theatres for literature: A practical aesthetics for group interpretation.* Sherman Oaks, CA: Alfred.

Langellier, K.M. (1983). Doing deconstruction: Sexuality and interpretation. *Literature in Performance, 4,* 45-50.

Langellier, K.M. (1986). From text to social context. *Literature in Performance, 6,* 60-70.

Langellier, K.M., (1988). [Forum: Cross-gender performance]. *Literature in Performance, 8,* 120-122.

Langellier, K.M. (1989). *Women's personal narratives: Strategies of resistance.* Paper presented at the Speech Communication Association Convention, San Francisco, CA.

Langellier, K.M., & Peterson, E.E. (1992). Spinstorying: A communication analysis of women storytelling. In E. Fine & J. H. Speer (Eds.), *Performance, culture, and identity.* New York: Praeger.

Lee, C.I. (1980). Roethke writes about women. *Literature in Performance, 1,* 23-32.

Leibman, N.C. (1988). Piercing the truth: Mildred and patriarchy. *Literature in Performance, 8,* 39-52.

Lundberg, P.L. (1989). Dialogically feminized reading: A critique of reader-response criticism. *Reader, 22,* 9-37.

Maclay, J.H., & Sloan, T.O. (1972). *Interpretation: An approach to the study of literature.* New York: Random House.

Maclean, M. (1987). Oppositional practice in women's traditional narrative. *New Literary History, 19,* 87-98.

Madison, S. (1988, November). *Unveiling ethnographic literature by women of color.* Paper presented at the Speech Communication Association Convention, New Orleans, LA.

Marranca B. (1987). Performance world, performance culture. *Performing Arts Journal, 10,* 21-29.

Martin, A. (Adapter & Director). (1987, October). *Women: Vietnam*

[Performance]. Carolinas Fall Festival, University of North Carolina, Wilmington.

Meese, E.A. (1986). *Crossing the double-cross: The practice of feminist criticism.* Chapel Hill, NC: University of North Carolina Press.

McDowell, D.E. (1985). New directions for black feminist criticism. In E. Showalter (Ed.), *The new feminist criticism* (pp. 186-199). New York: Pantheon.

Merrill, L. (1988, October). *Gender, ethnicity, and the politics of oral interpretation.* Paper presented at the Organization for the Study of Communication, Language, and Gender, San Diego, CA.

Merrill, L. (1989, November). *The politics of identification: Teaching group performance of literature.* Paper presented at the Speech Communication Association meeting, San Francisco, CA.

Miller, P.C. (1988). "Will you dance, Miss Austen?": A one woman show. *Literature in Performance, 8,* 65-75.

Modleski, T. (1986). Feminism and the power of interpretation: Some critical readings. In T. de Lauretis (Ed.), *Feminist studies/critical studies* (pp. 121-138). Bloomington, IN: Indiana University Press.

Nudd, D.M. (1986, November). *Undermining the romance plot: Feminist dramatizations of Jane Eyre.* Paper presented at the Speech Communication Association Convention, Chicago, IL.

Nudd, D.M. (1988). [Forum: Cross-gender performance]. *Literature in Performance, 8,* 123-125.

Nudd, D.M. (1991). Establishing the balance: Re-examining students' androcentric readings of Katharine Anne Porter's "Rope." *Communication Education, 40,* 49-59.

Owens, C. (1983). The discourse of others: Feminists and postmodernism. In H. Foster (Ed.),. *The anti-aesthetic: Essays on postmodern culture* (pp. 57-82). Port Townsend, WA: Bay.

Pace, P. (1988, November). *Victorian punk: The crisis of puberty in Wuthering Heights.* Paper presented at the Speech Communication Association Convention, New Orleans, LA.

Park-Fuller, L.M. (1983). Understanding what we know: Yonnondio: From the thirties. *Literature in Performance, 4,* 65-77.

Park-Fuller, L.M. (1986). Voices: Bakhtin's heteroglossia and polyphony, and the performance of narrative literature. *Literature in Performance, 7,* 1-12.

Pelias, R.J., & VanOosting, J. (1987). A paradigm for performance studies. *Quarterly Journal of Speech, 73,* 219-231.

Performance and critical theory: The Frankfurt school.[Symposium] (1988). *Literature in Performance, 8,* 1-38.

Peterson, E.E. (1983). Representation and the limits of interpretation. *Literature in Performance, 4,* 22-26.

Peterson, E.E. (1988). [Forum: Cross-gender performance]. *Literature in Performance, 8,* 122-123.

Pharr, S. (1988). *Homophobia: A weapon of sexism.* Inverness, CA: Chardon.

Pollock, D. (1988). The play as novel: Reappropriating Brecht's Drums in the Night. *Quarterly Journal of Speech, 74,* 296-311.

Poststructuralism and performance. (1983). [Symposium]. *Literature in Performance, 4,* 21-60.

Rakow, L. (1986). Rethinking gender research in communication. *Journal of Communication, 36,* 11-26.

Reinelt, J. (1987). Feminist theory and the problem of performance. *Modern Drama, 32,* 48-57.

Rice-Sayre, L. (1986). Domination and desire: A feminist-materialist reading of Manuel Puig's *Kiss of the Spider Woman.* In M.A. Caws (Ed.), *Textual analysis: Some readers reading* (pp. 245-256). New York: MLA.

Rich, A. (1986). *Blood, bread, and poetry.* New York: W. W. Norton.

Rothenberg, P. (1989). The hand that pushes the rock. *Women's Review of Books, 6*(5), 18-19.

Schweickart, P.P. (1986). Reading ourselves: Toward a feminist theory of reading. In E.A. Flynn & P.P. Schweickart (Eds.), *Gender and reading: Essays on readers, texts, and contexts* (pp. 31-62). Baltimore, MD: Johns Hopkins University Press.

Shields, R.E. (1988). [Forum: Cross-gender performance]. *Literature in Performance, 8,* 116-117.

Shields, R.E., & Arneson, P. (1989). Perspective taking as pedagogical goal in the beginning oral interpretation course. *Ohio Speech Journal, 27,* 23-32.

Showalter, E. (1971). Women and the literary curriculum. *College English, 32,* 855-862.

Showalter, E. (1984). Women's time, women's space: Writing the history of feminist criticism. *Tulsa Studies in Women's Literature, 3,* 29-44.

Showalter, E. (Ed.). (1985). *The new feminist criticism.* New York: Pantheon.

Sloan, T.O. (1962). A rhetorical analysis of John Donne's "The Prohibition." *Quarterly Journal of Speech, 48,* 38-45.

Sloan, T.O. (Ed.). (1966). *The oral study of literature.* New York: Random House.

Smith, B. (1985). Toward a black feminist criticism. In E. Showalter (Ed.), *The new feminist criticism* (pp. 168-185). New York: Pantheon.

Smith, B.H. (1983). Contingencies of value. *Critical Inquiry, 10,* 1-35.

Smith, R.E. (Ed.). (1988). [Forum: Cross-gender performance]. *Literature in Performance, 8,* 116-125.

Speer, J.H. (1985). Waulking o' the web: Women's folk performances in the Scottish isles. *Literature in Performance, 6,* 24-33.

Spitzack, C., & Carter, K. (1987). Women in communication studies: A typology for revision. *Quarterly Journal of Speech, 73,* 4-1-423.

Strine, M.S. (1983). Performance theory as science: The formative impact of Dr. James Rush's *The Philosophy of the Human Voice.* In D.W. Thompson (Ed.), *Performance of literature in historical perspectives* (pp. 509-527). Lanham, MD: University Press of America.

Strine, M.S. (1989). The politics of asking women's questions: Voice and value in the poetry of Adrienne Rich. *Text and Performance Quarterly, 9,* 24-41.

Strine, M.S., Long, B.W., & HopKins, M.F. (1990). Research in interpretation and performance studies: Trends, issues, priorities. In G.M. Phillips & J.T. Wood (Eds.), *Speech communication: Essays to commemorate the 75th anniversary of the Speech Communication Association* (pp. 181-204). Carbondale: Southern Illinois University.

Stucky, N. (1988). Unnatural acts: Performing natural conversation. *Literature in Performance, 8,* 28-39.

Sullivan, E.B. (1988). A feminist analysis of narrative in Spanish golden age honor plays. *Literature in Performance, 8,* 53-64.

Taft-Kaufman, J. (1985). Oral interpretation: Twentieth-century theory and practice. In T.W. Benson (Ed.), *Speech communication in the 20th century* (pp. 157-183). Carbondale: Southern Illinois University.

Taylor, J. (1990). Tracing connections between women's personal narratives and the short stories of Grace Paley. *Text and Performance Quarterly, 10,* 20-33.

Tompkins, J.P. (Ed.). (1980). *Reader-response criticism: From formalism to post-structuralism.* Baltimore, MD: Johns Hopkins University Press.

Trinh T.M. (1989). *Woman, native, other: Writing postcoloniality and feminism.* Bloomington: Indiana University Press.

Weedon, C. (1987). *Poststructuralist theory and feminist practice.* New York: Oxford.

Zimmerman, B. (1985). What has never been: An overview of lesbian feminist criticism. In E. Showalter (Ed.), *The new feminist criticism* (pp. 200-224). New York: Pantheon.

Chapter 5

New Voices in Organizational Communication: A Feminist Commentary and Critique

Marlene G. Fine
University of Massachusetts at Boston
Boston, MA

The purpose of this chapter is to offer and develop what I believe is a provocative thesis: that research in organizational communication should return to its pragmatic roots, albeit a pragmatism informed and guided by feminist theories. In this chapter, I critique three important research traditions in organizational communication from a feminist perspective and suggest directions for future research based on that perspective. My premise is that a feminist perspective provides a unique and useful critique of the existing work in organizational communication and offers a vision of research that transforms both our work as scholars in organizational communication and our lives as members of organizations.

I use the term *feminist perspective* here to indicate that I am bringing together ideas that represent different feminist theories. Feminist theory has emerged in all disciplines in the academy and ranges philosophically from liberal feminism through radical feminism. Also, feminist theorizing is based in women's experiences, which differ within classes, races, and cultures. There is, therefore, no single feminist theory. It is more accurate, instead, to talk of feminist theories or "feminisms" (Balsamo, 1985; Harding, 1987). All of these feminisms, however, reflect a concern with gender relations and social change.

The chapter is divided into five sections. In the first part, I provide a brief overview of the history of the study of organizational communication to give the reader a historical context for my thesis. In the second part, I identify five methodological and epistemological commitments of a feminist perspective that I believe would shape organizational communication in meaningful and powerful ways. These commitments create the lens through which I review and critique existing work in organizational communication in the third part. In the fourth part, I review some of the current feminist research in organizational communication, using the same lens to contrast feminist research with other work in the field. In the final section, I propose new directions for research in organizational communication based on the methodological and epistemological commitments of a feminist perspective outlined in the second section.

HISTORICAL OVERVIEW OF RESEARCH IN ORGANIZATIONAL COMMUNICATION

The development of research in organizational communication mirrors the development of research in other areas of the communication discipline in a variety of ways. The early work in the field began not in our discipline but in a different one—management. With its roots in a discipline that has always had a much more applied focus than ours, organizational communication research and theory began by dealing with highly pragmatic issues related to managing organizations effectively. That focus created an organizational and managerial bias in the research, which was intensified by the financial support for such work, which came from both major corporate organizations and the military (Redding, 1985). From its beginnings, then, researchers in organizational communication were interested in organizational contexts that were male-dominated and they focused their attention specifically on the men who managed those organizations[1].

Consistent with the emphasis on structuralism in the social sciences generally, management theorists in the late 1930s and throughout the next two decades talked about communication in organizations mainly in terms of networks and channels (Guetzkow, 1965; Roberts, O'Reilly, Bretton, & Porter, 1974). The early research findings reported in the management literature were extrapolated primarily from research in interpersonal communication and small group communication (Guetzkow, 1965). In the 1960s the focus shifted to communication as a medium through which organizational activities are carried out (Roberts et al., 1974). By the late 1960s the communication discipline had begun to recognize that organizations were a context in which communication occurred, primarily face-to-face interpersonal communication and small group communication. The early work in the field in organizational communication was highly derivative, using the current theories of interpersonal and small group communication, but applying them in organizational settings using organizational topics and assessing organizational outcomes.[2]

As communication theory moved away from the mechanistic model of communication that had guided it in its early years toward a more complex systems model that emphasized the processual nature of communication, the work in organizational communication also shifted. By the early 1980s, organizational communication was studied primarily from a systems perspective, although that perspective had generated few research studies, and the studies that were done did not use methods that were consistent with the systems assumptions (Monge, 1982).

Although the systems perspective continues to frame much of the work in organizational communication, a new approach, the interpretive perspective, has emerged in opposition to previous research in organizational communication, including that done from a systems perspective, and has gained increasing prominence in the field. Growing out of complementary theoretical and methodological developments in the humanities and the social sciences (including ethnography and other forms of naturalistic inquiry, cultural studies, critical theory, and feminist theory, among others), the interpretive perspective defines organizational communication as how people in organizations make sense of their activities. The interpretive perspective represents an important theoretical and methodological shift in organizational communication that has already produced interesting and useful documentations and interpretations of how organizational actors create and maintain organizations through discourse (see, for example, Putnam & Pacanowsky, 1983). The growing interest in the interpretive perspective in both communication and management has shifted researchers' attention away from controlling organizational outcomes to understanding the process of organizing and the role of discourse in that process.

I began by saying that the development of organizational communication has, in several ways, mirrored the development of the communication discipline in general. As our approach to understanding human communication has become more multifaceted and complex, our theory and research has become less and less accessible to those people who are not trained in the discipline. Even those of us who are trained in the discipline sometimes experience difficulty understanding the work of our colleagues. The sophisticated mathematical modeling procedures of those who are developing methods appropriate for testing complicated systems models of organizational communication are difficult to decipher without advanced statistical and mathematical study; the vocabulary and intellectual abstractions of the postmodernist critic cannot be understood without having completed an extensive reading list in critical theory, structuralism, cultural studies, hermeneutics, and various other contemporary philosophical and intellectual traditions. More important for those interested in organizational communication, our discussions as researchers often focus on narrow arguments about the statistical power of a particular test or the meaning of an arcane term. Our current work in organizational communication has moved us very far from a practical understanding of how people in organizations communicate, and what we as communication scholars can contribute to the larger community's understanding of communication and its potential to improve organizational effectiveness for both organizations and the individuals within them.

FEMINIST EPISTEMOLOGICAL AND METHODOLOGICAL COMMITMENTS

In this section, I identify five epistemological and methodological commitments of feminist research: women's problematics, women's knowledge, feminist synalytics, methodological integrity, and revolutionary pragmatism. These commitments are grounded in feminist theory and reflect theoretical assumptions about how research should proceed and about what we know and how we know it. I call them commitments rather than assumptions because feminist researchers are personally committed to the ways in which we do our research and the ways in which we come to understand and know our world, and we acknowledge those commitments throughout the research enterprise.

Women's Problematics

Feminist research generates its problematics from the perspective of women's experience (Harding, 1987). A feminist perspective takes women's experience off the margins and centers it, making women and the problems in their lives the central focus of research. The research questions that feminist researchers in the social sciences ask have to do with women's experiences in the political, economic, and social world. In the organizational context, for example, researchers study problems that have been central to women's experiences in organizations: sexual harassment, discrimination in hiring and promotion, lack of family care policies, and inflexible work structures. They also seek to identify ways in which women define and negotiate the organizational context: How do women define work-related concepts, such as work, success, and supervision? How do women make decisions, supervise subordinates, and communicate with other organizational members?

By making women's issues and experiences central, a feminist epistemology also focuses attention on the construct of gender, for gender has been central in women's lives in explicit and powerful ways. Although gender is also important in men's lives, one of the consequences of white male privilege is the ability to assume one's privileges are the result of merit and the concomitant inability to see gender as an important conceptual construct in men's, and, therefore, in anyone's lives (Fine, Morrow, & Quaglieri, 1990). Men have not been forced to consider the power of gender in shaping their lives because it has shaped their lives in ways that have privileged them over others, giving them no particular cause for concern[3]. Women, however, must deal with their gender every day. Many of their organizational experiences, such as sexual harassment, low wages, and lack of opportunity for promotion are the direct result of their gender. Feminist researchers seek to understand how gender is socially and symbolically constructed within organizations and how organizations themselves are gendered.

Following Millett's (1970) analysis of the political nature of relationships between men and women, feminist theory equates the personal with the political. If the personal equals the political, then the researcher has a responsibility to bring personal issues into the political arena. Further, by directing our attention to the relationship between the personal and the political, feminist theory reminds us that we should not create artificial separations between private life and public life, and organizational life and the larger social, economic, and political world in which we live, or the narrower, more personal context of daily life. The commitment to women's problematics requires feminist researchers to seek the connections in women's lives, and to study those experiences that are usually defined as either outside of or irrelevant to the organizational context.

In addition to focusing attention on gender, women's problematics also look at oppression. Oppression has been a central experience in women's organizational lives, for the patriarchal relationships and structures that shape the larger social world have also shaped the world of work and women's place within that world. Feminist research looks at the relationship between organizational structures and gender enactments, uncovering the ways that organizational ideologies, including hierarchy and bureaucracy, and modes of discourse silence and oppress women and other powerless members of organizations.

Women's Knowledge

Scholars in a variety of disciplines have argued theoretically and empirically that women come to understand the world in ways that are distinct from men's ways of knowing (Belenky, Clinchy, Goldberger, & Tarule,

1986; Gilligan, 1982; Keller, 1985). One of the most often acknowledged ways of knowing for women is through subjective knowledge. Subjective knowledge locates the place of truth within the individual, equating the scientific with the personal.

The shift from the objectivist stance of "normal" science, which separates objective and subjective knowledge and relegates the subjective to the nonscientific, to a feminist position which recognizes the "truthfulness" of personal knowledge has important implications for research. First, feminist research values women as important sources of information about their own experiences. Self-report data, which can be generated in a variety of ways (for example, through interviews, personal narratives, diaries, and questionnaires), are valid and important research data. Second, researchers and their personal experiences and knowledge become a fundamental and *acknowledged* part of the research. Harding (1987) says that feminist research locates the researcher in the same critical plane as the subject matter; the "beliefs and behavior of the researcher are part of the empirical evidence for (or against) the claims advanced in the results of the research" (p. 9). Feminist research reports often begin with a statement about the author's subjective knowledge of and connections to the subject matter; they are often written in the first person. Feminist research rejects the objectivist stance of normal science and embraces subjective knowledge as an important element of the research process.

In addition to changing the definition of appropriate knowledge, feminist epistemology also enlarges the definition of who can be a knower to include women. Feminist researchers do not look solely to male authority to legitimize their work; they listen to the voices of female authorities and acknowledge those voices as important guides in their work.

Feminist Synalytics

While feminist epistemology focuses our attention on problems derived from the experiences of women and seeks data from the voices of women recounting those experiences, feminist methodology directs the researcher to address those problems and make sense of that data through both analysis and synthesis. I use the term *synalytics* to describe this combination of analysis and synthesis because neither term alone sufficiently explains the methodological process, and the two terms simply juxtaposed are oxymoronic. To analyze is to separate into constituent elements; that which is analytical is, by definition, not synthetic. Synthesis involves bringing together or combining that which is separate; the synthetic is fabricated to replace the usual realities. In feminist synalytics, the researcher analyzes the constituent elements of social phenomena and synthesizes them into a new understanding of experience that replaces the usual male-defined definitions.

Consistent with the focus in women's problematics on the relationship between the personal and political, feminist synalytics looks for the connections in women's experiences and breaks the artificial boundaries between organizational, personal, and cultural life. The synalytic methodology commits the researcher to placing micro-analyses within a macro-analytic framework; organizational behaviors must be analyzed and synthesized within not just the organization but also a sociopolitical framework that is external to the organization. The deconstruction of experiences as we know them within organizations, and their subsequent reconstruction as we revision them in new cultural terms, gives new insight and meaning to organizational life.

Methodological Integrity

Feminist scholarship is cross- and interdisciplinary; it is not bound to the narrow focus or particular methods of a single discipline. Instead, it looks for broader visions and interpretations that integrate and synthesize a variety of perspectives and types of data. The methods that are appropriate to feminist scholarship vary. They include quantitative and qualitative methods, ranging from historiography to rhetorical criticism to content analysis to self-report surveys. A feminist perspective suggests that a variety of methods and perspectives be brought to bear to illuminate the questions the researcher asks. Thus, a feminist perspective values diversity.

Diversity of method, however, is a necessary but not sufficient characteristic of a feminist methodology, which posits that the researcher's methods and theories must be consonant with each other and with ontological assumptions that acknowledge the creative power of human existence and experience (e.g., people are proactive creators and interpreters of their environments). Methodological integrity is an essential characteristic of feminist research. Denzin (1970) likened research to a prism, with its many facets each reflecting light and illuminating an object from a different vantage point. The metaphor is particularly apt. The facets of a prism cannot lie randomly in different planes; they must lie in parallel planes in an integrated whole.

Theories that view human beings as reactive, and methods that treat people solely as objects of study, are not consistent with the assumptions of a feminist perspective. A feminist perspective rejects such research and theory on ethical grounds, regardless of their contribution to the knowledge base of organizational communication.

Revolutionary Pragmatism

Finally, a feminist perspective tells us why we study organizational communication—to create organizations that allow all people to express fully their human potential, and that allow them a genuine and free voice rather than a voice constrained by false ideology. A feminist perspective rejects research that is intended to further the economic goals of the organization without regard to the well-being of the people who constitute the organization.

The feminist researcher inquires in the name of change, for at its core, feminist theory is revolutionary. Gordon (1979) defines feminism as "an analysis of women's subordination for the purpose of figuring out how to change it" (p. 107). Eisenstein (1983) argues that feminism is revolutionary, visionary, and utopian because "the achievement of full freedom for women (all women, not a privileged few) presupposes such profound economic, social, and political changes that, were such a historical development to take place, the present status quo could not and would not survive" (p. xvii). Research on organizational communication that is informed by feminist methodology either explicitly or implicitly judges the status quo and argues for change; it is pragmatic in the philosophical and linguistic sense of that term.

The feminist imperative for change grows out of a unique characteristic of a feminist perspective. That characteristic is not some objective and measurable thing, such as a particular research method, or an intellectually reasoned theoretical position. It is, rather, an emotion that heightens the sense of identification between the researcher and the researched. In feminist research the researcher is bound intrinsically to her[4] subject; she cares passionately about the people whom she is studying[5]. She understands that she is one of them; that while she may have a different set of experiences and knowledge, speak a different language, or live within a different class, race, or culture, she shares a fundamental identity with those she studies and that identity is the basis of her passion for her subject.

Because feminist researchers acknowledge their connections with their subjects, we study organizational communication from the perspective of the "I": We acknowledge that we are studying ourselves. Thus, when we study oppressive ideologies enacted in organizations, we are studying our own oppression as members of organizations structured by the ideology of patriarchy. When we study ways to empower the powerless, we are studying ways to empower ourselves.

In this section, I identified five epistemological and methodological commitments of feminist research: feminist problematics, women's knowledge, feminist synalytics, methodological integrity, and revolutionary pragmatism. In the next section, I look at three research traditions that characterize much of the recent published work in organizational communication to see if they meet these commitments.

CRITIQUE OF LITERATURE IN ORGANIZATIONAL COMMUNICATION

When I began to examine the current literature in organizational communication, I decided to start with five major journals in communication and management: *Journal of Communication, Quarterly Journal of Speech, Communication Monographs, Academy of Management Journal,* and *Academy of Management Review.* I discovered, as Tompkins (1989) has pointed out, that most of the work in organizational communication has not been published in communication journals, particularly in our national journals. Instead it appears in journals from other fields, in some of our regional journals, and, most often, in edited volumes on organizational communication. To supplement my review, I also looked at the regional journals in communication, each of the volumes of *Communication Yearbook,* the September 1983 issue of *Administrative Science Quarterly,* which was devoted to articles on organizational culture, and three relatively recent edited volumes on organizational communication (Ferguson & Ferguson, 1988; Jablin, Putnam, Roberts, & Porter, 1987; McPhee & Tompkins, 1985). Much work in organizational communication has also been presented at professional conferences and remains unpublished. Because of the difficulty in gathering those studies, I have not included them in this review.

Tompkins hypothesizes that the scarcity of research in organizational communication in our field may be the result of having few graduate students in organizational communication who plan to pursue scholarly study. I suspect it is also the result of the "double whammy" of applied research. First, it is extremely difficult for outsiders to get permission to do research within organizations, especially if you are not pursuing management's research agenda. Second, the communication discipline has traditionally had a bias against applied research, which has most often been expressed in terms of the difficulty of working within the "normal science" paradigm of "clean" research in organizational settings.

Organizational research can be usefully classified into three perspectives: the functionalist, the interpretive, and the critical (Putnam, 1983). Using this organizational frame and a feminist lens, I next identify and critique the traditional research in organizational communication.

Functionalist Perspective

Definition of the Functionalist Perspective. The functionalist perspective comprises a variety of research traditions, including structural-functionalism, social systems, behaviorism, conflict functionalism, social exchange models, and abstracted empiricism, which carry, to different degrees, assumptions of logical positivism (Putnam, 1983). Defined in this way, functionalism has been the dominant perspective in organizational communication, as it has been in the disciplines of communication and management (administrative science) in general.

The work in organizational communication done from a functionalist perspective has been categorized by both theory and research tradition. Littlejohn (1983), for example, identified three theories of human organization as being most influential in focusing research concerns: classical, human relations, and social systems. Putnam and Cheney (1983), on the other hand, claimed that four traditions best characterized most of the extant research throughout the early 1980s: (a) organizational communication channels (the message-flow approach), (b) organizational communication climate (the psychological approach), (c) organizational communication networks (the structural approach), and (d) superior-subordinate communication (the dyadic approach). Both the theories and traditions of the functionalist perspective have focused researchers' attention on particular organizational topics, such as negotiation and bargaining (Donohue & Diez, 1985; Putnam & Jones, 1982a, 1982b; Theye & Seiler, 1979), leadership (Husband, 1985; Penley & Hawkins, 1985), organizational climate (Albrecht, 1979; Falcione & Kaplan, 1984; Jablin, 1980a), decision making (Stewart, Gudykunst, Ting-Toomey, & Nishida, 1986), superior-subordinate relationships (Jablin, 1980b; Remland, 1984; Watson, 1982), and employee satisfaction (Hatfield & Huseman, 1982; Richmond & McCroskey, 1979; Richmond, McCroskey, & Davis, 1982; Wheeless, Wheeless, & Howard, 1984). This diversity of theoretical models, research methodologies, and topical foci led to numerous debates about defining a single domain for organizational communication (Dennis, Goldhaber, & Yates, 1978; Redding, 1979; Richetto, 1977).

Regardless of theoretical position, research tradition, or topic, however, certain fundamental assumptions cut across the work in organizational communication done from a functionalist perspective. Within this perspective, organizational communication is defined as the transmission of messages within organizations. Functionalists "treat social phenomena as concrete, materialistic entities" (Putnam, 1983, p. 34) and "reify social processes" (p. 35). The organization is a fixed container in which messages are transmitted through channels—up, down, and across the organization—to people, who react to these messages and other organizational stimuli. Functionalists study the relationship between communication variables and organizational outcomes in order to predict and control those outcomes.

An examination of a representative article within the functionalist perspective best illustrates several assumptions of the perspective. One line of research in the organizational communication literature involves measuring the effectiveness of the Realistic Job Preview (RJP) (Reilly, Brown, Blood, & Malatesta, 1981; Wanous, 1980). The RJP is an attitude change technique which organizations use to give new employees a dose of "organizational reality" in order to reduce turnover among newly hired employees. The assumption is that if the employee's expectations of the organization can be made consonant with the reality of the organization, then the employee is less likely to be disappointed and leave. Popovich and Wanous (1982) develop a model of how the RJP affects turnover based on the Yale Persuasive Communication model; they argue that this particular model of persuasive communication provides the best model for specifying the process of persuasion so that organizations can control the outcome of the RJP.

Several important functionalist assumptions are evident in this analysis. First, the organization is a fixed container in which particular types of messages (for example, the RJP) are transmitted. Second, the communication process is reduced to a number of static, quantifiable variables (in this particular case—source, message, channel, and audience). Third, the goal of the research is to predict and control outcome variables (the reduction of employee turnover). In organizational research in particular, the outcome variables that interest the researcher are organizational outcomes that reflect a managerial bias. The RJP research doesn't question whether it is in the employee's best interest to remain with the company; reducing employee turnover is the managerial goal.

Critique of the Functionalist Perspective. Logical positivism has been thoroughly and persuasively critiqued by numerous scholars[6], so I will not belabor their points here. Instead, let me look specifically at the research in organizational communication generated by the functionalist perspective in terms of how well it meets the epistemological and methodological commitments of a feminist perspective.

Not surprisingly, organizational communication researchers did not take note of women or women's problematics until the 1970s, when increasing numbers of women began to enter corporations, especially in the managerial ranks. Although women had always been part of organizational life, most of them had roles that were peripheral to the concerns of management theorists (Kanter, 1977). The managerial bias of the functionalist perspective, which dominated the research in organizational communication, further marginalized women, making them virtually invisible in the research questions and designs.

Because functionalist research reduces social processes to constitutive elements and looks for causal relationships among those elements, the research design generally involves variable testing. Although some research in organizational communication began to include women, it did so by including gender as a variable in the research design[7]. At its worst, such research included gender simply to add a trendy new variable to the design. At its best, it included gender because of a genuine interest in discovering communication differences between men and women in organizations. In both cases, however, the research is suspect. By reducing gender to a variable, researchers equate gender with sex, denying the social construction of gender and falling into the trap of biological determinism, a position antithetical to most current theories of human behavior in general and human communication in particular. Focusing on gender as the determining variable in communication differences between women and men also hides the possibility that the relationship is reversed, in other words, that communication shapes gender (Foss & Foss, 1983; Putnam, 1982). By hiding the ways in which gender is constructed through communication, gender as variable research fails to reveal a central experience in women's lives that has oppressed them.

Looking at communication differences between women and men in organizations through a functionalist perspective fails to meet the feminist commitment to women's problematics in a second way. Because men's experience has historically defined normative behavior in organizations, studies comparing female and male communication use category systems derived from male experience to evaluate female communication against male norms. For example, Fairhurst (1986) reports that several studies on the use of power in organizational settings suggest that "males' influence strategies are assertive and direct in contrast to females' indirect, submissive, and 'people-oriented' tactics" (p. 103). While Fairhurst questions these conclusions because they come primarily from laboratory studies and not from observations of women's and men's actual behavior in organizations, a more critical conceptual flaw in such studies is that they assume a definition of power and the behaviors associated with the use of power that are based on male definitions. Recent research suggests that men and women define power differently (Belenky et al., 1986; Gilligan, 1982; Wyatt, 1984). Fine, Johnson, and Foss (1991) found that men equate power with a personal style characterized by aggressiveness towards others, and women see power as a cognitive attribute that accompanies intellect.

Although some functionalist researchers have recognized that women may perceive and use communication variables in ways that differ from men's perceptions and uses (Stewart et al., 1986), most tend to ignore or gloss over findings that suggest such differences between men and women (or white men and other minorities) exist. For example, in a study of the relationship between perceptual congruence in supervisor/subordinate communication and job satisfaction, Hatfield and Huseman (1982) found that congruence was a significant variable in predicting job satisfaction for whites but not for African Americans. Despite the lack of significance for African Americans, they concluded, however, that future research should identify ways of enhancing congruence between superiors and subordinates. The experiences and needs of white males dominate the problematics of functionalist research.

Functionalist research also fails to meet the commitment to women's knowledge. Within the functionalist perspective, subjective knowledge is generally not valued. Although some studies do use self-report data, such data are considered suspect. Quantitative data are considered more "accurate" than qualitative data (Dennis et al., 1978). The functionalist perspective also rejects the belief that the personal is the scientific. Research is conducted from an objectivist stance, which assumes that researchers are detached from and objective about the people and ideas they are studying. Functionalist researchers do not acknowledge that their experience and knowledge shape their research; research reports are written in objectivist language, which uses passive voice and dispassionate, presumably "neutral," vocabulary.

By definition, the functionalist perspective also rejects the commitments to feminist synalytics, methodological integrity, and revolutionary pragmatism. Functionalist research in organizational communication proceeds within an analytical framework: Social processes are reified and broken down into constituent elements, and the relationships among the elements are examined within the context of the organization as a closed container. A brief look at the research literature on tokenism demonstrates the shortcomings of the functionalist approach.

Tokens are individuals who enter a work environment in which members of their social category are numerically scarce (Kanter, 1977). Kanter (1977) asserts that this numerical imbalance, rather than the social category per se (e.g., gender or race), accounts for the social isolation, role conflict, and performance pressures that tokens (e.g., women and people of color) experience in organizations. Fairhurst (1986) identifies numerous studies of token dynamics that confirm Kanter's analysis. Two studies of male tokens (Fairhurst & Snavely, 1983a, 1983b; Snavely & Fairhurst, 1984) did not find, however, that the men experienced more social isolation, role conflict, or performance pressure than the women in the organization. Synthesizing these conflicting results within a larger sociopolitical framework that recognizes the power differentials between women and men that exist within the culture outside of the organization, provides a way to understand the different results. Fairhurst (1986) suggests that these power differentials "may have given male tokens a source of power with which to combat the loss of status due to numerical underrepresentation that female tokens do not have" (p. 90).

As I said earlier in this chapter, a feminist perspective rejects theories that view human beings as reactive and research methods that treat them solely as objects of study. The objectivist stance of the functionalist perspective, and the linear models of communication that are the foundation of much of the research, do not meet the feminist commitment to methodological integrity. Later work in the functional perspective is grounded in more complex theoretical understandings of human communication, but is limited by the research methods available within the functionalist perspective (Monge, 1982; Monge, Farace, Eisenberg, Miller, & White, 1984).

Revolutionary pragmatism commits the researcher in organizational communication to helping people in organizations create work environments that empower them and help them realize their human potential. The managerial bias of the functionalist perspective values organizational outcomes that often disempower employees and ignores the concerns of employees who are not in the managerial ranks. The functionalist research goal of prediction and control is antithetical to the empowerment of the individual inherent in revolutionary pragmatism.

In general, then, the functionalist perspective in organizational communication does not meet feminist epistemological and methodological commitments to women's problematics, women's knowledge, feminist synalytics, methodological integrity, or revolutionary pragmatism.

Interpretive Perspective

Definition of the Interpretive Perspective. The relatively recent interpretive perspective in organizational communication emerged in opposition to the functionalist perspective. Throughout the late 1960s and early 1970s, social scientists in a variety of disciplines began to critique prevailing theories of human behavior and to call for new conceptualizations that were based on how people use symbols to create meaning (Berger & Luckmann, 1967; Duncan, 1967; Harre & Secord, 1973; Stone & Farberman, 1970). As an emerging area of study in the communication discipline, organizational communication initially lagged behind in such debates, and the published work in the area continued to reflect the logical positivist assumptions of the functional perspective. A few tentative, questioning voices were heard, however, in graduate seminars and conference presentations. For example, in 1972 at the University of Minnesota, David Smith taught a graduate seminar in organizational communication in which students explored the utility of applying to organizational communication Bormann's fantasy theme analysis, which had been applied primarily to small group communication and political communication at that time[8].

The interpretive perspective gained national attention in communication in August 1981, when the Speech Communication Association and the International Communication Association jointly sponsored the first Summer Conference on Interpretive Approaches to the Study of Organizational Communication. Papers from the conference were published in the Spring 1982 issue of the *Western Journal of Speech Communication*. A similar debate about the utility of the interpretive perspective was simultaneously taking place in management, culminating in 1983 with the publication of a special issue of *Administrative Science Quarterly* devoted to papers that helped "illuminate the possibilities of culture as a root metaphor for organization studies" (Jelinek, Smircich, & Hirsch, 1983). That year was a watershed year for the interpretive perspective in organizational communication, marked also by the publication of an article in *Communication Monographs* (Pacanowski & O'Donnell-Trujillo, 1983) and the first edited volume of essays on the perspective (Putnam & Pacanowski, 1983).

The interpretive perspective starts with the theoretical assumption that individuals create and shape their own reality through communication (Krone, Jablin, & Putnam, 1987, p. 27); "interpretivists focus on the subjective, intersubjective, and socially constructed meanings of organizational actors" (Putnam, 1983, p. 34). Organizations are defined as social constructions created through discourse (Mumby, 1987), and organizational communication is defined as ways in which people in organizations make sense of their activities.

Methodologically, interpretivists reject the objectivist stance of logical positivism, focusing instead on the individuals' subjective accounts of their experience and becoming "immersed or involved in the lives of the people they study" (Putnam, 1983, p. 44). They seek to understand events in the here-and-now rather than predict and control the future. Interpretivists use a variety of research methods, most often those that grow out of naturalistic inquiry (Bantz, 1983), and they frequently triangulate their methods to gain additional understanding of issues (Albrecht & Ropp, 1982; Faules, 1982; Tompkins & Cheney, 1983).

Unlike researchers in the functionalist perspective, who are interested in identifying and controlling the variables that affect outcomes within organizations, researchers in the interpretive perspective are interested in understanding the processes of organizing and sense making in which organizational actors participate. To understand these processes, some interpretivists examine organizational culture[9] and symbolism. For example, Pacanowsky and O'Donnell-Trujillo (1983) suggested five types of cultural performances that researchers in organizational communication could profitably study: (a) ritual, including personal rituals, task rituals, social rituals, and organizational rituals; (b) passion, including passionate repartee; (c) sociality, including courtesies, pleasantries, sociabilities, and privacies; (d) politics, including showing personal strength, cementing allies, and bargaining; and (e) enculturation, including learning and teaching the roles and learning and teaching the ropes. Smith and Eisenberg (1987) studied a labor strike at Disneyland using a root-metaphor analysis that revealed that employees and management held conflicting world views. Bormann, Pratt, and Putnam (1978) analyzed fantasies of power, sex, and authority in an organization and linked the fantasies to how men responded to female leadership.

Interpretivists also look more microscopically at organizational discourse per se, looking for patterns of interaction and how they constitute meaning and regulate behavior in organizations. Fairhurst and Chandler (1989) attempted to extend Graen's Leader-Member Exchange theory (a leadership theory in management which grows out of a functionalist perspective and does not focus on communication) by looking at how a leader and three members display social structure through their use of power and social distance forms in their discourse.

Critique of the Interpretive Perspective. The interpretive perspective is theoretically and methodologically consistent with a feminist perspective. Both perspectives see people as proactive creators of meaning; both emphasize the social construction of reality and the subjective nature of experience; both acknowledge the truthfulness of personal knowledge; both value bringing diverse research methods together to illuminate problems. As it has been articulated in the literature, however, the interpretive perspective fails to meet the epistemological and methodological commitments of a feminist perspective in several important ways.

First, although the interpretive perspective is ideally suited for examining women's problematics, especially the social construction of gender, race, and class within organizations, most of the published research avoids issues of gender, race, or class. Further, despite acknowledging the subjective nature of experience as a defining assumption of the perspective, researchers often fail to acknowledge explicitly how their own experience has shaped their research. This lack of self-reflexivity on the part of researchers often produces research models and studies that are male-defined and highly ethnocentric. For example, in Eisenberg's (1984) study of how people in organizations use ambiguity purposefully to accomplish their goals, ambiguity is defined and valued in terms of the experiences of white males in the United States. Eisenberg says ambiguity is often valuable because it is deniable, thus allowing more options, safeguarding military plans, and generally allowing for the exercise of power. Nowhere in the essay does Eisenberg acknowledge that women (or anyone who does not conform to white male thinking) may not value strategic ambiguity for precisely the reasons that he claims it is valuable. Some research suggests that women do not conceptualize issues in the linear, hierarchical modes of thinking that would produce escalating options (Gilligan, 1982) and that they also do not define power as control over others (Fine et al., 1991). Given those differences, women in organizations may well reject strategic ambiguity as a means for accomplishing their goals.

Smith and Eisenberg (1987), in their analysis of the employee strike at Disneyland, illuminate how the conflicting metaphors of "drama," used by management, and "family," used by employees, became a source of organizational conflict that eventually led to the strike. The authors define family in patriarchal, male terms: Walt Disney presiding over his "family," a social structure that emphasizes nonviolence and intimacy. This definition is at odds with the reality of family life experienced by many women. I do not fault Smith and Eisenberg for their reading of this organizational text; their analysis yields many insights into the management-employee conflict at Disneyland. It is important to recognize, however, that their reading is only one of many, and that a feminist perspective would direct researchers to consider a different analysis. A commitment to women's problematics suggests that another critical concern for the researcher is how management created and maintained the paternalistic, patriarchal vision of family and the ways in which that vision denied employees, especially women, the opportunity to participate freely in shaping their organizational lives.

Second, the interpretive perspective generally does not meet the commitment to feminist synalytics. The interpretive work in the literature tends to focus on understanding the internal cultural context of the organization. In their introduction to the *Administrative Science Quarterly* special issue on organizational culture, Jelinek et al. (1983) conclude that although the perspective shows great promise, the collection of essays "lacks a broad, societal analysis exploring the modern corporation as a cultural form" (p. 338). For example, Schall (1983) uses a communication rules perspective to synthesize organizations, cultures, and cultural rules as communication phenomena. Using data from five sources that represent different job categories and hierarchical levels within a large organization, she describes the informal and formal rule systems in the organization. Schall's method is consistent with the methodological commitments of a feminist perspective: She uses insiders to evaluate her descriptions of the culture; she immerses herself within the work groups she studies as a learner rather than as an expert; and she shares her findings with all of the group members, both in writing and face to face. But Schall is ultimately unable to move beyond a description of the internal culture of the organization because her analysis provides no context in which to interpret and evaluate the culture.

The interpretive perspective does partially meet the commitment to methodological integrity. But it is caught in a conundrum over issues of diversity. The tendency in the published literature is to argue for diversity of perspectives and to refuse, in the name of diversity, to reject any particular mode of inquiry. All inquiry is seen as equally valid if it advances our knowledge of communication in organizations. Krone et al. (1987) say "no perspective is right or wrong" (p. 38), and Putnam, in the preface to the Putnam and Pacanowsky volume (1983) that introduced the interpretive perspective in organizational communication, says: "It is not our intent to eliminate existing paradigms; rather, we advocate a state of coexistence and mutual support between competing perspectives" (p. 7). The feminist commitment to methodological integrity includes an ethical imperative to reject theory and research which denies people's capacity for creating experience, their right to participate freely in shaping the organizations in which they work, and which furthers the economic interests of the organization without regard to the well-being of the people who constitute the organization. The nonideological stance of the interpretivists often leaves them in the position of valuing all work and unwilling to make ethical judgments about the methodological integrity of other perspectives.

Finally, their nonideological stance precludes interpretivists from becoming activists within the organizations they study. Interpretivists are not committed to revolutionary pragmatism. Their goal is explanation and understanding, not change. Although they place themselves in the same plane as their subjects and become involved with them, they have no commitment to their subjects beyond the research study itself. In the interpretive perspective, the researcher is an observer and interpreter of organizational life, not a proactive change agent within the organization. Only within the academy does the interpretivist researcher advocate for change, and even there, the advocacy is for inclusion, not radical restructuring.

Critical Perspective

Definition of the Critical Perspective. Although the critical perspective is often treated as part of the interpretive perspective (Putnam, 1983), research from a critical perspective differs from interpretive research in two significant ways. First, the two perspectives posit different goals for the research enterprise. Unlike interpretive research, which seeks understanding and explanation, critical research seeks to free people from domination and oppression. The goal of critical research is social reconstruction, which is effected by identifying and removing "illegitimate constraints on communication" (Deetz & Kersten, 1983, p. 148). The critical researcher has three tasks: understanding, critique, and education (Deetz, 1982). Second, the critical perspective focuses on "cultural structures as the only context within which organizational power relationships can be understood" (Conrad & Ryan, 1985). Unlike interpretive researchers, critical researchers are committed to understanding and critiquing organizational discourse by analyzing and synthesizing the discourse within a larger sociocultural context.

Although the critical perspective is not yet fully developed and is still marginalized within the organizational communication literature (Conrad & Ryan, 1985), it is gaining increasing prominence. Virtually all of the articles on organizational communication in *Communication Yearbook 13* (Anderson, 1990) represent the critical perspective. I include the perspective here both because of its increasing visibility in the literature in organizational communication and because it bears many similarities to feminist perspectives. The second point is particularly significant: Researchers who espouse the utility of a feminist perspective in communication are frequently asked how their ideas differ from those of critical theorists. (Both feminists and critical theorists should be interested in exploring why the reverse question is never asked.)

Two articles provide exemplars of the critical perspective in organizational communication. Mumby (1987) argues that narrative is "an ideological force that articulates a system of meaning which privileges certain interests over others" (p. 113). He examines a narrative about IBM and uncovers its deep structure, showing how the narrative reproduces the dominant ideology at IBM, reinforcing traditional sex-role stereotypes and hierarchical status differences. Wood and Conrad (1983) identify six recurring paradoxes that professional women experience and suggest ways that they can choose appropriate communication strategies for managing them. These paradoxes are created through mystification, the symbolic processes in which one group maintains its hegemony over another group by misrepresenting action. In evaluating the communication strategies available to women, the authors distinguish among those that perpetuate double-binding patterns, redefine the situation, and transcend the situation. They conclude that only transcendence "has the power to enrich not only individuals, but the possibility of a society dedicated to humane values" (p. 318).

Critique of the Critical Perspective. The critical perspective comes the closest of the research traditions in organizational communication to meeting the epistemological and methodological commitments of a feminist perspective. In theory, research done from the critical perspective can meet each of the commitments. In practice, however, the research often falls short.

Despite its central concern with power as a problematic (Conrad & Ryan, 1985), the critical perspective rarely yields research that examines patriarchy as a form of power[10]. Most often, power is problematized in economic terms, either using traditional Marxian economic analysis, or updating the Marxist terms, as Deetz and Mumby (1990) do when they argue that the logic of control has replaced the logic of profit in the modern corporation. Although the economic metaphor yields insights into the organization, it glosses over issues of gender and patriarchy, race and racism. Deetz and Mumby's (1990) argument that we need to shift from Marxian economic analysis to the concept of managerial capitalism masks the complex web of power relationships in modern organizations created and sustained through patriarchy and racism.

The commitment to women's problematics is especially important in organizational research precisely because we tend not to think of organizations as "gendered" (Acker, 1987). Instead, the organizational context is most easily apprehended in organizational terms that have been central in management theory. For example, when Haslett (1990) responds to Deetz and Mumby (1990) that organizations are too complex to be subsumed under one political ideology, she identifies organizational complexity in terms of size, type of industry, volatility of the industry, environmental uncertainty, and managerial decision making—the standard terms of analysis in business policy textbooks.

In addition to not meeting the commitment to women's problematics, the critical perspective also fails to acknowledge fully women's voices. Although researchers engage in analysis and synthesis, their analytical frame tends to be male. Conrad and Ryan (1985), for example, argue that when organizations engage in nonrational decision-making processes that are inconsistent with the socially constructed myths of individual and corporate rationality, managers rationalize nonrationality, thus maintaining organizational hierarchy and control. They conclude that this process of rationalizing nonrationality allows powerful individuals in the organization to continue "to be defined in terms of culturally legitimized, ontological superiority—their expertise and communicative or argumentative skills, superior access to information, broader `organization-wide' perspective, and so on" (p. 252). That analysis of organizational accounts is at odds with my own experience as a woman in an organization. The women I know often talk about the incompetence of powerful men in organizations; we account for their success not because they are ontologically superior but because they are male. Research suggests that I am not alone. In a study of the career aspirations of managerial and professional women and men in a public utility, one woman, who was asked to name the personal characteristics necessary for success in her company, responded, "You're male, you're white" (Fine et al., 1990, p. 57).

The critical perspective also rarely acknowledges female authorities. Instead, the theory and research are based primarily on the ideas of male thinkers, for example, Marx, Engels, Habermas, Gramsci, Foucault, Derridas, and Lukacs. My point is not that the ideas of these men are not important and valuable; many feminist writers acknowledge their intellectual debt to them. But where are the women's voices in the critical perspective?[11] The absence of women's voices in the intellectual grounding of critical theory makes it suspect as a basis for understanding human experience (if we are to define human inclusively). The lack of acknowledgment of female authorities in the published literature continues the devaluing of women's ideas and reproduces the existing genderized social structure within the academic community, putting the practice of the critical perspective at odds with its goal of social reconstruction.

Finally, despite its "emancipatory interest" (Smircich & Calas, 1987), the critical perspective in practice rarely meets the feminist commitment to revolutionary pragmatics. Most work in the critical perspective is highly theoretical and based on conceptual models rather than on empirical data. Researchers tend not to do their research inside organizations. Mumby (1987), for example, analyzed an IBM narrative he found in someone else's research; he never actually talked with anyone at IBM. Because the researchers are not working with employees in organizations, they have no need to write in forms that are accessible to employees or to develop pragmatic approaches for helping employees restructure their organizations in ways that encourage individual and organizational well-being. Even Wood and Conrad (1983), in their insightful analysis of the paradoxes professional women encounter, fail to provide practical advice for women in organizations. They suggest that women use transcendent communication strategies to respond to paradox, but never give examples of an actual response that a woman might use. The commitment to revolutionary pragmatics impels feminist researchers to work within organizations to develop pragmatic approaches to organizational problems.

In summary, the critical perspective has the potential to meet the epistemological and methodological commitments of a feminist perspective. In actual practice, however, the critical perspective does not fully meet the commitments to women's problematics, women's knowledge, and revolutionary pragmatism.

FEMINIST RESEARCH IN ORGANIZATIONAL COMMUNICATION

Although feminist concerns have influenced much of the recent research in many of the subfields of communication, they have not been as influential in organizational communication. Students and scholars with feminist interests may avoid organizational communication because they lack interest or are reluctant to work within traditional organizations, which are hierarchical, bureaucratic, and profit making. Feminist research in organizational communication tends to focus more on nontraditional organizations, which are women-run, nonhierarchical (in theory if not always in practice), and frequently not profit making.

Most of the feminist research in organizational communication has been presented at conferences and, as yet, little has been published. The lack of published work is not surprising considering the difficulty of publishing any work in organizational communication. Publishing feminist research in organizational communication is even more difficult because feminist research perspectives are not widely acknowledged and accepted. Further, organizations constrain the type and amount of feminist research. Feminist organizational research requires access to people in organizations. Such access is never easy to obtain; without having traditional managerial objectives as their research goals, feminist researchers face additional resistance in getting into organizations.

Feminist research in organizational communication comprises four lines of inquiry. The first line of inquiry does not focus on organizational communication per se; instead, it looks at the organizational context. For example, Ferguson (1984) examines how bureaucracies incorporate and sustain traditional patterns of dominance and control and suggests ways in which feminist perspectives could challenge those patterns and restructure organizational life. Acker (1987) posits a theory of gendered organizations by looking at the ways in which gender relationships are reproduced within organizations and work activities. Several researchers examine the genderized nature of research in organizational theory and suggest ways that feminist concepts could revise and rewrite that theory (Balsamo, 1985; Calas & Smircich, 1992; Jacobson & Jacques, 1990; Mumby & Putnam, 1992; Putnam, 1990). Putnam and Fairhurst (1985), in a brief critique of the research in organizational communication, provide an overview of its masculinist bias and suggest directions for future research. They also emphasize the need to focus research efforts on the communicative implications of the problematics that are studied and to update the research literature as more women move into managerial roles.[12].

The second line of inquiry focuses on women's problematics. As I said earlier, most of the research on women's problematics has been done from the perspective of gender as the variable.[13] There are, however, some exceptions. Two studies examine the rhetorical visions that are created in women's self-help books (Bate & Self, 1983; Koester, 1982). This type of research provides a foundation for understanding the ways in which gender, as it is enacted in organizations, is constructed and maintained through communication. Wood and Conrad (1983) identify some paradoxes women in organizations confront and offer strategies for dealing with them.

The third line of inquiry involves documenting women's voices by identifying the values, meanings, and aspirations women bring to the workplace. These studies include documenting young women's aspirations and work-related values (Fine et al., 1991; McCallister & Gaymon, 1989), identifying working women's perceptions of their communication skills (Fine, Johnson, Ryan, & Lutfiyya, 1987; Staley & Shockley-Zalabak, 1986), and revealing women's definitions of organizational experiences (Fine, Johnson, & Ryan, 1990; Fine, Morrow, & Quaqlieri, 1990). The results of these studies provide support for the theoretical perspective that views genders as cultural systems (Johnson, 1989).

The final line of inquiry comprises studies of alternative organizations that reflect women-defined values and assumptions. These studies are noteworthy both because they reveal organizational structures and enactments that challenge traditional conceptions of organizations and because they are exemplars for feminist research. Wyatt (1988), in her study of shared leadership in a community Weavers Guild with approximately 40 female members, offers a vision of leadership based on responsibility and interpersonal connection rather than power and status. She concludes that leadership is not a fixed construct, but one that emerges in response to particular situations and contexts. Seccombe-Eastland (1988) examines the interplay of ideology and action in a feminist bookstore, uncovering the tension inherent in the contradiction between the organization's radical separatist ideology and its identity as a business concern. She raises important questions about organizational goals and the definition of organizational success. Lont (1988) identifies similar tensions in her study of Redwood Records; unlike the feminist bookstore, however, Redwood chose to deal with the tension by adapting its organizational structure, finding what Lont calls "a middle ground" between lack of structure and hierarchy. In her study of Studio D of the National Film Board of Canada, Taylor (1988) looks at a small feminist organization that is embedded in, responsible to, and dependent on a large government bureaucracy. Her descriptions of the members' decision making, leadership strategies, and methods for resolving conflicts offer another perspective on the tensions between ideology and action that are inherent in organizations.

Each of these studies is noteworthy for its adherence to feminist methodological and epistemological commitments. The researchers engaged in naturalistic inquiry in which they acknowledged and valued the voices of the women they studied. They checked to ensure that the meanings they ascribed to what they heard and read were the meanings intended by their subjects. Lont, for example, circulated everything that she wrote about Redwood among the staff and solicited their oral and written comments. The researchers also either formed intimate connections with their subjects or developed their research out of existing intimate connections. Wyatt's research was prompted by her experience as a member of the Weaver's Guild; Seccombe-Eastland was an honorary member of the Collective that ran Twenty Rue Jacob, the bookstore she studied; and Taylor admits that she was not objective about Studio D and its goals.

The studies presented here represent current feminist work in organizational communication. Each of these lines of inquiry needs additional work. In the final section of this chapter, I suggest more specific directions for future research in organizational communication that grow out of the feminist epistemological and methodological commitments I outlined earlier.

FEMINIST DIRECTIONS FOR RESEARCH IN ORGANIZATIONAL COMMUNICATION

The epistemological and methodological commitments of a feminist perspective offer researchers in organizational communication a wealth of opportunities for studying organizations, both as they are constructed now and as they are reconfigured to meet the demands of the 21st century. In providing those research opportunities, a feminist perspective also offers researchers the opportunity to contribute directly to organizations in ways that enrich their own lives and the lives of organizational members. Embarking on a feminist research agenda also leads the researcher to make a personal commitment to the research enterprise and its role in the larger community.

In this final section, I identify three areas of research in organizational communication that are suggested by a feminist perspective: (a) documenting organizational experiences; (b) examining the social construction of gender, race, and class; and (c) constructing multicultural organizations. Finally, I propose that a feminist perspective commits the researcher to being a social activist within organizations.

Documenting Organizational Experiences

First, we need to begin to document the experiences of women and other marginalized groups in organizations. Such documentation requires that we allow women and others to speak for themselves, in their own voices. To do so, they must set their own research agendas and define their own organizational terms. Fine, Johnson, and Ryan (1990) surveyed 263 employees in managerial, professional, and clerical positions in a large Federal agency using a written questionnaire that was based on extensive interviews with a sample of employees that included white women, white men, men and women of color, executives, managers, technical specialists, and clerical workers. Their results indicated that the perceptions of women and men of color, white women, and white men were fundamentally different across a wide range of organizational experiences, including hiring and promotion, job satisfaction, sexual harassment, and affirmative action.

This study is interesting not just for its results, but also for its research methods. Asked by management to assess the training needs of women and people of color in the agency, the researchers began by asking employees to answer that question themselves. Their answers suggested that different groups within the organization experienced different realities and that they shared little understanding of each other's realities. The training programs that emerged out of the needs assessment were not the typical management training workshops. Instead, the survey results indicated that employees needed opportunities to share their experiences and to have others in the organization affirm and validate those experiences. The workshops allowed employees to identify and discuss stereotypes and communication styles based on gender, race, and ethnicity. More advanced workshops for managers focused on helping them see how white male norms for defining "appropriate" job performance standards, educational and work experience, and personal characteristics frequently precluded them from hiring and promoting white women and men and women of color.

In addition to documenting the experiences of women and people of color, researchers need to compile "dictionaries" of the meanings of work-related concepts so that we can begin to understand the voices of others. The current research in organizational communication assumes that we all speak the same language and share the same meanings for organizational terms. I have been struck by the number of times that I have heard white women and women and men of color use organizational concepts in ways that are very unlike the ways their white male counterparts use them. For example, at one meeting, a black male EEO officer was baffled when a group of white male managers said that the agency was unable to compete with private industry in recruiting young black women and men because starting salaries in the public sector lagged well behind starting salaries in the private sector. He told them that money was the wrong inducement. Instead, the managers should emphasize the importance of the agency's work in protecting the public good, since the black community highly values public service. In another instance, I was developing a workshop on success for managerial women and was taken aback when a woman in the planning group said that the definition of success we were using was too restrictive. She reminded us quite eloquently that women usually see their lives in larger patterns of interconnections and that success was not limited to movement up the organizational ladder. Such movement, in fact, often mitigates against women's opportunities for achieving success in other parts of their lives. Until we better understand the meanings that we each bring to the workplace, we cannot hear each other's voices.

Examining the Social Construction of Gender, Race, and Class

Another direction for research in organizational communication is to look at how gender, race, and class are socially constructed and reinforced within organizations. There are some obvious places that we can look to see both the construction of gender and the intersections of gender and class. Kanter's (1977) landmark study, *Men and Women of the Corporation*, details an organizational structure in which women are both marginalized and relegated to supporting roles, appearing only as secretaries and wives, and playing the same part regardless of the role in which they appear. The secretary provides her male boss with the same services at work as his wife does at home—making coffee, maintaining his calendar, keeping his environment clean and neat, even providing his emotional support. Although Kanter argues that gender roles in organizations are the result of structural constraints rather than social and political ideologies of power, her analysis suggests rich possibilities for places in which to examine the construction of gender in organizations.

L. Lederman (personal communication, November 19, 1989) suggests another place to look at gender role construction. She recalls in vivid detail attending a meeting at the home of a female executive for a major corporation. Until that meeting, Lederman had interacted with the executive only in corporate settings, where she presented herself as a competent professional and who did not dress, speak, or behave in stereotypically feminine ways. Lederman was surprised by the self she presented at home, however. The executive proudly told her that she had prepared their lunch herself, even baking the bread from scratch. Although the executive herself did not wear overly "feminine" clothing, her young daughter appeared in a frilly dress. As Lederman observed the familial scene, she realized that she was watching the executive construct at home the feminized gender role she did not seem to enact at work.

We need studies in which we observe how women construct gender roles both in the workplace and at home, and how those roles do or do not intersect. We should also look at the various ways that organizations reinforce and reward gender role behavior that is consistent with gender role stereotypes. Are women who speak up punished while men are rewarded? Are men who act unethically protected while women are left to hang for their crimes? Finally, we should look at the ways that social institutions outside of the organization, such as television, print media, religion, or schools create expectations of appropriate behavior for professional women and men.

Constructing Multicultural Organizations

The most serious issue facing organizations and their members as we approach the next century in the U.S. is how to construct multicultural rather than monocultural organizations. The slowest growing segment of the U.S. labor market is white males, who will account for less than half of the workforce by the year 2000. Historically, however, because the workforce was once mostly white and male, especially in the managerial ranks, organizational theorists developed their ideas about organizations and organizing based on the assumption of a homogeneous workforce.

Our existing organizational communication theories are also based on assumptions of homogeneity and are, therefore, unable to account for multicultural organizational forms. Functionalists "assume a *unitary view of organizations;* that is organizations are treated as cooperative systems in pursuit of common interests and goals" (Putnam, 1983, p. 36). The functionalist perspective assumes that all members of the organization are the same; those members who are different, for example, women and people of color, just need to be socialized or trained to be like everyone else, that is, white males. Although interpretivists take "a *pluralistic perspective* by treating the organization as an array of factionalized groups with diverse purposes and goals," their "primary unit of analysis centers on the values, goals, and interactions that create and sustain coalitions" (p. 37). The interpretivist perspective recognizes difference, but does not see it as important in organizing. Instead, commonality becomes the basis around which different groups organize; people in organizations look to values that they share to find the common ground on which to come together.

A multicultural organizational theory must confront difference directly, recognizing the assumption of difference as the organizational norm. Postmodern feminist theory provides a starting point for recognizing and valuing difference. Smircich and Calas (1987) offer postmodernism as a way to "read" organizational texts. Unlike modernism, which defines itself through opposition, postmodernism is defined through resistance. Rather than advocating a particular paradigm, postmodernism "*suspects* and *defers* acceptance of *any* notion of 'truth'" (p. 248). Participating in the postmodern world requires multiple discourses and interpretations of reality. Smircich and Calas say that we need "deconstructive readings" of our texts so that we are able to see the multiple discourses:

> Our participation in the *postmodernism of resistance depends on our ability to have a much wider and cultured view of the world*, on our ability to see ourselves as participants in the making of this world, and on our ability to speak "culturally" in the multiple voices of "the other participant's" discourse. It means not privileging one form of reading and saying over another. Postmodernism of resistance questions one's own and others' discursive strongholds. It is creating the critical "writing in the margin" of every writing that wants to "center itself on the page." (p. 256, emphasis in original)

Postmodernism provides the starting point for a theory of multicultural organizations by reminding us that we must always resist those voices that seek to dominate, and that we must insist that organizations not privilege one voice or one form of discourse over another. Both researchers and organizational members must work actively against organizational norms that privilege white male forms of discourse or definitions of organizational terms. For example, we need to question performance appraisals that conclude that an Asian American woman does not have managerial capability because she is too passive or that an African American male cannot be promoted to a position with greater responsibility because he is too confrontational and emotional. We must question the assumptions about discourse and the definition of communicative terms on which such conclusions are based.

Postmodern resistance, however, is a necessary but not sufficient condition of a theory of multicultural organizations. Resistance only helps us understand organizational texts by instructing us to question our assumptions about the rightness of a particular discourse. When we resist, we are static; we cannot move together in any direction. Organizations are essentially pragmatic entities; we organize in order to accomplish some end, to produce goods or services in the broadest sense of those terms. To accomplish those ends we must work together. I have felt enormous frustration as an organizational member as I watch members enact discourse styles that not only are not recognized and valued by others, but also are philosophically opposed to the other. For example, I recall sitting at a meeting of EPA senior staff, comprised of five white men, one African American man, and one white woman, where we were discussing affirmative action policy for the Agency. The African American male demanded that the other staff members discuss the issues in very direct terms. He accused the Agency of not being committed to affirmative action, and he became very angry when no one would respond or defend the Agency's actions. The white staff at the meeting became more and more uncomfortable, and the angrier the African American male became, the quieter and more uncomfortable the rest became. In separate conversations with me afterwards, each person gave me a different interpretation of what happened. The African American male was furious that no one in the Agency cared enough about affirmative action to engage in dialogue with him about the issue. The white staff members were furious that their African American colleague refused to talk calmly and rationally about the issue; they concluded that he had a chip on his shoulder about racial issues and, therefore, his comments couldn't be taken seriously. Telling each about their different rhetorical styles was insufficient. These people had been through workshops on communication styles across races and cultures; they understood that they were filtering their evaluations through their own communicative lenses. What they needed to know was how to get past those differences to create a discourse in which they could all participate.

Postmodern resistance is essentially nihilistic, for it can only resist oppression. Feminism, on the other hand, is essentially an affirmative perspective, for it affirms the integrity and value of all voices. Feminism is also essentially pragmatic because it calls for revolutionary change to create a world in which we affirm all voices. A theory of multicultural organizations needs the affirmative pragmatism of a feminist perspective.

One direction for future work in developing a theory of multicultural organizations is to reclaim women's voices, to look to female authority for new ideas about moving beyond resistance. Mary Parker Follett is one such voice. Others have suggested that researchers in organizational communication look more closely at Follett's work (Putnam & Fairhurst, 1985); I believe that Follett's ideas offer great potential for taking the critical perspective past postmodernism.

Basing her description on her own experiences as a member of civic groups, Follett describes effective group process as one in which the group begins by emphasizing the differences that each individual brings to the group and then integrating those differences into collective thought and collective will (Tonn, in press). Her definition of the difference between a crowd and a group highlights her conception of group process:

> There are no "differences" in the crowd mind. Each person is swept away and does not stop to find out his own difference. In crowds we have unison, in groups harmony. We want the single voice but not the single note; that is the secret of the group. (cited in Tonn, in press, p. 507)

I offer Follett here not to elaborate fully a theory of multicultural organizations, but to suggest that a feminist perspective offers possibilities for articulating such a theory.

Researcher as Social Activist

A feminist perspective does more than frame the researcher's questions or direct the application of theories to research methods and data. The feminist methodological commitment to revolutionary pragmatism provides an ethical imperative for the researcher to work *within* organizations to study real people in real situations and to work for changes that will improve the lives of those people. That imperative means that the researcher does more than just use organizations and their employees as subjects for academic study. It means that researchers use both the research process and research findings to help both organizations and their employees; it means that researchers commit themselves to following through with a project even after the data are collected; it means that whatever we learn from our research about organizational life must be shared with the members of that organization in forms that are intelligible, useful, and accessible to them. Let me provide a few examples of both ongoing and potential research projects that illustrate the concept of the researcher as social activist.

The research project that Fine, Johnson, and Ryan (1990) conducted in the EPA used interviews with employees representing a variety of constituencies in the Agency to develop the research agenda. Rather than assuming that they could impose a set of questions about race and gender issues in the workplace, the researchers asked employees what issues were most salient to them. After the employees identified the issues, the researchers developed a long questionnaire that asked employees both closed- and open-ended questions about the issues. After collecting and analyzing the data, the researchers briefed all employees on the findings and prepared a research report that was distributed to all employees of the Agency. I then spent another year working with an Employee Task Force, helping them develop workshops and other internal projects that would address the concerns and problems uncovered in the study.

In this particular study, the research process became as important as, or perhaps even more important than, the organizational projects that were developed based on the data. The creation of the Employee Task Force empowered employees to develop their own agenda for what they needed and how management could best meet those needs; the Task Force also gave employees an organized and legitimate voice in talking with management. Most important, the entire research process, from the initial interviews to the questionnaires to the employee briefings and subsequent workshops, started people thinking and talking about gender and race issues, and how these issues affected them individually and collectively both at work and in their social worlds outside of work. Throughout the three years that we worked on the project, I was constantly surprised and gratified by the many people who commented that they had learned something significant about themselves and their relationships with others during an interview or workshop or hallway conversation.

The difficult part of such research, however, is that you have to be available to have such discussions with employees and you have to have their trust. So employees could—and did—call me at my office to talk privately about issues they didn't want to discuss at more public sessions, or sometimes they would call just because they had been thinking about an issue and wanted to discuss it with me. I had to be open to and nondefensive about their criticism of me; I had to let them make decisions about how to proceed, even when I thought I knew a "better" way; and I had to be open to their pain, for many of the white women and men and women of color in the Agency had had enormously painful experiences negotiating a white male organization.

Two current projects also reflect the social activist stance of the feminist researcher in organizational communication. Bowen (personal communication, March 2, 1990) is a white female who is working with another white female to provide expertise in organizational communication issues to an all African American community education group called Blacks Educating Blacks about Sexual Health Issues (BEBASHI). The project began because Bowen thought it would be an excellent opportunity to study community organizing, and because she was committed to the social goals of the organization. Doing the work as a feminist researcher, however, is difficult. As the only whites involved in BEBASHI's activities, the researchers take particular care not to center themselves in the discussions, even though there are often occasions when their expertise in communication makes them believe that they "know" more about an issue. Learning to place yourself in the margins (as opposed to being marginalized by others) is hard work, and doing that when you allegedly have greater expertise stands in direct opposition to traditional conceptions of how we use our knowledge and what kinds of knowledge we value. But the process of placing ourselves in the margins both enlarges our own vision and empowers others to find their own voices, two necessary conditions for discovering and creating organizational forms that encourage everyone to participate to their fullest.

I am currently working on developing an Affirmative Action plan for the Committee for Boston Public Housing (CBPH), a nonprofit organization created by the Boston Housing Authority to work with the Tenant Boards of Boston's public housing developments to provide social services, education, and training for public housing tenants. I began the project because I am interested in understanding how to create multicultural organizations. CBPH has a diverse workforce; people of color constitute 51% of the central office and field staff for the organization. Hiring people of color, however, is only the start of true affirmative action. CBPH now needs to create an organization that allows these diverse peoples to work together in trusting, cooperative relationships. The current atmosphere in the organization is far from that goal. With a staff of only 25, CBPH has formed a White Caucus and a People of Color Caucus and each of the caucuses has internal splits among its members. Mistrust among the various factions keeps the organization embroiled in seemingly endless and painful discussions about process and makes it difficult to move ahead with the mission of the organization. The problem facing CBPH is enormously interesting to me as an academic and is even more important to me as someone who works in Boston. The work of CBPH is essential to the future well-being of the tenants of the major public housing developments in Boston, a city that is being torn apart by the drugs, crime, and violence that are rampant in the developments.

My purpose in participating in this project is not only to gather data on constructing multicultural organizations, but also to contribute to the welfare of the organization, its members, and the larger community in the city. Without that contribution, my work would have no meaning, except as a self-serving intellectual game that perpetuates the organizational ideology of academe. I am not arguing that the only studies of organizational communication that we should pursue are those that contribute directly to social causes. I am arguing that we should study real people in real organizations, and that when we do that, we take on an ethical commitment to those people—that we must be engaged with them in understanding their organizational discourse and we must be committed to working with them to enlarge that discourse in ways that allow them each to have a genuine voice.

CONCLUSION

In this chapter I have identified five epistemological and methodological commitments of a feminist perspective that characterize feminist research: feminist problematics, women's knowledge, feminist synalytics, methodological integrity, and revolutionary pragmatism. Using those commitments as a lens with which to critique current research traditions in organizational communication, I conclude that (a) the functionalist perspective fails to meet any of the commitments; (b) the interpretive perspective, although theoretically and methodologically compatible with many of the philosophical assumptions of a feminist perspective, has not yet yielded significant research that examines feminist problematics or engages in feminist synalytics, does not meet the ethical requirements of methodological integrity, and is not committed to revolutionary pragmatism; and (c) the critical perspective, although very close to a feminist perspective, has not fully met the commitments to women's problematics and women's knowledge, and, despite its emancipatory interest, has not been committed to revolutionary pragmatism. After reviewing some of the current work in organizational communication that does reflect a feminist perspective, I end by offering three directions for future research in organizational communication: documenting organizational experiences; the social construction of gender, race, and class; and constructing multicultural organizations. In addition, I emphasize the feminist commitment to revolutionary pragmatism by suggesting that researchers should be social activists within the organizations they study.

NOTES TO CHAPTER 5

1. For a description and analysis of the organizational roles of women and men and the "masculine" nature of management, see Kanter (1977).
2. It is important to note, however, that much of this early work was not done in "real world" organizational contexts. Rather, it was done in laboratory settings using student subjects.
3. As we have become more aware of the dysfunctional nature of gender for men, especially in relation to mortality statistics, men have become more interested in gender issues. Because the interest has been generated by health and medical concerns, however, the discussions have primarily focused on biological sex differences rather than the social construction of gender. Now that several recent medical studies suggest a direct relationship between stress and cholesterol levels, it will be interesting to see if the discussions shift to role expectations and gender construction. Some men have also become sensitized to gender as a legal issue in reverse discrimination suits for the rights of unmarried fathers, paternal custody in divorce cases, and related social welfare issues. In general,

however, women are much more aware than men are of the power of gender to shape their lives (see, for example, Fine, Morrow, & Quaglieri, 1990).

4.   I am not using the female pronoun here as a generic. I am identifying the researcher as female in this instance to emphasize that the commitment to revolutionary pragmatism arises out of the unique relationship formed when we have a female knower and a female known (Jacobsen & Jacques, 1990). I do not mean to suggest, however, that men cannot do feminist research; male thinkers have contributed to feminist ideas and male researchers are capable of embracing feminist commitments. Harding (1987) argues, however, that certain analyses are more appropriate for men than others. She suggests, for example, that male feminist researchers engage in "phallic critique": an examination of the gendered dimensions of men's thoughts and behaviors.

5.   The personal passion of the researcher for the people she studies is distinct from the intellectual passion (Polyani, 1962) of traditional male science. For an explanation of the distinction, see Fine (1988).

6.   For a review of the shortcomings of logical positivism in social science research, see Berger and Luckmann (1967), Harre and Secord (1973), and Pearce and Cronen (1980).

7.   The list of studies in organizational communication that include gender as variable is far too long to reproduce here. Fairhurst's (1986) review of the literature on male and female communication in the workplace includes numerous studies on male and female differences in leadership, which are representative of the "gender as variable" research.

8.   Starting in the early 1970s, Ernest Bormann introduced students in his rhetorical criticism and small group communication classes to the concept of group fantasy themes as a means of analyzing political discourse and small group discussions. Fantasy theme analysis first appeared in communication journals in articles on political discourse (Bormann, 1972; 1973).

9.   Some of the research on organizational culture, however, emerges out of the functionalist perspective. Smircich and Calas (1989) argue cogently that "'culture' has been incorporated into the positivist, technical interest as part of the 'traditional organizational literature'" (p. 229). To the extent that culture is defined as something that organizations "have" that can be manipulated and controlled, culture is reified as a static structure rather than being viewed, as the interpretist perspective would, as a socially constructed enactment of what an organization "is."

10. Hegemony is the term for power most often used in the critical perspective literature in organizational communication. The choice of hegemony as the central conceptual construct points to the male-defined nature of the literature. The Latin root of hegemony means leader or to

lead, and the term has been most often used to indicate the preponderant influence or authority of one nation over another. Leadership, authority, and nationalism are male constructs that neither derive from nor are directly inclusive of women's experience with power relationships. Hegemony refers to the activities of states or countries in the public arena; it glosses over the private oppression and violence experienced by women and people of color in patriarchal and racist societies.

11. Putnam and Fairhurst (1985) raise the same issue for all organizational theory and cite Mary Parker Follett and Joan Woodward as two female theorists who are rarely acknowledged in the organizational theory literature.

12. The Putnam and Fairhurst critique, although insightful and valuable, reflects a managerial bias. Most of the problematics they suggest for future research (role conflict and paradox, organizational romance, leadership, and mentoring) are issues of concern to women in professional and managerial positions or women who aspire to those positions. They mention women in other organizational roles only in the context of needing to document the history of women and work.

13. The research studies in organizational communication included in several edited volumes on gender and communication highlight the preponderance of gender as variable studies. See, for example, M. K. Nadler and L. B. Nadler (1987), L. B. Nadler and M. K. Nadler (1989), Rossi and Todd-Mancillas (1987), and Brusberg (1989).

REFERENCES

Acker, J. (1987, August). *Hierarchies and jobs: Notes for a theory of gendered organizations.* Paper presented at the annual meeting of the American Sociological Association, Chicago, IL.

Albrecht, T.L. (1979). The role of communication in perceptions of organizational climate. In D. Nimmo (Ed.), *Communication yearbook 3* (pp. 343-357). New Brunswick, NJ: Transaction Books.

Albrecht, T.L., & Ropp, V.A. (1982). The study of network structuring in organizations through the use of method triangulation. *Western Journal of Speech Communication, 46,* 162-178.

Anderson, J.A. (Ed.). (1990). *Communication yearbook 13.* Newbury Park, CA: Sage.

Balsamo, A. (1985). Beyond female as variable: Constructing a feminist perspective on organizational analysis. *Women and Language, 9,* 35-38.

Bantz, C.R. (1983). Naturalistic research traditions. In L.L. Putnam & M.E. Pacanowsky (Eds.), *Communication and organizations: An interpre-*

tive approach (pp. 55-71). Beverly Hills, CA: Sage.

Bate, B., & Self, L.S. (1983). The rhetoric of career success books for women. *Journal of Communication, 33*(2), 149-165.

Belenky, M.F., Clinchy, B.M., Goldberger, N.R., & Tarule, J.M. (1986). *Women's ways of knowing: The development of self, voice, and mind.* New York: Basic Books.

Berger, P.L., & Luckmann, T. (1967). *The social construction of reality.* Garden City, NY: Anchor Books.

Bormann, E. (1972). Fantasy and rhetorical vision: The rhetorical criticism of social reality. *Quarterly Journal of Speech, 58,* 396-407.

Bormann, E. (1973). The Eagleton affair: A fantasy theme analysis. *Quarterly Journal of Speech, 59,* 143-159.

Bormann, E.G., Pratt, J., & Putnam, L.L. (1978). Power, authority and sex: Male response to female leadership. *Communication Monographs, 45,* 119-155.

Brusberg, M.A. (1989). An investigation of sexual harassment, gender orientation, and job satisfaction. In C.M. Lont & S.A. Friedley (Eds.), *Beyond boundaries: Sex and gender diversity in communication* (pp. 189-208). Fairfax, VA: George Mason University Press.

Calas, M.B., & Smircich, L. (1992). Re-writing gender into organizational theorizing: Directions from feminist perspectives. In M. Reed & M. Hughes (Eds.), *Re-thinking organization: New directions in organizational research and analysis* (pp. 227-253). London: Sage.

Conrad, C., & Ryan, M. (1985). Power, praxis, and self in organizational communication theory. In R.D. McPhee & P.K. Tompkins (Eds.), *Organizational communication: Traditional themes and new directions* (pp. 235-257). Beverly Hills, CA: Sage.

Deetz, S.A. (1982). Critical interpretive research in organizational communication. *Western Journal of Speech Communication, 46,* 131-149.

Deetz, S.A., & Kersten, A. (1983). Critical models of interpretive research. In L.L. Putnam & M.E. Pacanowsky (Eds.), *Communication and organizations: An interpretive approach* (pp. 147-171). Beverly Hills, CA: Sage.

Deetz, S., & Mumby, D.K. (1990). Power, discourse, and the workplace: Reclaiming the critical tradition. In J.A. Anderson (Ed.), *Communication yearbook 13* (pp. 18-47). Newbury Park, CA: Sage.

Dennis, H.S., III, Goldhaber, G.M., & Yates, M.P. (1978). Organizational communication theory and research: An overview of research methods. In B.D. Ruben (Ed.), *Communication yearbook 2* (pp. 243-269). New Brunswick, NJ: Transaction Books.

Denzin, N.K. (1970). The methodologies of symbolic interaction: A critical review of research techniques. In G.P. Stone & H.A. Farberman (Eds.), *Symbolic interaction* (pp. 447-465). Waltham, MA: Xerox Publishing.

Donohue, W.A., & Diez, M.E. (1985). Directive use in negotiation interaction. *Communication Monographs, 52,* 305-318.

Duncan, H.D. (1967). The search for a social theory of communication in

American sociology. In F.E.X. Dance (Ed.), *Human communication theory: Original essays* (pp. 236-263). New York: Holt, Rinehart & Winston.

Eisenberg, E.M. (1984). Ambiguity as strategy in organizational communication. *Communication Monographs, 51,* 227-242.

Eisenstein, H. (1983). *Contemporary feminist thought.* Boston: G.K. Hall.

Fairhurst, G.T. (1986). Male-female communication on the job: Literature review and commentary. In M.L. McLaughlin (Ed.), *Communication yearbook 9* (pp. 83-116). Beverly Hills, CA: Sage.

Fairhurst, G.T., & Chandler, T. (1989). Social structure in leader-member interaction. *Communication Monographs, 56,* 215-239.

Fairhurst, G.T., & Snavely, B.K. (1983a). Majority and token minority group relationships: Power acquisition and communication. *Academy of Management Review, 8,* 292-300.

Fairhurst, G.T., & Snavely, B.K. (1983b). A test of the social isolation of male tokens. *Academy of Management Journal, 26,* 353-361.

Falcione, R.L., & Kaplan, E.A. (1984). Organizational climate, communication, and culture. In R. Bostrom (Ed.), *Communication yearbook 8* (pp. 285-309). Newbury Park, CA: Sage.

Faules, D. (1982). The use of multi-methods in the organizational setting. *Western Journal of Speech Communication, 46,* 150-161.

Ferguson, K.E. (1984). *The feminist case against bureaucracy.* Philadelphia: Temple University Press.

Ferguson, S.D., & Ferguson, S. (Eds.). (1988). *Organizational communication* (2nd. ed.). New Brunswick, NJ: Transaction Books.

Fine, M.G. (1988). What makes it feminist? *Women's Studies in Communication, 11*(1), 18-19.

Fine, M.G., Johnson, F.L., & Foss, K.A. (1991). Student perceptions of gender in managerial communication. *Women's Studies in Communication, 14*(1), 24-48.

Fine, M.G., Johnson, F.L., & Ryan, M.S. (1990). Cultural diversity in the workplace. *Public Personnel Management, 19,* 305-319.

Fine, M.G., Johnson, F.L., Ryan, M.S., & M.N. Lutfiyya. (1987). Ethical issues in defining and evaluating women's communication in the workplace. In L.P. Stewart & S. Ting-Toomey (Eds.), *Communication, gender, and sex roles in diverse interaction contexts* (pp. 105-118). Norwood, NJ: Ablex Publishing Corporation.

Fine, M.G., Morrow, A.A., & Quaglieri, P.L. (1990). Professional women in a male-dominated industry: What do they want and where are they going? *HR Horizons, 1*(1), 54-60.

Foss, K.A., & Foss, S.K. (1983). The status of research on women and communication. *Communication Quarterly, 31,* 195-204.

Gilligan, C. (1982). *In a different voice.* Cambridge, MA: Harvard University Press.

Gordon, L. (1979). The struggle for reproductive freedom: Three stages of feminism. In Z. Eisenstein (Ed.), *Capitalist patriarchy and the case for socialist feminism* (pp. 107-32). New York: Monthly Review Press.

Guetzkow, H. (1965). Communications in organizations. In J.G. March (Ed.), *Handbook of organizations* (pp. 534-573). Chicago: Rand McNally.

Harding, S. (1987). *Feminism and methodology.* Bloomington, IN: Indiana University Press.

Harre, R., & Secord, P.F. (1973). *The explanation of social behavior.* Totowa, NJ: Littlefield, Adams.

Haslett, B. (1990). Discourse, ideology, and organizational control. In J.A. Anderson (Ed.), *Communication yearbook 13* (pp. 48-58). Newbury Park, CA: Sage.

Hatfield, J.D., & Huseman, R.C. (1982). Perceptual congruence about communication as related to satisfaction: Moderating effects of individual characteristics. *Academy of Management Journal, 25,* 349-358.

Husband, R.L. (1985). Toward a grounded typology of organizational leadership behavior. *Quarterly Journal of Speech, 71,* 103-118.

Jablin, F.M. (1980a). Organizational communication theory and research: an overview of communication climate and network research. In D. Nimmo (Ed.), *Communication yearbook 4* (pp. 327-347). New Brunswick, NJ: Transaction Books.

Jablin, F.M. (1980b). Subordinate's sex and superior-subordinate status differentiation as moderators of the Pelz effect. In D. Nimmo (Ed.), *Communication yearbook 4* (pp. 349-366). New Brunswick, NJ: Transaction Books.

Jablin, F.M., Putnam, L.L., Roberts, K.H., & Porter, L.W. (Eds.). (1987). *Handbook of organizational communication: An interdisciplinary perspective.* Newbury Park, CA: Sage.

Jacobson, S.W., & Jacques, R. (1990, August). *Of knowers, knowing, and the known: A gender framework for revisioning organizational and management scholarship.* Paper presented at the annual meeting of the Academy of Management, San Francisco, CA.

Jelinek, M., Smircich, L., & Hirsch, P. (1983). Introduction: A code of many colors. *Administrative Science Quarterly, 28,* 331-338.

Johnson, F.L. (1989). Women's culture and communication: An analytical perspective. In C.M. Lont & S.A. Friedley (Eds.), *Beyond boundaries: Sex and gender diversity in communication* (pp. 301-316). Fairfax, VA: George Mason University Press.

Kanter, R.M. (1977). *Men and women of the corporation.* New York: Basic Books.

Keller, E.F. (1985). *Reflections on gender and science.* New Haven, CT: Yale University Press.

Koester, J. (1982). The Machiavellian princess: Rhetorical dramas for women managers. *Communication Quarterly, 30,* 165-172.

Krone, K.J., Jablin, F.M., & Putnam, L.L. (1987). Communication theory and organizational communication: Multiple perspectives. In F.M. Jablin, L.L. Putnam, K.H. Roberts, & L.W. Porter (Eds.), *Handbook of organizational communication: An interdisciplinary perspective* (pp.

18-40). Newbury Park, CA: Sage.

Littlejohn, S.W. (1983). *Theories of human communication* (2nd ed.). Belmont, CA: Wadsworth.

Lont, C. (1988). Redwood Records: Principles and profit in women's music. In B. Bate & A. Taylor (Eds.), *Women communicating: Studies of women's talk* (pp. 233-250). Norwood, NJ: Ablex Publishing Corporation.

McCallister, L., & Gaymon, D.L. (1989). Male and female managers in the 21st century: Will there be a difference? In C.M. Lont & S.A. Friedley (Eds.), *Beyond boundaries: Sex and gender diversity in communication* (pp. 209-229). Fairfax, VA: George Mason University Press.

McPhee, R.D., & Tompkins, P.K. (Eds.). (1985). *Organizational communication: Traditional themes and new directions*. Beverly Hills, CA: Sage.

Millett, K. (1970). *Sexual politics*. Garden City, NY: Doubleday.

Monge, P.R. (1982). Systems theory and research in the study of organizational communication: The correspondence problem. *Human Communication Research, 8*, 245-261.

Monge, P.R., Farace, R.V., Eisenberg, E., Miller, K.I., & White, L.L. (1984). The process of studying process in organizational communication. *Journal of Communication, 34*(1), 22-43.

Mumby, D.K. (1987). The political function of narrative in organizations. *Communication Monographs, 54*, 113-127.

Mumby, D.K., & Putnam, L. (1992). The politics of emotion: A feminist reading of bounded rationality. *Academy of Management Review, 17*, 465-486.

Nadler, L.B., & Nadler, M.K. (1989). Sex-role stereotypes in organizational conflict. In C.M. Lont & S.A. Friedley (Eds.), *Beyond boundaries: Sex and gender diversity in communication* (pp. 177-188). Fairfax, VA: George Mason University Press.

Nadler, M.K., & Nadler, L.B. (1987). Communication, gender, and intraorganizational negotiation ability. In L.P. Stewart & S. Ting-Toomey, (Eds.), *Communication, gender, and sex roles in diverse interaction contexts* (pp. 119-134). Norwood, NJ: Ablex Publishing Corporation.

Pacanowski, M.E., & O'Donnell-Trujillo, N. (1983). Organizational communication as cultural performance. *Communication Monographs, 50*, 126-147.

Pearce, W.B., & Cronen, V.E. (1980). *Communication, action, and meaning: The creation of social realities*. New York: Praeger.

Penley, L.E., & Hawkins, B. (1985). Studying interpersonal communication in organizations: A leadership application. *Academy of Management Journal, 28*, 309-326.

Polyani, M. (1962). *Personal knowledge: Towards a post-critical philosophy*. Chicago: University of Chicago Press.

Popovich, P., & Wanous, J. P. (1982). The Realistic Job Preview as a persuasive communication. *Academy of Management Review, 7*, 570-578.

Putnam, L.L. (1982). In search of gender: A critique of communication and sex-roles research. *Women's Studies in Communication, 5,* 1-9.

Putnam, L.L. (1983). The interpretive perspective: An alternative to functionalism. In L.L. Putnam & M.E. Pacanowsky (Eds.), *Communication and organizations: An interpretive approach* (pp. 31-54). Beverly Hills, CA: Sage.

Putnam L.L. (1990, April). *Feminist theories, dispute processes, and organizational communication.* Paper presented at the Arizona State University Conference on Organizational Communication: Perspectives for the 90s, Tempe, AZ.

Putnam, L.L., & Cheney, G. (1983). A critical review of research traditions in organizational communication. In M.S. Mander (Ed.), *Communications in transition* (pp. 206-224). Westport, CT: Praeger.

Putnam, L.L., & Fairhurst, G. (1985). Women and organizational communication: Research directions and new perspectives. *Women and Language, 9,* 2-6.

Putnam, L.L., & Jones, T.S. (1982a). Reciprocity in negotiations: An analysis of bargaining interaction. *Communication Monographs, 49,* 171-191.

Putnam, L.L., & Jones, T.S. (1982b). The role of communication in bargaining. *Human Communication Research, 8,* 262-280.

Putnam, L.L., & Pacanowsky, M.E. (Eds.). (1983). *Communication and organizations: An interpretive approach.* Beverly Hills: Sage.

Redding, W.C. (1979). Organizational communication theory and ideology: An overview. In D. Nimmo (Ed.), *Communication yearbook 3* (pp. 309-341). New Brunswick, NJ: Transaction Books.

Redding, W.C. (1985). Stumbling toward identity: The emergence of organizational communication as a field of study. In R.D. McPhee & P.K. Tompkins (Eds.), *Organizational communication: Traditional themes and new directions* (pp. 15-54). Beverly Hills, CA: Sage.

Reilly, R.R., Brown, B., Blood, M.R., & Malatesta, C.Z. (1981). The effects of realistic previews: A study and discussion of the literature. *Personnel Psychology, 34,* 823-834.

Remland, M.S. (1984). Leadership impressions and nonverbal communication in a superior-subordinate interaction. *Communication Quarterly, 32,* 41-48.

Richetto, G.M. (1977). Organizational communication theory and research: An overview. In B.D. Ruben (Ed.), *Communication yearbook 1* (pp. 331-346). New Brunswick, NJ: Transaction Books.

Richmond, V.P., & McCroskey, J.C. (1979). Management communication style, tolerance for disagreement, and innovativeness as predictors of employee satisfaction: A comparison of single factor, two-factor, and multiple-factor approaches. In D. Nimmo (Ed.), *Communication yearbook 3* (pp. 360-373). New Brunswick, NJ: Transaction Books.

Richmond, V.P., McCroskey, J.C., & Davis, L.M. (1982). Individual differences among employees, management communication style, and employee satisfaction: Replication and extension. *Human*

Communication Research, 8, 170-188.
Roberts, K.H., O'Reilly, C.A., Bretton, G.E., & Porter, L.W. (1974). Organizational theory and organizational communication: A communication failure? *Human Relations, 27,* 501-524.
Rossi, A.M., & Todd-Mancillas, W.R. (1987). Male/female differences in managing conflicts. In L.P. Stewart & S. Ting-Toomey (Eds.), *Communication, gender, and sex roles in diverse interaction contexts* (pp. 96-104). Norwood, NJ: Ablex Publishing Corporation.
Schall, M.S. (1983). A communication rules approach to organizational culture. *Administrative Science Quarterly, 28,* 557-581.
Seccombe-Eastland, L. (1988). Ideology, contradiction, and change in a feminist bookstore. In B. Bate & A. Taylor (Eds.), *Women communicating: Studies of women's talk* (pp. 251-276). Norwood, NJ: Ablex Publishing Corporation.
Smircich, L., & Calas, M.B. (1987). Organizational culture: A critical assessment. In F.M. Jablin, L.L. Putnam, K.H. Roberts, & L.W. Porter (Eds.), *Handbook of organizational communication: An interdisciplinary perspective* (pp. 228-263). Newbury Park, CA: Sage.
Smith, R.C., & Eisenberg, E.M. (1987). Conflict at Disneyland: A root-metaphor analysis. *Communication Monographs, 54,* 367-380.
Snavely, B.K., & Fairhurst, G.T. (1984). An examination of the male nursing student as a token. *Research in Nursing and Health, 7,* 287-294.
Staley, C., & Shockley-Zalabak, P. (1986). Communication proficiency and future training needs of the female professional: Self-assessment versus superiors' evaluations. *Human Relations, 39,* 891-902.
Stewart, L.P., Gudykunst, W.B., Ting-Toomey, S., & Nishida, T. (1986). The effects of decision making style on openness and satisfaction within Japanese organizations. *Communication Monographs, 53,* 236-251.
Stone, G.P., & Farberman, H.A. (Eds.). (1970). *Social psychology through symbolic interaction.* Waltham, MA: Xerox Publishing.
Taylor, A. (1988). Implementing feminist principles in a bureaucracy: Studio D The National Film Board of Canada. In B. Bate & A. Taylor (Eds.), *Women communicating: Studies of women's talk* (pp. 277-302). Norwood, NJ: Ablex Publishing Corporation.
Theye, L.D., & Seiler, W.J. (1979). Interaction analysis in collective bargaining: An alternative approach to the prediction of negotiated outcomes. In D. Nimmo (Ed.), *Communication Yearbook 3* (pp. 377-392). New Brunswick, NJ: Transaction Books.
Tompkins, P.K. (1989). Organizational communication: The central tradition. *Spectra, 25*(5), 2-3.
Tompkins, P.K., & Cheney, G. (1983). Account analysis of organizations: Decision making and identification. In L.L. Putnam & M.E. Pacanowsky (Eds.), *Communication and organizations: An interpretive approach* (pp. 123-146). Beverly Hills, CA: Sage.
Tonn, J. (in press). *The life and work of Mary Parker Follett.* Oxford: Oxford University Press.

Wanous, J.P. (1980). *Organizational entry: Recruitment, selection and socialization of newcomers.* Reading, MA: Addison-Wesley.

Watson, K. (1982). An analysis of communication patterns: A method for discriminating leader and subordinate roles. *Academy of Management Journal, 25,* 107-120.

Wheeless, L.R., Wheeless, V.E., & Howard, R.D. (1984). The relationships of communication with supervisor and decision-participation to employee job satisfaction. *Communication Quarterly, 32,* 222-232.

Wood, J.T., & Conrad, C. (1983). Paradox in the experiences of professional women. *Western Journal of Speech Communication, 47,* 305-322.

Wyatt, N. (1984). Power and decision making. In G.M. Phillips & J.T. Wood (Eds.), *Emergent issues in human decision making* (pp. 50-60). Carbondale, IL: Southern Illinois University Press.

Wyatt, N. (1988). Shared leadership in the Weavers Guild. In B. Bate & A. Taylor (Eds.), *Women communicating: Studies of women's talk* (pp. 147-176). Norwood, NJ: Ablex Publishing Corporation.

Chapter 6

Aristotle and Arimneste ("Nicanor's Mother"): Theatre Studies and Feminism *

Patti P. Gillespie

University of Maryland
College Park, MD

INTRODUCTION

From its recorded origins in sixth-century B.C. Greece, theatre has been a male art.[1] Perhaps because of the strong female characters in many Greek dramas, we forget that in the festival theatres of Athens women could participate only as audience members. Men paid for the productions, wrote the plays, performed the choruses, and acted all roles. Thus, characters such as Clytemnestra and Antigone, Medea and Lysistrata were conceived by male minds to be interpreted and performed by other male minds—and bodies.

Likewise, women were largely absent in the theatres of Republican Rome, in medieval Latin music dramas and civic cycles, and in the theatres of Shakespeare's time. Again, although figuring prominently as characters in plays, women were present only as spectators at the theatre. Women watched while men acted, designed, produced, performed, and wrote. Indeed, for the first 2,100 years of theatre's 2,500-year history, women were, almost without exception, excluded. The two consistent exceptions to this generalization were mimes and, of all people, nuns.

---

*Aristotle, like Shakespeare, seems to have had a sister. In a contemporaneous account, her name is given as Arimneste. Aristotle did not use her name in his extant writings, though he seems to have meant her when he spoke of "Nicanor's mother." (See Lipking, 1984).

Mimes (the word refers both to an improvised form of entertainment and to the entertainers who performed it) in Greece and Rome wore no masks.[2] Because they were early excluded from public festivals, Greek and Roman mimes performed wherever they could gather an audience. Considered socially inferior, mimes included female as well as male performers. During the Christian era, mimes grew increasingly influential and performed regularly at the growing number of festivals in both Rome and Byzantium. It was mime that provoked vigorous condemnation of theatre by the early church fathers, who found these entertainments sexual, violent, and blasphemous and who associated female mimes with prostitution. The church's condemnation of theatre and of actresses had begun. With the collapse of the western Roman empire, miming declined.

During the medieval period, clear—if rare—records prove that nuns both wrote and performed Christian dramas. Only three female playwrights are known by name: Hrostwith of Gandersheim (10th century), Hildegard of Bingen (12th century), and Katherine of Sutton (14th century). All three nuns were Benedictine (like Bishop Ethelwold), and all were from the upper levels of society. Their plays, when performed, were acted by female religieuses, probably for female audiences (Case, 1983; Cotton, 1978; Davidson, 1984; Hozeski, 1975).

The fact that nuns and mimes were the only regularly recorded female participants in the first 2,100 years of theatre can serve to remind us of the church's schizophrenic view of theatre. The fact that Hrostwith, the first known female playwright, appeared 1,600 years after the male Thespis can remind us of theatre's early public and civic (and thus male) role in male-dominated society.

At the Renaissance, theatre became less a communal event and more a commercial or court enterprise. Thereafter, more women participated in theatre. Women's presence, however, did not signal their equality. At court, women appeared occasionally in masques and plays, where they often sang or danced or simply displayed themselves in costume, leaving the speaking roles to men (Gilder, 1931). Outside of court, women appeared consistently only as performers in commedia dell arte troupes, which originated in Italy and later toured throughout Europe (Gilder, 1931). Even within commedia troupes, however, women were outnumbered, with typically six to eight men and only three or four women in a troupe (Nicoll, 1963). Female actors came to England with the Restoration (1660), to France somewhat earlier, and to Germany somewhat later.

Since the late 17th century, Western theatre has been unabashedly commercial, and female actors have been accepted almost everywhere. Women's equal participation in theatre, however, remains elusive. Extant plays offer far more roles for men than for women. The plays of Greece and Rome, for example, offer roughly three male roles for every female role; those of Shakespeare, five male roles for every female role. Stock companies of the 18th and 19th centuries typically hired two men for every woman, or three men for every two women, with women earning less than equivalently situated men. When husbands and wives were both company members, a single, unattributed amount was awarded; married women, of course, had few legal rights separate from their husbands (Cooley, 1986).

With changed hiring practices in the 19th and 20th centuries, almost twice as many male as female actors continued to be hired, evidence of the ratio of male to female roles in modern as well as historic plays (National Commission, 1976). Despite such clear inequities, female actors were both the earliest and the most accepted among female theatrical artists.

The first female English-language professional playwright, Aphra Behn, did not appear until the late 17th century; her reception may be adduced by remembering Virginia Woolf's (1957) observation: "Death would be better than living the life of Aphra Behn" (p. 67). Female playwrights remained rare into the 20th century. Not only were their numbers relatively few, but also their works were regularly ignored and quickly forgotten even when they won major prizes. For example, the plays of Susan Glaspell and Zona Gale, Pulitzer Prize winners in the 1920s and 1930s, dropped quickly from the repertory and the standard anthologies. Such cultural amnesia encourages the view that today's female playwrights (for whatever year "today" is invoked) constitute the first important instance of female authors of drama and helps account for such headlines as that of the *New York Times* in 1972, which asked, "Where are the Women Playwrights?" (p. D1).

Female directors, producers, and designers have been even rarer than female playwrights. Such artists as there were tended to cluster in positions of less prestige and to earn less money than males (Chinoy, 1987b; Hennigan, 1983; Johnson, 1984; Mason, 1983). Even today such artists in the United States are found more often in regional theatres and off-Broadway than in the large commercial houses of New York (Chinoy, 1987a; Chinoy & Jenkins, 1987, pp. 192-237, 353-371; National Commission, 1976).

In sum, the pattern of women in theatre mimics the pattern of women in society—the higher the position, the more the money, the fewer the women.

TRADITIONAL SCHOLARSHIP

Theatre studies are traditionally divided into three types: theory, criticism, and history, of which theory has, by far, the longest tradition. Given the male domination of the *art* of theatre, it is unsurprising that the *study* of theatre has also been an overwhelmingly male enterprise.

Theory

Dramatic theory began in Greece, fewer than 100 years after the last of the great dramas. Although Plato in *The Republic* (c. 373 B.C.) briefly treated drama (and banished it from his ideal state), Aristotle devoted a whole treatise, *The Poetics* (c. 335 B.C.), to it, proposing the first recorded theory of drama. Unsurprisingly, the male world of Athens and its drama found expression in his theory. For example, when Aristotle explained that dramatic characters should be both good and appropriate, he noted:

> Even a woman may be good, and also a slave; though the woman may
> be said to be an inferior being, and the slave quite worthless. . . . [and]
> valor in a woman, or unscrupulous cleverness, is inappropriate. (p.
> 44)[3]

With Aristotle, then, began the tradition of dramatic theories fully grounded in male culture and male presuppositions.[4]

Such presuppositions hardened in the Renaissance as theorists set about to prescribe, not merely describe, certain essential traits of good drama. In these theories, a central feature was decorum, which meant, among other things, that men should behave like men and women like women (in a culture ruled by men): "To weave nicely, to embroider, to spin are commendable in a woman; these things ought not to be esteemed in a man," and "If [strength of body] be attributed to a woman [or] if some poet or other portrays a woman in the same way Homer portrays Achilles, he would be severely censured" (Robortellus, 1548, p. 128). This Neoclassical theory persisted throughout most of the 18th century, when its gender-locked views were most succinctly summed up by Voltaire. When asked why no women had ever written a "tolerable tragedy," he explained, "Ah, the composition of tragedy requires *testicles*" (Byron, 1817; emphasis in the original).

In the early 19th century, Romantic theories, although revolutionary in shifting attention from the text to its effect on spectators, retained quite traditional views of women's place in drama:

> It is especially in female characters that love rises to its highest beauty;
> for it is in woman that this devotion, this self sacrifice, is the supreme

point; for she concentrates and develops her whole spiritual and actual life in this sentiment, finds in it alone a context of existence. (Hegel,
1818-1829, p. 529)

Although the early 20th century popularized a variety of new theories—for example, ritual, psychoanalytical, Marxist—none of these theories questioned (or perhaps even saw) the male domination within the theories. Marxist theory did offer two insights useful to later feminists: first,
that the historic moment accounted not only for the art and artist but also
for the critic; and second, that spectators were important to the art of the
theatre. Drawing upon these insights, black theorists of the 1960s alleged
that traditional art and criticism were means used by the powerful to
manipulate the powerless. Prefiguring feminists, some blacks repudiated
traditional artistic standards and substituted a black aesthetic that spoke
"directly to the needs and aspirations of Black Americans" (Neal, 1971, p.
272). "The question . . . is not how beautiful a melody, a play, a poem, or
a novel is, but how much more beautiful has the poem, melody, or play
made the life of a single Black man [sic]. . . " (Gayle, 1971, p. xxiii). In
less than a decade some feminists would build from this position, substi-
tuting the word *woman* for the word *black*, but, in the 1960s, few saw the
possibility of such a substitution. Fewer still saw any connection between
the political situation of blacks and women.

Meanwhile, in the field of linguistics, another, seemingly unrelat-
ed model for explaining literature and art was being developed—semiotics. Despite its formal, seemingly apolitical approach to theatre (Elam,
1980), semiotics would also prove useful to later feminist theorists of theatre.

Throughout the 1980s, then, women—let alone feminists—
remained generally outside academic writings on theatrical theory. For
example, within the two standard anthologies of theatrical theory (Clark,
1965; Dukore, 1974), no theoretical writings by women appeared, even
though Susanne Langer's influential *Feeling and Form* had been published
in 1953. Most recently, Marvin Carlson's *Theories of the Theatre* (1984)
cited only 15 women, mostly playwrights and actors rather than theorists
(of whom only three are named). Wholly absent in Carlson was any reference to feminist theatrical theory, although theories of black theatre were
treated briefly.

Criticism

Recorded criticism of individual plays dates from the Renaissance, when
both playwrights and scholars sought to evaluate plays in terms of an idealized (Neoclassical) model. Since then, criticism has paralleled shifts in

theoretical perspective.[5] Thus, in the 19th century, Romantic critics focused on central characters and strong emotional response, while later Realistic critics praised dramas for their social utility. During the 20th century, various theories have competed for the attention of critics: ritual, following Gilbert Murray (1912) or Northrop Frye (1957); psychoanalytic, following Sigmund Freud (1900) or Jacques Lacan (1977); Marxist, following George Lukacs (1909) or, more often, Bertolt Brecht (1964); neo-Aristotelian, new critical, structuralist, semiotic, deconstructionist, and on and on.

Given the male heritage of dramatic theory, it is not surprising to find critics and criticism also gender-locked. Like theorists, critics have been almost all white, well-educated, socially elevated, and male. Despite the critical shifts that aped shifting theoretical assumptions, critics have until recently held unchallenged their view that male-defined critical standards were universal and that in male-written plays gender was irrelevant. So long as playwrights were mostly male, critics (who were also mostly male) seemed to ignore gender. Long invisible, the biases of male critics can now be seen both in their interpretation of plays and in their critical statements.

A thoughtful analysis of traditional interpretations reveals assumptions about gender imbedded within them. It has recently become clear, for example, that the traditional interpretation of Aeschylus's *Oresteia* (that the trilogy offers a vision of an evolving, improving system of justice) requires readers to assume that women are by nature inferior to men. The explanation that Hedda Gabler retained her own name, rather than assuming her husband's, because she was a "daddy's girl" rests on the view that women take their identity from whatever man currently controls their life.

The appearance of female playwrights began to expose some of the previously hidden assumptions about gender and playwriting. Although critical responses to women's plays varied remarkably, they could hardly be considered gender-neutral. In the 17th and 18th centuries, for example, critics often praised a woman's work in terms of (male) gender: "Tis solid & tis manly all" (Cowley, 1667, p. 192)[6] and "Such things flow from a Woman's Pen as might be Envy'd by the Wittiest Men" (Ephelia, 1679, p. 194). Critics might even insist that a man had written the play—or at least had helped: "When any thing is written by a woman, that [critics] cannot deny their approbation to, [they] are sure to rob [women] of the glory of it, by concluding 'tis not her own; or at least, that she had some assistance" (Trotter, 1705, p. 187). Some critics condemned rather than patronized women's work, often in sexually charged language that conflated a woman with her play: "Since [Behn's] work had neither Witt enough for a Man, nor Modesty enough for a woman, she was to be look'd upon as a Hermaphrodite" (*A Journal from Parnassus*, 1688, p. 27).

Or, for another example:

> What a Pox have the Women to do with the Muses? I grant you the
> Poets call the Nine Muses by the Names of Women, but why so? Not
> because the Sex had anything to do with Poetry, but because in that
> Sex they're much fitter for prostitution. (Gildon, 1702, cited in
> Hampsten, 1980, p. 22)

In the 20th century, female playwrights have been more often
patronized than pummeled, but both sorts of responses can easily be cited.
For example, in 1916, Brander Matthews explained that women could not
be expected to write good plays, for they had "only a definitely limited
knowledge of life" and tended not to "submit themselves to the severe discipline which has compelled men to be more or less logical (pp. 124-125).
In 1937, Joseph Mersand found that, "When Ladies Write Plays," they are
more often successful as "reporters for the stage" than as artists because
"they rarely philosophize, their social consciousness is rarely apparent"
and "even the best of the daughters of the Muses" fail to reach "the heights
of aesthetic emotions" (p. 8). In 1942, George Jean Nathan thought that,
"Women, when it comes to the confection of drama, are most often inferi-
or to their boyfriends" (p. 34). In 1971, *The Mod Donna* so provoked
George Oppenheimer that he wondered if "maybe we were wrong in
allowing women to vote" (Lamb, 1971, back cover).[7]

Throughout the 1980s, in criticism as in theory, women—let
alone feminists—remained generally outside the mainstream. Fewer than a
quarter of theatrical reviewers in the United States were women. Of this
quarter, less than half worked in New York City, most often as "second
stringers" or as assistants to a drama editor. Most female critics reviewed
plays in cities and towns far outside the theatrical center, in such places as
Nashville and Houston (Latta, 1987).

The status of female academic critics is much harder to discern,
both because of the diverse venues in which they publish and because of
the difficulty in agreeing on a definition of an academic critic. However,
Books In Print 1989-1990 under "Theater-Reviews" lists 18 books, none
by a woman, and under "Dramatic Criticism," 20 books, of which 7
(including co-authored works) are by women. During 1988, in both
Modern Drama and *Comparative Drama*, women wrote about one out of
every four articles. Thus, in academic as well as journalistic criticism,
women apparently comprise slightly less than one-quarter of the total.

History

Of the three areas of study, theatre history was the last to develop. Although studies of an historical nature probably began about the time of Christ,[8] the first extant history of theatre as an independent study appeared only late in the 18th century (Signorelli, 1787-1790). The first theatre history—as distinct from literary history—did not appear until well into the 19th century (Bapst, 1893; Dunlap, 1832; Leclercq, 1869).

With intellectual roots in the 18th and 19th centuries, early theatre historians not surprisingly adopted the view that history was progressive (rather than cyclical or chaotic, for example) and that good historians were objective recorders and interpreters of data (that is, historians uncovered facts, got out of the way, and let the facts speak for themselves). Although related, these assumptions are separable, and each had consequences for the nature of the newly emerging field.

The idea that history progressed fitted well with Darwinian explanations of evolution and led early theatre historians to think in terms of movements from worse to better and from simple to complex. Drama, for example, evolved from religious rituals (e.g., Murray, 1912), and later styles of acting were better than earlier ones (e.g., Blunt, 1966, pp. 342-370). Such patterns of thinking obviously suggested ways of organizing evidence, attributing authorship, and naming events, as Young's early critique (1933) of Chambers' work (1903) so well demonstrated.

The idea that historians were objective, uninvolved observers made both theatre historians and their readers think that individual historians had no more influence on the historical record than individual physicists had on natural laws. Such notions of objectivity, of course, drew on then-current views of science, where observation and evidence were thought independent of the researcher and where "the scientific method" guided all inquiry. As appropriated to theatre history, the scientific method stressed discovering documents, acquiring facts, and cataloguing data more than speculating imaginatively about possible meanings of these documents, facts, or data. This approach to theatre history, grounded in logical positivism, dominated the field throughout the 1970s (Brockett, 1968, 1974, 1977, 1982; Nagler, 1959).

By the 1980s, however, many scholars had accepted the importance of the historian as well as the data to the writing of history. With this acceptance came self-aware attempts to understand the nature of historical scholarship. Some theatre historians therefore set about to explain differing views of history and to explore the consequences of certain previously invisible decisions made by historians—naming events, dividing time into discrete periods, and generalizing from data (Gillespie & Cameron, 1984; Gordon, 1986; McConachie, 1985; McLennan, 1981; Postlewait, 1988;

Vince, 1989).

Also, by recognizing the role of the historian as well as the data in making history, scholars could begin to see a history of theatre history, that is, to see ways in which historians of different countries and times saw, and therefore wrote, history. The political implications of this insight were not long in coming. Marxist historians again led the way, but others soon saw that if country, time, and class influenced the interpretation of evidence, then surely race and gender also must play a role.

Finally, as scholars came to understand that the single word *history* referred to more than one phenomenon (it denoted the past, the written record of the past, and the field of study), they saw more clearly the nature of history's exclusions. It had long been clear, for example, that women were excluded from much of theatre history (that is, from theatre's past); it only later became clear that they were also largely absent from the other theatre histories (that is, from the written records and the field of study). Again, suggestive data can be offered. Although *Books In Print 1989-1990* lists more than 200 titles under Theater-History and Theater-U.S.-History, fewer than 40 were by women (including co-authored books). Of 17 articles listed in *Theatre Research International* for 1988, 4 or possibly 5 were by women (one name does not reveal gender). The 1988 membership list of the American Society for Theatre Research suggests that about one-third of its members were women.

FEMINIST SCHOLARSHIP

With the women's movement of the late 1960s and 1970s came the first sustained challenge to male domination of theatrical art and scholarship.[9] Scholars—especially female scholars—began to question the assumption that male experience was universal experience, and so they began to study women and their experiences. A vital and energetic body of feminist scholarship has grown out of these tentative probings, scholarship

> distinguished by the systematic inclusion of women, by an absence of language and/or perspective that degrades women or minorities, by rigorous testing of assumptions that hark back to stereotypes and social mythology, and by a concern to rectify the omissions, the degradation, and the errors of the past. (Campbell, 1988, p. 4)

Feminist studies often differed in basic assumptions, methodologies, and conclusions, but they shared a commitment to the politics of feminism. Thus, they often included as a part of the study a critique of traditional scholarship that showed how it ignored or demeaned women while assuming and even asserting its own universality. By the late 1980s, such scholarship in theatre could be roughly categorized as one of four sorts: (a) studies of women's status in theatre; (b) criticisms of the depiction of women in drama and (later) theatre; (c) histories of female artists of theatre; and (d) theoretical studies of drama and theatre as informed by feminism. Although the four categories overlap, they are nonetheless useful in charting, however imperfectly, the directions of feminist scholarship in theatre.[10]

Status of Women in Theatre

Probably because of the visibility of actresses, theatre has had a reputation as a profession that welcomed women (e.g., Mohrmann, 1986). Women who tried to enter theatre, however, often found a situation starkly at odds with that reputation. Even before female scholars of theatre grappled with the theoretical implications of feminism, female artists noticed both the relatively small number of women who earned a living in theatre and the uneven distribution of women within the profession.

By the mid-1970s, several organizations had begun systematic inquiries into the status of women in theatre. The pivotal year was 1976, when several studies appeared: *The Creative Woman*, prepared as a part of International Women's Year, published information on the status of women in the arts, including theatre, and a bibliography of available resources (National Commission, 1976). Action for Women in Theatre surveyed both the status of female directors and the frequency of production of plays written by women; their surveys were later expanded to include designers and were periodically updated thereafter. The Women's Program of the American Theatre Association formed and quickly devised plans for research.[11] Other women's theatre organizations were formed: in 1978, the Women's Project of the American Place Theatre; in 1979, the Committee for Women of the Dramatists Guild; in 1982, the League of Professional Theatre Women/New York. All offered forums for collecting information on the position of women in theatre.

The emerging picture of the profession was troubling. Of the several hundred plays produced in major regional theatres between 1969 and 1975, only 7% were written by women (National Commission, 1976, p. 6). Of the several thousand roles available in Broadway plays between 1953 and 1972, only one-third were for women (National Commission, 1976, p. 6). Of the 261 plays produced on Broadway between 1977 and 1982, only 3% were directed by women (League, 1983, p. 391). Of the union-certified designers interviewed in 1983, only one had worked on

Broadway (League, 1983, p. 360). Among professors of theatre, few
women were full professors; most were clustered in the untenured and
part-time ranks (Becker, Selzer, & Choi, 1983; Emmert & Clevenger, 1983;
Hall, 1971). Although data continued to be collected and updated
throughout the 1980s, most feminist scholars turned to studies that sought
to understand the reasons for these patterns.[12]

Women's Depiction in Drama and Theatre

Early studies exploring the depiction of women in plays assumed that such
depictions both reflected and helped shape the public's view of women in
real life; that is, drama not only showed women's position in society but
also offered a way of changing that position. Because such research
promised political as well as intellectual rewards, it took on a sense of
urgency. Feminist scholars of drama began to construct a model of women
as they appeared in the plays of the past and present, drawing both their
assumptions and many of their methodologies from similar studies in the
criticism of mass media and nondramatic literature (e.g., Cornillon, 1972;
Haskell, 1974).

Early research focused on negative or stereotypical images of
women. Later investigations revealed—or at least stressed—more positive
and more complex female characters. Doubtless many factors explain this
shift, but its similarity to a change within feminism itself is clear. Early
studies, like early feminism itself, needed to "name the enemy" (Campbell,
1972; Hancock, 1972); therefore, to accumulate examples of women's
being ignored or demeaned in literature as in life served the political (and
rhetorical) needs of the moment. But, as the larger feminist movement
shifted attention from the differences between men and women to the differences among women (Alcoff, 1988; Freedman, 1988; Hawkesworth,
1989; Offen, 1988), research into images of women in literature, media,
and theatre likewise shifted to capture this new interest. Therefore, in
many venues, feminism and feminist studies began to focus on various
kinds of women—women of color, women of various ethnicities, women
in careers, women at home, and women alone and in relationships (celi-
bate, lesbian, and heterosexual) (Arnold, 1989; Awkword, 1989; Bassnett,
1987; Bulbeck, 1988; Gonzales, 1989; hooks, 1984; Lorde, 1981;
McDowell, 1985; Smith, 1985; Yarbro-Bejarno, 1986).

But this shift in theatre awaited evidence as well as perception;
that is, only later studies were able to focus on a body of plays that portrayed women in interesting new ways in part because such plays had
become available for the first time. These newly available works had two
sources: (a) the rediscovery of some gender-sensitive older works, once
"lost" from the canon but now restored because they were reread in terms

of gender; and (b) the creation of new plays by contemporary feminist and other playwrights.

By the end of the 1980s, scholars had examined the depiction of women in plays by, among others, Imamu Baraka (Richards, 1982), S.N. Behrman (Baxter, 1973), Moliere (Gutwirth, 1982), Eugene O'Neill (Vunovich, 1966), William Shakespeare (e.g., Bamber, 1982; Dash, 1981; Dusinberre, 1979), Ntozake Shange (Richards, 1983), G.B. Shaw (Adams, 1974; Crane, 1974), August Strindberg (Dawson, 1964), and Tennessee Williams (Mraz, 1967). They had studied female characters in plays of such diverse venues as Jacobean tragedy (Finke, 1984), Tony-Award winning plays (O'Brien, 1983), Pulitzer Prize plays (Stephens, 1981), musical plays (E.S. Klein, 1962; K.G. Klein, 1984), serious American drama (Schaffer, 1966), and dramas of the 1920s (Wiley, 1957). Some studies chronicled the continuing power of well-known stereotypes, like "the bitch, the goddess, and the whore," identified by Megan Terry (Gussow, 1972). Others described "the new woman" (Kolb, 1975; Stephens, 1982; Wiley, 1989), "the liberated woman" (Shafer, 1974), "the black woman" (Tener, 1975; Turner, 1982), "women in melodrama" (Bank, 1981), and "the wife" (Zahler, 1973), among others. When Helen Krich Chinoy and Linda Walsh Jenkins published their *Women in American Theatre* (1981), such studies were numerous enough to comprise one of the book's six sections—"Images"—a section expanded in their revised edition (1987).

Also during the 1980s, scholars began to consider not only women's depiction in drama but also their depiction on stage, perhaps in response to Jenkins's (1981) call: "We need research that considers the visual image/icon on stage. . . .[that answers questions like] What gender values are being reinforced or created by the `stage picture' alone?" (p. 237). Thus, scholars pondered the effect on audiences of male characters having been played by women (L. Adler, 1981; Shafer, 1981). Alternatively, and with greater relish, they considered the significance of female characters having been played by men or boys throughout much of theatre's history (Case, 1985; Helms, 1989). Did this practice mask a deep fear that gender identity was fragile (Levine, 1986); allow homosexual eroticism a public, if cloaked, expression (Case, 1988, pp. 21-27; Jardine, 1983); or manifest a view that male and female sexuality were interchangeable (Orgel, 1989)? Also, scholars probed ways by which performance might alter or call into question depictions in texts—by casting against gender, for one example (Jenkins & Ogden-Malouf, 1985), or by casting against stereotypes of lesbian behavior, for another (Davy, 1989; Dolan, 1988, pp. 59-81). By the end of the decade, an occasional scholar studied ways by which women's image could be manipulated through the arrangement of space, lights, properties, and sound (Greeley, 1989).

By the decade's end as well, the putative correspondence

between women in the real world and women on the stage was being questioned. Increasingly, theatre scholars, following the directions pointed by literary and film scholars (e.g., De Lauretis, 1984; Natoli, 1987), sought to differentiate women in the world and the constructed image of women (often designated as "Woman") on the page or stage. The issue became not, as it was earlier, how women and Woman were similar, but rather how they differed and how Woman as created served to perpetuate the goals of patriarchy. At the same time, feminist scholars wanted to understand how audience members, especially women, saw and interpreted Woman and why spectators, especially female spectators, seemed able to accept and enjoy characterizations that showed Woman as unimportant, inferior, or evil. Interest in spectators moved the attention of critics away from the text, whether written or performed, to the audience as the maker of meaning (Dolan, 1988; Pribram, 1988).

Female Artists in Theatre's History

Studies of female artists in the real world were rarer than those of female characters in drama, a point easily verified by consulting any standard index. The disparity existed for at least two reasons. First, studies of drama were routinely undertaken by scholars in language and literature as well as theatre departments, while studies of theatre as an institution were usually confined to scholars in departments of theatre alone. Second, published play texts were more readily accessible for study than were reliable records of long-forgotten women.

Feminist historians shared with Marxist historians the assumption that the writing of history was neither neutral nor objective, that it favored the predispositions of its writers—almost all of whom were middle-class, white, Eurocentric, and (the feminists added) male. From this assumption, it followed that theatre history's overwhelming attention to male artists might reflect not only the theatrical events themselves but also the biases of those historians who recorded and transmitted the events. It followed further that standard accounts of the few women included in the historical record might be warped and so would deserve reassessment.

Accordingly, early feminist historians set for themselves two major tasks: first, to write compensatory histories aimed at uncovering and recording the contributions of those female artists whom history (that is, historians) had erased; and, second, to review and perhaps revise the accounts of those female artists included in standard histories. Compensatory histories sought both to position women within the traditional histories of theatre (the male historical canon) and also to uncover and establish a history of female artists in the theatre (a female tradition). Revisionist histories sought to reinterpret events, taking into account the effects of gender on those events. Thus, compensatory histories might, for example, recover women's contributions to medieval theatre (Case, 1983; Cotton, 1978; Davidson, 1984; Hozeski, 1975). Revisionist histories might also ask why Bishop Ethelwold rather than Hrostwith is usually credited with the reintroduction of drama in the 10th-century church, a study yet to be undertaken.

In both sorts of studies, feminist historians sought to go beyond chronicling the careers of specific women; that is, they aimed to go beyond the now largely discredited "great man" [sic] approach to history. Feminist historians wanted to consider the artists and practices as part of larger social and economic systems, which in public life favored men over women. Thus, when focusing on the career of a single artist, feminist historians made gender relevant to an explanation of her successes and failures (e.g., Gardiner, 1980; Gillespie, 1989a, 1989b; Hart, 1989a; Langdell, 1985). When focusing on a group of female artists in theatre, feminist historians related their experiences to those of other women of the time (e.g., Carlson, 1988; Chinoy, 1982; Colvin, 1977; Davis, 1988; Day, 1980; Hampsten, 1980; Johnson, 1975; MacDonald, 1988; Morgan, 1981; Olauson, 1981; Parrott, 1988; Sutherland, 1978; Vincinus, 1979).

Feminist historical studies clustered in significant patterns. Studies of female actors and playwrights, for example, far outnumbered those of female directors, designers, and producers (calculated from "Sourcebook," in Chinoy & Jenkins, 1987, pp. 391-404, but see also Robinson, Roberts, & Barranger, 1989). Thus, the number of studies roughly mirrored the proportion of such artists in the world. Although studies of trends and groups increased after the mid-1970s, studies of individual artists continued to dominate, with, for example, dissertations on individual artists outnumbering those on groups and trends by about two to one (calculated from "Sourcebook," Chinoy & Jenkins, 1987, pp. 400-404). Some feminist historians also studied and published analyses of contemporary people and events, a practice generally avoided by traditional historians (e.g., Brown, 1980; Gillespie, 1978, 1981; Leavitt, 1980; Natalle, 1985). This decision seems to have been a conscious one. Suspicious of history's repeated erasure of women, feminist historians attempted to guarantee contemporary women a position in the theatre histories of the future.

Theories of Drama and Theatre as Informed by Feminism

Literary and film scholars were interested in feminist theory long before theatre scholars. As early as 1968, for example, Mary Ellman was thinking about "Phallic Criticism;" by 1981, Elaine Showalter had offered "gynocriticism" as both a method and theory for literature. Feminism entered film practice and study in 1972 with the First International Festival of

Women's Films; by 1975, Laura Mulvey had published her seminal essay and thus laid the groundwork for a feminist theory of film. Theatre lagged well behind.

Among the earliest studies relevant to feminist theories of drama were those that examined female characters in plays, for such studies sharpened understanding of differences among such concepts as female, feminine, and feminist and underscored disjunctions between the conventions of literary form and the reality of the world. Soon joining such studies were those of the works and careers of female playwrights (Abramson, 1969; Austin, 1983; Betsko & Koening, 1987; Cotton, 1980; Coven, 1982; Gottlieb, 1979; Malpede, 1983; Spencer, 1987).

With this information available, and again following paths charted earlier by literary scholars, some theatre scholars sought to compare female with male playwriting. Scholars generally agreed, for example, that contemporary female playwrights often abandoned causally organized plots and psychologically driven characters in favor of plays described as circular, quilted, contiguous, or web-like (e.g., Case, 1988; Gillespie, 1981; Greeley, 1989). Theorists disagreed, however, on the reasons for this shift. Some sought answers in biology, arguing (for example) that causal, linear plots—with their rising action, climax, and falling action—reproduced male orgasm, while circular or contiguous plots reproduced female sexuality—with its smaller, contained, repeating patterns (e.g., Boesing, 1981). Others instead sought answers in theatrical practice and economics, arguing (for example) that female playwrights appropriated forms already explored by contemporary male playwrights of theatre's avant garde, in which female artists tended to cluster because of a more welcoming production situation (e.g., Gillespie, 1981).

As distinctions *among* women and *between* sex and gender grew clearer, so did differences among feminists—their assumptions and working methods (Hawkesworth, 1989; Kolodny, 1980; Offen, 1988; Rich, 1976). As these differences gained attention in the larger feminist movement, differences among female playwrights grew clearer. By the mid-1980s, therefore, biological explanations were greeted with increased skepticism, and explanations based on historic and economic circumstances gained favor (Barrett, 1985; Case, 1988; Dolan, 1988, 1989c; Nachlin, 1971). Nonetheless, theoretical studies of women's writing, including women's playwriting, continued to probe its connections, if any, with sex and gender (Bovenschen, 1986; Bryony & Todd, 1984; Feral, 1984; Gottner-Abendroth, 1986; Marre, 1985; Weigel, 1986; Willis, 1985).[13]

Although theoretical attention to production elements other than text lagged behind, studies of producing and acting were not uncommon. The proliferation of feminist theatres during the 1970s, for example, occasioned theories that sought to explain both their existence and their traits (e.g., Bardsley, 1984; Gillespie, 1978; Keyssar, 1985; Leavitt, 1980; Natalle, 1985; Rea, 1972, 1974; Zivanovic, 1989). The clustering of female (and feminist) artists off- and off-off-Broadway likewise led to theories seeking to account for their position outside the commercial theatre (Chinoy, 1987a; Segal & Sklar, 1983). There were efforts to develop theories of acting and actor training that took into account the experiences of female actors (Jenkins & Ogden-Malouf, 1985; Zeig, 1984). By the late 1980s, some scholars focused on the spectator as a maker of meaning instead of on the performance as a source of meaning (Davy, 1986; Dolan, 1988; Maus, 1987). Although both design and directing would seem especially fertile areas for theoretical work, little such work was underway when the 1980s ended (Adler, 1982; Reinhardt, 1981).

Throughout most of the 1980s, a variety of voices and approaches could be heard in feminist theoretical studies of drama and theatre. Theorists stressed what have been called "bottom-up" or "piecemeal" theories (Carroll, 1988), theories that sought to explain specific, limited phenomena within theatre. They did so from several perspectives (e.g., liberal, radical, Marxist), using methods that ranged from the strictly empirical to the highly speculative. By the decade's end, however, a strong preference for a different kind of analysis had emerged, based on a so-called postmodern perspective and arrived at through new methods.

Again, theorists of theatre were following directions previously pointed by theorists in literature and film, toward an imaginative blend of semiotics (following especially Peirce, 1981, and Eco, 1984), psychoanalysis (especially Lacan, 1977), Marxism (especially Althusser, 1970, 1971, and Brecht, 1964), and deconstruction (Derrida, 1976, 1978) dominated feminist literary theory and almost all film theory. Following this lead, the most active and vocal feminist theorists of theatre in the late 1980s seized upon this same blend. They abandoned piecemeal theorizing, seeking instead a general theory of feminist practice in theatre (e.g., Case, 1988; Dolan, 1989c; Phelan, 1988; Reinelt, 1986). Therefore, theorists of theatre increasingly turned to consider how ideology (especially that connected with gender) was imbedded in texts and performances, how spectators were positioned to accept such ideologies unquestioningly, how feminists might best come to understand texts and performances in order to subvert them, and how performances might contribute to the disruption of such ideologies (Davy, 1989; Diamond, 1988; Dolan, 1989a, 1989b; Feral, 1982; Forte, 1985; Stephens, 1989a, 1989b).

FUTURE RESEARCH

It seems clear that, for the near future, feminist researchers in theatre must continue the sorts of research already underway. Without current data on the status of women in the professions (theatre *and* education), efforts at improving that status will languish. Unless the ubiquity of patriarchal images of female characters in drama is exposed, both audiences and scholars may underestimate their pervasiveness and so their power. Unless recent feminist images are examined and recorded, their potential for provoking change may be squandered. Without knowledge of female artists and scholars from the past, those of the future will lack a tradition from which to draw and will seem to lack a heritage. Without the analyses of feminist theories, some data will yield few patterns and, therefore, limited insights. Whatever additional sorts of research may be undertaken, future feminist scholars of theatre must preserve and extend the work of their predecessors. This much is necessary for the health of the feminist enterprise in theatre. It is not, however, sufficient. Some new directions are needed— and are already being identified.

In literary studies, for example, feminists have launched sustained attacks on "the canon"—those models of excellence traditionally taught in classes, anthologized in volumes, enshrined in scholarly publications, and praised for their universality (von Hallberg, 1984). Although literary canons are the most often discussed, the same sort of masterpiece mentality is clearly echoed in theatre's theory, criticism, history, and indeed practice itself (through hierarchies based on physical locations, acting companies, and dramatic repertories, for example). But feminist scholars in theatre have only begun to address the issues surrounding canons (e.g., Dolan, 1988, pp. 19-40). Feminists in other fields have offered several possible courses of action with respect to canons, and each has implications. For example, feminist theatre scholars might choose to expose the way a canon is made, to include selected women within it, to establish a female alternative to it, or to reject the very idea of a canon as elitist. But the mere act of arguing that a canon is nothing more than a series of choices made by (male) scholars at some time in the past can help to clarify yet again the role of historians in making the historical record and critics in defining art and good art (Lauter, 1983).

Also, feminists in theatre studies, having seen some of the traps of feminist scholarship, must begin to confront them. Feminists see, for example, that the language and explanatory structures they have inherited predispose them toward certain ways of thinking, ways not always consonant with their radical needs (e.g., Hawkesworth, 1989; Messer-Davidow, 1989). They see, further, that critiquing traditional art and its scholarship inevitably keeps male ideas at the center of the discussion—and of the citation indexes.[14] They see, as well, that adapting, rather than jettisoning, traditional explanations of phenomena to guide feminist inquiries also keeps male ideas central to the issues and males' names central to the citation indexes. They see, finally, that to jettison (male) traditions in theatre's art and scholarship would be to impoverish both. The dilemma is formidable. If men remain at the center, then women remain at the margins, and feminist scholars do not disrupt patriarchal patterns. If, on the other hand, feminist scholars reject or ignore theatre's traditions, they lose the wisdom of over 2,000 years. Feminist scholars must confront these dilemmas in every area of specialization. In addition to these new directions, applicable throughout the whole discipline of theatre, some trends seem specific to the specialties within theatre.

Criticism

Hart (1989b) seems to describe accurately the near future of feminist criticisms of drama: Critics will shift "from discovering and creating positive images of women in the context of drama to analyzing and disrupting the ideological codes embedded in the inherited structures of dramatic representation" (p.4). That is, feminist critics will increasingly explore plays in light of currently fashionable literary and film theories—semiotics, deconstruction, Marxism, and Lacanian psychoanalysis. Such investigations seem likely to focus special attention on certain kinds of playwrights (Benmussa, 1979; Diamond, 1985; Marohl, 1987) and on certain kinds of performing units (Case & Hughes, 1989; Schneider, 1989; Solomon, 1985). We can also anticipate that critics will continue to study the images of female characters (Woman), but that they will increasingly consider ways in which language (including metaphor), structure, and form function to establish or undermine expectations. Feminist critics exploring language will follow the leads offered by, among others, Margaret Wilkerson (1989) in "Music as Metaphor" and Mary K. Deshazer (1989) in "Rejecting Necrophilia." Those feminist critics interested in pursuing how form serves to manipulate expectations will profit from such articles as Susan Carlson's "Women in Comedy" (1985) and "Revisionary Endings" (1989) and Jonnie Guerra's "Beth Henley: Female Quest and the Family-Play Tradition" (1989).

Other feminist critics, however, will likely focus on theatre rather than drama and so will increasingly study ways by which acting, directing, and design have been (or can be) harnessed to shape interpretation. Given the recent focus on lesbian performance as a tactic for transcending gender stereotypes on stage, more studies of acting style, cross-casting, and cross-dressing are likely. Such directions have been well charted by Case (1985, 1989), Davy (1986, 1989), Dolan (1989a, 1989b), and Schneider (1989), among others. But as the force of semiotics invades theatre scholarship, more studies of other elements of production can be anticipated. Indeed, in light of the shifting interest away from written text and toward

plays-in-performance and performance art, such studies may well consti-
tute a major direction of future criticism. If so, then such studies as Lynn
Greeley's "Martha Boesing: Playwright of Performance" (1989) and
Catherine Schuler's "Spectator Response and Comprehension: The
Problem of Karen Finley's *Constant State of Desire*" (1990) will offer useful
models.

Other critics will probably focus on "the feminist spectator as critic," to borrow the title of Jill Dolan's book (1988). Here the goal will be to
allow female and male spectators to reveal the tensions within the performance—between spoken and visual messages, overt and covert meanings,
author's intentions and realized performance. As spectators learn to see
the often hidden persuaders that lurk within texts and performances and to
discover how the persuaders work, they can imagine ways of subverting
them when the messages undercut the political agenda of feminism. To
this end, feminists may wish to draw more fully on contemporary reception theories, as modified for theatrical use by Carlson (1989, pp. 82-98).

In addition, it seems quite likely that feminist critics must expand
their interest beyond the form and content of plays, whether in text or performance, to the very procedures of critics and criticism. This shift would
indicate an increasing emphasis on theory.

Theory

Two major shifts within feminist theories of theatre seem to be underway,
and they seem likely to chart the course of feminists' theories of theatre in
the coming decades. First, *dramatic* theory, so evident during the first
2,100 years of theoretical reflection, is expanding to a more comprehensive *theatrical* theory. This shift means that as much attention will be paid
to elements of performance and to spectators as to text. Although this shift
is occurring throughout the field of theatre, it is likely to be especially pronounced among feminist theorists because of their wish to stress spectators. Feminists, following Brecht, see spectators as agents of political
change. But feminists also see in the shift from an aesthetics of text (with
its effects on the spectator) to an aesthetics of reception (where spectators
are central to the event) an opportunity to study and celebrate those differences to which feminism is currently dedicated. That is, when a text is
central, a single controlling element is conceptualized, but when spectators are central, different responses of diverse individuals are the issue.
Explaining differing responses in terms of differing experiences—experiences rooted in time and place—underscores the historic nature of life and
art and so the possibility of change.

Second, feminists' early treatment of women in theatre, with the
emphasis clearly on theatre, is yielding to a study of women and theatre

within feminism, with the emphasis clearly on feminism. In this respect, feminists in theatre are repeating tendencies now visible in the larger intellectual community, where theory has taken the place of philosophy and "intertextual references" have taken the place of traditions of inquiry (Jameson, 1984). Thus, if the admittedly small sample offered by recent books (Case, 1988; Dolan, 1988; Hart, 1989b) and articles (e.g., Speakman, 1989) is any guide, feminist theories in theatre will probably continue to ignore or repudiate the long tradition of theatrical theory (except Brecht's) in favor of contemporary theories developed in literary and film studies, with their blend of Althusserian Marxism, Lacanian psychoanalysis, semiotics, and deconstructionism (Ecker, 1986; Felski, 1989; Kauffman, 1989; Miller, 1986; Monteith, 1986).

Some feminist theorists in theatre may wish to examine the wisdom of this trend, inasmuch as replacing traditional dramatic theories with contemporary film and literary theories that are themselves under severe attack from several directions may be an unwise decision, politically as well as intellectually (Carroll, 1988; Christian, 1988; Hawkesworth, 1989; Jameson, 1988). Moreover, a theoretical hegemony within theatrical scholarship would appear at odds both with current feminism and with traditional theatrical theory. Perhaps what is needed is not a feminist theory of theatre, but rather feminists' theories of theatre, theories as richly diverse as those of the current canon but without its heritage of oppressions. Perhaps Kolodny (1980) is correct in that a "playful pluralism" is what feminists' political agenda prescribes.

History

> It is the relationship of women to history which explains the nature of female subordination, the causes for women's cooperation in the process of their subordination, the condition for their opposition to it, [and] the rise of feminist consciousness. (Lerner, 1986, p. vii)

If Lerner is correct, then feminist historians in all disciplines have an awesome task, which they have scarcely begun. In theatre, for example, compensatory histories are still badly needed, for some of the most basic questions about women's advent and place in organized theatre remain unasked as well as unanswered. Revisionist histories are also relatively rare in theatre, and surely critiques of the traditional accounts must precede the writing of a balanced history of the theatre.

Clearly, feminist historians in theatre have much more work to do in uncovering the past. In this pursuit, they will find Davis' (1989) three questions helpful: "How does the ideology of the dominant culture affect women's status?" "How do social, class, and economic factors affect privilege?" and "How is the status quo maintained or challenged in artistic media?" (pp. 68-71). Such questions should, of course, be asked by any good historian of theatre, feminist or not. The fact that Davis must list these questions in order to call attention to the inadequacies of the current accounts says much about traditional histories of theatre: They tend to be "tunnel histories" that divorce theatre from the culture that produced it (Gillespie & Cameron, 1984, pp. 3-34).

But feminist historians must do more. They must also address the process of historical study as well as the content of the past. They must consider ways by which historical methods have helped shape (and change) the past-as-lived into the past-as-written. At the end of the 1980s, little such work had been undertaken.

For example, historical definitions, historical periods, and historical generalization have all exerted effects on women that are only dimly understood. The Greek definition of *theatre* excluded mime, the only form to include women. Although African-American theatre historians have analyzed the ways in which the very definitions of theatre have worked to exclude African-Americans, feminist historians of theatre leave the issue all but unaddressed.[15] The Neoclassical definition of *tragedy*, with its emphasis on affairs of state, heavily favored male experience, *Phedre* notwithstanding. Women seemingly belonged in comedy, in which domestic issues and ordinary people were the subjects. But theorists, at least since the time of Aristotle, have deemed comedy an inferior genre. Has the effect of genre extended beyond the written text? Female actors, specializing in tragedy, might aspire toward social acceptance even in the 17th or 18th century; female actors specializing in comedy, however, remained socially suspect. The relationship, if any, between definitions, genres, and genders remains unexplored.

Similarly, historical periods in theatre, as in history generally, are demarked by political and economic changes growing out of wars or technological shifts. Yet, conceiving periods through such criteria seems likely to stress male over female experience. (And indeed, periods of great advance for men are often those of special trial for women.) Moreover, perceptual shifts advantageous to feminists might accompany changes in periods, or even in the naming of periods. A chapter entitled "Theatre Between the Wars" sets expectations different from one called "Theatre During Feminist Protest."

Likewise, historical generalization, although unavoidable, inevitably shapes thinking. Generalization, by asserting similarity, obscures differences among and within actors, theatres, audiences, women, and so on. Do generalizations about actors and acting apply equally well to women and men? Do generalizations about class and the location and architecture of theatre buildings apply equally to men and women? Few of the usual generalizations within theatre have been examined for their applicability to women. Many questions have not yet been asked, much less answered. Indeed, they have not yet been correctly phrased.

In sum, what Hatch (1989, p. 148) cites as the five major obstacles facing African-American historians, when reworded to apply to women, also face feminist historians of theatre: (a) scarcity of primary materials, (b) a severely circumscribed definition of theatre, (c) a paucity of publication outlets, (d) a disgraceful absence of scholars who know women's as well as men's roles in and relationship to theatre history, and (e) an abundance of institutionalized sexism. Future feminist scholarship in theatre history will need to address each of these problems.

African-American historians, delving beneath the surface of traditional histories, have found a rich heritage of African-American contributions to mainstream culture. For example, Martin Bernal's *Black Athena: The Afroasiatic Roots of Classical Civilization* (1987), questioning traditional accounts, argues persuasively that the contributions of African-Americans have been deliberately suppressed and distorted in order to uphold the supremacy of European civilization. Feminist historians have yet to formulate a detailed account of the culture that first produced theatre, and so women's contributions to its origins, if any, remain unknown. Feminist historians might profit from emulating their African-American predecessors and from reconsidering the traditional accounts of theatre's history from its beginning.

CONCLUSIONS

Twenty years of feminist scholarship enriches the understanding of both theatre and education. Twenty years, however, cannot repair the damage of centuries, and so much work remains to be done. We—by which I mean feminist scholars (male and female)—must continue collecting new names, facts, and documents; we must continue finding new artists and developing new theories. But we must also build on the past and do so in ways that will not taint the future. Feminist scholars must keep the data of the past but question the interpretations, hold fast to the framework of fact but reject the male histories written from it. We must retain and expand the repertory, while reassessing the canon. We must admire the erudition of past theorists while rejecting their biases.

We must also respect differences among scholars, non-feminist as well as feminist. We can be helped in this goal by recognizing that the future can no more be the property of one feminist criticism, history, or theory of theatre than the past could be possessed by a single male tradition. What we seek as feminist scholars, then, is not a feminist explanation of theatre's richness but instead feminists' explanations that are as richly diverse as their predecessors', but without the legacy of patriarchal bias.

In these ways the insights of Arimneste can balance and correct those of Aristotle.

NOTES TO CHAPTER 6

1. The information from which I build the following narrative is readily available in any standard theatre text (e.g., Brockett, 1987; Gillespie & Cameron, 1984). The interpretation is, of course, my own.

2. Despite references to *mimi, ioculatores,* and *histriones* during the Middle Ages, no clear evidence establishes an unbroken tradition of mime through the Middle Ages and into the Renaissance, although several scholars have asserted one.

3. The standard APA citation form does not permit me to make points about dating that are important to my argument. I have therefore adapted it. All quotations of dramatic theory come from Dukore (1974), which is a sourcebook of original documents. In the text I will cite the theorist and his [sic] date, followed by page numbers in Dukore.

4. Aristotle's views of women's unsuitability as tragic figures derive not from an isolated aesthetic sensibility, but from his views on real women, whom he saw as mutilated and inferior men. Thus, *The Poetics* merely points to a system of belief more fully explained in Aristotle's writings on biology and philosophy. (See Horowitz, 1976).

5. The words *critic* and *criticism* are now often used to describe two quite different sorts of activities: writing scholarly analyses and evaluations intended for publication in academic journals, on the one hand, and, on the other hand, writing personal responses intended for publication in newspapers and popular magazines. Some scholars prefer to call the first *criticism* and the second *reviewing,* or alternately, *academic* and *journalistic* criticism. The separation of these two practices arose in the late 18th century and has become increasingly rigid since. I shall treat both, distinguishing them only when their divergence appears relevant to my major argument.

6. Again standard APA citation obscures matters of dating that are important to my argument. The citations in this paragraph, unless otherwise attributed, are found in Cotton (1980). In the text I will cite the original source and date, followed by page numbers in Cotton.

7.   In theatre, the responses of female as well as male critics betrayed (and sometimes still betray) strong assumptions concerning gender. These same tendencies (to describe the good as masculine, to consider women as imitative of men, to assert a male source for a good female work) are equally present in the history of visual arts. (See Parker & Pollock, 1981, especially pp. 50-81).

8.   Although the work did not survive, references to *Theatrike Historia* by King Juba II of Mauretania appear in both Pollux and Athenaeus. Scholars interested in reviewing the history of theatre history are referred to Vince (1989).

9.   Throughout this piece the sex-gender system is the issue. As first identified by the anthropologist Gayle Rubin, it is usefully summarized by Lerner (1986) as "that institutionalized system which allots resources, property, and privileges to persons according to culturally defined gender roles. Thus, it is sex which determines that women should be child bearers, it is the sex-gender system which assures that they should be child-rearers" (p 238). In using *male* and *men, female* and *women,* I refer to this system, not merely to biological sex. I define a feminist as someone, male or female, who wishes to transform the sex-gender system.

10. Although the new feminist movement appeared throughout the world and throughout academic disciplines, only its manifestations in the United States and in theatre can be treated here. Occasional references are made to foreign scholars whose influence has been both strong and direct and to studies in other disciplines when the parallels seem likely to strengthen my argument. For general comparisons of national differences in feminism, interested readers may consult Savona (1984), Humm (1986), Bulbeck (1988), and Offen (1988).

Because the body of scholarly work was still far too vast to allow comprehensiveness, I selected for citation: (a) those works whose representativeness allowed them to serve as examples of many such studies; (b) works which (because early) marked a new direction which others followed; and (c) those works that I found unusually provocative.

11. Although the American Theatre Association went bankrupt during 1985, the Women's Program continues, now affiliated with ATHE, the Association for Theatre in Higher Education. Originally committed to serving the needs of women in theatre, the Women's Program became a "feminist forum" in the mid-1980s.

12. Again, the pattern is not limited to the United States. See, for example, Venables (1980) and Wandor (1980, 1984, 1986).

13. Playwriting seems to share these issues with other writing; see, for example, Showalter (1986). But the relationship between biological and cultural causes is a question throughout film and visual arts as well as literary ones; see, for example, Nachlin (1971), Lippard (1976), Rosenberg

(1983), and Parker and Pollock (1981). It is, indeed, an argument among feminists in most disciplines .

14. Case and Forte (1985, pp. 63-64), in discussing performance strategies, show how deconstructing oppression leaves the oppressors on stage—and the oppressed off stage and therefore invisible.

15. Parker and Pollock's work (1981) is an exploration of the relationship between the changing definitions of art, the changing acceptance and role of female artists, and the intersections of these two traditions (see also, Clark, 1979). There is no such study among feminists in theatre, although Case (1988), in the chapter "Personal Theatre," offers a glimpse of possible findings were such a study to be undertaken.

REFERENCES

A journal from Parnassus. (1688). (Cited in Cotton, N. (1980). *Women playwrights in England c. 1363-1750.* Lewisburg, PA: Bucknell University Press).

Abramson, D.E. (1969). *Negro playwrights in the American theatre, 1925-1959.* New York: Columbia University Press.

Adams, E. (1974). Feminism and female stereotypes in Shaw. *The Shaw Review, 17,* 17-22.

Adler, D. (1982). The unlacing of Cleopatra. *Theatre Journal, 34,* 450-466.

Adler, L. (1981). Adah Isaacs Menken in *Mazeppa.* In H.K. Chinoy & L.W. Jenkins (Eds.), *Women in American theatre* (pp. 81-87). New York: Crown.

Alcoff, L. (1988). Cultural feminism versus post structuralism. *Signs, 13,* 405-436.

Althusser, L. (1970). *For Marx* (B. Brewster, Trans.). New York: Vintage.

Althusser, L. (1971). *Lenin and philosophy and other essays* (B. Brewster, Trans.). New York: Monthly Review Press.

Aristotle. (c. 335 B.C.). Poetics. Reproduced in B.F. Dukore (Ed.). (1974). *Dramatic theory and criticism: Greeks to Grotowski* (pp. 31-55). New York: Holt, Rinehart, and Winston.

Arnold, S. (1989). Dissolving the half shadows: Japanese American women playwrights. In L. Hart (Ed.), *Making a spectacle* (pp. 181-194). Ann Arbor: University of Michigan Press.

Austin, G. (Ed.). (1983). The "woman" playwright issue. *Performing Arts Journal 21, 7*(3), 87-102.

Awkword, M. (1989). Appropriative gestures: Theory and Afro-American literary criticism. In L. Kauffman (Ed.), *Gender and theory: Dialogues on feminist criticism* (pp. 238-246). New York: Basil Blackwell.

Bamber, L. (1982). Comic women, tragic men: A study of gender and genre in Shakespeare. Stanford, CA: Stanford University Press.

Bank, R.K. (1981). The second face of the idol: Women in melodrama. In

H.K. Chinoy & L.W. Jenkins (Eds.), *Women in American theatre* (pp. 238-242). New York: Crown.

Bapst, G. (1893). *Essai sur l'histoire du theatre: La mise en scene, le decor, le costume . . .* Paris: Librairie Hachette.

Bardsley, B. (1984). The young blood of theatre: Women's theatre groups. *Drama, 152*, 25-29.

Barrett, M. (1985). Ideology and the cultural production of gender. In J. Newton & D. Rosenfelt (Eds.), *Feminist criticism and social change: Sex, class, and race in literature and culture* (pp. 65-85). New York: Methuen.

Bassnett, S. (1987). The Magdalena experiment: New directions in women's theatre. *The Drama Review, 31*(4), 10-17.

Baxter, M. (1973). *Modern woman as heroine in representative plays by S. N. Behrman.* Unpublished doctoral dissertation, University of Wisconsin, Madison.

Becker, S.L., Selzer, J.A., & Choi, H.C. (1983). Theatre programs in American colleges and universities. *ACA Bulletin, 46*, 32-35.

Benmussa, S. (1979). *Benmussa directs: Playscript 91.* Dallas: Riverrun Press.

Bernal, M. (1987). *Black Athena: The Afroasiatic roots of classical civilization.* New Brunswick, NJ: Rutgers University Press.

Betsko, K., & Koenig, R. (Eds.). (1987). *Interviews with contemporary women playwrights.* New York: Beech Tree Books.

Blunt, J. (1966). *The composite art of acting.* New York: Macmillan.

Boesing, M. (1981). The web. In *Plays in progress* (Vol. 4, No. 1, pp. 1/1-2/36). New York: Theatre Communications Group.

Bovenschen, S. (1986). Is there a feminine aesthetic? In G. Ecker (Ed.), *Feminist aesthetics* (pp. 23-50). Boston: Beacon Press.

Brecht, B. (1964). *Brecht on theatre* (J. Willet, Trans. & Ed.). London: Methuen.

Brockett, O.G. (1968). *History of the theatre.* Boston: Allyn & Bacon. (Later editions in 1974, 1977, 1982, 1987).

Brockett, O.G. (1987). *History of the theatre* (5th ed.). Boston: Allyn & Bacon.

Brown, J. (1980). *Feminist drama: Definitions and critical analysis.* Metuchen, NJ: Scarecrow Press.

Bryony, L., & Todd, S. (1984). But will men like it? Or, living as a feminist writer without committing murder. In S. Todd (Ed.), *Women and theatre: Calling the shots* (pp. 24-32). New York: Faber.

Bulbeck, C. (1988). *One world women's movement.* London: Pluto Press.

Byron, G.N.G., Lord. (1817). Letter to John Murray. In *The Oxford dictionary of quotations* (3rd ed., 1979). *s.v.* Voltaire.

Campbell, K.K. (1972). The rhetoric of women's liberation: An oxymoron. *Quarterly Journal of Speech, 59*, 74-86.

Campbell, K.K. (1988). What really distinguishes and/or ought to distinguish feminist scholarship in communication studies? *Women's Studies in Communication, 11*, 4-5.

Carlson, M.A. (1984). *Theories of the theatre: A historical and critical survey from the Greeks to the present.* Ithaca, NY: Cornell University Press.
Carlson, M.A. (1989). Theatre audiences and the reading of performance. In T. Postlewait & B.A. McConachie (Eds.), *Interpreting the theatrical past: Essays in the historiography of performance* (pp.82-98). Iowa City: University of Iowa Press.
Carlson, S. (1985). Women in comedy: Problem, promise, paradox. In J. Redmond (Ed.), *Drama, sex, and politics: Vol. 7: Themes in drama* (pp. 159-172). Cambridge: Cambridge University Press.
Carlson, S. (1988). Process and product: Contemporary British theatre and its communities of women. *Theatre Research International, 13,* 249-263.
Carlson, S. (1989). Revisionary endings: Pam Gems's Aunt Mary and Camille. In L. Hart (Ed.), *Making a spectacle* (pp. 103-117). Ann Arbor: University of Michigan Press.
Carroll, N. (1988). *Mystifying movies: Fads and fallacies in contemporary film theory.* New York: Columbia University Press.
Case, S.E. (1983). Re-viewing Hrosvit. *Theatre Journal, 35,* 533-542.
Case, S.E. (1985). Classic drag: The Greek creation of female parts. *Theatre Journal, 37,* 316-328.
Case, S.E. (1988). *Feminism and theatre.* New York: Methuen.
Case, S.E. (1989). Toward a butch-femme aesthetic. In L. Hart (Ed.), *Making a spectacle* (pp. 282-299). Ann Arbor: University of Michigan Press.
Case, S.E., & Forte, J. (1985). From formalism to feminism. *Theater, 16*(2), 62-66.
Case, S.E., & Hughes, H. (1989). A case concerning Hughes: Letters from Sue-Ellen Case and Holly Hughes. *The Drama Review, 33*(4), 10-17.
Chambers, E.K. (1903). *The mediaeval stage* (2 vols.). London: Oxford University Press.
Chinoy, H.K. (1982). Suppressed desires: Women in the theatre. In K.W. Wheeler & V.L. Lussier (Eds.), *Women, the arts, and the 1920s in Paris and New York* (pp. 126-132). New Brunswick, NJ: Transaction Books.
Chinoy, H.K. (1987a). Art vs. business. In H.K. Chinoy & L. W. Jenkins (Eds.), *Women in American theatre* (pp. 1-9). New York: Theatre Communications Group.
Chinoy, H.K. (1987b). Women backstage and out front. In H.K. Chinoy & L.W. Jenkins (Eds.), *Women in American theatre* (pp. 353-363). New York: Theatre Communications Group.
Chinoy, H.K., & Jenkins, L.W. (Eds.). (1981). *Women in American theatre.* New York: Crown.
Chinoy, H.K., & Jenkins, L.W. (Eds.). (1987). *Women in American theatre* (rev. ed.). New York: Theatre Communications Group.
Christian, B. (1988). The race for theory. *Feminist Studies,14,* 67-80.
Clark, B.H. (Ed). (1965). *European theories of the drama, with a supple-

ment on the American drama (rev. ed.). New York: Crown.

Clark, V.A. (1979). The archeology of black theatre. *Black Scholar, 10,* 43-56.

Colvin, C. (1977). Feminism in the theatre. *Contemporary Review, 230,* 316-317.

Cooley, E.H. (1986). *Women in American theatre, 1850-1870: A study in professional equity.* Unpublished doctoral dissertation, University of Maryland, College Park.

Cornillon, S.K. (Ed.). (1972). *Images of women in fiction: Feminist perspectives.* Bowling Green, OH: Bowling Green State University Press.

Cotton, N. (1978). Katherine of Sutton: The first English woman playwright. *Theatre Journal, 4,* 475-481.

Cotton, N. (1980). *Women playwrights in England c. 1363-1750.* Lewisburg, PA: Bucknell University Press.

Coven, B. (1982). *American women dramatists of the twentieth century: A bibliography.* Metuchen, NJ: Scarecrow Press.

Cowley, A. (1667). Poem. In K. Philips, *Poems.* London: Herringman. sig. cl. (Cited in Cotton, N. (1980). *Women playwrights in England c. 1363-1750.* Lewisburg, PA: Bucknell University Press).

Crane, G. (1974). Shaw and women's lib. *The Shaw Review, 17,* 23-32.

Dash, I.G. (1981). *Wooing, weddings, and power: Women in Shakespeare's plays.* New York: Columbia University Press.

Davidson, C. (1984). Women and the medieval stage. *Women's Studies, 11,* 99-114.

Davis, T. (1988). Actresses and prostitutes in Victorian London. *Theatre Research International, 13,* 221-233.

Davis, T. (1989). Questions for a feminist methodology in theatre history. In T. Postlewait & B.A. McConachie (Eds.), *Interpreting the theatrical past: Essays in the historiography of performance* (pp. 59-81). Iowa City: University of Iowa Press.

Davy, K. (1986). Constructing the spectator: Reception, context, and address in lesbian performance. *Performing Arts Journal, 10,* 43-52.

Davy, K. (1989). Reading past the heterosexual imperative: Dress suits to hire. *The Drama Review, 33*(3), 153-170.

Dawson, W.M. (1964). *The female characters of August Strindberg, Eugene O'Neill, and Tennessee Williams.* Unpublished doctoral dissertation, University of Wisconsin, Madison.

Day, R.A. (1980). Muses in the mud: Female wits anthropologically considered. *Women's Studies, 7,* 61-74.

De Lauretis, T. (1984). *Alice doesn't: Feminism, semiotics, cinema.* Bloomington: Indiana University Press.

Derrida, J. (1976). *On grammatoloy* (G.C. Spivak, Trans.). Baltimore, MD: Johns Hopkins University Press. (Original work published 1967).

Derrida, J. (1978). *Writing and difference* (A. Bass, Trans.). Chicago: University of Chicago Press. (Original work published 1967).

Deshazer, M.K. (1989). Rejecting necrophilia: Ntozake Shange and the warrior revisited. In L. Hart (Ed.), *Making a spectacle* (pp. 86-102).

Ann Arbor: University of Michigan Press.

Diamond, E. (1985). Refusing the romanticism of identity: Narrative interventions in Churchill, Benmusa, Duras. *Theatre Journal, 37*, 273-286.

Diamond, E. (1988). Brechtian theory/feminist theatre: Toward a gestic feminist criticism. *The Drama Review, 32*(1), 82-94.

Dolan, J. (1988). *The feminist spectator as critic.* Ann Arbor, MI: UMI Research Press.

Dolan, J. (1989a). Desire cloaked in a trenchcoat. *The Drama Review, 33*(1), 59-67.

Dolan, J. (1989b). Feminists, lesbians, and other women in theatre: Thoughts on the politics of performance. In J. Redmond (Ed.), *Women in theatre: Vol. 11: Themes in drama* (pp. 199-207). Cambridge: Cambridge University Press.

Dolan, J. (1989c). In defense of the discourse: Materialist feminism, postmodernism, poststructuralism . . . and theory. *The Drama Review, 33*(3), 68-102.

Dukore, B.F. (Ed.). (1974). *Dramatic theory and criticism: Greeks to Grotowski.* New York: Holt, Rinehart, and Winston.

Dunlap, W. (1832). *A history of the American theatre.* New York: J. & J. Harper.

Dusinberre, J. (1979). *Shakespeare and the nature of women.* New York: Barnes and Noble.

Ecker, G. (Ed.). (1986). *Feminist aesthetics* (H. Anderson, Trans.). Boston: Beacon Press.

Eco, U. (1984). *Semiotics and the philosophy of language.* Bloomington: Indiana University Press.

Elam, K. (1980). *The semiotics of theatre and drama.* London: Methuen.

Ellman, M. (1968). *Thinking about women.* New York: Harcourt, Brace, Jovanovich.

Emmert, P., & Clevenger, T. (1983). Gender and academic specialization in graduate theatre programs in the United States. *ACA Bulletin, 43*, 49-55.

Ephelia. (1679). Female poems on several occasions. (Cited in Cotton, N. (1980). *Women playwrights in England c. 1363-1750.* Lewisburg, PA: Bucknell University Press).

Felski, R. (1989). *Beyond feminist aesthetics: Feminist literature and social change.* Cambridge, MA: Harvard University Press.

Feral, J. (1982). Performance and theatricality: The subject demystified. *Modern Drama, 25*, 170-184.

Feral, J. (1984). Writing and displacement: Women in theatre. *Modern Drama, 27*, 549-563.

Finke, L.A. (1984). Painting women: Images of femininity in Jacobean tragedy. *Theatre Journal, 36*, 357-370.

Forte, J. (1985). Rachel Rosenthal: Feminism and performance. *Women and Performance, 2*(2), 27-37.

Freedman, B. (1988). Frame up: Feminism, psychoanalysis, theatre.

Theatre Journal, 40, 375-397.

Freud, S. (1900). On Oedipus and Hamlet. Reproduced in B.F. Dukore (Ed.). (1974). *Dramatic theory and criticism: Greeks to Grotowski* (pp. 827-831). New York: Holt, Rinehart, and Winston.

Frye, N. (1957). *Anatomy of criticism.* Princeton, NJ: Princeton University Press.

Gardiner, J.K. (1980). Aphra Behn: Sexuality and self respect. *Women's Studies, 7,* 67-78.

Gayle, A. (1971). Introduction. In A. Gayle (Ed.), *The black aesthetic* (pp. xv-xxiv). Garden City, NY: Doubleday.

Gilder, R. (1931). *Enter the actress: The first women in the theatre.* New York: Theatre Arts Books.

Gildon, C. (1702). *Pamphlet.* (Cited in Hampsten, E. (1980). Petticoat authors: 1660-1720. *Women's Studies, 7,* 21-38).

Gillespie, P.P. (1978). Feminist theatre: A rhetorical phenomenon. *Quarterly Journal of Speech, 64,* 284-294.

Gillespie, P.P. (1981). America's women dramatists, 1960-1980. In H. Bock & A. Wertheim (Eds.), *Essays on contemporary American drama* (pp. 187-206). Munich: Max Hueber Verlag.

Gillespie, P.P. (1989a). Anna Cora Ogden Mowatt Ritchie's *Fairy Fingers:* From Eugene Scribe's? *Text and Performance Quarterly, 2,* 125-134.

Gillespie, P.P. (1989b). Wendy Wasserstein. In P.C. Kolin (Ed.), *American playwrights since 1945: A guide to scholarship, criticism, and performance* (pp. 447-456). Westport, CT: Greenwood Press.

Gillespie, P.P., & Cameron, K.M. (1984). *Western theatre: Revolution and revival.* New York: Macmillan.

Gonzalez, Y.B. (1989). Toward a re-vision of Chicano theatre history: The women of El Teatro Campesino. In L. Hart (Ed.), *Making a spectacle* (pp. 239-259). Ann Arbor: University of Michigan Press.

Gordon, L. (1986). What's new in women's history? In De Lauretis (Ed.), *Feminist studies/critical studies.* Bloomington: Indiana University Press.

Gottlieb, L.C. (1979). *Rachel Crothers.* Boston: Twayne Publishers.

Gottner-Abendroth, H. (1986). Nine principles of a matriarchal aesthetic. In G. Ecker (Ed.), *Feminist aesthetics* (pp. 81-94). Boston: Beacon Press.

Greeley, L. (1989). Martha Boesing: Playwright of performance. *Text and Performance Quarterly, 9,* 207-215.

Guerra, J. (1989). Beth Henley: Female quest and the family play tradition. In L. Hart (Ed.), *Making a spectacle* (pp. 118-130). Ann Arbor: University of Michigan Press.

Gussow, M. (1972, Feb. 22). New group to offer plays by women. *New York Times,* p. 44.

Gutwirth, M. (1982). Moliere and the woman question. *Theatre Journal, 34,* 344-359.

Hall, L. (1971). In the university. In T.B. Hess & E.C. Baker (Eds.), *Art and sexual politics* (pp. 130-146). New York: Macmillan.

Hampsten, E. (1980). Petticoat authors: 1660-1720. *Women's Studies, 7,* 21-38.

Hancock, B.R. (1972). Affirmation by negation in the women's liberation movement. *Quarterly Journal of Speech, 58,* 164-271.

Hart, L. (1989a). Megan Terry. In P.C. Kolin (Ed.), *American playwrights since 1945: A guide to scholarship, criticism, and performance* (pp. 447-456). Westport, CT: Greenwood Press.

Hart, L. (Ed.). (1989b). *Making a spectacle.* Ann Arbor: University of Michigan Press.

Haskell, M. (1974). *From reverence to rape: The treatment of women in the movies.* New York: Holt, Rinehart, and Winston.

Hatch, J.V. (1989). Here comes everybody: Scholarship and black theatre history. In T. Postelwait & B.A. McConachie (Eds.), *Interpreting the theatrical past: Essays in the historiography of performance* (pp. 148-165). Iowa City: University of Iowa Press.

Hawkesworth, M.E. (1989). Knowers, knowing, known: Feminist theory and claims to truth. *Signs, 14,* 533-557.

Hegel, G.W.F. (1818-1829). *The philosophy of art.* Selections reproduced in B. F. Dukore (Ed.). (1974). *Dramatic theory and criticism: Greeks to Grotowski* (pp. 526-532). New York: Holt, Rinehart, and Winston.

Helms, L. (1989). Playing the woman's part: Feminist criticism and Shakespearean performance. *Theatre Journal, 41,* 190-200.

Hennigan, S. (1983). *The woman director in the contemporary, professional theatre.* Unpublished doctoral dissertation, Washington State University, Pullman.

hooks, b. (1984). *From margin to center.* Boston: South End.

Horowitz, M.C. (1976). Aristotle and woman. *Journal of the History of Biology, 9,* 183-213.

Hozeski, B. (1975). Hildegard of Bingen's *Ordo Virtutum*: The earliest discovered liturgical morality play. *American Benedictine Review, 26,* 251-259.

Humm, M. (1986). Feminist literary criticism in America and England. In M. Monteith (Ed.), *Women's writing: A challenge to theory* (pp. 90-116). New York: St. Martin's Press.

Jameson, F. (1984). Periodizing the 60s. In *The ideologies of theory: Vol. II: Syntax of history* (pp. 178-208). Minneapolis: University of Minnesota Press.

Jameson, F. (1988). Beyond the cave: Demystifying the ideology of modernism. In *The ideologies of theory. Vol. II: Syntax of history* (pp.115-132). Minneapolis: University of Minnesota Press.

Jardine, L. (1983). *Still harping on daughters.* Sussex: Harvester.

Jenkins, L.W. (1981). Images. In H.K. Chinoy & L.K. Jenkins (Eds.), *Women in American theatre* (pp. 236-237). New York: Crown.

Jenkins, L.W., & Ogden-Malouf, S. (1985). The (female) actor prepares. *Theater, 17*(1), 66-69.

Johnson, C.D. (1975). That guilty third tier: Prostitution in nineteenth century American theatre. *American Quarterly, 27,* 574-584.

Johnson, C.D. (1984). *American actress: Perspective on the nineteenth century*. Chicago: Nelson Hall.

Kauffman, L. (Ed.). (1989). *Gender and theory: Dialogues on feminist criticism*. New York: Basil Blackwell.

Keyssar, H. (1985). *Feminist theatre*. New York: Grove.

Klein, E.S. (1962). *The development of the leading feminine character in selected librettos of American musicals from 1900 to 1960*. Unpublished doctoral dissertation, Columbia University, New York, NY.

Klein, K.G. (1984). Language and meaning in Megan Terry's 1970s musicals. *Modern Drama, 27*, 574-583.

Kolb, D.S. (1975). Rise and fall of the new woman in American drama. *Educational Theatre Journal, 27*, 149-160.

Kolodny, A. (1980). Dancing through the minefield: Some observations on the theory, practice, and politics of a feminist literary criticism. *Feminist Studies, 6*, 1-25.

Lacan, J. (1977). *Ecrits*. New York: Norton.

Lamb, M. (1971). *Plays of women's liberation: The Mod Donna & Scyklon Z*. New York: Pathfinder Press.

Langdell, C.D. (1985). Aphra Behn and sexual politics: A dramatist's discourse with her audience. In J. Redmond (Ed.), *Drama, sex, and politics: Vol. 7: Themes in drama* (pp. 109-128). Cambridge: Cambridge University Press.

Langer, S. (1953). *Feeling and form: A theory of art*. New York: Scribner.

Latta, C.J.D. (1987). The lady is a critic. In H.K. Chinoy & L.W. Jenkins (Eds.), *Women in American theatre* (pp. 226-233). New York: Theatre Communications Group.

Lauter, P. (1983). Race and gender in the shaping of the American literary canon: A case study from the twenties. *Feminist Studies, 9*, 435-464.

League of Professional Theatre Women/New York. (1983). *The director and designers report on sex discrimination in theatre*. New York: Author.

Leavitt, D. (1980). *Feminist theatre groups*. Jefferson, NC: McFarland.

Leclercq, L. (1869). *Les decors, les costumes et la mise en scene au XVIIe siecle, 1615-1680*. Paris.

Lerner, G. (1986). *The creation of patriarchy*. Oxford: Oxford University Press.

Levine, L. (1986). Men in women's clothing: Anti-theatricality and effeminization from 1579-1642. *Criticism: A Quarterly for Literature and the Arts, 28*, 121-142.

Lipking, L. (1984). Aristotle's sister: A poetics of abandonment. In R. von Hallberg (Ed.), *Canons* (pp. 85-105). Chicago: University of Chicago Press.

Lippard, L. (1976). *From the center: Feminist essays on women's art*. New York: E. P. Dutton.

Lorde, A. (1981). The master's tools will never dismantle the master's house. In E. Moraga & G. Anzaldua (Eds.), *This bridge called my back* (pp.98-101). Watertown, MA: Persephone Press.

Lukacs, G. (1909). The sociology of modern drama. Reproduced in B.F. Dukore (Ed.). (1974). *Dramatic theory and criticism: Greeks to Grotowski* (pp. 933-941). New York: Holt, Rinehart, and Winston.

MacDonald, J. (1988). Lesser ladies of the Victorian stage. *Theatre Research International, 13*, 234-249.

Malpede, K. (Ed.). (1983). *Women and theatre: Compassion and hope.* New York: Drama Book Publishers.

Marohl, J. (1987). De-realized women: Performance and identity in *Top Girls. Modern Drama, 30*, 376-388.

Marre, D. (1985). What to do when thrust is out. In J. Redmond (Ed.), *Drama, sex, and politics: Vol. 7: Themes in drama* (pp. 221-228). Cambridge: Cambridge University Press.

Mason, L.C. (1983). *The fight to be an American woman and a playwright: A critical history from 1772 to the present.* Unpublished doctoral dissertation, University of California-Berkeley.

Matthews, B. (1916). *A book about the theatre.* New York: Scribner's Sons.

Maus, K. (1987). Horns of a dilemma: Jealousy, gender, and spectatorship in English Renaissance drama. *ELH, 54*, 561-562.

McConachie, B.A. (1985). Towards a postpositivist theatre history. *Theatre Journal, 37*, 465-486.

McDowell, D. (1985). New directions for black feminist criticism. In E. Showalter (Ed.), *The new feminist criticism* (pp. 186-199). New York: Pantheon.

McLennan, G. (1981). *Marxism and the methodologies of history.* London: Verso.

Mersand, J. (1937). When ladies write plays. *Players Magazine, 14*(1), 8.

Messer-Davidow, E. (1989). The philosophical bases of feminist literary criticism. In L. Kauffman (Ed.), *Gender and theory: Dialogues on feminist criticism* (pp. 63-106) . New York: Basil Blackwell.

Miller, N. (1986). *The poetics of gender.* New York: Columbia University Press.

Mohrmann, R. (1986). Occupation: Woman artist—on the changing relations between a woman and artistic production. In G. Ecker (Ed.), *Feminist aesthetics* (pp. 150-161). Boston: Beacon Press.

Monteith, M. (Ed.). (1986). *Women's writing: A challenge to theory.* New York: St. Martin's Press.

Morgan, F. (1981). *The female wits.* London: Virago.

Mraz, D. (1967). *The changing image of female characters in the works of Tennessee Williams.* Unpublished doctoral dissertation, University of Southern California, Los Angeles.

Mulvey, L. (1975). Visual pleasure and narrative cinema. *Screen, 16*(3), 6-18.

Murray, G. (1912). Excursus on the ritual forms preserved in Greek tragedy. In J.E. Harrison (Ed.), *Themis* (pp. 341-363). Cambridge: Cambridge University Press.

Nachlin, L. (1971). Why have there been no great women artists? In T.B.

Hess & E.C. Baker (Eds.), *Art and sexual politics* (pp. 1-39). New York: St. Martin's Press.

Nagler, A.M. (1959). *A sourcebook in theatrical history.* New York: Dover.

Natalle, E.J. (1985). *Feminist theatre: A study in persuasion.* Metuchen, NJ: Scarecrow Press.

Nathan, G.J. (1942). *The entertainment of a nation, Or three sheets in the wind.* New York: Alfred A Knopf.

National Commission on the Observance of International Women's Year. (1976). *The creative woman: A report of the committee on the arts and humanities.* Washington, DC: Department of State.

Natoli, J. (Ed.). (1987). *Tracing literary theory.* Chicago: University of Chicago Press.

Neal, L. (1971). Black arts movement. In A. Gayle (Ed.), *The black aesthetic* (pp. 272-290). Garden City, NY: Doubleday.

Nicoll, A. M. (1963). *The World of Harlequin: A critical study of the Commedia dell' Arte.* Cambridge: Cambridge University Press.

O'Brien, S. (1983). The image of women in Tony-award winning plays. *Journal of American Culture, 6,* 45-49.

Offen, K. (1988). Defining feminism: A comparative historical approach. *Signs, 14,* 132-143.

Olauson, J. (1981). *The American woman playwright: A view of criticism and characterization.* Troy, NY: Whitston Publishing.

Orgel, S. (1989). Nobody's perfect: Or, why did the English stage take boys for women. *The South Atlantic Quarterly, 88,* 7-29.

Parker, R., & Pollock, G. (1981). *Old mistresses: Women, art and ideology.* New York: Pantheon.

Parrott, S.F. (1988). Networking in Italy: Charlotte Cushman and the white marmorean flock. *Women's Studies, 14,* 305-338.

Peirce, C.S. (1981). *Writings of Charles S. Peirce: A chronological edition* (4 vols.) (Ed. M. Fisch). Bloomington: Indiana University Press.

Phelan, P. (1988). Feminist theory, poststructuralism, and performance. *The Drama Review, 32*(1), 107-127.

Plato. (c.373 B.C.). *The Republic, Book X.* Reproduced in B.K. Dukore (Ed.). (1974). *Dramatic theory and criticism: Greeks to Grotowski* (pp. 12-31). New York: Holt, Rinehart, and Winston.

Postlewait, T. (1988). The concept of periodization in theatre history. *Theatre Journal, 40,* 299-318.

Pribram, E.D. (Ed.). (1988). *Female spectators: Looking at film and television.* New York: Verson.

Rea, C. (1972). Women's theatre groups. *The Drama Review, 16*(2), 79-89.

Rea, C. (1974). Women for women. *The Drama Review, 18*(4), 77-87.

Reinelt, J. (1986). Beyond Brecht: Britain's new feminist drama. *Theatre Journal, 38,* 154-164.

Reinhardt, N. (1981). New directions for feminist criticism in theatre and the related arts. *Soundings: An Interdisciplinary Journal, 64,* 361-387.

Rich, A. (1976). Women's studies: Renaissance or revolution. *Women's Studies, 3*, 121-126.

Richards, S.L. (1982). Negative forces and positive non-entitities: Images of women in the dramas of Baraka. *Theatre Journal, 34*, 233-240.

Richards, S.L. (1983). Conflicting images in the plays of Ntozake Shange. *Black American Literature Forum, 17*, 73-78.

Robinson, A.M., Roberts, V.M., & Barranger, M.S. (Eds.). (1989). *Notable women in the American theatre*. Westport, CT: Greenwood Press.

Robortellus, F. (1548). On comedy. Reproduced in B.F. Dukore (Ed.). (1974). *Dramatic theory and criticism: Greeks to Grotowski* (pp. 125-130). New York: Holt, Rinehart, and Winston.

Rosenberg. J. (1983). *Women's reflections: The feminist film movement*. Ann Arbor, MI: UMI Research Press.

Savona, J.L. (1984). French feminism and theatre: An introduction. *Modern Drama, 27*, 540-545.

Schaffer, P.W. (1966). *The position of women in society as reflected in serious American dramas from 1890-1928*. Unpublished doctoral dissertation, Stanford University, Stanford, CA.

Schneider, R. (1989). Holly Hughes: Polymorphous perversity and the lesbian scientists. *The Drama Review, 33*, 171-183.

Schuler, C. (1990). Spectator response and comprehension: The problem of Karen Finley's *Constant State of Desire*. *The Drama Review, 34*(1), 131-145.

Segal, S., & Sklar, R. (1983). The women's experimental theatre. *The Drama Review, 27*, 74-75.

Shafer, Y. (1974). The liberated woman in American plays of the past. *Players Magazine, 49*(3/4), 95-100.

Shafer, Y. (1981). Women in male roles: Charlotte Cushman and others. In H.K. Chinoy & L.W. Jenkins (Eds.), *Women in American theatre* (pp. 74-81). New York: Crown.

Showalter, E. (1981). Feminist criticism in the wilderness. *Critical Inquiry, 8*, 179-205.

Showalter, E. (1986). Piecing and writing. In N.K. Miller (Ed.), *The poetics of gender* (pp. 222-247). New York: Columbia University Press.

Signorelli, P.N. (1787-1790). *Storia critica dei teatri antichi e moderni, 6* vols. Naples, Italy: Presso Vincenzo Orsino.

Smith, B. (1985). Toward a black feminist criticism. In E. Showalter (Ed.), *The new feminist criticism* (pp. 168-185). New York: Pantheon.

Solomon, A. (1985). The WOW cafe. *The Drama Review, 29*(1), 92-101.

Speakman, D. (1989). The next stage: Devaluation, revaluation, and after. In J. Redmond (Ed.), *Women in theatre. Vol. 11: Themes in drama* (pp. 221-252). Cambridge: Cambridge University Press.

Spencer, J. S. (1987). Norman's 'Night Mother. *Modern Drama, 30*, 364-375.

Stephens, J.A. (1981). Women in Pulitzer prize plays, 1918-1949. In H.K. Chinoy & L.W. Jenkins (Eds.), *Women in American theatre* (pp. 243-251). New York: Crown.

Stephens, J.L. (1982). *Why marry?* The new woman of 1918. *Theatre Journal, 34,* 183-196.
Stephens, J.L. (1989a). Subverting the demon-angel dichotomy: Innovation and feminist intervention in twentieth-century drama. *Text and Performance Quarterly, 1,* 53-64
Stephens, J.L. (1989b). Gender ideology and dramatic convention in progressive era plays, 1890-1920. *Theatre Journal, 41,* 45-55.
Sutherland, C. (1978). American women playwrights as mediators of the woman problem. *Modern Drama, 21,* 319-336.
Tener, R.L. (1975). Theatre of identity: Adrienne Kennedy's portrait of the black woman. *Studies in Black Literature, 6,* 1-5.
Trotter, C. (1705). *Works.* (Cited in Cotton, N. (1980). *Women playwrights in England c. 1363-1750* (pp. 81-121). Lewisburg, PA: Bucknell University Press).
Turner, S.H.R. (1982). *Images of black women in the plays of black female playwrights.* Unpublished doctoral dissertation, Bowling Green State University, Bowling Green, OH.
Venables, C. (1980). The woman director in the theatre. *Theatre Quarterly, 10*(38), 3-8.
Vince, R.W. (1989). Theatre history as an academic discipline. In T. Postelwait & B.A. McConachie (Eds.), *Interpreting the theatrical past* (pp. 1-18). Iowa City: University of Iowa Press.
Vincinus, M. (1979). Happy times if you can stand it: Women entertainers during the interwar years in England. *Theatre Journal, 31,* 357-360.
von Hallberg, R. (Ed.). (1984). *Canons.* Chicago: University of Chicago Press.
Vunovich, N. (1966). *The women in the plays of Eugene O'Neill.* Unpublished doctoral dissertation, University of Kansas, Lawrence.
Wandor, M. (1980). Political theatre for the eighties. *Theatre Quarterly, 9,* 28-30.
Wandor, M. (1984). The fifth column: Feminism and theatre. *Drama, 152,* 5-9.
Wandor, M. (1986). *Carry on, understudies.* New York: Routledge & Kegan Paul.
Where are the women playwrights? (1972, May 20). *New York Times,* pp. D1-3.
Weigel, S. (1986). Double focus: On the history of women's writing. In G. Ecker (Ed.), *Feminist aesthetics* (pp. 59-80). Boston: Beacon Press.
Wiley, C. (1957). *A study of the American woman as she is presented in the American drama of the 1920s.* Unpublished doctoral dissertation, University of New Mexico, Albuquerque.
Wiley, C. (1989). The matter with manners: The new woman and the problem play. In J. Redmond (Ed.), *Women in theatre. Vol. 11: Themes in drama* (pp. 109-128). Cambridge: Cambridge University Press.
Wilkerson, M.G. (1989). Music as metaphor: New plays of black women. In L. Hart (Ed.), *Making a spectacle* (pp. 61-75). Ann Arbor:

University of Michigan Press.

Willis, S. (1985). Helene Cixous' *Portrait de Dora*: The unseen and the un-scene. *Theatre Journal, 37*, 287-301.

Woolf, V. (1957). *A room of one's own*. New York: Harcourt, Brace, Jovanovitch.

Yarbro-Bejarno, Y. (1986). The female subject in Chicano theatre: Sexuality, race, and class. *Theatre Journal, 38*, 389-407.

Young, K. (1933). *The drama of the medieval church* (2 vols.). Oxford: Clarendon Press.

Zahler, W.P. (1973). *The husband and wife relationship in American drama from 1919-1939*. Unpublished doctoral dissertation, Kent State University, Kent, OH.

Zeig, S. (1984). The actor as activator: Deconstructing gender through gesture. *Women and Performance, 2*(2), 12-17.

Zivanovic, J. (1989). The rhetorical and political foundations of women's collaborative theatre. In J. Redmond (Ed.), *Women in theatre. Vol. 11: Themes in drama* (pp. 209-220). Cambridge: Cambridge University Press.

Chapter 7

Opposites in an Oppositional Practice: Rhetorical Criticism and Feminism

Celeste Michelle Condit
University of Georgia
Athens, GA

In the Western academy, rhetoric is the oldest profession. The first teachers in classical Greece were sophists, who sought to educate Greek males in the art of statesmanship by teaching them the art of public deliberation (Murphy, 1983). Like most academic disciplines, rhetoric has always been male dominated, but unlike other disciplines, the gendering of rhetoric has been ambiguous. Rhetoric was "run out of town" by the highly masculine culture of the Romans in favor of the more manly practice of philosophy. In the Middle Ages, when top-down control by the patriarchal church was pervasive, rhetoric was defrocked as the "harlot of the arts." When the heavily male enlightenment and the exclusive privileging of objectivized rationality replaced the patriarchal church, the academic marginalization of "dame" rhetoric continued.

Historically, rhetoric has thus been treated largely as the despised and feared old maid of the Western academy. Rhetoric, however, is not only a realm of study, but also a real-world practice, and in the world of public politics it has always been of great importance. The gendering of rhetoric as a political practice has been equally problematic. Some believe that rhetoric as a practice has provided the feminized alternative to male violence as a central organizing tool and method for constructing social behavior. As McGee (1980b) has pointed out, it was through the feminine rhetorical practices of a woman ruler, Queen Elizabeth I, that liberty's encroachment on monarchy was accomplished.

The contrary perspective holds that rhetoric has historically been a "manly" art because it is the tool of the public sphere—a sphere that men have allocated to themselves. It has thus frequently been a coercive art (Gearheart, 1979). The ambiguity of the gender preferences of rhetorical practice has been further emphasized by Jamieson (1988), who points out that the rise of the mass media has resulted in the replacement of a "manly" style of speaking with a feminine style.

This deeply based disagreement about the gendering of rhetoric suggests that rhetoric, rather than being either a masculine pursuit or a feminine deviation, may constitute a true hermaphrodite. As such, it may be capable of generating a gynandrous world—one in which persons of any biological sex, employing ranges of the qualities we have historically misallocated to "masculine" and "feminine" realms, work playfully together in a variety of shapes and combinations. To realize the full fertility of rhetoric, however, we must make revisions in theory, for the fact that rhetoric has been dressed primarily in the past by men has left it with a scanty wardrobe. This chapter will, therefore, proceed by offering a broad sketch of the current knowledge of rhetoric, especially in rhetorical criticism. It will then describe some of the major shortcomings that have arisen from the biases engendered by male domination. Finally, it will suggest some directions for future gynandrous work in rhetorical studies.

THE HERMAPHRODITIC POTENTIAL OF RHETORIC

Rhetoric was defined by Aristotle as "the faculty [power] of discovering in the particular case, what are the available means of persuasion" (Aristotle/1932/350 B.C., p. 7). Today, the term is usually defined more broadly, and most rhetorical theorists are distinguished by their adoption of a perspective that sees communication (especially language use) as *situated historical action*. This perspective defines rhetoric as a distinctive discipline by adopting basic assumptions unshared in other academic departments. First, by placing language in a specific *historical context*, rhetoricians set their work off from that of philosophers, the majority of whom have tended to view language use in terms of timeless truths. A philosopher, for example, might ask "what is *justice*?" whereas a rhetorician would ask "how did Hitler employ linguistic resources to construct an understanding of public *justice* that legitimized the killing of Jews as scapegoats for Germany's financial woes?"

The second distinctive component of the rhetorical perspective focuses on the treatment of language as serious and efficacious public *action*. Mainstream sociologists, political scientists, and historians might be interested in how Hitler accomplished his evil deeds, but they would tend to look to causes other than language usage. They would assume that language was merely some epiphenomenon of "underlying forces." In contrast, most rhetorical theorists assume that the rhetoric itself is a significant action. They believe either that language alone constructs the social judgments upon which governments act, or that linguistic processes mediate underlying political and economic forces to produce unique social compromises.

Rhetorical theory thus tends to posit language usage as a vital component of human life. By viewing language usage as action, rhetoricians also assume a strategic dimension to communication. They presume that people are often trying to accomplish particular goals with their auditors when they engage in speaking. Rather than simply "expressing" themselves in a reflexive manner, according to rhetorical perspectives, people may sometimes *intend* to bring about specific conditions when they speak in the ways they do (at least within the bounds of their knowledge).

The character of rhetorical knowledge forms the last definitional boundary of rhetorical theory. In the Western philosophical and scientific traditions, rhetoric has been placed at the opposite pole from knowledge. Plato contrasted rhetoric to philosophical dialectic, suggesting that rhetoric was incapable of providing knowledge of "permanent forms" so that it could not give us any Truths worth knowing. After the scientific enlightenment, scientists similarly disparaged rhetoric, suggesting that only scientific methods could produce truths of any value. Both the philosophical and scientific arguments are based on the assumption that there is permanent and certain knowledge, and that this is the only kind of knowledge worth having. It is true that rhetoric does not give certain knowledge: that is not what it is designed to do. Rhetoric, as Aristotle recognized, gives knowledge of the probable. That is, rhetoric as a way of knowing calls on us to bring to bear all the human resources we have, and to employ human communication as a collective means of coming to the best understanding of an issue that our time and situation will allow. This kind of probabilistic knowledge is extremely vital, for it forms the basis of most human action. We can never know with certainty whether a given piece of legislation or an act of foreign policy will be the best choice, but if we do not act on the basis of the best arguments we have, we are behaving in a fashion that is irresponsible. Even in the minor case where we believe that we are probably going to be happier with owning car "A" than "B" (on the basis of consumer information, personal taste, recommendations by friends, and salespersons' pitches), it would be foolish to flip a coin and take whatever chance gives us on the grounds that we cannot know which choice is better "for certain." The limitations of such probabilistic knowledge are frustrating only to those who posit the false possibility of having certain knowledge over such contingent affairs.

Rhetoric thus explores the role of language usage in the crucial

area of collective human decision making. It does so through three different approaches—rhetorical theory (and its history), the history of public
address, and rhetorical criticism. These three approaches to the understanding of strategic language usage are intertwined with each other and
they share a political stance. They tend to presume that a political system
is good to the extent that it makes its decisions based on open argument
and bad to the extent that those decisions are based on other factors (especially economic and other forms of coercion). Consequently, rhetorical
criticism has always included a strong oppositional practice. Rhetorical
critics, precisely because they believe that public knowledge is arrived at
through the agonistic practices of public rhetoric, are comfortable situating
themselves in opposition to mainstream rhetorics and in support of con-
testing groups and ideas. Often, the "mainstream" is precisely that which
is already receiving substantial and ordinary social support. If the critic is
to make a social contribution, based on insight and knowledge beyond the
norm, this may even *require* an oppositional stance (Klumpp & Hollihan,
1989; Scott & Smith, 1969; Wander & Jenkins, 1972). Such a stance can
be either progressive, leftist, or reactionary conservative, but it is often progressive, again because the tenets of rhetorical theory support a progressive, evolutionary method of social change, rather than conservative stasis
or force-engendered revolution.

As a consequence of these oppositional elements, rhetorical criticism has a relationship to feminism that is somewhat unusual in the academy. Rhetorical criticism is incorporating progressive feminism with relatively minor hostility. If we define feminist studies broadly as those scholarly efforts that seek to increase our understanding of women's lives, their
interests, and the social structures that gender human beings, we might
perceive two by-products of the assimilation process. First, that the
absorbed feminism has influenced rhetorical criticism to make changes of
degree (see below), and second, that a separate feminist critical doctrine
has not developed with any breadth and depth. Some feminists would
applaud and celebrate this easy evolutionary incorporation of feminist perspectives into rhetorical criticism, others (usually of radical and socialist
persuasions) would lament it as a lost opportunity for revolution.

Before adopting condemnatory or celebratory stances, it is probably best to explore in greater detail the parameters of current critical practice in rhetoric. I will divide this exploration along the lines of the two
overarching approaches to rhetorical theory that are most common. The
oldest school is that described by Bitzer (1968) as the "situational"
approach. The other perspective is the "positional" school.

Situational theories focus on an individual rhetor and the rhetor's
immediate audience. They assume that a speaker intentionally responds to
some preexisting exigence by particular and largely intentional communi-

cation choices, which are constrained by various factors in a fairly narrowly defined historical context. Those employing the situational perspective tend to assume that the context, as viewed from the perspective of the speaker or the immediate audience, is the *full* context. Thus, election-year speeches are analyzed in terms of those factors that relate directly to the campaign (e.g., the issues at stake, the images constructed by the various candidates, or the events that happen during the campaign). Similarly, a eulogy is viewed in the historical context framed by the death of the person who is the subject of the eulogy, the goals and purposes of that individual's life, as well as the goals and purposes of the speaker and audience. Therefore, from the situational perspective, the relatively immediate response to the speech by the immediate audience provides a major criterion for judgment of the speech.

In contrast to this individualistic perspective, the positional orientation focuses on broader historical contexts and more numerous rhetorical agents. Advocates of this perspective, including Hariman (1986), McGee (1980a), McKerrow (1989), and Wander (1984), assume that any successful speaker is the representative of a large number of other persons. The speaker has experienced some set of social conditions shared by a large number of people and is articulating those conditions in a way that others find convincing. From this positional perspective, the context is probably broader than the specific issue the speaker addresses. The speaker will target some event, institution, or other social element that can be used cogently to represent the broad and diffuse social conditions at issue, but will not be able to name and explain all of the factors underlying the urge to speak and the audience's urge to listen. In this view, the rhetorician's job is to understand the speech in terms of the broad context of social forces in operation. Often, these broader forces will include the shape of the economic system and the modes of reproduction in the society, but other forces may be important as well (e.g., environmental deterioration, technological developments, or ethnic relations). Finally, from a positional perspective, the immediate audience is not the end point of the event. Instead, the greatest importance rests in the habits of vocabulary that are either created or reinforced by the speaker and the fit of such usages within the entire score of the public vocabulary.

Both of these perspectives—the situational and the positional— posit rhetoric as human action situated in specific historical contexts. They simply focus on broader or more narrow contexts; ultimately, of course, this makes the difference between the two approaches a matter of degree. This difference, however, has led to substantially different critical practices.

Situational Criticism

The situational perspective has grown out of the pedagogical tradition. That is, the situational perspective is closely tied with the sophistic practice of teaching individual speakers how to give persuasive speeches. It is therefore generally a prescriptive theory—offering guidelines for desirable rhetorical practices, rather than simply describing what the normal rhetorical practices are. For this reason, situational criticism tends to evaluate the speaking of individuals on a variety of grounds including truthfulness, morality, and artistry. The central ground, however, is usually effectiveness, that is, the success of the discourse in doing all that is possible to achieve the goals of the rhetor.

The oldest method of rhetorical criticism to employ the situational perspective is neo-Aristotelianism. The neo-Aristotelian critic utilizes the classical writings of rhetorical theorists as a kind of template by which to judge a single speech, usually by an important rhetor. Most frequently, the inventional skills of the speaker are evaluated: How sound is the logic? How appropriate are the emotional appeals? How good a job does the speaker do at using and crafting an effective ethos (Hill, 1972)? Another frequent object of attention is stylistic choice. Critics evaluate the use of metaphors, the sound of the language, and other stylistic dimensions (Weidhorn, 1972). Often, the delivery skills and arrangement are also open to comment (Fulkerson, 1979).

The major limitation of this approach was that it requires the critic to accept the values and concerns of the audience and the speaker as though they were adequate and all encompassing. As the work of Hill suggests, if a speaker makes an argument that the audience is likely to accept, no matter how repugnant that argument, the critic is put in the position of labeling the argument "good rhetoric." For this reason and others, many critics, led by feminists (Campbell, 1972b; S. K. Foss, 1989), have abandoned neo-Aristotelian criticism.

There have been, however, less constrained uses of the situational perspective. The award-winning essay by Patton (1977) provides one classic example (see also the essays in Leff & Kauffeld, 1989). Patton explores Carter's rhetorical choices in terms of their fitness for the times, but he also manages to promote a positive value norm for political campaigning in the process. Similarly, by focusing on laudable rhetoric, Leff and Mohrmann (1974) have managed to employ the situational perspective in a series of studies that illuminate and laud inclusive and important human values. More technical studies have taken situationalism in other directions as well. Ryan's work (1981) has provided insight into the crafting of important speeches, thus illuminating the process of rhetorical composition by major political leaders. Additionally, a large group of formalists have worked within the situational perspective. Influenced by literary criticism or structuralist approaches, these additional areas of study are illustrated by Benson's (1980) depiction of the rhetorical structure of the Wiseman films, Olson's (1983) exploration of the rhetorical iconography of Norman Rockwell, and McGuire's (1977) examination of the mythic structure of *Mein Kampf*.

The situational perspective has housed feminist works of importance, as well as works on progressive topics of interest to feminists. The study of Elizabeth Cady Stanton's rhetoric by Campbell is one classic example (1980; see also 1989). This is joined by essays on a variety of other feminist figures (Japp, 1985; Kendall & Fisher, 1974), as well as by progressive works on topics of interest to feminists, such as African-American rhetoric (Jefferson, 1967) and the environment (Oravec, 1984). Feminist situational criticism has also been active in expanding the focus of rhetoricians to popular movies as situated action (Rushing, 1986, 1989).

As Campbell (1973), Solomon (1988a), and others have noted, however, there are inherent tensions between the situational perspective and feminism. Given that women rhetors have traditionally had problems of ethos that ran very deep, and that their rhetoric has always demanded a great deal from their audiences, the situational perspective, because it focuses on successful adaptation to immediate audiences, is more likely than not to find women deficient as orators. This has resulted in a call for new criteria, a call in part for new rhetorical theories (Jenefsky, 1989).

Positional Criticism

In contrast to the situational perspective, which highlights the actions of individuals in very narrowly defined historical events, the positional perspective highlights the broad and mostly anonymous shifts and forces of language in history. Burke's (1945) claim that language has "substance" is of particular importance. If language has substance, then the coming and going of different terms as guides for a collectivity is of significance. The shift away from the 18th-century term "liberty" towards "equality" and "freedom" in the 20th century is, by this account, of great consequence. Those studying rhetorical position thus explore the broad changes in the vocabularies used by various collectives to express themselves and, thereby, to coordinate social action through laws, attitudes, and practices. McGee and Martin's (1983) charting of the historical development of the term "public servant" is illustrative of this approach. Some social movement studies are thus positional (Newman, 1975), while others are more situational (Andrews, 1973; Zarefsky, 1986).

The concept of rhetoric as "expression" is, from the positional perspective, of central importance. The use of terms, if they are to be "substantial," is tied to the experiences of the audience members who affirm them. Terms may be linked to the experience of fairly narrow groups, as, for example, the term "right to choice" is arguably of most interest to women, especially white women of the American middle and working classes. Terms may also be more general in their linkages to the broad interests of many human beings—although the claim to generality is usually disputed (thus, I believe that "freedom" is an important term for most human beings, but some socialists would disagree; some might even challenge the universality of the term "justice"). The study of which terms get included at which periods of time is therefore an extremely important gauge of the overall representativeness and fairness of a society. If some members do not have their interests and experiences expressed in the public vocabulary, it is virtually impossible to have their interests protected in the laws of the land. Thus, the work of Wander (1984) has pointed out repeatedly that one of the most important tasks of the rhetorician is to study the silences in the public vocabulary, to trace out the "third persona" missing from the discourse. His studies join the substantial body of work by those who have explored various vocabularies as expressions of the different interests and experiences of competing groups (S.K. Foss, 1979; Solomon, 1979).

Like the situationalists, positionalists are interested in judging rhetoric. Rather than making their criteria those of pedagogically based rhetorical theories, however, positionalists tend to look at broader criteria. Most frequently, their judgment tends to be based on criteria of social morality (see Fisher 1987; Frentz, 1985). These criteria can arise from a number of sources, but often they are linked to the component of the discourse on which the critic is focusing. Sometimes these criteria arise from inventional factors such as logical adequacy (Bormann, 1973). At other times they transform the concept of individual ethos into a social concept—assessing the adequacy of the inclusion of a range of voices and images in the public vocabulary (Condit 1987; Wander 1984). At still other times, these criteria arise from stylistic concerns (Black, 1970). For example, in a brilliant analysis of metaphor, Ivie has traced the adequacy of the rhetorics of pro- and anti-nuclear advocates (1987).

The character of positional studies also allows them to work at times without explicit judgments. Scholars may simply describe the competing visions of those speaking from different historical positions without making formal judgments about them, or they may describe the development of discursive units (Osborne, 1977) or the characteristics of historical eras and their causes (Black, 1976). It is in this manner that feminist interests entered positional studies of rhetoric. The work of S.K. Foss (1979) and Solomon (1979) on the ERA maintained this nonjudgmental stance, as did that of Railsback (1984) and Vanderford (1989) on abortion, and Jablonski (1988) on feminists in the Catholic church. This nonpartisan stance eased the introduction of issues of concern to women by limiting the range of controversies with which the authors had to deal.

As a whole, the positionalist perspective on rhetoric is younger than that of situationalism, and is yet underdeveloped. It has produced fewer textbooks, although it has a growing body of critical studies. Its basic direction, however, leads toward an exploration of how people in groups and broader collectives cooperate and contest to construct shared public vocabularies that form the substance of human collectivity. Positionalism experiences no fundamental tensions with feminism, and similar to situational criticism, it has been productive in both feminist studies and in other works of broad interest to women, as well as having produced works that consider a broader range of media (Kidd, 1975; Schwichtenberg, 1983). Both major perspectives in rhetorical criticism have thus been employed in some ways by feminist critics. But in neither arena have feminists yet addressed all the pertinent issues. Several concerns need further attention.

The Short-Comings of Male-Dominated Rhetorical Theories

The simplest problem for rhetorical studies from a feminist point of view is the continued linguistic sexism of some writers. Some authors continue to make their work unpalatable and unusable for feminist critics when they persist in using *non*generic pronouns (i.e., "he" and "man" when they mean "she or he" and "humans," e.g., Black, 1988; Hauser, 1986). Let us rehearse the issues one more tedious time. First, using "he" except when one means to denote males violates the first and most important canon of rhetorical style—it is unclear. The audience cannot be sure whether the talk is only about males, or whether females are to be included too.

Second, the term is not truly inclusive. Many of us read some works and feel deliberately and completely excluded when the author speaks about scholars as "he." Third, quite a few studies show that for many people masculine pronouns call up only masculine images. Read the following paragraph by Black (1988) and ask yourself if you and he are thinking of men and women or only of men:

> the ascetic is initiated into a higher mystery, and he proclaims himself wealthy.
>   He is himself now possessed, secured, but by a supernal agent. He has become the proprietary equivalent of an unpossessable natural object. He has broken through to a different realm of reflexive vocabulary, and he becomes mystifying in a different way. (p. 142)

Black uses masculine pronouns because he is still thinking exclusively about men. We have only to compare the way in which female asceticism turns outward to other love to grasp this (see Kuseki, 1988). When the Speech Communication Association bestowed its Golden Anniversary award on this prose, it continued to sanction this antiquated male-biased approach to scholarship. The reaction to this essay should have been embarrassment at its datedness, not accolades.

A second and more complex problem created by the male domination of rhetorical criticism is the dependency of situationalism on a closed and male-dominated "canon." The canon is the set of speeches and other rhetorical documents that are taken as models of human eloquence. They help form the standards of good speaking, and are most frequently taught to students as touchstones. This canon is overwhelmingly biased towards men, especially towards white men of the Western tradition. Campbell (1989) has launched a sustained attack on this closed canon, and is working diligently to recover the eloquence of women and to force the inclusion of women's works in the standard texts and histories (the same thing needs to be done with regard to other historically underrepresented groups). This entails, however, much more than simply adding new names to our indexes, for the ways in which women's speech is eloquent are sometimes different from the conventional criteria applied to eloquence (that of formal grammar, elite "taste," or poetic "sublimity"). Groups that are not educated by elite institutions or taught the rules of classic western poetry often express themselves with stunning power and in beautiful ways, but they often violate the classic norms of Western rhetoric to do so. Rewriting the canon thus involves rewriting the sets of criteria that are used in evaluating rhetorical performances as well. It may also require the production of multiple canons and multiple criteria, rather than singular ones (Condit, 1990b).

A third fundamental problem in contemporary rhetorical criticism arises from the public/private split. Historically, rhetoric has been a study of the public realm. Because men have dominated that realm, men are bound to dominate any historical studies. There are several ways to address that historical bias. One is simply to accept it, realizing that as social change continues, more and more women are being included in public oratory. To some extent, as academics who wish to retain an accurate account of history, we must admit the inadequacies of the past. Such acceptance is subject to a revision of the historical record to recover those many important speakers who have been neglected.

A second approach to the public/private split is to denounce the public realm, urging the dissolution of this split. Many feminists have done so, especially those influenced by socialism. They argue that we should attempt to create a world in which the concept of private life becomes

obsolete, as the concept of the individual is effaced in notions of relationships (Jagger, 1988). They argue further that relationality is a woman's
concept and that individuality is a male concept. Thus, to create a relational society in place of an individualist one is to replace a male-favoring
society with a female-favoring one. I tend to disagree—I think human
beings are best served by a *combination* of relationship and individuality,
and, hence, I believe that the concept of a private life, in which a person
can develop his/her own potential, sheltered from duties and the coercion
of others, is as important for women as it is for men. I would suggest that
there is a need to realign the definition of public responsibilities and private rights so that they are just to women and encourage them to develop
their own capabilities in the areas they want. Whichever path we take—
whether it be socialist or a combined individual/social approach—we are
talking about fairly radical revisions in rhetorical practice and theory.

A third way to address the bias constituted by the grounding of
rhetoric in the public sphere is to transfer rhetorical studies to private and
organizational spheres as well. It is fully legitimate to study interpersonal
decision making and organizational decision making in line with the classic rhetorical model and little of this has been done. Some work in this
area explores the power relations implicit in interpersonal practices; other
studies examine the interpersonal transmission of vocabularies that shape
and influence women's personal lives (e.g., images of female slenderness;
Spitzack, 1988).

A final approach has been to suggest the sublation of rhetorical
studies in favor of communication studies (Gearheart, 1979; and in part,
Foss & Foss, 1991). To some extent that has occurred. The majority of
methodologically explicit feminist studies in the last 10 years have been in
the realm of interpersonal communication. Not surprisingly, I disagree
with this path. I believe that, whatever its flaws, for the foreseeable future
rhetoric will continue to be the way in which democratic governments
make decisions. For feminists to abandon the study of rhetoric is to abandon an important arena of power.

In addition to the issues of canon formation and the status of the
public focus of rhetoric, a feminist critique also challenges specific areas
and tools of rhetorical studies. It would be impossible to examine all of the
available tools, but let us glance briefly at one as an example of the kind
of gaps that are hiding in male-stream work. In the second half of the 20th
century, rhetorical criticism has returned repeatedly to narratively based
tools, whether in the form of Bormann's fantasy theme analysis, Fisher's
narrative paradigm, or Burke's dramatism. In some ways, these perspectives have been hospitable to feminist insights, but there are problems that
require further analysis. Burke's dramatism provides the single largest
source of critical activity, so I will use it to indicate the direction and

depth of the issues that require exploration.

Burke's dramatistic perspective has been employed with good effect by many female scholars (e.g., Carlson, 1988; Kuseki, 1988). However, serious problems are embedded in Burke's masculinist biases. These can be pointed to in a most concise fashion if we simply consider his definition of "man." Burke's use of the *non*generic male designation accurately points out only male culture, not female culture, as is evident if we contrast his view with other possibilities. Note how inauthentic it sounds if we replace Burke's "man" with "woman" to see if the definition truly is generic. His definition might then read:

> Woman is
> the symbol-using (symbol-making, symbol-misusing) animal
> inventor of the negative (or moralized by the negative)
> separated from her natural condition by instruments of her own making
> goaded by the spirit of hierarchy (or moved by the sense of order)
> and rotten with perfection. (Burke, 1968, p.16)

For me, it does not ring true. Contrast this definition with our culture's purely feminine definition of woman:

> Woman is
> the symbol-receiving (hearing, passive) animal
> inventor of nothing (moralized by priests and saints)
> submerged in her natural conditions by instruments of man's making
> goaded at the bottom of hierarchy (moved to a sense of orderliness)
> and rotted by perfection.

Finally, let me propose Celeste's definition of gynandrous humanity

> People are
> players with symbols
> inventors of the negative and the possibility of morality
> grown from their natural condition by tools of their collective making
> trapped between hierarchy and equality (moved constantly to reorder)
> neither rotten nor perfect.
> Arguing, talking, chatting.

I hope that the differences in these three versions suggest to you that Burke's rhetorical theory is shot through with a deep-seated negativity toward what humanity can be, and a blindness toward feminine creativity. Burke's view is not inaccurate, but merely one-sided—rotten with a negative perfection. It needs a feminist balance. I believe we will find a similar lack of balance in most methods of criticism produced by the male stream.

In addition to revisions of specific critical methods, feminists also need to address whole areas of research. One of the hottest areas of rhetorical criticism currently is the "Rhetoric of Inquiry." The featuring of science as the object of inquiry for rhetoricians is somewhat problematic since it is one means of depoliticizing rhetoric. Instead of studying social movements, we are now studying punctuated equilibria and Nova, and endlessly rehashing old epistemological battles (without, I might add, much attention to extant feminist critiques of the relevant epistemologies). There is the possibility for feminist and progressive work in this area, of course. Given that science has become such a driving force, a rhetorical critique of science might help give some greater space to humane Being. Solomon's (1985) work on the Tuskegee Syphilis Project, arrived at independently from the Project on the Rhetoric of Inquiry, is a brilliant demonstration of this potential. However, most of the work in the Rhetoric of Inquiry is celebratory, or at least blind to political problems. Major advocates of the approach have maintained that to say that science is rhetorically constructed is not to say that scientific decisions are arrived at politically. Instead, they portray rhetoric as a neutral, almost "objective," tool, akin to scientific methodology. Most dramatically, they address and consider none of the cases in which the rhetoric of science has produced blatant abuse of women (Bleier, 1984; Harding, 1986; Spallone, 1989). Clearly, the Rhetoric of Inquiry project needs to be dramatically altered by feminist practice; other areas have similar needs.

Feminists have already isolated other important revisions needed in rhetorical practice. One pressing problem is the tendency of situational studies to view audiences as homogeneous, usually isomorphic with white northern male critics, rather than accounting for their diversity (Solomon, 1988b). Another gap is the devaluing of regional and local discourse. Another is the dismissing of rhetoric that is not focused on changing laws of the state (where is our study of the southern black women's self-help organizations? lesbian social networks? the garden clubs?). Most important, we need explicit theorization of the new feminist perspectives. In line with what much of the literature says about the predispositions of women as scholars, feminist rhetorical critics have spent their time involved in the relatively concrete arena of practice, as opposed to the abstract arena of theory. This has left them open to attacks by theoretical feminists who have denied the progressive critics their feminism (Steeves, 1987), and it has also made it more difficult to consolidate our efforts together. The tradeoff has been the relatively easy mainstreaming of feminist criticism, evident in the inclusion of feminist criticism in three of the major anthologies of rhetorical criticism currently on the market (Brock, Scott, & Chesebro, 1989; S. K. Foss, 1989; Hart, 1990).

One final shortcoming in contemporary rhetorical criticism, from a feminist perspective, is methodological. Some feminists have launched an attack on the concept of rationality that undergirds much rhetorical theory. Some would modify the concept of rationality, and others would eliminate it altogether. The extension of this issue, for critics, is the concern with objectivity of method. As I suggested before, those feminist studies with the most radical potential (the positional ones) have frequently chosen to eschew judgment in favor of objectivity. This choice is theoretically defensible, I believe, but it requires a modification of our understanding of and criteria for objectivity (Condit, 1990a). We need to retheorize the meaning of scholarly objectivity in the context of feminist commitments, epistemologies, and practices, especially as they are related to the particular concerns of studying linguistic phenomena. Simultaneously, we might want to increase the number of judgmental studies we do. We should, I believe, resist the tendency to label either choice as *the* feminist practice, since both routes may prove productive for women.

Feminist Labors

I have suggested both that academic rhetorical criticism has incorporated feminist work, and that it falls short in some areas. I would now like to focus in more detail on existing feminist contributions.

It is popular these days to argue that feminism has not penetrated deep enough because it has not altered the methodologies of communication practice. To some extent, it is clear that mainstream methods in communication research, dominated as they are by numbers, by objectification of persons, and by unreflective categorization, suffer from this problem. I would suggest that the case of rhetoric is quite different. In the first place, rhetorical methods start out being qualitative and engaged with individual judgment—or at least a large portion of the field has been that way since the 1970s (Wander & Jenkins, 1972). Second, rhetorical practice, because it does not study private experience, has not objectified persons into "subjects" (nor have rhetoricians tended to employ the demeaning concept of "masses" popular in other fields: they have preferred the term "people"). For these and other reasons, rhetoric starts out as a practice whose methods are already more sympathetic to feminist interests than are most academic practices. This is probably related to the historical stance of rhetoric as an oppositional practice to the mainstream philosophical and scientific academy.

Therefore, I see the feminist revolution in rhetorical criticism as being one that is incremental and ongoing, rather than a visible and sudden replacement. Feminist rhetorical critics are gradually changing each brick in the structure of criticism, one by one, rather than razing the building to the ground and starting over. (There are several advantages to this approach if you want to continue to accept the shelter of the structure.)

This quiet revolution is evident in the works of women scholars such as Karen and Sonja Foss, Martha Solomon, Karlyn Campbell, Marsha Vanderford, and Carol Jablonski. All of their work has contained differences in question and methodology from the broad tendencies of their male counterparts. These scholars did not all explicitly label their work as feminist in terms of its approach and methodology, but in the process of thinking from a feminist perspective and women's experience, they generated a body of research that looks different from male-stream scholarship.

The first striking difference is that many feminist scholars tend to look at both sides of a controversy, exploring the interactions and differences of the competing views. I suspect this is the case because the duality induced by being female in a male-dominated world sensitized these scholars to such interactions and made them wary of oppressing other groups by exclusion or biased treatment.

The second difference in feminist rhetorical studies resides in the data on which they focus. On the whole, feminists are less likely to focus on a single "great" orator or a single text. They are more likely to look at large numbers of texts that share similarities. Additionally, they are more likely to look at texts other than great speeches in pivotal historical movements. They are likely to study jokes, cartoons, romance novels, popular magazines, soap operas, and other rhetorical vehicles of everyday life. Rather than abandoning the model of rhetoric as social decision making, they see these alternate media as participating in important ways in social decision-making processes because of their contact with average persons in their daily lives. Finally, women have been crucial in incorporating subjects of concern to women into the academic discussion—ending the silencing of concerns about the human system of reproduction, but also increasing attention to the environment in which we live.

In addition to these broad tendencies, it seems to me that women have subtly and importantly altered male-stream notions of rhetorical phenomena in specific fields by producing models that are more dynamic and process-oriented than male models. The best example is the work of Jamieson and Campbell (1982) on genre. They elaborated a notion that portrays genre as fluid and changeable. This model contrasts sharply with the rigid categorical approach of Ware and Linkugel (1973).

I would not want to claim that these ways of going about research are *the* feminist methods. Speech Communication has long had a strong contingent of relationally oriented men (Dervin, Grossberg, O'Keefe, &

Wartella, 1989), who have pushed the field in some of these directions. Hence, the contribution of feminists is additional to these works, rather than simply oppositional to all men. Additionally, it is possible for these methods to be used by chauvinists—no method is immune from use to ill ends. Moreover, many feminists use other methods. Nonetheless, these tendencies have been evident in recent feminist scholarship, and they have expanded the possibilities of scholars and of our understanding of ordinary women. In addition to expanding attention to women's issues, women orators, and the sites of women's speaking, feminist rhetoricians have also made important contributions by increasing the range of studies and by shifting the emphasis of the mainstream methodologically.

All this being said, this feminist work is not immune to conflict. I believe that a fairly large and healthy body of feminist scholarship has been done in the area of rhetorical studies, but I believe that too few people (feminists included) would recognize it as such (K. A. Foss, 1989; Spitzack & Carter, 1987; Steeves, 1987). This is due in part to the fact that progressive feminist rhetorical critics have tended to shirk theorization. The problem is deepened, however, because many feminist rhetoricians are liberal feminists, rather than essentialists (e.g., radical or socialist feminists). Given the dominance of essentialist feminisms in women's studies programs and feminist theory generally, this results in a tendency to dismiss these progressive liberal studies as "accommodationist" or inadequately radical.

In exploring this problem, let me first note that when I say that feminist rhetoric has been "liberal" I do not intend either the cardboard version of liberalism offered by conservatives such as George Bush, nor the straw demons summoned by leftists such as Allison Jagger. Liberal feminism has evolved beyond Locke and Milton; it retains the goals of tolerance of difference, mutual respect, individual growth, and rational agreement, but adds to them social support for the basics of personal growth, preservation of human emotion, and respect for differences between men and women, but also between groups of women. It is important, I believe, that feminist rhetoricians tend to be liberal because rhetoric itself is an essentially liberal practice. A social system structured around rhetoric presumes that audiences are constructed of human beings who are capable of making sound decisions that are in both their own interests and the general interest. It further presumes that social systems can change without violent revolution and that it is probably good that they do so. It presumes that arguing for such change on the basis of good reasons is the best option we have for a better way of living for all.

It is not too surprising, therefore, that there is a substantial body of feminist work in rhetoric, that it blends into the tradition comfortably without explicit theorization of its feminist stance, and that this makes radical feminists unhappy with it. Part of the feminist agenda must, therefore, be not only attendance to the shortcomings of male-stream scholarship, but also the working out of ways to allow diversity in feminism itself.

Toward a Gynandrous Rhetoric

To move in that direction, I urge the building of a gynandrous rhetoric. I use the word "gynandrous" to denote respect for a variety of differences of human gender—not just between men and women, but among a broad range of the different ways people have gendered themselves, all containing their positive elements, including androgynous, lesbian, feminine, tough, wimp, butch, gay, and even the flexible multifaceted few who can dance through many of these genderings in different rhetorical contexts. (For if you believe that gender really is socially constructed, and you believe that individuals are capable of manipulating social codes, you leave open the possibility that we are not necessarily trapped in single ways of gendering ourselves.) I use the term "gynandrous" quite seriously, in opposition to all the alternatives I know that have been postulated—masculine culture, feminine culture, feminist culture, and androgyny.

Obviously, my proposal sounds most like androgyny, a term proposed almost two decades ago. There were several problems with this goal of making each and every human being into a full person with a full range of so-called "masculine" and "feminine" characteristics. The first problem was that, by putting the male "andro" before the female "gynous" in a historical milieu dominated by men, one inadvertently supported the social trend to make women more masculine, without making men more feminine. In the present historical context it is essential to put women first.

The second problem arose from the fact that people are not homogeneous. Some of us are physically strong and others are not. Some are tall and others are short. We will never consist of some ideal median (and would we want that monotony?). As we see our task today, it is not to promote the same model for every person. Rather, it is to preserve those feminine qualities that are positive and to promote them, so that individuals of any biological sex may choose among the widest possible varieties of paths, rather than being chained either to the split stereotypes of femininity and masculinity, or to the single stereotype of watered-down masculinity that some believed androgyny represented. The ultimate ideal may be for each person to have flexibility, to have a range of ways of being-in-the-world from sensitivity through strength. In the present historical context, the social task is to promote those positive values historically associated with the female social role (as opposed to the ridiculous caricatures of the stereotype of femininity), while simultaneously allowing women the pleasures of the so-called masculine ways of being-in-the-world.

The roles of rhetorical criticism in this endeavor are multifold. One activity we might pursue is to begin judging rhetorical acts based on feminine and/or gynandrous criteria. This is obviously appropriate with regard to speakers such as Katherine Davalos Ortega and Geraldine Ferraro, but it will be more fun and of equal importance with regard to Daniel Webster, Ronald Reagan, Andrew Young, and Mikhail Gorbachev (see, e.g., Jenefsky, 1989). This should give situational criticism a fresh new influence. It will require additional theoretical work to elaborate gynandrous criteria.

Positional critics can engage in a related activity—exploring the types of objectivity available for performing broad-scale historical analyses of changes in public vocabulary. We have as yet no studies that address a single rhetorical phenomenon from multiple objective frameworks. This calls upon us to generate more team projects among women, for feminist rhetorical critics still work almost exclusively in isolation in spite of our explicit support of relational values. In addition, positional critics need to add judgmental elements to some of their analyses.

Another activity that feminist rhetorical critics might want to engage in is to continue to draw attention to issues that have a major impact on the lives of women. We have had no exploration of the current day care crisis, of the new reproductive technologies, of coerced sex, of pornography, and too few explorations of the rhetoric of doing politics as a female candidate. There are clearly other areas of importance that I have forgotten about or do not know about because they do not have sufficient presence in our discourse. Most important, we need to have issues of concern to women of all colors, sexual orientations, economic classes, and abilities brought to our attention. Feminists need to fill in the gaps for each other.

Surprisingly, perhaps, we also need to continue producing studies that reveal the sexism in our politics and cultures. There are very few of these studies in our mainstream journals (see Klumpp & Hollihan, 1989; Payne, 1989). Until men are forced to read and understand the pervasiveness of the problem, their ignorance will dampen more innovative research.

In addition to these revisions of conventional studies, I think some critics might want to push the boundaries of critical practice by exploring the ways in which rhetoric is experienced in women's lives. Examining both the construction of speeches by women and the experience of listening on a positional and situational basis would help us to reformulate our concepts of criticism. This can be done in terms of individuals, but also by exploring the female as auditor and speaker in the public space (Oravec, 1990).

Finally, I think feminist critics may want to reexamine the notion of a critical voice on two planes. First, we need to examine the displace-ment between the public realm and the academic realm, and second, we need to explore the bipolarity of criticism. Throughout its history, rhetoric has had an unstable position in the academy. As a consequence, it has been eager to prove its academic legitimacy by separating itself from the real world. One of the most damning critiques one could level at the works of rhetorical critics has been to call their scholarship "merely jour-nalistic." Consonant with such values, we have lauded arcane pieces that have the least possible real-world relevance. I believe that there are differ-ences between what academics do and what journalists do, but I also believe that we distort what we do when we define it in opposition to journalists and run away from rhetoric being interesting to the general public. Campbell (1972a) provided an excellent model when she broad-cast rhetorical critiques to the public over radio. She provided a model of the rhetorical critic as social activist and teacher—trying to enlighten the public, rather than trying to escape from it. We need more theoretical dis-cussion of the boundaries between the academy and other institutions, but we clearly need to make those boundaries more permeable.

Finally, we need to reexamine the concept of "critique" itself. Feminist criticism across the academy has tended to be oppositional—solely oppositional—and has tended to define criticism as "to find fault with, especially to trace the patriarchal influence in." There has been a tendency to assume that anything that exists must be patriarchal in its essence, because everything that exists was created during the tenure of the patriarchs. Neither clause is true. It may be time that we begin to parse more carefully the influence of the patriarchy from other influences.

Feminist rhetorical critics are well positioned to provide leader-ship to feminist scholarship generally with regard to those elements of lan-guage and communication that are the result of the innate structures of language and the process of communication and those which are more historically bound to male privilege. This will cause us to turn our critical skills back on ourselves as well. Recently, it has been claimed in many spaces that women's research has been denied a hearing in the main-stream journals of Speech Communication (e.g., K. A. Foss, 1989). While it is true that the past failure to index Women's Studies in Communication was a ghettoizing of the research that appeared in that volume, in my experience it is not true that women's research has received wholesale rejection either on grounds that it is uninteresting, or because it doesn't take appropriate forms (i.e., it is "soft"). That is, it is rejected no more fre-quently on political grounds than are other kinds of work—for example, situationalists routinely reject the work of positionalists, and vice versa. I have been a reviewer for both the Quarterly Journal of Speech and Communication Monographs for several years, and I simply have not seen many feminist pieces come across my desk; I have certainly not seen anything that seemed particularly radical. I have encouraged those few feminist-leaning manuscripts that I have reviewed, but in at least half the cases, authors of feminist manuscripts who have received "revise and resubmit" notices from the editor have never sent their articles back revised (and very few articles on any subject, with any methodology, receive any more encouragement than a revise and resubmit notice the first time around).

In my opinion, the climate toward women's research in the Speech Communicatin Association (SCA) is no more chilly than the climate to any other kind of research in this highly competitive arena. It may be that some people's versions of feminist values are incompatible with competition per se, but then complaining because they do not win the competition seems inappropriate. I believe that one major reason that womanist scholarship has not appeared widely is that not enough women have been submitting and going through the process of multiple revisions necessary to produce a piece of writing polished enough to satisfy an audience that spends much of their lives reading the best of human eloquence. If nothing else, women scholars need to take rejection less finally. From personal experience I assure you that it is possible to rewrite a paper even after receiving a rejection notice and to get the same editor who rejected it to print it (though it requires persistence and insistence).

There are structural, economic, and cultural barriers that impede women's ability to take the time and to adopt the narcissistic personality necessary for this process, and I would not have us forget those impediments. But, by contrast to many academic disciplines, in SCA we live in a climate that is reasonably willing to accept our work if we overcome those external barriers to writing it.

If there is a problem with the reception of our work, I believe that it lies in the now well-discussed "glass ceiling" effect. The power structure is willing to tolerate our work and to allow it to be published, but it continues to keep it from having influence by controlling the award structures. Only about 15% of the lead articles in the *Quarterly Journal of Speech* in the past decade have been authored by women. Fewer still have been awarded prizes, and the prizes are distributed unevenly. It is possible for a young male rhetorical scholar to receive national prizes; to date, it has not seemed possible for young feminist scholars. In SCA, men have been rewarded for potential, women have been rewarded only for hard-fought accomplishments.

Ultimately, the question of whether to worry about such structures of influence comes down to whether we see our future as "separate but equal" or mainstreamed. I fear that the separatist course is suicidal. I suspect that if there is to be a feminist presence in this academy, we have to recognize that the criterion for presence in the academy is changing and that it is increasingly necessary to garner prizes and to publish in mainstream journals in order to get tenure. But even if this is not true, and we are able to establish, from the ground up, a force sufficient to sustain feminist practice, I personally remain opposed to separatism. It is important for all groups to have a space in which to think together with those of similar concerns. However, it is also important to recognize that we share a planet with others and that we must communicate with them in order to cohabitate successfully. This requires that we collectively construct a mainstream to replace the male stream. We need to be active players in that mainstream at all levels—some women must sacrifice family to win prizes, others must sacrifice scholarship to administrate, others must sacrifice fame for family and friends. Such sacrifices are necessitated by the fact that no human being can do everything in a short mortal life.

Someday I want to find that the best-selling public speaking text is written by a feminist and that it features an entirely different stance toward public speaking than the manipulative, self-glorification-oriented texts that now dominate the publishing lists. I want to see a writer informed by feminism produce a theory of the role of rhetoric in social life to replace that of Burke. I want to participate in a project that produces a book that overviews the field of communication by including feminist insights, rather than setting those insights off as separate from the normal practice (as I believe this book does).

To prefer the approach of mainstreaming is simply to say that as rhetoricians, we recognize the power of our audiences and respect that power when we wish to lead. I think feminist rhetorical criticism has begun to construct a laudable model of all-fronts, incremental change, which in some ways stands, as rhetoricians have always stood, in opposition to the mainstream academy. In this case that means some opposition to the feminist academy to the extent that what is now the mainstream of academic feminist theory is dominated by essentialist perspectives. To work through an oppositional stance in an oppositional practice may prove difficult in theory, but in critical practice we seem to be getting the housework done.

CONCLUSIONS

For feminists in rhetorical criticism it is neither the best of times nor the worst of times. We rest in a fluid field that has permitted some entree to feminist ideas and activities, but wherein much more activity is needed. Rhetorical criticism has always been an oppositional practice; it has opposed the norms of the academy, and it has opposed the taken-for-grantedness of the mainstream of American political life. Moreover, rhetoric as a practice has often represented feminine modes of relating to other human beings. Even to this day, however, the rhetorical academy continues to be dominated by men and masculinity. There is, therefore, much that remains to be done. The first solution to the problem is for women to write more rhetorical studies.

REFERENCES

Andrews, J.A. (1973). The passionate negation: The Chartist movement in rhetorical perspective, *Quarterly Journal of Speech, 59,* 196-208.

Aristotle. (1932). *The rhetoric of Aristotle* (trans. L. Cooper). Englewood Cliffs, NJ: Prentice-Hall. (Originally published circa 350 B.C.).

Benson, T.W. (1980). The rhetorical structure of Frederick Wiseman's *High School. Communication Monographs, 47,* 233-261.

Bitzer, L.F. (1968). The rhetorical situation. *Philosophy and Rhetoric, 1,* 1-14.

Black, E. (1970). The second persona. *Quarterly Journal of Speech, 56,* 109-119.

Black, E. (1976). The sentimental style as escapism, or the devil with Dan'l Webster. In K.K. Campbell & K.H. Jamieson (Eds.), *Form and genre: Shaping rhetorical action* (pp. 75-86). Falls Church, VA: Speech Communication Association.

Black, E. (1988). Secrecy and disclosure as rhetorical forms. *Quarterly Journal of Speech, 74,* 133-150.

Bleier, R. (1984). *Science and gender: A critique of biology and its theories on women.* New York: Pergamon Press.

Bormann, E. (1973). The Eagleton affair: A fantasy theme analysis. *Quarterly Journal of Speech, 59,* 143-159.

Brock, B.L., Scott, R.L., & Chesebro, J.W. (1989). *Methods of rhetorical criticism: A twentieth-century perspective* (3rd ed., rev.). Detroit: Wayne State University Press.

Burke, K.B. (1945). *A grammar of motives.* New York: Prentice-Hall.

Burke, K.B. (1968). *Language as symbolic action.* Berkeley, CA: University of California Press. (Originally published 1966).

Campbell, K.K. (1972a). An exercise in the rhetoric of mythical America. *Critiques of contemporary rhetoric.* Belmont, CA: Wadsworth Publishing Co., Inc.

Campbell, K.K. (1972b). The forum: Conventional wisdom—traditional form: A rejoinder. *Quarterly Journal of Speech, 58,* 451-460.

Campbell, K.K. (1973). The rhetoric of women's liberation: An oxymoron. *Quarterly Journal of Speech, 59,* 74-86.

Campbell, K.K. (1980). Stanton's "The solitude of self": A rationale for feminism. *Quarterly Journal of Speech, 66,* 304-312.

Campbell, K.K. (1989). *Man cannot speak for her* (2 vols.). New York: Praeger.

Carlson, A.C. (1988). Limitations on the comic frame: Some witty American women of the nineteenth century. *Quarterly Journal of Speech, 74,* 196-310.

Condit, C.M. (1987). Democracy and civil rights: The universalizing influence of public argumentation. *Communication Monographs, 54,* 1-18.

Condit, C.M. (1990a). *Decoding abortion rhetoric: Communicating social change.* Urbana, IL: University of Illinois Press.

Condit, C.M. (1990b). Rhetorical criticism and audiences: The extremes of McGee and Leff. *Western Journal of Speech Communication, 54,* 330-345.

Dervin, B., Grossberg, L., O'Keefe, B., & Wartella, E. (1989). *Rethinking communication: Paradigm issues* (Vol. 1). Newbury Park, CA: Sage.

Fisher, W.R. (1987). *Human communication as narration: Toward a philosophy of reason, value, and action.* Columbia, SC: University of South Carolina Press.

Foss, K.A. (1989). Feminist scholarship in speech communication: Contributions and obstacles. *Women's Studies in Communication, 12*(1), 1-10.

Foss, K.A., & Foss, S.K. (1991). *Women speak: The eloquence of women's lives.* Prospect Heights, IL: Waveland Press.

Foss, S.K. (1979). Equal rights amendment controversy: Two worlds in conflict. *Quarterly Journal of Speech, 65,* 275-288.

Foss, S.K. (1989). *Rhetorical criticism: Exploration and practice.* Prospect Heights, IL: Waveland Press.

Frentz, T.S. (1985). Rhetorical conversation, time, and moral action. *Quarterly Journal of Speech, 71,* 1-18.

Fulkerson, R.P. (1979). The public letter as a rhetorical form: Structure, logic, and style in King's "Letter from Birmingham jail." *Quarterly Journal of Speech, 65,* 121-136.

Gearheart, S.M. (1979). The womanization of rhetoric. *Women's Studies International Quarterly, 2,* 195-201.

Harding, W. (1986). *The science question in feminism.* Ithaca, NY: Cornell University Press.

Hariman, R. (1986). Status, marginality, and rhetorical theory. *Quarterly Journal of Speech, 72,* 38-54.

Hart, R.P. (1990). *Modern rhetorical criticism.* Glenview, IL: Scott, Foresman/Little, Brown Higher Education.

Hauser, G.A. (1986). *Introduction to rhetorical theory.* New York: Harper and Row.

Hill, F.I. (1972). Conventional wisdom—traditional form: The President's message of November 3, 1969. *Quarterly Journal of Speech, 58,* 373-386.

Ivie, R. (1987). Metaphor and the rhetorical invention of cold war "idealists." *Communication Monographs, 54* (June 1987), 165-182.

Jablonski, C.J. (1988). Rhetoric, paradox, and the movement for women's ordination in the Roman Catholic Church. *Quarterly Journal of Speech, 74,* 164-183.

Jagger, A.M. (1988). *Feminist politics and human nature.* Totowa, NJ: Rowman & Littlefield. (Originally published ,1983, Sussex, England: Harvester Press).

Jamieson, K.H. (1988). *Eloquence in an electronic age.* New York: Oxford University Press.

Jamieson, K.H., & Campbell, K.K. (1982). Rhetorical hybrids: Fusions of generic elements. *Quarterly Journal of Speech, 68,* 146-157.

Japp, P.M. (1985). Esther or Isaiah? The abolitionist-feminist rhetoric of Angelina Grimke. *Quarterly Journal of Speech, 71,* 335-348.

Jefferson, P. (1967). The magnificent barbarian at Nashville. *Southern Speech Communication Journal, 33,* 77-87.

Jenefsky, C. (1989, November). *Integrity as a rhetorical strategy in Andrea Dworkin's intercourse.* Paper presented at the meeting of the Speech Communication Association, San Francisco, CA.

Kendall, K.E., & Fisher, J.Y. (1974). Frances Wright on women's rights: Eloquence versus ethos. *Quarterly Journal of Speech, 60,* 56-58.

Kidd, V. (1975). Happily ever after and other relationships styles: Advice on interpersonal relations in popular magazines, 1951-1973. *Quarterly Journal of Speech, 61,* 31-39.

Klumpp, J.F., & Hollihan, T.A. (1989). Rhetorical criticism as moral action. *Quarterly Journal of Speech, 75,* 84-97.

Kuseki, B.K. (1988). Kenneth Burke's "five dogs" and Mother Teresa's love. *Quarterly Journal of Speech, 74,* 323-333.

Leff, M.C., & Kauffeld, F.J. (Eds.). (1989). *Texts in context: Critical dialogues on significant episodes in American political rhetoric.* Davis, CA: Hermagoras Press.

Leff, M.C., & Morhmann, G.P. (1974). Lincoln at Cooper Union: A rhetorical analysis of the text. *Quarterly Journal of Speech, 60,* 346-358.

McGee, M.C. (1980a). The "ideograph": A link between rhetoric and ideology. *Quarterly Journal of Speech, 66,* 1-17.

McGee, M.C. (1980b). The origins of "liberty": A feminization of power. *Communication Monographs, 47,* 23-45.

McGee, M.C., & Martin, M.A. (1983). Public knowledge and ideological argumentation. *Communication Monographs, 50,* 47-65.

McGuire, M. (1977). Mythic rhetoric in Mein Kampf: A structuralist critique. *Quarterly Journal of Speech, 63,* 1-13.

McKerrow, R.E. (1989). Critical rhetoric: Theory and praxis. *Communication Monographs, 56,* 91-111.

Murphy, J.J. (Ed.). (1983). *A synoptic history of classical rhetoric.* Davis, CA: Hermagoras Press.

Newman, R.P. (1975). Lethal rhetoric: The selling of the China myths. *Quarterly Journal of Speech, 61,* 113-128.

Olson, L.C. (1983). Portraits in praise of a people: A rhetorical analysis of Norman Rockwell's icons in Franklin D. Roosevelt's "four freedoms" campaign. *Quarterly Journal of Speech, 69,* 15-24.

Oravec, C. (1984). Conservationism vs. preservationism: The "public interest" in the Hetch Hetchy controversy. *Quarterly Journal of Speech, 70,* 444-458.

Oravec, C. (1990). The sublimation of mass consciousness in the rhetorical criticism of Jacksonian America. *Communication, 11,* 291-314.

Osborne, M. (1977). The evolution of the archetypal sea in rhetoric and poetic. *Quarterly Journal of Speech, 63,* 347-363.

Patton, J.H. (1977). A government as good as its people: Jimmy Carter and the restoration of transcendence to politics. *Quarterly Journal of Speech, 63,* 249-257.

Payne, D. (1989). The Wizard of Oz: Therapeutic rhetoric in contemporary media ritual. *Quarterly Journal of Speech, 75,* 25-39.

Railsback, C.C. (1984). The contemporary American abortion controversy: Stages in the argument. *Quarterly Journal of Speech, 70,* 410-424.

Rushing, J.H. (1986). Ronald Reagan's "star wars" address: Mythic containment of technical reasoning. *Quarterly Journal of Speech, 72,* 415-433.

Rushing, J.H. (1989). Evolution of "the new frontier" in *Alien* and *Aliens: Patriarchal co-optation of the feminine archetype. *Quarterly Journal of Speech, 75,* 1-24.

Ryan, H.R. (1981). Roosevelt's fourth inaugural address: A study of its composition. *Quarterly Journal of Speech, 67,* 157-166.

Schwichtenberg, C. (1983). Dynasty: The dialectic of feminine power. *Central States Speech Journal, 34,* 151-161.

Scott, R.L., & Smith, D.K. (1969). The rhetoric of confrontation. *Quarterly Journal of Speech, 55,* 1-8.

Solomon, M. (1979). The "positive woman's" journey: A mythic analysis of STOP ERA. *Quarterly Journal of Speech, 65,* 262-274.

Solomon, M. (1985). The rhetoric of dehumanization: An analysis of medical reports of the Tuskegee Syphilis Project. *Western Journal of Speech Communication, 49,* 233-247.

Solomon, M. (1988a). Ideology as rhetorical constraint: The anarchist agitation of "red Emma" Goldman. *Quarterly Journal of Speech, 74,* 184-200.

Solomon, M. (1988b). "With firmness in the right": The creation of moral hegemony in Lincoln's second inaugural. *Communication Reports, 1,* 32-37.

Spallone, P. (1989). *Beyond conception: The new politics of reproduction.* Granby, MA: Bergin & Garvey Publishers, Inc.

Spitzack, C. (1988). Body talk: The politics of weight loss and female identity. In B. Bate & A. Taylor (Eds.), *Women communicating: Studies of women's talk* (pp. 51-74). Norwood, NJ: Ablex Publishing .

Spitzack, C., & Carter, K. (1987). Women in communication studies: A typology for revision. *Quarterly Journal of Speech, 73,* 401-423.

Steeves, H.L. (1987). Feminist theories and media studies. *Critical Studies in Mass Communication, 4,* 95-135.

Vanderford, M.L. (1989). Vilification and social movements: A case study of pro-life and pro-choice rhetoric. *Quarterly Journal of Speech, 75,* 166-182.

Wander, P. (1984). The third persona: An ideological turn in rhetorical theory. *Central States Speech Journal, 35,* 197-216.

Wander, P., & Jenkins, S. (1972). Rhetoric, society, and the critical response. *Quarterly Journal of Speech, 59,* 441-450.

Ware, B.L., & Linkugel, W.A. (1973). They spoke in defense of themselves: On the general criticism of apologia. *Quarterly Journal of Speech, 59,* 273-283.

Weidhorn, M. (1972). Churchill the phrase forger. *Quarterly Journal of Speech, 58,* 161-174.

Zarefsky, D. (1986). *President Johnson's war on poverty: Rhetoric and history.* University, AL: University of Alabama Press.

Chapter 8

Feminist Critique of Mass Communication Research

Cynthia M. Lont

George Mason University
Fairfax, VA

Mass communication research is, and continues to be, in a state of flux encumbered (or enhanced) by divergent approaches in methodology and theory. Researchers study the general—the relationship between mass media and society—to the specific—the use of television by the individual. Methodologies range from content analysis to critical studies.

Due to the multitude of approaches to the study of mass communication and the massive amount of material, this chapter focuses on specific mass communication research approaches to the study of women and media. This focus narrows the field for a more thorough analysis and exposes the reader to a specific group of research, which although diverse in methodology, is similar in intent. The three approaches include: content analysis of the portrayal of women in media; historical narratives of individual women as processors of the media; and feminist critical analysis of media and society. The chapter concludes with a discussion of new directions for feminist research in mass communication.

CONTENT ANALYSIS

Up until a very few years ago, what came to the minds of many students and scholars in mass communication when discussing "feminist" research was the content analysis of the roles assigned to women in the media. Studies revolved around the portrayal of women in such mainstream media as television commercials (Courtney & Whipple, 1974), prime-time television (Goff, Goff, & Lehrer, 1980; Haskell, 1979; McNeil, 1975; Turow, 1974; Weigel & Loomis, 1981), and Saturday morning cartoons (Mayes & Valentine, 1979); in print media such as magazine photographs (Sparks & Fehlner, 1986), newspaper comics (Brabant, 1976; Brabant & Mooney, 1986), and print advertisements (Bonelli, 1989); and in Top 40 radio music lyrics (Hyden & McCandless, 1983) and DJ chatter (Lont, 1990).

The National Organization for Women (NOW) (1972) was one of the first groups to use content analysis to study the roles of women on television. The Screen Actor's Guild (1974) reinforced NOW's findings through a study of the roles assigned to males and females in television commercials. Two communication journals (*Journal of Communication*, Spring 1974; *Journal of Broadcasting*, Summer 1975) devoted issues to women and media using content analysis to study women in television (Courtney & Whipple, 1974), prime-time television (McNeil, 1975; Seggar, 1975; Tedesco, 1974), daytime television (Downing, 1974), cartoons (Streicher, 1974), and fiction (Franzwa, 1974). In general, these studies found:

1. More male than female characters on television programs (Tedesco, 1974), except during daytime television when the number of male and female characters were the same (Downing, 1974).

2. More diverse and less stereotypical roles assigned to males than females during television programs (Downing, 1974; McNeil, 1975).

3. Younger and more attractive female characters during daytime television (Downing, 1974).

4. Less competent female characters than male characters on television (Seggar, 1975).

5. Predominantly male voice-overs (spoken or sung) in television commercials (Courtney & Whipple, 1974; Screen Actors Guild, 1974).

6. Females in "nonspeaking" roles as often as males in commercials (Screen Actors Guild, 1974).

7. Males used more often as product representatives during commercials with the exception of daytime programming (Courtney & Whipple, 1974).

8. Two males for every female in the average commercial (Screen Actors Guild, 1974).

These findings were further documented by *Hearth and Home* (Tuchman, Daniels, & Benet, 1978) and *Window Dressing on the Set* (U.S. Commission on Civil Rights, 1977, 1979). *Hearth and Home*, a collection of studies and essays, reaffirmed the limited roles assigned to women in television, women's magazines, and newspapers, and detailed the effect on children and youth who watch television. *Window Dressing on the Set* (U.S. Commission, 1979) found television drama did not reflect the sexual and racial/ethnic make-up of the United States, and that sex stereotyping occurred more often than race stereotyping.

Content analysis of women's roles in the media during the 1980s found little change. Females are portrayed less often and have fewer major roles than males (Henderson, Greenberg, & Aitken, 1980). Television promotes the notion that employment outside the home jeopardizes a female's chances for marital success (Weigel & Loomis, 1981). Female characters are portrayed more often than male characters as confined to the home environment (Downs, 1981). Females are depicted as more passive, dependent, and weaker than males (Geis, Brown, Jennings, & Porter, 1984), and females are portrayed as younger and more attractive than their male counterparts (Downs & Harrison, 1985).

Although television has been the focus of many content analysis studies, other media studies show little difference. A replication study (Brabant, 1976) of Sunday comics by Brabant and Mooney (1986) found "with the exception of a substantial increase in the percentage of appearances by males and females in leisure activities, a change in the portrayal of males and females in the Sunday comics was minimal for the decade studied" (p. 148). In magazine advertisements directed toward women, Bonelli (1989) found a concentration on relationships, romance, and on looking good to attract men. This is reinforced by a study of women's magazines which found living alone portrayed as something a woman must "live through" (Clark, 1980).

Content analysis of music reinforces sex-role stereotypes. Saucier (1986) found women in country music to be portrayed as housewives, mothers, or lovers while the images of women in rock music most often portray the ideal, the evil, or the victim (Butruille & Taylor, 1987). Even disc jockeys who introduce music on the radio are predominantly male, and their chatter portrays females as family members (mother, daughter, wife) more often than males (Lont, 1990).

Strengths

One of the strengths of content analysis is its ability to quantify the portrayal of females and males in the media. The consistently negative and always deferent roles assigned to females show little has changed. While some believe that women on television, for example, have gained stature, content analysis undermines this belief. No matter the target audience, the time of day, or the media used, sex-role stereotypes pervade the media.

A second strength is the use of content analysis as a foundation for further research or in conjunction with another methodology. For example, one research perspective, "cultivation analysis," uses content analysis and questionnaire data to study the relationship between television portrayal and audience behavior. Developed by George Gerbner and his associates at the Annenberg School of Communication, television is viewed as the central cultural enforcer of American society. Its function is to order, extend, and maintain the social order rather than alter, threaten, or weaken it. Television, therefore, socializes people into standard roles and behaviors. Gerbner believes researchers must move past studying specific acts or their amount (of violence) and seek the impact of the collection of these images in the "world" as depicted by television (Gerbner & Gross, 1976). Gerbner first uses a detailed content analysis of a representative sampling of programs to reveal the "world" of television. Second, viewers who complete opinion surveys are divided into "heavy," "moderate," or "light" viewers. Gerbner's hypothesis is that "heavy" viewers are more likely to give "world of television" answers. For example, respondents are asked to estimate the proportion of people employed in law enforcement or what their chances are of being involved in a crime. "Heavy" viewers are more likely to give answers that reflect the television world, that is, overestimates, making the world seem a "mean and scary" place (Gerbner, Gross, Jackson-Beeck, Jeffries-Fox, & Signorelli, 1978).

Cultivation analysis is used in the study of sex-role stereotypes. Buerkel-Rothfuss and Mayes (1981), in a study of soap opera viewing, found "an important relationship between what a person watches on daytime serials and what he or she believes to be true about those aspects of the real world which tend to be portrayed with exaggerated frequency on soap operas" (p. 114). Morgan and Rothschild (1983) found a relationship between television viewing and sex-role stereotypes reported by adolescents.

Although cultivation analysis has critics (Hirsch, 1981; Hughes, 1980; Newcomb, 1981), Hawkins and Pingree (1981) found in an analysis of 48 studies using cultivation analysis that there is evidence for a link between viewing and beliefs.

Limitations

One of the limitations of content analysis is its tendency to remain at the descriptive level, ignoring relationship(s) between content and the social structures which produce content.

A second limitation of content analysis in the study of media messages is the lack of messages available for study. Many topics and characters receive little exposure in media (Wimmer & Dominick, 1987). For example, to learn how lesbians are portrayed on television would be difficult because they are rarely portrayed. Of course, the lack of exposure of a group is significant, as it is a "symbolic annihilation" of this group in the media (Tuchman et al., 1978).

A third criticism relates directly to the analysis of women in the media and the way content analysis organizes evidence within preconceived categories. Studies set out with "a set of original hypothesis, such as 'women are represented as less intelligent than men,' and then organizes empirical evidence which serves to confirm the original hypothesis" (Jaddou & Williams, 1981, p. 105). Content analysis reveals little as to why women are portrayed certain ways. Focus on the content and its simplistic categories steers the researcher and the reader away from other aspects of the media process which may impact the final product.

Many scholars using content analysis to study women and their role in the media would not identify themselves as feminists (especially many of the researchers who published studies in the 1970s), yet a majority of their work reflects a liberal feminist perspective. Liberal-feminists focus on the legal and economic difficulties women face, using the political style of a pressure group as a primary influence. The major goal is to integrate women seeking a piece of the present economic pie into mainstream American society. Their views are the least "offensive" to nonfeminists, because the only change sought is the redistribution of wealth within the present economic and social order rather than a radical change in society as a whole. Although underlying feminist assumptions are rarely identified within the content analysis of women and media, certain common beliefs are uncovered:

1. The fundamental cause for the oppression of women in society is the existence of male supremist ideology and the male chauvinist attitudes which result.

2. Sexual oppression exists independently of other human divisions and, therefore, the struggle against sexism does not necessarily involve any other social issue.

3. Women of all classes, races, and nationalities must subordinate their differences and unite around that which they all have in common—their sex—in order to fight male supremacy (Janus, 1977, p. 20).

Therefore, the major goals of liberal feminism are the elimination of oppression and exploitation of women and the integration of women into society as equals with men.

The intent of content analysis is to document differences within the media and equalize the quality and quantity of roles assigned to males and females. Are women seen outside the home more often than men? Are women depicted as more dependent, more passive, or more emotional than men? The assumption is that if women are seen as "different" they have less chance of competing with men in terms of jobs, advancement, and so on. There is little discussion as to the appropriateness of competition, capitalism, or other societal structures that are reflected in the media.

The fundamental problem with this approach is the separation of discrimination based on sex from that based on race, class, and/or age. Although the fundamental cause for the oppression of women in society is the existence of male chauvinist attitudes, they completely ignore that male chauvinist attitudes reflect white, upper-middle-class attitudes and, therefore, the elimination of the oppression of women alone is insufficient.

The final criticism of content analysis of women's roles in the media is the assumption that if females were portrayed in the same roles as males, the media message would be different. This belief that a mere change in the sex of a character would significantly change the program and its potential effect demonstrates little understanding of the capitalist, patriarchal system in which the media messages are made. A character which embodies the competitive nature of society, for example, would change little whether played by a male or female. Not only would the content remain unchanged (the basic storylines, underlying values of the characters, etc.), but the structure (commercial breaks, plot development, etc.) and the role media play as a business within a capitalist society would continue.

HISTORICAL NARRATIVES

In the early 1970s, feminist academicians began to rediscover and reclaim past women who had influenced their discipline. Realizing women in media history were virtually invisible, feminist communication scholars documented their predecessors. Although women communicators traced "their history to Dinah Nuthead, a colonial printer in Maryland in 1696" (Smith, 1982, p. 146), a major movement fully documenting the history of women and media did not begin until 250 years after her death.

Women as media "processors" (Smith, 1982) were studied via historical descriptive narrative, rectifying the absence of historical figures who made significant contributions to the formation of media, both mainstream and feminist. The resulting works identified and described contributions by many women. The most noted collections include Beasley and Gibbon's (1977) *Women in Media: A Documentary Sourcebook*, Marzolf's (1977) *Up From the Footnote: A History of Women Journalists*, Gelfman's (1976) *Women in Television News*, Belford's (1986) *Brilliant Bylines*, Ross's (1974) *Ladies of the Press*, and Schilpp's (1983) *Great Women of the Press*.

The interest in past media processors led easily to the study of present media processors (Craft, 1988; Mills, 1988; Sanders, 1988). In addition, the problems of women employed in the media came to the surface. *Window Dressing on the Set: Women and Minorities in Television* (U.S. Commission on Civil Rights, 1977) and its update (1979) verified that women and minorities were "not being fully utilized at all levels of station management nor at all levels of local station operations" (p. 153). Women, particularly minority women, were concentrated in clerical jobs. A number of minority women were in visible positions, but without comparable representation in decision-making positions, suggesting that minorities and women serve merely as "window dressing" (U.S. Commission, 1977).

Butler and Paisley (1980) found men in the media work force more likely than women to be managers, to have higher salaries, and to receive promotions. This underrepresentation of women in the media reinforced Singleton and Cook's (1982) findings which discovered women were relegated to less seemingly "important" tasks, even when they held the same positions as men. Women news correspondents reported significantly less foreign affairs, economy, disaster, and feature stories than did their male counterparts. Editors overassigned women significantly more stories dealing with U.S. government, environment, and social problems.

The Women's Institute for the Freedom of the Press (WIFP) was of prime importance to the reclamation project. WIFP published Beasley and Gibbon's (1977) *Women and Media: A Documentary Sourcebook*, one of the first collections focusing on the contributions of individual women to journalism and broadcasting. In addition, WIFP became a clearinghouse for local, national, and international issues concerning women and media through its monthly newsletter, *Media Report to Women*. A portion of *Media Report* is devoted to studies which quantify and qualify women's place in mainstream and feminist media. Examples (1990) include a study which found that 70% of Denver women journalists saw sexism at work; a survey from Britain which showed that women in the advertising business are not in the top jobs; and another which announced that television portrays childless black females as superficial, unskilled, and dependent.

WIFP also publishes a directory of women's media which includes groups and individuals, mainstream and feminist. The directory provides a list of women speakers, courses on women and media, distributors, women's bookstores, and selected directories on women and library collections, all in order to document and make accessible women's media and women's history[1].

In addition to the collections, the newsletter, and studies of women employed in the media, the reclamation of historic women in media is furthered by the study of women and media in the classroom. WIFP sponsors and publishes a collection edited by Densmore entitled *Syllabus Sourcebook on Media and Women* (1980), containing over 60 syllabi on women and media forms (journalism, media, art, broadcasting, communication theory, feminist press, film, history, image, language, photography, radio, soap operas, sports writing, theater, video, and women's magazines). The purpose of the book is to help departments and instructors who want to institute courses on women and media. Dr. Donna Allen, founder of the WIFP, suggests the reader use it to improve "your own courses, or to draw up new ones, and in short, to join us as pioneers in this new movement" (1980, p. v).

Strengths

Historical narrative, in its purest form, serves as a historical framework, providing the reader with a context for struggle in the present day. Biography provides a base for analysis. For example, *Notable Women/The Modern Period* (Sicherman & Green, 1980) presents biographies which are a helpful background for researchers. Many of the women included in this collection are media processors. Although the narrative alone does not provide analysis, researchers can use the narrative as a springboard for further sociocultural analysis.

When people think of women in the media they conjure up such names as Barbara Walters or Margaret Bourke-White, while a woman such as Ida Lupino is known more for her abilities in front of the camera (as an actress) than behind it (as one of the first women television directors). A strength of the historical narrative, therefore, is to verify that there were and continue to be a multitude of strong women in the media. Women such as: Ida B. Wells, a journalist and one of the most effective black leaders; Judith Carey Waller, the first station manager of WMAQ, Chicago and the first to produce play-by-play college football; Charlotte Spears Bass, editor of *The California Eagle*, the oldest black newspaper on the West Coast; and Alicia Patterson, publisher of *Newsday*, are among those who were lost until researchers began this reclamation process. The mere reclaiming of women in media history provides role models for women to emulate, credibility for women working in the media, and a historic tradition of which women in the media can be proud.

Limitations

Once again, an underlying assumption within the historic narrative tradition is if more women were processors, past or present, mainstream media would be different. My argument is that the socialization process of most media processors, male or female, is so complete that little change would occur. Training by journalism schools and other media institutions teaches students certain accepted attitudes and values. Media organizations reinforce this socialization through evaluation and advancement. Peer pressure and audience expectations solidify these aspects until a person, male or female, would find it difficult to rebel. Therefore, it may not be the sex of the media processor which would change the media, but the ability to question traditional media values.

Historic narratives give the details of a person's life, but tell the reader little else. There is no way the reader can understand the cultural setting of the time or the complex interactions of that era. Historic narratives are discrete units with little connection among them. In order to get a better understanding, many historic narratives must be written, interwoven, and read.

CULTURAL STUDIES

Critical studies are based, directly or indirectly, on a Marxist position in which mass media are considered "a means of production," and part of "the monopolistic ownership of the capitalist class, nationally or internationally organized" to serve the interests of that class (McQuail, 1989, p. 63). Those who work in the media—cultural workers—are used to manufacture and distribute the ideological message the ruling class wishes to be seen or heard. Those who are exposed to the media are manipulated into accepting the ideological messages presented. If indeed the media mirror society, the mirror is a distorted one, reflecting only the dominant ruling class's ideological views. This limited view subjugates questions of sex under questions of class, thus reducing the importance of women's position within society, their unique contribution, and women's oppression, unless it is connected to a discussion of class. Part of the Marxist position is the belief that economics is a prime influence on ideology, and therefore, the study of class within society is the focus. One critical approach, cultural studies, challenges this "vulgar" Marxist analysis by including economic, cultural, and political factors as influential in the formation of ideology through media content (Williams, 1958).

Feminist scholars who sought the study of women's experiences and cultures or women's role in the present culture found cultural studies very appealing. Feminist cultural studies scholars view the media as a means of transmitting "sexist ideology" which justifies a patriarchal society. Sexist ideology assures that women will accept their inferior status (low-paying jobs, little authority, traditional roles in the family). Feminist cultural studies examines how dominant ideologies are integrated throughout the media and "how they function within a patriarchal culture where 'preferred' meanings reside in male discourse" (Baehr, 1981, p. 145).

Cultural studies, especially its U.S. outgrowth, should have provided fertile ground in which feminist media studies could grow. This did not occur. Cultural studies continued to ignore women's "ways of life" in the analysis of media. In studies of youth subcultures and popular music (Chambers, 1985; Grossberg, 1983-1984; Hebdige, 1979; Willis, 1973), for example, female experiences are subsumed into "youth" experiences (which really means male), ignored, or used to reinforce the stereotypical image of females in general.[2] While concentrating on class values, issues of gender (and race) go unexplored.

In opposition to male-dominated cultural studies, feminist scholars began to study the experiences of females in British society. McRobbie and Garber (1975), for example, studied working-class teenage girls. Although they adopted some of the guidelines used in the study of boys and subcultures, "the centrality of class; the importance of the spheres of school, work, leisure, and the family," they also "added the crucial dimension of sex and gender structuring" (p. 210). While detailing various roles girls played which differed from boys, McRobbie and Garber also found that girls negotiated a different space than boys, and offered "a different type of resistance to what can at least in part be viewed as their sexual subordination" (p. 221).

McRobbie and Garber have been followed by other cultural scholars who study women and their relationship to media and society. Dorothy Hobson (1982) analyzed the female audience of *Crossroads*, by using multiple methods and studying various sources to examine this British soap opera. Baehr and Dyer include in their book, *Boxed In: Women and Television* (1987), a section which focuses on women and programming strategies and another section which highlights women's roles on television.

In the United States, feminist scholars with slight modifications to the cultural studies approach analyze media forms which range from soap operas to feminist media. Perhaps one of the most well-known studies is Janice Radway's *Reading the Romances* (1984). Her approach may seem wide in scope but it enables her to gain a broader perspective which is true of the cultural studies approach. For example, she not only studies the texts from a feminist perspective, she assesses the publication and distribution process of the novels, and ties this together through interviews with women who are heavy readers of romance novels. Her analysis brings together the various factions which make up the culture of the romance novel reader.

Other examples which are similar in scope include: Rakow's (1988) analysis of gender and technology; Lont's (1984) study of a women's music recording label, Redwood Records; Brown's (1991) study of Australian soap opera viewing by adolescents; and Steeves and Smith's (1987) socialist feminist analysis of prime-time television.

Strengths

A cultural studies approach is both holistic and historic, recognizing that events and institutions can never be viewed apart from their social context. In order to understand an "event or institution one must study the historical conditions which shape it" (Janus, 1977, p. 24).

Differing from a content analysis approach to the study of media, a cultural studies approach includes more than a study of sex roles. A multitude of social/cultural relationships are analyzed. Taking a Marxist approach to the study of class further, feminist scholars take into consideration the interaction of class and gender (often race) in their study of the media (Steeves, 1987). The move away from a liberal-feminist approach to a more Marxist-feminist approach, where the point of departure must be that we live in a capitalist-society which oppresses people in many diverse ways, is imperative. Media images reflect not only sexism but also other forms of oppression based on class, race, and nationality.

A feminist cultural approach is activist in nature, acknowledging that representations of women (and men) cannot change unless the structures of patriarchal economic and social relations also change. A feminist cultural studies approach opens up questions about the special nature of women's relationship to the media. In other studies, vital questions are left unasked. Cultural studies allow one to seek answers which go beyond the roles women play in the media to the roles women play in patriarchal relations under capitalism and, then, to the representation of those relations in the ideological domain.

Limitations

In general, cultural studies lack any methodological rigidness. Although the theories behind cultural studies are abundant, the "how-to" of cultural studies is absent. Each researcher must determine her/his own best method for analysis.

Much cultural studies research is overly theoretical with little practical application to specific cultures. This is a problem both for the discipline itself and, most important, for students interested in cultural studies. Theoretical pieces abound focusing on the philosophical issues of cultural studies, but few examples are available detailing how to implement these theories.

Scholars who study cultures from a cultural studies perspective, no matter what the specific methods used, find they must synthesize great amounts of information in order to "read" the culture. As with any qualitative approach, problems exist for both the researcher and the reader. The researcher, to more fully understand the culture, must be concerned with massive amounts of information in a variety of forms, and then synthesize this material into a comprehensible form. Cultural studies research on specific cultures, by their very nature, are much longer than the average published article. Although there are now journals which will accept longer pieces, the majority of the communication journals have standard length requirements which are problematic for cultural studies. In addition, we as readers are used to articles with a structure, which is easily scanned and condenses the results.

The limits which affect cultural studies are no different than the limits on any approach using qualitative methods. The results are not generalizable and the studies not replicable, nor are they intended to be. Depending on your research philosophy, this may or may not be seen as a limitation.

NEW DIRECTIONS

The three approaches to the study of women and mass communication are all important in their own right. Content analysis helps verify the differences between women's and men's roles in the media. Historic narratives provide valuable material to reclaim women in the media and to further our understanding of specific periods of media development. Cultural studies view cultures (including women's and feminist cultures) from a more holistic view, detailing the interaction of media and society. Each approach continues to enhance the understanding of women and the media.

Feminist mass communication researchers continue to try to understand women and their connection to the media by melding various approaches. Content analysis is used to form a foundation on which to build a critical analysis; historical narratives are used to situate a critical analysis; and cultural studies approaches are incorporating economics as an important component of what Garnham (1983) entitles "cultural materialism." The traditional limits placed on research methodologies and perspectives are being eradicated.

Feminist researchers are calling for more activism within research (Condit, 1988). The mandate that research be shrouded in "objectivity" is ignored as feminist scholars not only report results but recommend changes in society. Feminist scholars further social change by studying the media's crucial role in the construction of meaning and the reconstruction of feminism and feminist issues within patriarchal discourse (Baehr, 1981, p. 148).

To continue to understand the role of media and its impact on women (and men), other issues must be addressed. Scholars must redefine the ideology of "professionalism" within the media. Hochschild (1971) discusses the clockwork of the male career which focuses the attention of the researcher on the important roles most often filled by males. Support staff such as production assistants, production secretaries, continuity, copy editors, and so on most often filled by females, are left unnoted. The contribution of women's work must be identified and discussed. The role of women within the economics of a capitalist, patriarchal society continues to be of prime importance in order to fully understand the ideological messages embedded within the media.

Research on feminist media (media which have as one of their main goals the elimination of sexist ideology) is severely limited (Lont, 1984; Taylor, 1988). The majority of feminist media and their structure is completely different from the mainstream, yet little research has focused on these alternative means of communicating and working. If one intention of feminist scholars is to change the media's role in society, the study of feminist media and its alternate view of media is imperative.

Within the historic narrative, more research needs to focus on women of color and their roles in the media process (employment and portrayal) (Rhodes, 1991). The absence of lesbians in media is another area which needs further exploration.

Studies of women and the media must look beyond a simple, directional connection between media and the impact on audience that content analysis or historic narrative assumes. These approaches err in their view of the relationship between media and user. It is not the media alone which determine what women are, but culture in conjunction with the media which contributes to women's subordinated positions.

Finally, research on the roles assigned to women within our own discipline needs to be addressed. In many areas of communication research there has been an increase in the academic ranks of women. Yet, many women and men continue to believe that mass communication, especially the area of study which involves technologies, is a male bastion. The most visible women in mass communication are known for their work in such traditional areas as children and television (Wartella, 1979, 1980; Wartella & Ettema, 1974; Wartella & Reeves, 1985) or soap operas (Alexander, 1985): admirable work but acceptable "women's" areas of study. Questions of academic bias need to be addressed. Are women only interested in these traditional female areas of study or are they guided into these areas by their graduate advisors? Are there no women studying the traditional male areas of mass communication study or do they find less support by publishers and editors for their work? Indeed, how can we expect strong women researchers if they are limited to certain areas of study or given less credibility if they chose to study the more male areas of technology? Perhaps our study of the roles assigned to women in the media needs to be expanded to the roles assigned to women in the study of the media. The charge that many fields have been male-centered is undeniable (Bleier, 1988). Although some women study mass communication, change will take more than the acceptance of a few tokens in the field. As more women study mass communication, work together within the same department, and receive and give support for their views and approaches, which may differ from the male-defined approaches and research of the past, changes may occur.

NOTES TO CHAPTER 8

1. As of 1991, *The Directory of Women's Media* was transferred to a new publisher, The National Council for Research on Women, The Sara Delano Roosevelt Memorial House, 47-49 East 65th Street, New York, NY 10021.

2. This point is reinforced by Corrigan and Frith (1975) in "The Politics of Youth Culture:" "In this piece we have (in common with almost every other writer on youth culture) ignored women—our notion of 'the working class kid' is a male one. We have no excuse except ignorance—we know very little about the culture of teenage girls—but we don't want to conceal the serious political problems of working class sexism, adult and young" (p. 239).

REFERENCES

Alexander, A. (1985). Adolescents' soap opera viewing and relational perceptions. *Journal of Broadcasting and Electronic Media, 29,* 295-308.

Baehr, H. (1981). The impact of feminism on media studies—just another commercial break? In D. Spender (Ed.), *Men's studies modified: The impact of feminism on the academic disciplines.* Oxford: Pergamon Press.

Baehr, H., & Dyer, G. (1987). *Boxed in: Women and television.* New York: Pandora.

Beasley, M., & Gibbons, S. (1977). *Women in media: A documentary sourcebook.* Washington, DC: Women's Institute for Freedom of the Press.

Belford, B. (1986). *Brilliant bylines: A biographical anthology of notable newspaper women.* New York: Columbia University Press.

Bleier, R. (1988). *Feminist approaches to science.* New York: Pergamon Press.

Bonelli, L. (1989). Sex-role stereotyping in fragrance advertisements In C.M. Lont & S.F. Friedley (Eds.), *Beyond boundaries: Sex and gender diversity in communication* (pp. 265-282). Fairfax, VA: George Mason University Press.

Brabant, S. (1976). Sex role stereotyping in the Sunday Comics. *Sex Roles, 2,* 331-337.

Brabant, S., & Mooney, L. (1986). Sex role stereotyping in the Sunday Comics: Ten years later. *Sex Roles, 14,* 141-148.

Brown, M.E. (1991). Strategies and tactics: Teenagers' readings of an Australian soap opera. *Women and Language, XIV* (1), 22-28.

Buerkel-Rothfuss, N., & Mayes, S. (1981). Soap opera viewing and the cultivation effect. *Journal of Communication, 31,* 108-115.

Butler, M., & Paisley, W. (1980). *Women and the mass media.* New York: Human Sciences Press.

Butruille, S.G., & Taylor, A. (1987). Women in American popular song. In L.P. Stewart & S. Ting-Toomey (Eds.), *Communication, gender and sex roles in diverse interaction contexts* (pp. 179-188). Norwood, NJ: Ablex.

Chambers, I. (1985). *Urban rhythms: Pop music and popular culture.* London: MacMillan.

Clark, R.L. (1980). How women's magazines cover living alone. *Journalism Quarterly, 58,* 292-294.

Condit, C.M. (1988). What makes our scholarship feminist? A radical/liberal view. *Women's Studies in Communication, 11,* 6-8.

Corrigan, P., & Frith, S. (1975). The politics of youth culture. *Working Papers in Cultural Studies,* 7-8, 231-242.

Courtney, A.E., & Whipple, T.W. (1974). Women in TV commercials. *Journal of Communication, 24,* 110-118.

Craft, C. (1988). *Too old, too ugly, and not deferential to men.* Rocklin, CA: Prima Publishing and Communications.

Densmore, D. (Ed.). (1980). *Syllabus sourcebook on media and women.* Washington, DC: Women's Institute for Freedom of the Press.

Downing, M. (1974). Heroine of the daytime serial. *Journal of Communication, 24,* 130-137.

Downs, A.C. (1981). Sex-role stereotyping on prime-time television. *The Journal of Genetic Psychology, 138,* 253-258.

Downs, A.C., & Harrison, S.K. (1985). Embarrassing age spots or just plain ugly: Physical attractiveness stereotyping as an instrument of sexism on American television commercials. *Sex Roles, 13,* 9-19.

Franzwa, H.H. (1974). Working women in fact and fiction. *Journal of Communication, 24,* 104-109.

Garnham, N. (1983). Toward a theory of cultural materialism. *Journal of Communication, 33,* 314-329.

Geis, F.L., Brown, V., Jennings, J., & Porter, N. (1984). TV commercials as achievement scripts for women. *Sex Roles, 10,* 513-525.

Gelfman, J.S. (1976). *Women in television news.* New York: Columbia University Press.

Gerbner, G., & Gross, L. (1976). Living with television: The violence profile. *Journal of Communication, 26,* 173-179.

Gerbner, G., Gross, L., Jackson-Beeck, M., Jeffries-Fox, S., & Signorelli, N. (1978). Cultural indicators: Violence profile #9. *Journal of Communication, 28,* 176-207.

Goff, D.H., Goff, L.D., & Lehrer, S.K. (1980). Sex-role portrayals of selected female television characters. *Journal of Broadcasting, 24,* 467-477.

Grossberg, L. (1983-1984). The politics of youth culture: Some observations on rock and roll in American culture. *Social Text, 8,* 104-126.

Haskell, D. (1979). The depiction of women in leading roles in prime time television. *Journal of Broadcasting, 23,* 191-196.

Hawkins, R., & Pingree, S. (1981). Using television to construct social reality. *Journal of Broadcasting, 25,* 347-364.

Hebdige, D. (1979). *Subculture: The meaning of style.* London: Methuen.

Henderson, L., Greenberg, B.S., & Aitken, C.K. (1980). Sexual differences in giving orders, making plans and needing support on television. In B.S. Greenberg (Ed.), *Life on television: Content analyzes of U.S. TV drama* (pp. 49-63). Norwood, NJ: Ablex.

Hirsch, P.M. (1981). On not learning from one's mistakes: A reanalysis of Gerbner et al's findings on cultivation analysis part II. *Communication Research, 8,* 73-95.

Hobson, D. (1982). *Crossroads: The drama of a soap opera.* London: Methuen.

Hochschild, A. (1971). Inside the clockwork of the male career. In F. Howe (Ed.), *Women and the power to change* (pp. 47-80). New York: Carnegie Foundation.

Hughes, M. (1980). The fruits of cultivation analysis: A reexamination of some effects of television watching. *Public Opinion Quarterly, 44,* 287-302.

Hyden, C., & McCandless, N.J. (1983). Men and women as portrayed in the lyrics of contemporary music. *Popular Music and Society, 9,* 19-26.

Jaddou, L., & Williams, J. (1981). A theoretical contribution to the struggle against the dominant representation of women. *Media, Culture and Society, 3,* 105-124.

Janus, N. Z. (1977). Research on sex-roles in the mass media: Toward a critical approach. *Insurgent Sociologist, 7,* 19-32.

Lont, C.M. (1984). *Between rock and a hard place: A model of subcultural persistence and women's music.* An unpublished dissertation, University of Iowa, Iowa City.

Lont, C.M. (1990). The roles assigned to females and males in non-music radio programming. *Sex Roles, 22,* 661-668.

Marzolf, M. (1977). *Up from the footnote: A history of women journalists.* New York: Hastings House.

Mayes, S.L., & Valentine, K.B. (1979). Sex role stereotyping in Saturday morning cartoon shows. *Journal of Broadcasting, 23*, 41-45.

McNeil, J.C. (1975). Feminism, femininity, and the television series: A content analysis. *Journal of Broadcasting, 19*, 259-271.

McQuail, D. (1989). *Theories of mass communication.* London: Sage.

McRobbie, A., & Garber, J. (1975). Girls and subcultures: An exploration. *Working Papers in Cultural Studies, 7-8*, 209-222.

Media Report to Women. (1990, March/April). 18.

Mills, K. (1988). *A place in the news: From the women's pages to the front page.* New York: Dodd, Mead.

Morgan, M., & Rothschild, N. (1983). Impact of the new television technologies: Cable TV, peers, and sex-role cultivation in the electronic environment. *Youth and Society, 15*, 33-50.

National Organization for Women, National Capital Area Chapter. (1972). *Women in the wasteland fight back.* Washington, DC: NOW, National Capital Area Chapter.

Newcomb, H. (1981). Assessing the violence profile studies of Gerbner and Gross: A humanistic critique and suggestion. In M. Janowitz & P. Hirsch (Eds.). Reader in public opinion and mass communication. New York: Free Press.

Radway, J.A. (1984). *Reading the romances: Women, patriarchy, and popular literature.* Chapel Hill: The University of North Carolina Press.

Rakow, L.F. (1988). Gendered technology: Gendered practice. *Critical Studies in Mass Communication, 5*, 57-70.

Rhodes, J. (1991). Television's realist portrayal of African-American women and the case of "L.A. Law." *Women and Language, XIV* (1), 29-34.

Ross, I. (1974). *Ladies of the press.* New York: Arno Press.

Sanders, M. (1988). *Waiting for prime time: The women of television news.* Urbana, IL: University of Illinois Press.

Saucier, K.A. (1986). Healers and heartbreakers: Images of women and men in country music. *Journal of Popular Culture, 20*, 147-166.

Schilpp, M.G. (1983). *Great women of the press.* Carbondale, IL: Southern Illinois University Press.

Screen Actors Guild. (1974). *The relative roles of men and women in television commercials.* New York: Screen Actors Guild.

Seggar, J.F. (1975). Imagery of women in television drama: 1974. *Journal of Broadcasting, 19*, 273-281.

Sicherman, B., & Green, C.H. (Eds.). (1980). *Notable American women/The modern period* (Vol. 2). Cambridge, MA: Belknap Press.

Singleton, L.A. & Cook, S.L. (1982). Television network news reporting by female correspondents: An update. *Journal of Broadcasting, 26*, 487-491.

Smith, M.Y. (1982). Research retrospective: Feminism and the media. *Communication Research, 9*, 146-160.

Sparks, G.G., & Fehlner, C.L. (1986). Faces in the news: Gender comparisons of magazine photographs. *Journal of Communication, 36*, 70-

79.

Steeves, H.L. (1987). Feminist theories and media studies. *Critical Studies in Mass Communication, 4,* 95-135.

Steeves, H.L., & Smith, M.C. (1987). Class and gender in prime-time television entertainment: Observations from a socialist feminist perspective. *Journal of Communication Inquiry, 11*(1), 43-63.

Streicher, H.W. (1974). The girls in cartoons. *Journal of Communication, 24,* 125-129.

Taylor, A. (1988). Implementing feminist principles in a bureaucracy: Studio D The National Film Board of Canada. In B.Bate & A. Taylor (Eds.). *Women communicating: Studies of women's talk* (pp. 277-302). Norwood, NJ: Ablex.

Tedesco, N.S. (1974). Patterns in prime time. *Journal of Communication, 24,* 119-124.

Tuchman, G., Daniels, A.K., & Benet, J. (1978). *Hearth and home: Images of women in the mass media.* New York: Oxford University Press.

Turow, J. (1974). Advising and ordering: Daytime, prime time. *Journal of Communication, 24,* 138-141.

U.S. Commission on Civil Rights. (1977). *Window dressing on the set: Women and minorities in television.* Washington, DC: U.S. Government Printing Office.

U.S. Commission on Civil Rights. (1979). *Window dressing on the set: An update.* Washington, DC: U.S. Government Printing Office.

Wartella, E. (1979). *Children communicating: Media in development of thought, speech, understanding.* Beverly Hills, CA: Sage.

Wartella, E. (1980). Children and television: The development of the child's understanding of the medium. In G. Wilhoit & H. deBrock (Eds.), *Mass communication review yearbook* (pp. 516-553). Beverly Hills, CA: Sage.

Wartella, E., & Ettema, J. (1974). A cognitive developmental study of children's attention to television commercials. *Communication Research, 1,* 46-49.

Wartella, E., & Reeves, B. (1985). Historical trends in research on children and the media: 1900-1960. *Journal of Communication, 35,* 118-133.

Weigel, R. H., & Loomis, J.W. (1981). Televised models of female achievement revisited: Some progress. *Journal of Applied Social Psychology, 11,* 58-63.

Williams, R. (1958). *Culture and society.* New York: Columbia University Press.

Willis, P. (1973, March). The triple X boys. *New Society,* 693-695.

Wimmer, R.D., & Dominick, J.R. (1987). *Mass media research* (2nd ed.). Belmont, CA: Wadsworth Publishing.

Women's Institute for Freedom of the Press. (1989). *1989 Directory of women's media.* Washington, DC: Women's Institute for Freedom of the Press.

Chapter 9

Enlarging Conceptual Boundaries: A Critique of Research in Intercultural Communication

Alberto Gonzalez
Bowling Green State University
Bowling Green, OH

Tarla Rai Peterson
Texas A&M University
College Station, TX

As we reviewed the essays to be included in *Feminist Visions*, we noticed how "culture" figured prominently in the future of feminist communication research. The literature reviews from each chapter reveal that feminism does not yet reflect a diversity of women's cultural voices and that the development of new questions and methods for understanding the communication of marginalized cultural communities represents an exciting challenge, not only for feminist communication research, but for the communication field as a whole.

Attention to culture arises from the realization that a woman's symbolic construction of exploitation is framed by her cultural experience. Indeed, her concept of womanhood is largely constructed from the distinct meanings and values of her cultural community. Further, the symbolic images of inclusion and self-determination will manifest themselves variously, according to the world view of her cultural community. Feminist visions, then, anticipate cultural analysis as a ground for research in women's communication.

In this chapter, we begin by describing a feminist perspective that could enrich the study of communication cultures. Second, we review the traditional questions and methods used in three branches of intercultural communication research and assess the possibilities for the incorporation of feminist concerns. Third, we present examples of feminist research in intercultural communication and discuss how they introduce intercultural and cultural possibilities that are omitted from malestream[1] research. Fourth, we propose our vision for feminist research of communication cultures. Finally, we discuss concepts and projects, including some suggested in this volume, that illustrate how a culturally sensitive feminist perspective could radicalize communication inquiry, while "interculturalizing" feminist theory.

A FEMINIST PERSPECTIVE TOWARD COMMUNICATION CULTURES

By "feminist perspective," we mean initially, as Offen (1988) stated, "recogniz[ing] the validity of women's own interpretations of their lived experience and needs and acknowledg[ing] the values women claim publicly as their own" (p. 152). Among other things, feminism identifies the patriarchal structures and processes of exclusion and calls for the reinterpretation of history and social hierarchy. For many feminism entails activism. Foss and Foss (1988) concluded:

> [T]he feminist perspective seeks to understand human behavior and through that understanding, to change social life. Feminist scholars see how gender has been constructed to denigrate women and seek to change that construction (p. 10).

The orienting values that guide feminist scholarship feature equal participation and authenticity. Fine (1988) argues that feminist scholars should employ "research methods that do not exploit those who are the subjects of research; that do not impose the researcher's reality on the subjects; that let the researched speak for themselves in their own voices" (p. 19).

The implications of a rapproachment between a feminist perspective and intercultural communication research are advanced through the following claims:

1. The inherently political stance of a feminist perspective is compatible with the primary motive behind intercultural research. At its best, intercultural research bestows legitimation to all voices in cross-cultural dialogue and provides insights about the communication of previously marginalized voices. This move is not solely an epistemological mandate. It is a political recognition of ethnocentrism within the academy.

Feminism is also political in its open opposition to women's subordination to men and in its search to alter the patriarchal basis of social organization and control. Fowlkes (1987) wrote that, "Feminist epistemology recognizes the political nature of our attempts to know and accepts the responsibility for carrying on a politics of knowledge" (p. 2). Accepting this responsibility means that feminist work cannot stop with the recognition of injustice. It advocates the elimination of injustice through efforts to intervene in coercive power relationships.

2. A feminist perspective inherently provides criticism. However, the critique of gender and other historical power configurations must demonstrate sensitivity to cultural diversity regarding notions of womanhood, manhood, and personhood. Offen (1988) points out that feminist theory in the United States has been biased toward the "assumption that equality of rights is the essence of feminism" (p. 124). This United States conception of individual equality and rights may be inappropriate for many cultures. For example, Bassnet (1986) writes that her upbringing in a Mediterranean family with Marxist politics led her to perceive that, "The needs of the one exist in a dialectical relationship with the needs of the many" (p. 10). She finds feminism in the United States alien to this world view and is "disturbed by the tendency in the women's groups towards what seemed to [her] to be a somewhat egotistic emphasis on self-development" (p.10). Like interculturalists, feminist critics should carefully reflect on how their constructions of gender are inevitably a product of their cultural milieu.

3. Intercultural communication research from a feminist perspective reveals how discursive media (structures of power, knowledge, ideology, myth, etc.) are used to construct and maintain culture-specific images of gender in the actual interactions between members of culturally distinct communities. Only if feminism transcends the boundaries of Western society, resonating with the experiences of women in other societies, will its politics of transformation be realized. We support these claims in the sections that follow.

INTERCULTURAL COMMUNICATION: AN OVERVIEW

While occasionally taking into account the social facticity of gender, intercultural communication inquiry as undertaken by United States scholars has yet to incorporate the construction of gender in the explication of discourse produced from culturally varied sources (Offen, 1988). We argue that in the portrayal of monolithic culture, the majority of intercultural studies published in the 1970s and 1980s privileged Anglo-masculine analyses of culture, social structures, and behavior. An ironic consequence is that reductionist approaches, most visible in the equation of nationality with culture, suppressed and distorted the phenomenon of cultural diversity at a time when it claimed to enlighten previously unexplored ways of living and communicating.

Intercultural communication scholars have yet to produce germinal area-defining articles, what might be referred to as "classic" intercultural communication studies, or guides that go much beyond transplanting familiar recommendations for good communication (empathy, openness, equality) into the intercultural context. Popular texts on intercultural communication mirror the predominant topics in intercultural research, namely relationships between culture and language, self-identity, interpersonal conflict, social context, nonverbal communication systems, and cultural sensitivity (Borden, 1991; Dodd, 1987; Samovar & Porter, 1991; Singer, 1987).

While intercultural communication inquiry has only recently become a legitimate focus for communication scholars, it has developed rapidly. Divisions in our national and regional organizations, 13 volumes of the Speech Communication Association's *International and Intercultural Communication Annual*, numerous journal articles, and prescriptive texts attest to the expanse of the subject as well as to the urgency of addressing issues of theory and method.

There is fair consensus on the precise human phenomenon that is the purview of intercultural communication research. In 1980, Asante described the fundamental object of intercultural study. "Cultural differences," he wrote, "not cultural similarity, is [sic] the premise of the field of intercultural communication. If this were not the case then all our discussions would be pointless" (p. 401). Kim's (1984) definition also is centered on the notion of difference: "Intercultural communication, then, refers to communication phenomena in which participants, different in cultural backgrounds, come into direct or indirect contact with one another" (p. 16). Beyond a consensus on scene, there is little that unites intercultural researchers, a condition that prompted Gudykunst (1983) to describe intercultural inquiry as "aparadigmatic [implying] a somewhat immature area" (p. 14). Methodologically, intercultural inquiry has included empirical-quantitative measurement (Ting-Toomey, 1986), rhetorical criticism (Starosta, 1984), and hermeneutics, (Deetz, 1984; Pilotta, 1983).

The traditional questions in intercultural study emphasize theory building and fidelity in representing the native's symbolic world: What is the relationship between culture and communication? How can "culture" and "communication" be construed to produce a plausible theory for intercultural communication? What characteristics of communication, if any, are unique to the intercultural communication context? By what methods can the intercultural communication context be studied? These questions have been addressed generally in three very different ways. The approaches compose three active and often contentious research branches: cultural measurement, cultural description, and cultural criticism.[2]

The Cultural Measurement Branch

Kim (1986) introduced Volume 10 of the *ICC Annual* with a clear definition of the cultural measurement branch:

> The central research focus in the communication approach to interethnic relations is the communication process itself, that is, the process of contact and interaction between individuals of differing ethnicity through sending, receiving, and interpreting verbal and nonverbal messages. (p. 12)

Although Kim attempted to cast the widest net in calling for multidisciplinary approaches to the process of intercultural interaction, her methodological preference was clearly toward experimental design. This preference repeats a bias expressed in an earlier Annual in which Sarbaugh and Asuncion-Lande (1983) asserted that intercultural inquiry has "attracted many amateurs" who "sometimes do not adhere to established standards for scientific research" (pp. 45-46).

The cultural measurement approach has dominated intercultural inquiry in the 1980s. Utilizing quantitative methods in experimental design, Gudykunst, Kim, Ting-Toomey, and others have set out to build a theory of intercultural communication, and they advocate theory building as the primary goal for intercultural inquiry.

This branch has been attacked for relying too heavily on empirical psychology and its embodiment of Western rationalism—a rationalism that is not amenable to cross-cultural application. Asante and Vora (1983) observed: "[O]ur analysis of the interaction must not impose Western categories. Few scholars have been willing to relinquish their hold on methods designed for nonintercultural forms of dialogue and interaction" (pp. 293-294). Tsuda (1986) stated: "Still today, empirical positivist methodology with its objective, functional, and apolitical tendency makes most social scientists become an accomplice to the social injustices and inequalities the ruling class has created and wanted so much to keep unexplored" (p. 10).

Shuter (1990) argued that this branch simply exploits the intercultural context to validate more general communication theories such as uncertainty reduction, communication apprehension, and initial interaction perception (p. 238). He stated:

> [R]esearchers in communication who conduct intercultural research do not generally exhibit in their published studies a passion for culture, an interest in descriptive research, or a desire to generate intracultural theories of communication. Instead, much of the published research in intercultural communication, particularly in the national and regional speech-communication journals, is conducted to refine existing communication theories: culture serves principally as a research laboratory for testing the validity of communication paradigms.
>
> While this research agenda has produced significant insights on selected communication theories, it has virtually ignored the heart and soul of intercultural research: culture. (p. 238)

Put another way, Shuter seems to ask: *Where is the culture* in intercultural research?

As currently practiced, much quantitative research still equates culture with nationality and adopts a monolithic view of culture. The problem occurs when broad sampling techniques come to represent attitudes of "a culture" without regard to intracultural diversity. In her review of *Culture and Interpersonal Communication*, Stanback (1990) identified a weakness of broad sampling techniques used in the study of culture: "Because the authors consider `culture' as synonymous with `nation' and `society,' they do not emphasize research on ethnic groups within nations, although some of their conclusions are applicable to certain genres of interethnic research" (p. 329). In another instance, Ting-Toomey (1988) used survey responses from 246 French undergraduate students, 279 undergraduates from Japan, and 256 communication students "from a moderate-sized university on the east coast" of the United States (p. 32). From these samples she derived, as the title of the article states, "Rhetorical Sensitivity Style in Three Cultures: France, Japan, and the United States." Although key information is absent—Are the universities public or private? What socioeconomic classes are involved? What are the ethnic groups represented? From what regions do the students come?—the reader is expected to accept each sample as representative of a single national identity.

The debate over how to study communication among cultures is not new. In 1978, Hepworth advocated that "more pre-empirical study of the instruments used in cross-cultural attitude and personality measurement must be conducted. In addition, more field work is necessary to collect and assess ethnographic data from foreign cultures in which experiments are to be conducted" (p. 42). At the same time, Casmir (1978), though stressing a holistic approach, dismissed the kinds of data sought by ethnographers in stating that: "*Episodic*, highly limited, but often interesting and informative reports of culture-specific ways of dealing with such matters as food, time, sex, family relations, and age have unfortunately done little to allow broader, generally applicable, or generalizable insights" (p. 4, emphasis in the original).

As currently practiced, the experimental design paradigm of explain-predict-control is not friendly to a feminist perspective that seeks to reveal and change patterns of women's oppression.[3] The paradigm is inherently manipulative where the feminist resists manipulation; it reduces human experience where the feminist seeks to understand the simultaneous facets and conditions of human experience. The central values of the paradigm are male-defined standards of validity and reliability, constructs that bring to the status of knowledge only those events that are judged familiar by the researcher.

The Cultural Description Branch

An alternative approach relies on descriptive detail as the basis for cultural analysis. The symbolic elements of cultural life are at the forefront of this approach. Cultural members are observed in their native environments and "produce" data as they move through daily routines. Here, validity is the presentation and description of a social world that is not only recognizable to its inhabitants, it is confirmed by them. In contrast to the cultural measurement branch, the ethnography branch views culture as an intricate mosaic, one whose overall form is yet unclear, in which individual communities perform variations on broader cultural norms.

Philipsen's (1975, 1976, 1986) programmatic elucidation of the cultural dimensions of "Teamsterville" talk successfully established (a) the utility of ethnographic detail in the interpretation of discourse, (b) that the interpretation of "culturally situated speech" is informed by the native speaker's conceptualization of the role of speech, and (c) that the cultural interpretation of discourse is a viable and occasionally necessary means for providing accounts of how meanings are understood by various publics.

Using participant observation and extensive interview techniques, Philipsen described how members of an urban neighborhood sustained a specific social identity (maleness) through unique styles and codes for speaking. Katriel and Philipsen (1981) interviewed respondents, examined respondent's logs, and observed the communication conduct of two women from the northwest United States. Their study showed that in *some* American speech the term "communication" refers to an intimate and rare interaction whereby the self is validated and problems of identity are addressed.

Others have extended Philipsen's ethnographic approach to the study of culturally situated discourse (Carbaugh, 1987; Katriel, 1987; Kochman, 1986). These studies have produced insights at the intracultural level and acknowledge implications for the intercultural context only indirectly (for recent exceptions see Carbaugh, 1989; Gonzalez 1989; Philipsen, 1989).

The ethnographer's desire for nonevaluative thick description, however, has precluded explanations of how talk is used to suppress. For example, it is clear from Philipsen's description of Teamsterville that status-equal males in the presence of a female will not include her in conversation in order to assert their dominance. Her efforts to be included in conversation, according to the Teamsterville cultural code, would be met with physical force. The nonrepresentation of women's voices in Philipsen's Teamsterville studies reproduces the Teamsterville code that silences women. As currently practiced, ethnographers of speech are not inclined to describe such codes as oppressive.

But the ethnographer need not jeopardize nonjudgmental description by presenting the possible implications of such cultural codes. The male "places for speaking" in Teamsterville, the neighborhood street and corner, can also be described as female "places of silence." In Teamsterville, women's discourse is confined to the "front porch." What kind of female talk occurs on the front porch? A feminist perspective would seek to discover and represent the speech of marginalized cultural members.

Thus, with a new feminist awareness, this descriptive approach to cultural analysis is capable of making available to the critic the discursive forms from which members of women's communities order and perform strategies to enact their identity and to induce change. The ethnographer's efforts to allow interpretation to emerge from and represent authentically the lived experiences of cultural members in as complete a way as possible complements the feminist's goal of empowering women's voices.

The Cultural Criticism Branch

Asante, Newmark, and Blake (1979) view the intercultural communication context as essentially problematic. Intercultural studies, "seek to explicate the dissimilarities and similarities which impede or enhance communication across cultures. The task is to elucidate the problems and issues of intercultural communication" (p. 11). Building on the presumption of intercultural communication as problematic, recent texts prescribe varying sets of variables, strategies, and ethics for satisfying intercultural interaction (Brislin, 1981; Dodd, 1987; Samovar & Porter, 1987; Sitaram & Cogdell, 1976).

The issues extend beyond evaluations of communication in intercultural settings to critiques of the ways in which scholars conceptualize those settings. Asante (1980) argued that American theoretical frameworks and prescriptions for intercultural communication competence contain Western biases that limit understanding of "Afrocentric" and "Asiocentric" perspectives (p. 402). Similarly, in a critique on the cultural measurement approaches to intercultural communication research, Yum (1988) stated:

> [T]here has been increasing dissatisfaction with the use of North American models of communication to explain communication processes in Asia. . . . Most cross-cultural studies of communication simply describe foreign communication patterns and compare them to those of North America. Rarely do they go beyond the surface to explore the roots of such differences. (p. 374)

As a corrective, Asante advocated a new direction for intercultural research, a "refocusing [of] attention on the broad ideological questions that impinge on our communication with persons from other cultures" (p. 402).

At the heart of the cultural criticism branch is opposition to the centrality in United States scholarship of economically privileged, white, male culture. Tsuda (1986) claims that the goal of the critical perspective is "to bring about emancipation from distorted communication" (p. 13). Like the feminist perspective, this is an inherently political stance.

The movement toward critical qualitative, non-United States based intercultural inquiry is growing. For example, the Spring 1990 issue of *The Southern Communication Journal* presented research that for the most part employed as starting points non-United States cultural traditions and assumptions.[4]

These latter two branches are of particular interest for an intercultural feminist perspective. The ethnographic approach gains access to traditionally devalued styles of discourse used by women and other marginalized co-cultures. The critical approach examines the cultural assumptions and motives of particular research methods and resists those methods that repress full participation. New questions are being advanced for development within particular cultural contexts: How does the relationship formed from intercultural dialogue reflect cultural ideology? How do the forces of history and ideology influence that dialogue? What cultural assumptions are brought to bear in the theory-generating process? What is the potential for critical methods in the examination of politically invested intercultural interaction?

FEMINIST SCHOLARSHIP IN INTERCULTURAL COMMUNICATION

The historical reluctance to directly examine the interaction between aspects of women's cultural experience with the factors of race, gender, and class emerges from prevailing patterns of privilege and functions to stabilize those patterns further. Unless these interrelated factors are discussed, feminist work will fail to account for the complexity and diversity of female experience. Feminists who avoid discussing racism will find it difficult to pursue intercultural research, for the researcher in an intercultural environment should be both capable of and willing to examine a broad range of human perspectives.

Marginalized Voices in Feminist Studies

Unfortunately, the reproduction of race and class prejudices of the dominating culture has attended the growth of feminist scholarship. We concur with feminist scholars who argue that United States feminist criticism suffers from an ethnocentrism that stresses Anglo middle-class individualism and pragmatism (Bassnet, 1986; Cannon, Higginbotham, & Leung 1988; Offen, 1988). This bias has resulted in what we assess as a reluctance of American feminist critics in communication to undertake gender studies that amplify the lived cultural experiences of people of color and other marginalized co-cultures of non-Anglo/European origin.

   Facilitating this reluctance is the situation facing individuals attempting to explicate the culturally situated experiences of women. Kramarae (1989) observes that, "White middle-class women are the gatekeepers of most of the `women's' publications and presses" and that these women generally are interested in stressing feminist community rather than variance through "sisterhood because it is a way to avoid talking about racism and classism" (pp. 320-321). If Johnson (1989) is correct in concluding that, "in a more pragmatic vein, the `two cultures' perspective clearly places interaction between women and men in the domain of intercultural communication" (p. 311), we must also conclude that women's co-cultures—communities in which women create and maintain distinct ways of thinking and speaking—exist, and that interaction among these co-cultures requires attention to the variables that influence dialogue within an intercultural communication context.

   A few feminist critics in the United States recently have embraced the turn toward ethnic and racial diversity in feminist literature, which we think warrants a review of how intercultural research findings and approaches might facilitate a renewed appreciation for intercultural sensitivity in feminist research. Sensitivity to cultural constructs can enable feminists who explore women's "cultures" to focus more directly on the symbolic enactments of those cultures. Johnson (1989) pointed out that feminists have grounded their approaches to culture in anthropology. Anthropological inquiry, however, tends to examine culture as context rather than focusing on the intermediatory role of the native-as-social/symbolic-actor in structuring intracultural meaning in the creation of identity and intercultural meaning in communication between cultures. An intercultural feminist perspective provides a theoretical framework that will sustain conceptualizations that include all dimensions of inequality as called for by Cannon et al (1988).

An Intercultural Feminist Perspective

Hooks (1984) wrote that in order for feminist theory to encompass a wider variety of human experiences, the women who guide its formulation must confront racial, sexual, and economic aspects of Western culture that combine to privilege some women over others. She suggested that one reason feminist theory is perceived by many women as irrelevant to their lives is that "much feminist theory emerges from privileged women who live at the center, whose perspectives on reality rarely include knowledge and awareness of the lives of women and men who live in the margin" (p. x). The resulting differences among women create barriers that pleas for sisterhood cannot transcend.

Many feminists who claim that women's common oppression provides a basis for sisterhood advocate that women should present a united front to the non-female world. Hooks argued that this idea is:

> a false and corrupt platform disguising and mystifying the true nature of women's varied and complex social reality. Women are divided by sexist attitudes, racism, class privilege, and a host of other prejudices. Sustained woman bonding can occur only when these divisions are confronted and the necessary steps are taken to eliminate them. Divisions will not be eliminated by wishful thinking or romantic reverie about common oppression despite the value of highlighting experiences all women share. (p. 44)

While Hooks recognizes the value of unified resistance by all women, she refuses to accept shared victimization as the basis for bonding. Not only does this concept of bonding alienate women who are oppressed by other women, but it naturalizes the patriarchal ideology that women are victims. Hooks suggested that stronger bonds will be formed "on the basis of our political commitment to a feminist movement that aims to end sexist oppression" (p. 47). Although it may be easier to avoid conflict and minimize disagreement, only by engaging in constructive confrontation can feminists transcend the divisions between women. If feminist theory is to radicalize the study of intercultural communication, feminism itself must be radicalized to encompass the lives and ideas of women on the margin.

A culturally sensitive feminist perspective would radicalize intercultural communication research by emphasizing cultural specificity and by encouraging analysis of symbolic achievement and maintenance of gender as inseparable from other aspects of culture. Combining this feminist perspective with aspects of the cultural description and cultural criticism orientations enables two outcomes. First, descriptions of gender are legitimate only to the extent that they are understood and recognized within the social world being explored. Second, the term "gender," like culture, becomes an idea that is not premised on difference from, or comparison with, "male" culture or what is often called the "dominant" culture. Instead, the term is based on its situated use as it inscribes a particular social world and is inclusive of factors such as race and class.

This emphasis on culture as an ongoing process simultaneously structured by gender and structuring gender encourages interpreting women's and men's experiences as "co-cultures," rather than interpreting women's experiences as subcultures within a traditional patriarchal culture.

Language and Culture

The language used by women and men to communicate with each other is central in human society because it connects individuals with a cultural order that embodies group perceptions, interpretations, thoughts, and values. Variety among languages maintains social structures. Language not only transmits human culture, but also creates and naturalizes it. Humans know of no world that is not organized as a language, and much of our shared consciousness is structured as a language.

Men have structured language to feature male perspectives while silencing women's perspectives (Spender, 1985; West & Zimmerman, 1987). Nowhere is this emphasis on male perspectives more dangerous than in a culture's religious creed. When discussing the language of religion, Spender (1985) pointed out that the Biblical record inherited by Christianity has been carefully edited by men. Although many descriptions named the deity as unisexual, androgynous, or female, male editors chose to eliminate all female names from the classification of the deity. The resulting male God reinforces the world views whereby men, by reason of their superior nature, can relegate women to the periphery (pp. 166-168).

The Judeo-Christian tradition is not alone in this prejudice against woman. Anzaldua (1987) describes a similar process among the

Toltecs/Aztecs. The deity Coatlicue balanced the dualities of male and female for the Toltecs until one of the Toltec tribes (Aztecs) joined with the Mexitin. The Mexitin deity gained control of the religious system, then assigned the Aztec-Mexitin people to unify all people. In carrying out this mandate they evolved a new culture based on class rather than clan and patrilineal rather than matrilineal descent. When the Aztec ruler Itzcoatl came to power, he had only to destroy the people's historical documents and rewrite a new history that validated the new social order. Women, who formerly had possessed property, held important administrative positions, and served as healers and priestesses in the old culture, were written out of the new history (pp. 31-35).

According to traditional accounts of language in use, when members of one group are in an asymmetrical power relationship with members of another group, the dominant group engulfs the subordinate group and renders it mute. This process can be seen in the linguistic characterization of the male as an unmarked and the female as a marked category. Anzaldua (1987) points out that male bias is encoded into the basic grammar of Spanish. She wrote that the first time she heard women refer to themselves as nosotras, "I was shocked. I had not known the word existed. Chicanas use *nosotros* whether we're male or female. We are robbed of our female being by the masculine plural. Language is a male discourse" (p. 54). Spender (1985) points to the same prejudice in English, asserting that, "By promoting the use of the symbol *man* at the expense of *woman*, it is clear that the visibility and primacy of males is supported. We learn to see the male as the worthier, more comprehensive and superior sex and we divide and organize the world along these lines" (p. 153). Similarly, the pronoun "he" can refer to either a male person, or a person whose sex is not specified; whereas "she" refers only to females.

From an intercultural perspective, the political potential of feminist critique lies in explicating the nature of gender relations from cultural community to cultural community and, where appropriate, in excavating women's voices from their tombs. Because language is so fundamental to cultural identity, feminists should search for new approaches to explore language, as well as point out inadequacies of conventional techniques of linguistic analysis. Language, which has been the means of silencing women, can also invigorate them. Anzaldua's (1987) description of the painful experience suffered by Chicanas points out that social attitudes and language use intertwine to create a sense of personal legitimacy or illegitimacy:

> If you want to really hurt me, talk badly about my language. Ethnic identity is twin skin to linguistic identity—I am my language. Until I can take pride in my Language, I cannot take pride in myself. . . Until I

am free to write bilingually and to switch codes without having always to translate, while I still have to speak English or Spanish when I would rather speak Spanish, and as long as I have to accommodate the English speakers rather than having them accommodate me, my tongue will be illegitimate. (p. 59)

Her critique suggests alternatives to the current demands for an "official" language that could establish a woman's point of view. The intent is not the exclusion of others—which would lead to partial and therefore false results—but the reforming of time and space in such a way that women's perspectives are integrated into, rather than effaced from, the totality of experience.

Data and Methods

Since cultural codes have excluded many of women's experiences from the realm of public communication, communication researchers must seek nontraditional data for analysis. Rather than assuming, for example, that significant communication artifacts are constructed or presented in public contexts, the feminist critic seeks out women's symbolic expressions in the contexts where they have most often occurred. Rakow (1987) argues that, "At the very least, we need to be sure we are studying real women in their real contexts" (p. 83). The contexts seen as important for study are those that women across cultures designate as important in their daily lives, for significant experience is that which the experience designates as such. Contexts may include such nontraditional data sources as housework, child care, markets, and factories. Linguistic texts passed through women's cultures can be found in sources and activities such as singing, story-telling, diaries, poetry, cookbooks, and letters. Although these mundane activities may be judged insignificant by male-stream, elitist society, they are contexts in which women have had some opportunity for self-expression.

While we realize that focusing on the traditional aspects of women's lives may valorize them, we are more distressed when feminists denigrate social roles traditionally performed by women. In a 1988 interview, Herrmann (1989) said that those women who have joined the ranks of corporate executives or professionals have internalized patriarchy even more exclusively than have their less fortunate sisters. They have been "hoodwinked" into trading in one form of colonization for another. Herrmann illustrated the new colonization of women with popular magazines meant for the "executive woman:" "They teach the art of pleasing the boss (who may even be female) and of dressing with elegance for business meetings. In them we find `quizzes' meant to reassure the ever nervous reader of her intelligence" (p. xxvii). The only significant differences between magazines targeting these women and their "unliberated" sisters are the contexts within which women are taught to exhibit appropriately deferential behavior. Herrmann also expressed dismay at how little a women's world has changed during the past 15 years:

> If a few women now hold important posts, I don't find this phenomenon new or particularly meaningful. . .The masses are what count. And the great majority of women continue to occupy subordinate positions, to receive mediocre salaries, and to assume responsibility for family life without any serious support from society. . . The only values that continue to triumph remain virile values: power and domination. Which is why our society is sick to the point of devouring itself. (p. xxvii)

The fact that men have allowed selected women to join them in welding "power and domination" does not help those members of society who remain outside the patriarchal elite. Even worse, it creates the false appearance that their oppression is self-imposed, rather than locating responsibility for oppression in cultural ideology. Hooks (1984) argues that a feminism designed to provide to privileged women social equality with men of their class is, at best, irrelevant to the vast majority of women. She quotes Ehrlich's (1981) claim:

> Feminism is not about dressing for success, or becoming a corporate executive, or gaining elective office; it is not being able to share a two career marriage and take skiing vacations and spend huge amounts of time with your husband and two lovely children because you have a domestic worker who makes all this possible for you, but who hasn't the time or money to do it herself; it is not opening a Women's Bank, or spending a weekend in an expensive workshop that guarantees to teach you how to become assertive.(pp. 7-8)

While Hooks focuses primarily on the relations between white women and women of color in the United States, her analysis generalizes to an international scope. Feminism's potential for radicalizing intercultural communication research cannot be realized in a framework that reproduces patriarchy by replacing privileged men with privileged women and provides no structural critique of the ideology of liberal individualism.

A 1987 issue of *Women's Studies* illustrates the variety of communicative texts and methodologies available to feminist scholars. The essays all began with a close study of a female text. After demonstrating that their texts constitute part of a specifically female form of communication, feminist concepts were employed to critique the male modes of theory that would have been applied to these texts in the past.

Davis (1987) develops the theme of diaries as mediators in a structural sense and shows them to be crucial tools in coping with change. Her analysis of pioneer women's diaries shows how diaries can provide useful evidence in the study of frontier challenge and adaptation. While she does not deny the private aspects of diaries, her analysis shows how women's private writings are crucial to developing a historical record. Her essay effectively challenges the judgment made by traditional historians that diaries are "merely" valuable to those who are interested in women's private feelings (pp. 5-14). Lensink (1987) studied the extended diary of one woman, Emily Hawley Gillespie, rather than examining the more elliptical diaries of several women. She suggests that the extended diary be studied as a form of female autobiography. By carefully unraveling the forms used by Gillespie in writing her diary, Lensink enables us to view the diary in personal and literary terms simultaneously. Her essay shows both that careful analysis of the mundane can yield important theoretical insights, and that feminist theory can help alleviate the rigidity of existing theories of autobiography (pp. 39-53).

Barker-Nunn (1987) also examined female autobiography. Her analysis of the autobiographies of Kim Chernin and Maxine Hong Kingston shows that blurring the boundaries between mother and daughter leads to the blurring of other social boundaries. She also points out that both autobiographies begin as the mother's stories, reminding us that oral sources are essential to efforts to recover women's experiences. Gilligan's (1982) and Chodorow's (1978) work provides a feminist theoretical basis for Barker-Nunn's analysis (pp. 55-63). Communicative interaction between mother and daughter was also explored by Hall and Langellier (1988). They take a phenomenological approach to the activity of mother/daughter storytelling. The major strength of their approach is that they avoid dividing the text into preexisting categories and allow categories to emerge from the talk. This approach allows a definition of women's communication to emerge on its own terms by including varied aspects of public and private performance that otherwise might have been ignored.

Nomura (1987) demonstrates the broad range of sources available to document the lives of women in her analysis of tanka poems written by Teika Tomita, a Japanese-American pioneer woman. Tomita's poetry sustained her throughout almost her entire life cycle, from her early struggles with natural elements to later struggles with social prejudice in the United States. The discussion of Tomita's changing use of poetry throughout her life cycle introduces the question of change over time, while the form of the tanka poem provides both cultural and literary diversity to the study of ways in which words become coping mechanisms.

In addition to using data from sources that have been traditionally denigrated as "feminine," feminists can co-opt topics men have claimed as their exclusive property, such as technology. Altman (1990) exemplified this tactic in her research about technologies of housework. She juxtaposed "housework," a term that has been defined as central to women's culture and peripheral to men's culture, against "technology," a term that has been defined as peripheral to women's culture and central to men's culture. The apparent incongruity resulting from combining the concept of technology with the concept of housework focuses attention on the disparity between men's and women's cultural experiences. The new perspective also represents women's traditional culture rather than men's as archetypal for the generic human experience.

A feminist perspective does not preclude intercultural communication researchers from studying more publicly legitimated communication performances such as speeches, political debates, or novels. Male-centered texts are especially appropriate for studying how various cultures have embodied gender in male-stream texts, and how those texts in turn naturalize the culture's gender definitions. With male-centered texts, however, the researcher neither assumes equal significance to both women and men nor affirms the gender presentation made in them.

Campbell's (1989) analysis of public speeches delivered during the late 1800s and early 1900s by Afro-American women Ida B. Wells and Mary Church Terrell provide an example of an insightful exploration of the interrelationship of sex, race, and class. Campbell limits her study of early feminists to women who were central to the movement, nationally known, and for whom extant texts of speeches are available. While neither Wells or Church Terrell met the centrality criterion, she chose to include them. Campbell claims that these two women attempted unsuccessfully to persuade white women that discrimination based on race was linked to discrimination based on sex. In her analysis of their speeches, Campbell accepts these women's decisions to present and adapt their messages to a predominantly white, male, professional audience. Rather than judging Wells or Church Terrell, she explores possible motives for this choice. While Campbell chose to examine publicly legitimated discourse, her analysis questions the validity of male-stream audience responses to that discourse. She explores what those texts, adapted to a male-stream audience, communicate about social hierarchies experienced by the Afro-American women who participated in the Woman's Rights Movement.

However carefully we select the communication contexts to explore, feminists should also seek to avoid confusing communication contexts with communication performances. For example, intercultural communication researchers need to focus on communication behaviors used to create gender while preparing food, rather than on the food preparations themselves, in order to unpack the symbol systems used unobtrusively to reproduce oppressive gender stereotypes. Stacy (1988) argues that accounts of culture enhanced by the application of feminist perspectives emerge only when the researcher is rigorously aware of both the context and the process of constructing accounts to describe situations.

Finally, a feminist perspective on intercultural communication research is more compatible with holistic, qualitative methods than with reductionist, quantitative approaches, for the goals of prediction and control are at best irrelevant, and at worst, antagonistic to feminist scholarship (Lather, 1988; Rakow, 1987). Chen (1990) claims that the process of selecting variables, which is essential to the positivist research agenda, creates the false impression that gender and culture are variables that can be added and subtracted at will. If we seek understanding of how our informants make sense of their own reality, we must use methods such as detailed case studies that are more compatible with this holistic perspective. Rakow suggests in-depth interviewing, ethnography, life histories, and storytelling as appropriate data gathering techniques. Steeves (1988) argues that feminist scholarship should be distinguished by its incorporation of participatory methods into research and by conscious attempts to extend traditional methodologies. However, Muto (1988) cautions against taking a position that advocates a single correct way of doing feminist principles. Ultimately, methods chosen to undertake a feminist critique of culture should be those that encourage the researcher to assume a self-consciously reflexive stance. As Wood (1988) points out, "Method is subordinate to the questions posed" (p. 25).

FUTURE DIRECTIONS FOR CULTURALLY SENSITIVE FEMINIST SCHOLARSHIP

Feminist scholarship not only encourages reexamination of existing cultural concepts but development of new ones that incorporate women's experiences and are directed toward a specific social purpose. A feminist critic focuses on how gender has been constructed and on how women's perspectives have been treated in that construction. If a communication process mutes women's perspectives, the critic seeks to change it. However, we can also view women's oppression as an example of the broader issue of domination within social hierarchies (Wood, 1988). From this perspective, feminist scholarship would focus primarily on the process of oppression, and thus concern itself with all oppressed groups. An intercultural feminist perspective, then, is one in which the researcher believes that all people should have opportunities to participate in creating knowledge, and that perspectives drawn from members of oppressed groups should be an integral part of communication theory and practice.

Intercultural communication inquiry, when radicalized by a feminist perspective, would include selecting persons who appear to be dispossessed by male-stream culture and learning from them. Hooks (1984) pointed out that the experience of living on the edge of culture provides marginalized people with an oppositional world view. Because their survival depends on being able to please those who live in the center, oppressed people develop the "knowledge of both margin and center" that is essential to the development of systemic feminist theory (p. ii).

While researchers advocate the elimination of "injustice by challenging . . . the coercive power, force, or authority that upholds male prerogatives," they should also "recognize the validity of women's own interpretations of their lived experience. . . in that particular culture" (Offen, 1988, p. 152). The researcher should be prepared to gain more from these "dispossessed" persons than she will provide them, for understanding how gender is produced clarifies both social structures and the social control processes that sustain them (West & Zimmerman, 1987). For example, Jackson (1986) reported that her feelings about her gender were crystallized during her fieldwork among Tukanoan people in the Central Northwest Amazon. She wrote that "even though for Tukanoan women being female is the identity feature of the most significance, and even though Tukanoan, one is not frustrated and invalidated" in the ways women living in the United States are (p. 270). Tukanoan women appeared to feel less of a conflicted sense of gender identity than women Jackson had known in the United States. She determined that this was related to the existence of group rituals, as well as to less formalized means of openly acknowledging the opposition between the sexes in Tukanoan society. The overt sex segregation gave rise to female solidarity and political clout that are denied to women in societies where male dominance is hidden beneath the surface. Jackson returned home

> better equipped to understand how varied the forms of female subordination can be . . . This, in turn, allowed [her] to comprehend sex roles and related issues, among Tukanoans and in general, in a more sophisticated and objective fashion, even though the route to that objectivity involved much subjectivity and introspection. (p. 272)

Pitfalls and Potential of Activist Politics

The assumption that cultures perpetuate inequality between women and men and other culturally distinct human groups is implicit to feminist activism. A corollary is that feminism should and will improve women's lives. Unfortunately, when dealing in intercultural contexts such assumptions occasionally lead feminists into ethnocentric traps. For example, Papandreou (1988) has drawn attention to the ways in which aid provided to Third World countries emphasizes men's needs and generally ignores women's needs. However, when urging reexamination of such aid in terms of how it affected women's lives, she uncritically accepted Western "development" as a transcultural good. She wrote:

> For those of us in the privileged western world. . .we have an obliga-
> tion, a moral duty, if you like, to explore what can be done to reduce
> the enormous gap in wealth between rich and poor nations. We as
> concerned women must give serious attention to the special needs
> and situations of women in these countries and determine whether
> development has improved or worsened their lot. (p. xviii)

Rather than *determining* whether the lot of women has improved or worsened, feminists studying intercultural communication should demonstrate their respect for those women they study by *asking them*.

Feminists who assume the "moral duty" to determine the quality of another person's life contradict the feminist concern for the human right to develop one's full potential and to speak in one's own voice. A holistic approach to feminist-intercultural study requires the researcher to appreciate and learn from, rather than merely tolerate, cultural diversity. If researchers believe that women are oppressed, their critique should involve a knowledge of the deep structure meanings of the dispossessed which is gained only by access to the situated talk which reveals how informants perceive their lot. These perceptions will sometimes differ dramatically from scholarly expectations. Abyaneh's (1989) analysis of power relationships in Iranian families who had immigrated to the United States illustrates the potential value of such studies. The dominant sociological tradition explains patriarchy in United States immigrant families as a part of the cultural heritage they bring with them. She found that among Iranian families, husband domination increased after immigration to the United States. Women spent more hours on weekly housework and received less domestic help from their husbands than they had in Iran. They also had less control over family finances. Abyaneh suggested that her conclusions should lead us to ask, "What is it about the United States that encourages male domination?" (p. 69). Kelly (1989) found similar patterns of change in Somali families that immigrated to the United States. Addressing these issues can assist feminist-intercultural researchers in creating theory that embraces the complexity of women's lives. Kramarae (1989) claimed that gender describes both inequality and hierarchy. This condition led her to suggest a research agenda that is especially significant for those who study communication in intercultural settings. She suggested that:

> Instead of constructing a pretend research world in which race, age and class are variables separate from gender, we look at the connections—at, for example, the ways that a gender hierarchy is used in the construction of what we call class or race. (p. 319)

Stanback (1988) makes the same point, stating that, "at its best, feminist theory is systemic; it can account for the interrelated influences of culture, class, and gender—and of racism, classism, and sexism" (p. 188). She argues that, "The presence of each form of oppression in black women's lives affects our experience of all the others" (p. 29). Without an intensified focus on the process of oppression within social hierarchies, cross-cultural research will continue to produce results that mirror the lives of the predominantly white professionals who conduct the studies.

Some feminists are beginning to explore these relationships. Cannon et al.'s (1988) study of the financial and informational support provided by middle-class women's families during the transition period between high school and college demonstrates the interconnections between these systems and illustrates the difficulties encountered by researchers who attempt to generalize about women's lives. Recognizing that many such studies have (both inadvertently and advertently) excluded women of color, they felt that it was essential to include such women in their study. They made a conscious attempt to treat class, race, and gender as political, sexualized hierarchies. They found that different techniques were required to recruit black women volunteers than to recruit white women volunteers. Their results showed that black women had received less support from their families than had white women. However, most black woman volunteers had been raised in working-class families, while most white woman volunteers had been raised in middle-class families. After reexamining their data, Cannon et al. decided that the difference in support levels should be attributed primarily to class rather than to race—working-class women had received less support than had middle-class women.

The challenge for feminist research in intercultural contexts is to critique the interconnections between concepts such as age, race, and class without assuming that the hierarchies will be the same in all cultures. For example, Zavella (1989) points out that, "when white feminists were demanding reproductive rights, including the right to abortions, Chicana activists were fighting forced sterilizations and defending the right to bear children" (p. 27). Christian (1989) and Zavella (1989) both credit the hostility towards feminism expressed by many women of color to an early feminist emphasis on separatism. They argue that although family bonds may have been primarily constraining to middle-class white feminists, such bonds provided the only support system for many women of color.

Additionally, texts for analysis, whether they function primarily as symbols or artifacts, should emerge from the culture itself. When describing Somali women's immigration experiences, Kelly (1989) cautions researchers that in order to understand women's perspectives, they should avoid decontextualizing women's experiences. Critics should also attempt to privilege the experiential reason of the culture under study. That is, as in intercultural inquiry, interpretations of women's cultures must be accessible and understood to the social world being investigated.

Passaro's (1987) discussion of Nicaraguan women, which explores the structure of language used in Sandanista literature, exemplifies this kind of inquiry. Passaro accepts the Sandanista's claim that cultural equality is both desirable and as yet unfulfilled. Her analysis suggests that despite the overt revolutionary intent of establishing cultural equality, the language categories used to talk about men and women negate the possibility of cultural equality between them. Terms for women are syntactically categorized with terms for children rather than with terms for men, suggesting that men are responsible for and thus dominant over both women and children.

Miyake's (1989) exploration of the feminine voice in Japanese literature provides a different yet equally valuable example of feminist cross-cultural research. Instead of accepting the Western presumption that women's writing has been muted, Miyake examines Japanese poetry and prose to learn what she can about women's existences in that culture. She shows how the development of Japanese prose is directly influenced by poetry written primarily by women, concluding that Japanese tradition "provides an example of women's writings being not muted versions of but rather central to the development of the mainstream culture" (p. 98).

Feminist Critiques of Communication Inquiry

Just as feminist critiques have challenged and brought into relief the taken-for-granted assumptions of male privilege that has rendered the practices of patriarchy invisible, so too are feminists examining the role of culture in shaping communication contexts. For example, when reviewing the research on interpersonal communication, Wood explains that the exchange model of interpersonal relations gains its explanatory power from its alignment with the expectations and interests of the dominant society. She states that the exchange model is inadequate to a feminist approach to interpersonal communication because of:

> its limited recognition of how practice is constrained by particular social and cultural beliefs, and, especially, by the hegemony of a given culture. It should surprise no one that exchange as a way of being in relationships thrives in western culture where many voices and visions of human relationships have been systematically suppressed or made peripheral to the "real business" of the culture. . . . Exchange flourishes in America (and elsewhere) because it is suited to relations in the public sphere, which has been privileged, and because it is consistent with values and preferred interpersonal modes of those who hold power in our society, i.e., white males.

She continues, describing how various models of interpersonal relationships are derived from the norms of the dominating culture in the U.S. Thus, her research further focuses on dominant groups, and reflects their ways of being. The norms of other cultural groups are assessed as deviant, or simply left unexplored. In this way, a cycle of suppression emerges. According to Wood, feminism can break this cycle by gaining access to a variety of interpersonal ontologies. The description and understanding of patterns of interpersonal relations between cultural communities leads the feminist researcher to intercultural inquiry.

Feminist critiques of other communication contexts also illuminate theories and practices that help establish and reinforce cycles of suppression. In this volume Condit points out that rhetorical criticism has depended on a closed and male-dominated canon that is "overwhelmingly biased . . . towards white men of the Western tradition." Gillespie adds that the "masterpiece mentality" that has dominated theater's theory, criticism, and history suppresses alternative perspectives. She claims that the "models of excellence [that have been] praised for their universality" have helped to justify the status quo.

The concept of universality has been questioned throughout this volume. As Wood's comment regarding the exchange model suggests, universality is simply a covering term that naturalizes stereotypes held by the dominating culture. So-called "universal" standards for public speaking, decision making, managing organizations, and so on provide barriers against diversity that may be introduced by persons of a different ethnicity,

272 González & Peterson

gender, or race than the Western white male.

Feminist performance theory rejects the notion of universality, and instead focuses on differences of class, ethnicity, gender, or race that might confuse current hierarchical structures. Langellier, Carter, and Hantzis claim that feminist performance is grounded in a commitment to diversity. Similarly, Condit suggests that a feminist rhetorical practice could undermine the patriarchy of traditional rhetorical practice by analyzing broader historical contexts and more varied rhetorical agents than have traditionally been analyzed. We would add that cultural inclusiveness is a goal of feminist approaches to communication, rather than merely a means to an end.

Langellier et al. claim that by focusing on difference, feminists perform "a political act in the interest of women in their racial, ethnic, class, and other social diversities." Similarly, Fine's review of the organizational communication literature indicates that "although the interpretive perspective is ideally suited to examining women's problematics, especially the social construction of gender, race, and class within organizations, most of the published research avoids issues of gender, race, or class." Although the interpretivist perspective rejects notions of objectivity and universality, its emphasis on shared-meaning systems within the organization often blinds researchers to the significance of difference.

In Lont's review of mass communication research the major criticism of three primary approaches—content analysis, narrative history, and cultural studies—centers on the narrow conceptions, even among feminists, of women's experience. Women's constructions of exploitation and integration reflect varying cultural frames. The intercultural potential in the intersection between media producer and media consumer is found in Lont's conclusion that, "it is not the media alone which determines what women are but the culture in conjunction with the media which contributes to women's subordinated positions." Lont's call for audience-based feminist research on media entails greater cross-cultural awareness.

Not only does this volume call for emphasizing diversity, but also for rethinking the category systems used to legitimize contexts for study. In her assessment of small group research, Wyatt approaches this issue of cultural inclusion directly. "We must study groups of women and minorities in their own contexts," she recommends. Not only must variable group composition be expanded to include women's cultural heritages, but the locations and types of groups must be expanded as well. She states that,

> perhaps our first step should be to look around and inventory what kinds of groups are currently operating in our communities. We should figure out how groups contribute to the social welfare of the

communities and organizations in which we live and begin to develop some new taxonomies of group types. (p. 77)

Langellier and her co-authors extend the call to seek new systems for categorizing communication performances by claiming that, because of its Western emphasis on individuality, adoption of the humanistic perspective maintains, rather than subverts, existing power relations. Pluralism is also suspect in that it "hides oppression by its taken-for-granted assumption that all have the freedom to choose." She concludes that feminist performance studies that ignore the fact that "every performance . . . is unavoidably gendered and socially marked . . . [are] partial and critically flawed." Acknowledging that any description of culture is partial, the culturally sensitive feminist researcher attempts to reveal dimensions of communication that, although shared by other women, will be expressed so as to reflect a unique cultural community.

CONCLUSION

By listening to women from culturally differentiated settings talk about how they perceive changes that could lessen their oppression, what they find attractive or threatening about the struggle for equality, and what sorts of opportunities for self-expression they find attractive, researchers can enhance the liberating potential of their work. As Kramarae (1989) points out, perspectives that destabilize current ways of doing research "can help change conditions even as they express conditions" (p. 320). A feminist perspective that represents gender as part of an interdependent, continually constructed, cultural hierarchy can reduce the macroscopic bias in intercultural communication studies.

Sensitivity to cultural constructs can also help feminist criticism overcome its ethnocentrism. Pratt (1984) suggests that women should question the pressures they put on other women "to be like us, to assimilate to our culture, be like our family, so we can feel comfortable." She argues that when "feminists" press women to "talk like us, think like us, fight like us. . . [we do not] differ from the obliteration practiced by the rest of the dominant culture" (p. 49). A feminist critique of intercultural communication enables us to undertake the urgent task of engaging in scholarship that is both multicultural and grounded in the daily lives of women.

In summary, the situation is not simply one in which a feminist perspective on communication expands areas of inquiry within the communication discipline. Rather, the two areas of investigation are enhanced by recognizing each other's primary concerns. Thus, the focus of this volume is on how feminist praxis and cultural explanations for communication practices can enrich each other. A culturally sensitive feminist approach can radicalize—that is, provide new possibilities for—the study of communication.

NOTES TO CHAPTER 9

1. Our use of "malestream" follows Daly (1978).
2. We do not attempt a survey of intercultural research. A 10-year overview is presented by Shuter (1990). See also Kim (1984).
3. The work of van Dijk is a notable exception. See, for example, van Dijk (1987).
4. Essays include: Asante (1990), Broome (1990), Gonzalez (1990), Frye (1990), and Mare (1990) in *The Southern Communication Journal,* 55.

REFERENCES

Abyaneh, P. (1989). Immigrants and patriarchy: The case of Iranian families. *Women's Studies, 17,* 67-69.
Altman, K.E. (1990). Public discourse on American home technologies. In M. Medhurst, A. Gonzalez, & T. Peterson (Eds.), *Communication and the culture of technology* (pp. 95-111). Pullman, WA: Washington State University Press.
Anzaldua, G. (1987). *Borderlands la frontera: The New Mestiza.* San Francisco: Spinsters/Aunt Lute Press.
Asante, M.K. (1980). Intercultural communication: An inquiry and overview into research directions. In D. Nimmo (Ed.), *Communication yearbook 4* (pp. 401-410). New Brunswick, NJ: Transaction Books.
Asante, M.K. (1990). The tradition of advocacy in the Yoruba courts. The *Southern Communication Journal, 55,* 250-259.
Asante, M.K., Newmark, E., & Blake, C.A. (1979). The field of intercultural communication. In M.K. Asante, E. Newmark, & C.A Lake (Eds.), *Handbook of intercultural communication* (pp. 11-22). Beverly Hills, CA: Sage.
Asante, M.K., & Vora, E. (1983). Toward multiple philosophical approaches. In W.B. Gudykunst (Ed.), *Intercultural communication theory: Current perspectives* (pp. 293-298). Beverly Hills, CA: Sage.
Barker-Nunn, J. (1987). Telling the mother's story: The autobiographies of Maxine Hong Kingston and Kim Chernin. *Women's Studies, 14,* 55-63.

Bassnet, S. (1986). *Feminist experiences: The women's movement in four cultures.* London: Allen & Unwin.

Borden, G.A. (1991). *Cultural orientation: An approach to understanding intercultural communication.* Englewood Cliffs, NJ: Prentice-Hall.

Brislin, R.W. (1981). *Cross-cultural encounters: Face-to-face interaction.* New York: Pergamon Press.

Broome, B.J. (1990). "Palevome": Foundations of struggle and conflict in Greek interpersonal communication. *The Southern Communication Journal, 55,* 260-275.

Campbell, K.K. (1989). *Man cannot speak for her* (Vol. 1, pp. 145-156). New York: Praeger.

Cannon, L.W., Higginbotham, E., & Leung, M.L.A. (1988). Race and class bias in qualitative research on women. *Gender & Society, 2*(4), 449-462.

Carbaugh, D. (1987). Communication rules in Donahue discourse. *Research on Language and Social Interaction, 21,* 31-61.

Carbaugh, D. (1989). Fifty terms for talk. In S. Ting-Toomey & F. Korzenny (Eds.), *Language, communication and culture: Current directions* (pp. 93-120). Newbury Park, CA: Sage.

Casmir, F.L. (1978). A theoretical framework for the study of intercultural and international communication. In F.L. Casmir (Ed.), *Intercultural and international communication* (pp. 2-6). Washington, DC: University Press of America.

Chen, V. (1990, March). *What are the consequences of treating gender and ethnic culture as separate variables in communication research?* Paper presented at the 1990 Conference on Research in Gender and Communication, Atlanta, GA.

Chodorow, N. (1978). *The reproduction of mothering: Psychoanalysis and the sociology of gender.* Berkeley, CA: University of California Press.

Christian, B. (1989). But who do you really belong to—Black Studies or Women's Studies? *Women's Studies, 17,* 17-24.

Daly, M. (1978). *Gyn/ecology, the metaethics of radical feminism.* Boston: Beacon Press.

Davis, G.R. (1987). Women's frontier diaries: Writing for good reason. *Women's Studies, 14,* 5-14.

Deetz, S. (1984). Metaphor analysis. In W.B. Gudykunst & Y.Y. Kim (Eds.), *Methods for intercultural communication research* (pp. 215-228). Beverly Hills, CA: Sage.

Dodd, C.H. (1987). *Dynamics of intercultural communication* (2nd ed.). Dubuque, IA: Wm. C. Brown Publishers.

Ehrlich, C. (1981). The unhappy marriage of Marxism and feminism. In L. Sargent (Ed.), *Women and revolution* (pp. 109-133). Boston, MA: South End Press.

Fine, M.G. (1988). What makes it feminist? *Women's Studies in Communication, 11,* 18-19.

Foss, S.K., & Foss, K.A. (1988). What distinguishes feminist scholarship in communication studies? *Women's Studies in Communication, 11,* 9-

11.

Fowlkes, D.L. (1987). Feminist epistemology is political action. *Women and Politics, 7*, 1-4.

Frye, P.A. (1990). Form and function of North Yemeni qat sessions. *The Southern Communication Journal, 55*, 292-304.

Gilligan, C. (1982). *In a different voice: Psychological theory and women's development.* Cambridge, MA: Harvard University Press.

Gonzalez, A. (1989). "Participation" at WMEX-FM: Interventional rhetoric of Ohio Mexican Americans. *Western Journal of Speech Communication, 53*, 398-410.

Gonzalez, A. (1990). Mexican "otherness" in the rhetoric of Mexican Americans, *The Southern Communication Journal, 55*, 276-291.

Gudykunst, W.B. (1983). Theorizing in intercultural communication. In W.B. Gudykunst (Ed.), *Intercultural communication theory: Current perspectives* (pp. 13-20). Beverly Hills, CA: Sage Publications.

Hall, D., & Langellier, K. (1988). Storytelling strategies in mother-daughter communication. In B. Bate & A. Taylor (Eds.), *Women communicating: Studies of women's talk* (pp. 107-126). Norwood, NJ: Ablex Publishing Corporation.

Hepworth, J.C. (1978). Some pre-empirical considerations for cross-cultural attitude measurements and persuasive communications. In F.L. Casmir (Ed.), *Intercultural and international communication* (pp. 42-71). Washington, DC, University Press of America.

Herrmann, C. (1989). *The tongue snatchers* (trans. N. Kline). Lincoln: University of Nebraska Press. (Original work published 1976).

hooks, b. (1984). *Feminist theory: From margin to center.* Boston: South End Press.

Jackson, J. (1986). On trying to be an Amazon. In T.L. Whitehead & M.E. Conaway (Eds.), *Self, sex, and gender in cross-cultural fieldwork* (pp. 263-274). Urbana & Chicago: University of Illinois Press.

Johnson, F. (1989). Women's culture and communication: An analytical perspective. In C.M. Lont & S.A. Friedley (Eds.), *Beyond boundaries: Sex and gender diversity in communication* (pp. 301-316). Fairfax, VA: George Mason University Press.

Katriel, T. (1987). *Talking straight: Durgi speech in Israeli Sabra culture.* Cambridge: Cambridge University Press.

Katriel, T., & Philipsen, G. (1981). What we need is communication: "Communication" as a cultural category in some American speech. *Communication Monographs, 48*, 301-317.

Kelly, H. (1989). Somali women's immigration experiences: A study in diversity. *Women's Studies, 17*, 57-61.

Kim, Y.Y. (1984). Searching for creative integration. In W.B. Gudykunst & Y.Y. Kim (Eds.), *Methods for intercultural communication research* (pp. 13-30). Beverly Hills, CA: Sage.

Kim, Y.Y. (1986). A communication approach to interethnic relations. In Y.Y. Kim (Ed.), *Interethnic communication: Current research* (pp. 9-18). Newbury Park, CA: Sage.

Kochman, T. (1986). Black verbal dueling strategies in interethnic communication. In Y.Y. Kim (Ed.), *Interethnic communication: Current research* (pp. 136-157). Newbury Park, CA: Sage.

Kramarae, C. (1989). Redefining gender, class, and race. In C.M. Lont & S.A. Friedley (Eds.), *Beyond boundaries: Sex and gender diversity in communication* (pp. 317-329). Fairfax, VA: George Mason University Press.

Lather, P. (1988). Feminist perspectives on empowering research methodologies. *Women's Studies International Forum, 11,* 569-581.

Lensink, J.N. (1987). Expanding the boundaries of criticism: The diary as female autobiography. *Women's Studies, 14,* 39-53.

Mare, L.D. (1990). Ma and Japan. *The Southern Communication Journal, 55,* 319-328.

Miyake, K.L. (1989). Woman's voice in Japanese literature: Expanding the feminine. *Women's Studies, 17,* 87-101.

Muto, J. (1988). If I'm reading this, I must not be by the pool. *Women's Studies in Communication, 11,* 20-21.

Nomura, G.M. (1987). Tsugiki, a grafting: A history of a Japanese pioneer woman in Washington State. *Women's Studies, 14,* 15-37.

Offen, J. (1988). Defining feminism: A comparative historical approach. *Signs: A Journal of Women in Culture and Society, 14,* 119-157.

Papandreou, M. (1988). Feminism and political power: Some thoughts on a strategy for the future. In E. Boneparth & E. Stoper (Eds.), *Women power and policy: Toward the year 2000* (pp. xi-xix). New York: Pergamon Press.

Passaro, J. (1987). Conceptualizations of gender: An example from Nicaragua. *Feminist Issues, 7*(2), 49-60.

Philipsen, G. (1975). Speaking "like a man" in Teamsterville: Culture patterns of role enactment in a urban neighborhood. *Quarterly Journal of Speech, 61,* 13-22.

Philipsen, G. (1976). Places for speaking in Teamsterville. *Quarterly Journal of Speech, 62,* 15-25.

Philipsen, G. (1986). Mayor Daley's council speech: A cultural analysis. *Quarterly Journal of Speech, 72,* 247-260.

Philipsen, G. (1989). Speech and the communal function in four cultures. In S. Ting-Toomey & F. Korzenny (Eds.), *Language, communication, and culture: Current directions* (pp. 79-92). Newbury Park, CA: Sage.

Pilotta, J.J. (1983). The phenomenological approach. In W. B. Gudykunst (Ed.), *Intercultural communication theory: Current perspectives* (pp. 271-282). Beverly Hills, CA: Sage.

Pratt, M.B. (1984). Identity: Skin, blood, heart. In E. Bulkin, M.B. Pratt, & B. Smith (Eds.), *Yours in struggle* (pp. 11-63). Brooklyn, NY: Long Haul Press.

Rakow, L.F. (1987). Looking to the future: Five questions for gender research. *Women's Studies in Communication, 10,* 79-86.

Samovar, L.A., & Porter, R.E. (1991). *Communication between cultures.* Belmont, CA: Wadsworth.

Samovar, L.A., & Porter, R.E. (Eds.). (1987). *Intercultural communication: A reader* (5th ed.). Belmont, CA: Wadsworth.

Sarbaugh, L.E., & Asuncion-Lande, A. (1983). Theory building in intercultural communication: Synthesizing the action caucus. In W.B. Gudykunst (Ed.), *Intercultural communication theory: Current perspectives* (pp. 45-60). Beverly Hills, CA: Sage.

Shuter, R. (1990). The centrality of culture. *The Southern Communication Journal, 55*, 237-249.

Singer, M.R. (1987). *Intercultural communication: A perceptual approach.* Englewood Cliffs, NJ: Prentice-Hall.

Sitaram, K.S., & Cogdell, R.T. (1976). *Foundations of intercultural communication.* Columbus, OH: Charles E. Merrill Publishing Company.

Spender, D. (1985). *Man made language* (2nd ed.). London: Routledge & Kegan Paul.

Stacy, J. (1988). Can there be a feminist ethnography? *Women's Studies International Forum, 11*, 21-27.

Stanback, M.H. (1988). Feminist theory and black women's talk. *The Howard Journal of Communication, 1*, 187-194.

Stanback, M.H. (1990). Review of Gudykunst, W.B., Ting-Toomey, S., & Chua, E. (1988). *Culture and interpersonal communication.* Beverly Hills, CA: Sage. In *The Southern Communication Journal, 55*, 329-30.

Starosta, W.J. (1984). On intercultural rhetoric. In W.B. Gudykunst & Y.Y. Kim (Eds.), *Methods for intercultural communication research* (pp. 229-238). Beverly Hills, CA: Sage.

Steeves, H.L. (1988). What distinguishes feminist scholarship in communication studies? *Women's Studies in Communication, 11*, 12-17.

Ting-Toomey, S. (1986). Conflict communication styles in black and white subjective cultures. In Y.Y. Kim (Ed.), *Interethnic communication: Current research* (pp. 75-88). Newbury Park, CA: Sage Publications.

Ting-Toomey, S. (1988). Rhetorical sensitivity style in three cultures: France, Japan, and the United States. *Central States Speech Journal, 39*, 28-36.

Tsuda, Y. (1986). *Language inequality and distortion in intercultural communication.* Amsterdam: John Benjamins.

van Dijk, T.A. (1987). *Communicating racism: Ethnic prejudice in thought and talk.* Newbury Park: Sage.

West, C., & Zimmerman, D.H. (1987). Doing gender. *Gender and Society, 1*, 125-151.

Wood, J.T. (1988). Feminist scholarship in communication: Consensus, diversity, and conversation among researchers. *Women's Studies in Communication, 11*, 22-27.

Yum, J.O. (1988). The impact of Confucianism on interpersonal relationships and communication patterns in East Asia. *Communication Monographs, 55*, 374-390.

Zavella, P. (1989). The problematic relationship of feminism and Chicana Studies. *Women's Studies, , 25-36.*

Author Index

Abramson, D. E., 181, *191*
Abyaneh, P., 268, *274*
Acker, J.,144, 146, *159*
Acock, A., 21, *47*
Adams, E., 178, *191*
Adler, D., 182, *191*
Adler, L., 178, *191*
Aitken, C., 233, *246*
Albrecht, T. L., 134, 139, *159*
Alcoff, L., 177, *191*
Alderton, S. M., 73, *82*
Alexander, A., 243, *244*
Althusser, L., 182, *191*
Altman, I., 21, 25, *46*
Altman, K. E., 265, *274*
Anderson, J. A., 143, *159*
Andrews, J. A., 211, *226*
Anzaldua, G., 260, 261, *274*
Argyle, M., 21, *46*
Aries, E. J., 63, *82*
Aristotle, 170, *191*, 206, *226*
Arneson, P., 95, *122*
Arnold, S., 177, *191*
Asante, M. K., 252-253, 256-257, *274, 274*
Asch, S., 53, *82*
Asuncion-Lande, A., 253, *278*
Austin, G., 181, *191*
Awkword, M., 177, *191*
Bacon, W. A., 89, 92, 110, *117*
Baehr, H., 239-240, 242, *244*
Baird, Jr., J. E., 60, 70, *82*
Balsamo, A., 125, 146, *159*

Bamber, L., 178, *191*
Bank, R. K., 178, *191*
Bantz, C. R., 139, *159*
Bapst, G., 174, *192*
Bardsley, B., 182, *192*
Barker-Nunn, J., 264, *274*
Barranger, M. S., 180, *201*
Barrett, M., 181, *192*
Bassnett, S., 177, *192*, 251, 258, *275*
Bate, B., 8, *16*, 30, 31, 36, 37, 43, *46*, 74, 82, 147, *160*
Baxter, L., 25, *46*
Baxter, M., 178, *192*
Beasley, M., 236-237, *244*
Becker, S. L., 177, *192*
Belenky, M., 23, 35, 36, 42, *46*, 60, 61, 66, 67, 71, *82*, 129, 136, *160*
Belford, B., 236, *244*
Benet, J., 232, 235, *248*
Benmussa, S., 184, *192*
Benson, T. W., 9, *16*, 211, *226*
Berger, C., 25, *46*
Berger, P. L., 135, 138, 158, *160*
Bernal, M., 188, *192*
Bernard, J., 23, *46*
Betsko, K., 181, *192*
Bitzer, L. F., 208, *226*
Black, E., 212-214, *226*
Blake, C. A., 256, *274*
Bleier, R., 30, 40, *46*, 217, *226*, 244, *245*
Blood, M. R., 135, *164*

Blunt, J., 174, *192*
Bochner, A., 19, 20, 21, *46*
Boesing, M., 181, *192*
Bonelli, L., 232-233, *245*
Booth-Butterfield, M., 74, *82*
Booth-Butterfield, S., 74, *82*
Borden, G. A., 252, *275*
Bormann, E. G., 65, 66, 67, *82*, 139, 140, 158, 160, 212, *226*
Bovenschen, S., 181, *192*
Bowman, M., 107, *117*
Brabent, S., 232-233, *245*
Bradley,. P. H., 70, *83*
Brecht, B., 172, 182, *192*
Brehm, S., 21, *46*
Brislin, R. W., 256, *275*
Brock, B. L., 218, *226*
Bretton, G. E., 126, *165*
Brockett, O. G., 167, 174, 189, *192*
Broome, B. J., 257, 274, *275*
Brown, B., 135, *164*
Brown, J., 180, *192*
Brown, M. E., 240, *245*
Brown, V., 233, *245*
Brusberg, M. A., 147, 159, *160*
Bryony, L., 181, *192*
Buerkel-Rothfuss, N. 234, *245*
Bulbeck, G., 176, 177, 190, *192*
Burke, K. B., 211, 216, *226*
Butler, J., 106, 107, 109, 112, 113, *117*
Butler, M., 237, *245*
Butruille, S, G., 233, *245*
Byron, G.N.G., Lord, 170, *192*
Calabrese, R., 25, *46*
Calas, M. B., 140, 145, 146, 152, 158, *160, 165*
Camden, C.T., 71, *84*
Cameron, K. M., 174, 187, 189, *196*
Campbell, K. K., 40, *46*, 175, 177, *192*, 210-211, 214, 218,. 223, *226, 228*, 265, *275*

Capo, K. E., 88, 99, 101, 102, 107, *117*
Cannon, L.W., 258-259, 269, *275*
Carbaugh, D., 256, *275*
Carlin, P.S., 90, *117*
Carlson, A.C., 216, *227*
Carlson, M.A., 171, *193*
Carlson, S., 180, 184-185, *193*
Carroll, N., 182, 186, *193*
Carter, K., 8, *16, 18,* 38, 39, *48,* 88, 91, 106, 111, 113, *117, 118, 122,*. 220, *229*
Case, S. E., 89, 98, 105, 116, *118,* 168, 178-179, 181-183, 184, 186-187, *193*
Casmir, F. L., 254, *275*
Chambers, E. K., 174, *193*
Chambers, I., 240, *245*
Chandler, T., 140, *161*
Chen, V., 266, *275*
Cheney, G., 134, 139, *164, 165*
Chesebro, J. W., 218, *226*
Chodorow, N., 264, *275*
Choi, H.G., 177, *192*
Chinoy, H. K., 169, 178, 180, 182, *193*
Christian, B., 186, *193*, 270, *275*
Cirksena, K., 29, 30, *46*
Clark, B. H., 171, *193*
Clark, M. S., 22, *46*
Clark, R. L., 233, *245*
Clark, V. A., 187, 191, *194*
Clevenger, T., 177, *195*
Clinchy, B. Mcv., 23, *46*, 60, *82,* 83, 129, 136, *160*
Cline, R., 21, *46*
Coch, L., 54, 81, *83*
Cogdell, R. T., 256, *278*
Cohn, F., 69, *84*
Colson, T., 94, *118*
Colvin, G., 180, *194*
Condit, C. M., 40, *46,* 212, 241, 218, *227,* 242, *245*

Conquergood, D., 91, 105, 107, 108, 111, 112, *118*
Conrad, C., 143, 144, 145, 147, *160, 166*
Cook, S. L., 237, *247*
Cooley, E. H., 169, *194*
Cooper, P. J., 12, *18*, 43, *49*
Coote, A., 62, *83*
Cornillon, S. K., 177, *194*
Corrigan, P., 240, 244, *245*
Cotton, N., 168, 172, 179, 181, 189, *194*
Couch, C. J., 55, *83*
Courtney, A. E., 231-232, *245*
Coven, B., 181, *194*
Cowley, A., 172, *194*
Coyle, J., 19, *46*
Craft, C., 236, *245*
Cragan, J. F., 58, 70, *83*
Crane, G., 178, *194*
Cronen, V. E., 7, *17*, 135, 158, *163*
Culler, J., 102, *118*
Culley, M., 91, *119*
Dailey, S. J., 99, *118*
Daly, M., 250, 274, *275*
Daniels, A. K., 232, 235, *248*
Darley, J. G., 54, 55, 81, *83*
Dash, I. G., 178, *194*
Davidson, C., 168, 179, *194*
Davis, G. R., 264, *275*
Davis, L. M., 134, *164*
Davis, T., 180, 187, *194*
Davy, K., 178, 182, 184, *194*
Dawson, W. M., 178, *194*
Day, R. A., 180, *194*
de Beauvoir, S., 106, *118*
DeLauretis, T., 110, *118*, 179, *194*
Deetz, S. A., 143, 144, *160*, 252, *275*
Densmore, D., 237, *245*
Dennis, H. S., 134, 137, *160*
Denzin, N. K., 131, *160*
Derrida, J., 182, *194*

Dervin, B., 8, *16*, 219, *227*
Deshazer, M. K., 184, *194*
Diamond, E., 182-183, *195*
Diamond, I., 23, *46*
Diez, M. E., 134, *160*
Dindia, K., 71, *83*
Dodd, C. H., 252, 256, *275*
Dolan, J., 105, 107, 109, 117, *118*, 178-179, 181-186, *195*
Donohue, W. A., 134, *160*
Donovan, J., 89, *118*
Dominick, J. R., 234, *248*
Downing, M., 232, *245*
Downs, A. C., 233, *245*
Drewal, M. T., 108, *118*
Duck, S., 19, *46*
Duelli-Klein, R., 88, *118*
Dukore, B. F., 170-171, 189, *195*
Duncan, H. D., 138, *160*
Dunlap, W., 174, *195*
Dusinberre, J., 178, *195*
Dyer, G., 240, *244*
Eagleton, T., 97, *118*
Eakins, B., 71, *83*
Eakins, R. G., 71, *83*
Ecker, G., 186, *195*
Eco, U., 182, *195*
Edelsky, C., 70, 71-73, *83*
Edwards, J., 21, *47*
Ehrlich, C., 263, *275*
Eisenberg, E. M., 138, 140, 141, *161, 163, 165*
Eisenstein, H., 132, *161*
Elam, K., 171, *195*
Ellman, M., 180, *195*
Emmert, P., 177, *195*
Entin, E., 71, *85*
Eron, L. D., 69, *85*
Ephelia, 172, *195*
Eskilson, A., 73, *83*
Ettema, J., 243, *248*
Fairhurst, G. T., 136, 137, 138, 140, 145, 146, 153, 158, 159,

161, 164, 165
Falcione, R. L., 134, *161*
Farace, R. V., 138, *163*
Farberman, H. A., 138, *165*
Farnham, C., 6, *16*, 44, *47*
Faules, D., 139, *161*
Favreau, O. E., 59, *83*
Fehlner, C. L., 232, *247*
Felski, R., 186, *195*
Feral, J., 181-182, *195*
Ferguson, K. E., 146, *161*
Ferguson, S. D., 133, *161*
Ferguson, S., 133, *161*
Fine, E. C., 91, *118*
Fine, M. G., 40, *47*, 129, 132, 136,
    141, 145, 147, 149, 154, 158,
    161, 250, *276*
Finke, L. A., 178, *195*
Fisher, B. A., 57, 73, *83*
Fisher, J. Y., 211, *228*
Fisher, W. R., 212, *227*
Fitzpatrick, M. A., 19, *46*
Flynn, E. A., 102, 116, *118*
Forte, J., 182-183, 191, *193, 195*
Foss, K. A., 7, 8, *16, 17*, 32, 44, 45,
    47, 73, 80, *83*, 136, 141, 145,
    147, *161*, 215, 220, 223, *227*,
    250, *275*
Foss, S.K., 7, 8, *16, 17*, 32, 44, 45,
    47, 73, 80, 83, 136, *161*, 210,
    212, 215, 218, *227*, 250, *275*
Fowlkes, D. L., 251, *276*
Franzwa, H. H., 232, *245*
Freedman, B., 177, *195*
French, M., 35, *47*
French, Jr., J. R. P., 54, 81, *83*
Frentz, T. S., 212, *227*
Freud, S., 172, *196*
Friedley, S. A., 8, 12, 17, *18*, 43, *49*
Frith, S., 240, 244, *245*
Frye, N., 172, *196*
Frye, P. A., 257, 274, *276*
Fulkerson, R. P., 210, *227*

Fuoss, K., 108, 109, *118*
Garber, J., 240, *247*
Gardiner, J. K., 179, *196*
Garnham, N., 242, *245*
Gayle, A., 171, *196*
Gaymon, D. L., 147, *163*
Gearheart, S. M., 206, 215, *227*
Geiger, D., 92, 98, *119*
Geis, F. L., 233, *245*
Gelfman, J. S., 236, *246*
Gerbner, G., 234, *246*
Gershenfeld, M. K., 57, *85*
Gibbons, S., 236-237, *244*
Giddens, A., 62, *83-84*
Gilbert, S. M., 96, *119*
Gilder, R., 168, *196*
Gildon, C., 173, *196*
Gill, T., 62, *83*
Gillespie, P. P., 167, 174, 179-182,
    187, 189, *196*
Gilligan, C., 7, *17*, 26, 34, 37, 42,
    47, 60, 62, 67, *84*, 130, 136, 141,
    161, 264, *276*
Goff, D. H., 232, *246*
Goff, L. D., 232, *246*
Goldberger, N., 23, *46*, 60, 82,
    129, 136, *160*
Goldhaber, G. M., 134, *160*
Gonzalez, A., 256-257, 274, *276*
Gonzalez, Y. B., 177, *196*
Goodall, Jr., H. L., 7, *17*
Gordon, J., 69, *84*
Gordon, L., 104, *119*, 132, *161*,
    174, *196*
Gottlieb, L. G., 181, *196*
Gottner-Abendroth, H., 181, *196*
Gouran, D. S., 52, 53, 55, 58, 70,
    84
Gray, P. H., 90, *119*
Greeley, L., 101, *119*, 178, 181,
    185, *196*
Green, C. H., 238, *247*
Greenberg, B. S., 233, *246*

Greenberger, D., 21, *49*
Greene, L. R., 73, *84*
Gross, L., 234, *246*
Grossberg, L., 219, *227*, 240, *246*
Gudas, F., 98, 116, *119*
Gudykunst, W. B., 134, *165*, 252, 276
Guerra, J., 184, *196*
Guetzkow, H., 53, 81, *84*, 126, 162
Gussow, M., 178, *196*
Gutwirth, M., 178, *196*
Hall, D., 34, 36, 37, *47*, 264, *276*
Hall, R. M., 56, 66, *84*
Hall, L., 177, *196*
Hamera, J., 108, 109, 111, *119*
Hampsten, E., 173, 180, *197*
Hancock, B. R., 177, *197*
Hantzis, D. M., 88, 108, 109, 113, *117, 118, 119*
Haraway, D., 38, *47*
Harding, S., 9, *17*, 27, 30, 33, *47*, 125, 128, 130, 132, 158, *162*
Harding, W., 217, *227*
Hariman, R., 209, *227*
Harre, R., 135, 138, 158, *162*
Harris, D. H., 53, 81, *84*
Harrison, S. K., 233, *245*
Hart, L., 105, 117, *119*, 179, 184, 186, *197*
Hart, R. P., 218, *227*
Hartsock, N., 23, *46*
Haskell, D., 232, *246*
Haskell, M., 177, *197*
Haslett, B., 144, *162*
Hatch, J. V., 188, *197*
Hatfield, E., 21, *49*
Hatfield, J. D., 134, 137, *162*
Hauser, G. A., 213, *227*
Hawkesworth, M. E., 177, 181, 183, 186, *197*
Hawkins, B., 134, *163*
Hawkins, R., 234, *246*

Hebdige, D., 240, *246*
Hegel, G. W. F., 171, *197*
Heilbrun, C. G., 63, 79, *84*
Helms, L., 178, *197*
Henderson, L., 233, *246*
Henderson, M., 21, *46*
Hennigan, S., 169, *197*
Hepworth, J. C., 254, *276*
Herrmann, C., 262-263, *276*
Hewes, D., 19, 20, *47*
Higginbotham, E., 258-259, 269, 275
Hill, F. I., 210, *227*
Hill, R. T., 108, 109, *118, 119*
Hirokawa, R. Y., 58, 61, 68, *84*
Hirsch, M., 7, *17*
Hirsch, P. M., 139, 141, *162*, 234, 246
Hobson, D., 240, *246*
Hochschild, A., 243, *246*
Hoffman, L., 91, *119*
Hollihan, T. A., 208, 222, *228*
hooks, B., 113, 117, *119*, 177, *197*, 259, 263, 267, *276*
HopKins, M. F., 88, 106, 111, *119*, 122
Horowitz, M. C., 170, 189, *197*
Howard, R. D 134, *166*
Hozeski, B., 168, 179, *197*
Huesmann, L. R., 69, *85*
Hughes, H., 184, *193*
Hughes, M., 234, *146*
Humm, M., 176, 190, *197*
Huseman, R. C., 134, 137, *162*
Husband, R. L., 134, *162*
Hutcheon, L., 109, *119*
Hyden, C., 232, *246*
Irigaray, L., 109, *120*
Isbell, T., 99, *120*
Ivie, R., 212, *227*
Jablonski, C. J., 213, *228*
Jablin, F. M., 133, 134, 139, 142, 162

Jacklin, C. N., 71, *85*
Jackson, J., 267, *276*
Jackson-Beeck, M., 234, *246*
Jacobson, S. W., 132, 146, 158, *162*
Jacques, R., 132, 146, 158, *162*
Jaddou, L., 235, *246*
Jaffe, J., 71, *85*
Jagger, A. M., 13, *17*, 215, *228*
Jameson, F., 186, *197*
Jamieson, K. H., 206, 219, *228*
Janus, N. Z.,235, 240, *246*
Japp, P. M., 211, *228*
Jaquette, J., 23, *47*
Jardine, L., 178, *197*
Jefferson, P., 211, *228*
Jeffries- Fox, S., 234, *246*
Jelinek, M., 139, 141, *162*
Jenefsky, C., 211, 222, *228*
Jenkins, L. W., 56, 59, 63, 64, 67, 74, 75, 81-82, *84*, 169, 178, 180, 182, *193, 197*
Jenkins, M. M., 68, 69, 70, *86*, 91, *120*
Jenkins, S., 208, 218, *230*
Jennings, J., 233, *245*
Johnson, C. D., 169, 180, *197-198*
Johnson, F. L., 7, 15, *17*, 136, 141, 145, 147, 149, 154, *161, 162*, 258-259, *276*
Jonasdottir, A., 38, *47*
Jones, A. R., 112, *120*
Jones, D. J., 60, 66, *84*
Jones, K., 38, *47*
Jones, T. S., 134, *164*
Jurma, W. E., 73, *82*
Kalcik, S., 60, 66, 67, 75, *84*
Kanter, R. M., 79, *84*, 126, 135, 137, 150, 157, *162*
Kaplan, E. A., 134, *161*
Katovich, M. S., 55, *83*
Katriel, T., 255-256, *276*
Kauffeld, F. J., 210, *228*

Kauffman, L., 186, *198*
Keller, E. F., 7, *17*, 27, 30, 33, *47*, 130, *162*
Kelly, H., 269-270, *276*
Kelly-Gadol, J., 7, *17*
Kendall, K. E., 211, *228*
Kennard, J. E., 100, *120*
Kennedy, C. W., 71, *84*
Kersten, A., 143, *160*
Keyssar, H., 182, *198*
Kidd, V., 213, *228*
Kim, Y. Y., 252-253, 274, *276*
Klein, E. S., 178, *198*
Klein, K. G., 178, *198*
Kleinau, M., 99, 108, *120*
Klumpp, J. F., 208, 222, *228*
Knapp, M., 21, 25, 27, 28, *47*
Kochman, T., 256, *277*
Koenig, R., 181,.*192*
Koester, J., 147, *162*
Kohlberg, L., 60, *85*
Kolb, D. S., 178, *198*
Kolodny, A., 181, 186, *198*
Kraemer, H. C.,71, *85*
Kramarae, C., 79, *85*, 258, 269, 273, *277*
Kramer, C., 56, 59, 63, 64, 67, 74, 75, 81-82, *84*
Krone, K. J., 139, 142, *162*
Kuhn, T. S., 3, *17*
Kulka, R. A., 11, *17*
Kuseki, B. K., 214, 216, *228*
Lacan, J., 172, 182, *198*
Lamb, M., 173, *198*
Langdell, C. D., 179, *198*
Langellier, K. M., 34, 36, 37, *47*, 88, 91, 92, 94, 95, 102, 113, *120*, 264, *276*
Langer, S., 171, *198*
Lather, P., 266, *277*
Latta, C. J. D., 173, *198*
Lauter, P., 183, *198*
League of Professional Theatre

Women/New York, 176-177, *198*

Leavitt, D., 180, 182, *198*

Leclercq, L., 174, *198*

Lee, C. I., 90, *120*

Leff, M. C., 210, *228*

Lefkowitz, M., 69, *85*

Lehrer, S. K., 232, *246*

Leibman, N. C., 101, *120*

Lensink, J. N., 264, *277*

Lerner, G., 175, 186, 190, *198, 275*

Leung, M A., 258-259, *269*

Levine, J. M., 53, 68, *85*

Levine, L.,, 78, *198*

Levinger, G., 21, *47*

Linkugel, W. A., 219, *230*

Lipking, L., 167, *198*

Lippard, L., 181, 190, *198*

Littlejohn, S. W., 134, *163*

Locke, A., 19, *46*

Long, B. W., 88, 106, *122*

Lont, C. M., 8, *17*, 147, *163*, 232-233, 240, 243, *246*

Loomis, J. W., 232-233, *248*

Lorde, A., 177, *198*

Luckmann, T., 135, 138, 158, *160*

Lukacs, G., 172, *199*

Lund, M., 21, 22, *47*

Lundberg, P. L., 113, *120*

Lutfiyya, M. N., 147, *161*

MacDonald, J., 180, *199*

Maclay, J. H., 98, *120*

Maclean, M., 113, *120*

Macmillan, J. W., 53, *85*

Madison, S., 101, *120*

Malatesta, C. Z., 135, *164*

Malpede, K., 181, *199*

Mare, L. D., 257, 274, *277*

Marohl, J., 184, *199*

Marcuse, H., 24, *47*

Marre, D., 181, *199*

Marranca, B., 107, 110, *120*

Martin, A., 90, *120*

Martin, J., 11, *17*

Martin, M. A., 211, *228*

Marzolf, M., 236, *246*

Mason, L. C., 169, *199*

Matthews, B., 173, *199*

Maus, K., 182, *199*

Mayes, S., 232, 234, *245, 247*

McCall, G., 19, *46*

McCallister, L., 147, *163*

McCandless, N. J., 232, *246*

McConachie, B. A., 174, *199*

McCroskey, J. C., 134, *164*

McDowell, D. E., 100, *121*, 177, *199*

McDonald, G., 22, *47*

McFarlane, P. T., 63, *86*

McGee, M. C., 205, 209, 211, *228*

McGrath, J. G., 11, *17*, 56, *85*

McGuire, M., 211, *228*

McHughes, J., 108, *120*

McIntosh, P., 8, *17*

McKerrow, R. E., 209, *228*

McLennan, G., 174, *199*

McNeil, J. C., 232, *247*

McPhee, R. D., 62, *85*, 133, *163*

McQuail, D., 239, *247*

McRobbie, A., 240, *247*

Mead, M., 53, 55, 81, *85*

Meese, E. A., 96, 104, *121*

Merrill, L., 95, 113, *121*

Mersand, J., 173, *199*

Messer-Davidow, E., 183, *199*

Michaels, J., 21, *47*

Milberg, S., 22, *46*

Miller, D., 55, *83*

Miller, G., 21, 29, *47-48*

Miller, J., 23, 42, *48*

Miller, K. I., 138, *163*

Miller, N., 186, *199*

Miller, P. C., 90, *121*

Millett, K., 129, *163*

Mills, K., 236, *247*

Miyake, K. L., 270, *277*

Modleski, T., 102, 104, 105, 106,

110, 116, *121*
Mohrmann, G. P., 210, *228*
Mohrmann, R., 176, *199*
Monge, P. R., 126, 138, *163*
Monteith, M., 186, *199*
Mooney, L., 232-233, *245*
Moreland, R. L., 53, 68, *85*
Morgan, F., 180, *199*
Morgan, M., 234, *247*
Morrison, T. L., 73, *84*
Morrow, A. A., 129, 147, 158, *161*
Mraz, D., 178, *199*
Mulvey, L., 181, *199*
Mumby, D. K., 139, 143, 144, 145,
Murphy, J. J., 205, *228*
Murray, G., 172, 174, *199*
Muto, J., 266, *277*
Nachlin, L., 181, 190, *199*
Nadler, L. B., 147, 159, *163*
Nadler, M. K., 147, 159, *163*
Nagler, A. M., 174, *200*
Napier, R., 57, *85*
Natale, M., 71, *85*
Natalle, E. J., 180, 182, *200*
Nathan, G. J., 173, *200*
National Commission on the
   Observance of International
   Women's Year, 169, 176, *200*
National Organization for Women,
   232, *247*
Natoli, J., 179, *200*
Neal, L., 171, *200*
Nelson, M. W., 36, *48,* 74, 75, *85*
Newcomb, H., 234, *247*
Newman, R. P., 211, *228*
Newmark, E., 256, *274*
Nicoll, A. M., 168, *200*
Nielsen, J. M., 3, 6, *17*
Nishido, T., 134, *165*
Nomura, G. M., 264, *277*
Nudd, D. M., 92, 94, 95, 101, *121*
O'Barr, W. M., 79, *85*
O'Brien, S., 178, *200*

O'Connell, L., 21, 22, *48*
O'Donnell-Trujillo, N., 139, 140,
   163
O'Keefe, B., 219, *227*
O'Reilly, C. A., 126, *165*
Oakley, A., 57, 62, *85*
Offen, J., 250-251, 258, 267, *277*
Offen, K., 176-177, 181, 190, *200*
Ogden-Malouf, S., 178, *182*
Olauson, J., 180, *200*
Olson, L. C., 211, *228*
Oravec, C., 211, 222, *229*
Orgel, S., 178, *200*
Osborne, M., 212, *229*
Owens, C., 103, 109, *121*
Pacanowsky, M. E., 127, 139, 140,
   142, *163, 164*
Pace, P., 109, *121*
Page, H. E., 53, *85*
Paisley, W., 237, *245*
Papandreou, M., 268, *277*
Park-Fuller, L. M., 90, 111, *121*
Parker, R., 173, 181, 187, 190-191,
   200
Parrott, S. F., 180, *200*
Passaro, J., 270, *277*
Patton J. H., 210, *229*
Payne, D., 222, *229*
Pearce, W. B., 7, *17,* 135, 158, *163*
Pearson, J. C., 12, *17,* 43, 48, 69,
   70, *85*
Peirce, C. S., 182, *200*
Pelias, R. J., 88, 103, 105, *121*
Penley, L. E., 134, *163*
Petchesky, R., 23, *48*
Peterson, E. E., 91, 95, 108, *120,
   121*
Pharr, S., 95, *121*
Phelan, P., 182, *200*
Philipsen, G., 255-256, *276-277*
Phillips, G. M., 9, *18,* 25, 27, *48*
Pilotta, J. J., 252, *277*
Pingree, S., 234, *246*

Planalp, S., 19, *47*
Plato, 170, *200*
Pollock, D. 107, *122*
Pollock, G., 173, 181, 187, 190-191, *200*
Polyani, M., 132, 158, *163*
Poole, M. S., 62, 63, 64, 68, *85*
Popovich, P., 135, *163*
Porter, L. W., 126, 133, *162, 165*
Porter, N., 233, *245*
Porter, R. E., 252, 256, *278*
Postlewait, T., 174, *200*
Powell, M. G., 22, *46*
Pratt, J., 66, *82*, 140, *160*, 273, *277*
Pratt, M. B., 273
Presnell, M., 59, 60, 66, 79, *85*
Pribram, E. D., 179, *200*
Putnam, L. L., 66, *82*, 127, 133, 134, 136, 139, 140, 142, 145-146, 151, 153, 159, *160, 162, 163, 164*
Quaglieri, P. L., 129, 147, 158, *161*
Quellette, R., 22, *46*
Radway, J. A., 240, *247*
Railsback, C. C., 213, *229*
Rakow, L., 40, *48*, 105, 106, *122*, 240, *247*, 262, 266, 278
Rawlins, W., 19, 20, *48*
Rea, C., 182, *200*
Redding, W. C., 126, 134, *164*
Reeves, B., 243, *248*
Reilly, R. R., 135, *164*
Reinelt, J., 108, 113, *122*, 182, *200*
Reinhardt, N., 182, *200*
Remland, M. S., 134, *164*
Rhodes, J., 243, *247*
Rice-Sayre, L., 103, *122*
Rich, A., 104, *122*, 181, *201*
Richards, S. L., 178, *201*
Richetto, G. M., 134, *164*
Richmond, V. P., 134, *164*
Roach, S., 60, 66, 75, *86*
Roberts, K. H., 126, 133, *162, 165*

Roberts, V. M., 180, *201*
Robinson, A. M., 180, *201*
Robortellus, F., 170, *201*
Roloff, M., 19, 21, *47, 48*
Ropp, V. A., 139, *159*
Rose, H., 30, *48*
Rosenberg, J., 181, 190, *201*
Rosenfeld, L. B., 57, *86*
Ross, I., 236, *247*
Rossi, A. M., 147, 159, *165*
Rothenberg, P., 96, *122*
Rothschild, N., 234, *247*
Rubin, L., 27, 37, *48*
Rushing, J. H., 211, *229*
Ryan, H. R., 210, *229*
Ryan, M. S., 143, 144, 147, 149, 154, *160, 165*
Sacks, O., 1, *18*
Samovar, J. A., 252, 256, *277-278*
Sanders, M., 236, *247*
Sandler, B. R., 56, 66, *84*
Sanford, F. H., 53, 81, *86*
Sarbaugh, L. E., 253, *278*
Saucier, K. A., 233, *247*
Savona, J. L., 176, 190, *201*
Scarf, M., 28, *48*
Schaef, A., 23, 27, *48*
Schaffer, P. W., 178, *201*
Schall, M. S., 141, *165*
Schilpp, M. G., 236, *247*
Schneider, R., 184, *201*
Schuler, C., 185, *201*
Schultz, M., 79, *85*
Schweickart, P. P., 100, 102, 103, 116, *118, 122*
Schwichtenberg, C., 213, *229*
Scott, R. L., 208, 218, 226, *229*
Screen Actors Guild, 232, *247*
Seccombe-Eastland, L., 147, *165*
Secord, P. F., 135, 138, 158, *162*
Segal, S., 182, *201*
Seggar, J. F., 232, *247*
Seibold, D. R., 19, *47*, 62, *85*

Seiler, W. J., 134, *165*
Self, L. S., 147, *160*
Selzer, J. A., 177, *192*
Shafer, Y., 178, *201*
Shields, R. E., 94, 95, *122*
Shimanoff, S. B., 68, 69, 70, *86*
Shockley-Zalabak, P., 147, *165*
Showalter, E., 96, 100, 102, 103, *122*, 180-181, 190, *201*
Shuter, R., 253, 274, *278*
Sicherman, B., 238, *247*
Signorelli, P. N., 174, *201*, 234, *246*
Singer, M. R., 252, *278*
Singleton, L. A., 237, *247*
Siteram, K. S., 256, *278*
Sklar, R., 182, *201*
Sloan, T. O., 92, 98, *120, 122*
Smircich, L., 139, 141, 145, 146, 152, 158, *160, 162, 165*
Smith, B., 100, 177, *122, 201*
Smith, B. H., 97, *122*
Smith, D. K., 208, *229*
Smith, M. C., 240, *248*
Smith, M. Y., 236, *247*
Smith, R. C., 140, 141, *165*
Smith, R. E., 94, *122*
Snavely, B. K., 137, 161, *165*
Snoek, J., 21, *47*
Solomon, A., 184, *201*
Solomon, M., 211-212, 217, *229*
Spallone, P., 217, *229*
Sparks, G. G., 232, *247*
Speakman, D., 186, *201*
Speer, J. H., 91, *118, 122*
Spencer, J. S., 181, 201
Spender, D., 23, 35, *48*, 62, *86*, 260-261, *278*
Spitzack, C., 8, *16, 18*, 34, 37, 38, *39, 48*, 88, 91, 106, *118, 122*, 215, 220, *229*
Stacy, J., 266, *278*
Stanback, M. H., 39, *48*, 254, 269, *278*

Staley, C., 147, *165*
Starosta, W. J., 252, *278*
Steeves, H. L., 10, 11, 12, *18*, 217, 220, *229*, 240-241, *248*, 266, *278*
Steinberg, M., 21, *48*
Stephens, J. A., 178, *201*
Stephens, J. L., 178, 182, *202*
Stewart, L. P., 12, *18*, 43, *49*, 134, 137, *165*
Stoll, C. S., 63, *86*
Stone, G, P., 138, *165*
Streicher, H. W., 232, *248*
Strine, M. S., 88, 89, 101, 106, 107, 113, *122, 123*
Stucky, N., 91, *122*
Sullivan, E. B., 101, *123*
Sutherland, C., 180, *202*
Swanson, G., 53, *86*
Taft-Kaufman, J., 88, 98, 99, 116, *123*
Tarule, J., 23, *46*, 60, *82*, 129, 136, *160*
Taylor, A., 8, *16*, 74, *82*, 147, *165*, 233, 243, *245, 248*
Taylor, D., 21, 25, *46*
Taylor, J., 101, *123*
Tedesco, N. S., 232, *248*
Tener, R. L., 178, *202*
Theye, L. D., 134, *165*
Ting-Toomey, S., 134, *165*, 252, 254, *278*
Tischler, N. C., 73, *84*
Todd, S., 181, *192*
Todd-Mancilles, W. R., 147, 159, *165*
Tompkins, J. P., 99, 100, *123*
Tompkins, P. K., 133, 139, 163, *165*
Tonn, J., 153, *165*
Traupmann, J., 21, *49*
Trinh, T. M., 110, 112, *123*
Trotter, C., 172, *202*

Tsuda, Y., 253, 257, *278*
Tuchman, G., 232, 235, *248*
Turner, S. H. R., 178, *202*
Turow, J., 232, *248*
U.S. Commission on Civil Rights, 232-233, 237, *248*
Utne, M., 21, *49*
Valentine, K. B., 232, *247*
Vanderford, M. L., 213, *230*
van Dijk, T. A., 255, 274, *278*
Van Oosting, J., 88, 103, 105, *121*
Venables, C., 177, 190, *202*
Vince, R. W., 174, 190, *202*
Vincinus, M., 180, *202*
Von Hallberg, R., 183, *202*
Vora, F., 253, *274*
Vunovich, N., 178, *202*
Walder, W. O., 69, *85*
Wander, P., 208-209, 212, 218, *230*
Wandor, M., 177, 190, *202*
Wanous, J. P., 135, *163, 166*
Ware, B. L., 219, *230*
Waring, M., 54, 62, 81, *86*
Warren, C., 33, *49*
Warren, C. A. B., 79, *86*
Wartella, E., 220, *227*, 243, *248*
Watson, K., 134, *166*
Weedon, C., 89, 91, *123*
Weidhorn, M., 210, *230*
Weigel, R. H., 232-233, *248*
Weigel, S., 181, *202*
West, C., 71, *86*, 260, 267, *278*
Wheeless, L. R., 134, *166*
Wheeless, V. E., 134, *166*
Whipple, T. W., 231-232, *245*

White, L. L., 138, *163*
Whyte, W., 79, *86*
Wieder-Hatfield, D., 74, *86*
Wiley, C., 178, *202*
Wiley, M. G., 73, 83, 178, *202*
Wilkerson, M. G., 184, *202*
Williams, J., 235, *246*
Williams, R., 239, *248*
Williams, S. J., 70, 71, *86*
Willis, F. N., 70, 71, *86*
Willis, P., 240, *248*
Willis, S., 181, *203*
Wimmer, R. D., 234, *248*
Women's Institute for Freedom of the Press, 237-238, *248*
Wood, J. T., 9, 12, *18*, 23, 25, 27, 29, 34, 40, 42, *48, 49*, 79, *86*, 143, 145, 147, *166*, 266, *278*
Woolf, V., 169, *203*
Wyatt, N., 63, 67, 74, *86*, 136, 147, *166*
Wright, D. W., 58, 70, *83*
Yarbro-Bejarno, Y., 177, *203*
Yates, M. P., 134, *160*
Yocum, M. R., 60, 75, *86*
Young, K., 174, *203*
Yum, O., 257, *278*
Zahler, W. P., 178, *203*
Zander, A., 53, *86*
Zarefsky, D., 211, *230*
Zavella, P., 270, *278*
Zeig, S., 182, *203*
Zimmerman, B., 100, *123*
Zimmerman, D. H., 71, *86*, 260, 267, *278*
Zivanovic, J., 182, *203*

Subject Index

Abusive Relationships , 35,41
  See also Relationships, abusive
Academy of Management Journal, 133
Academy of Management Review, 133
Access, 146
Action for Women in Theatre, 176
Activist, 2, 3, 15, 154
Actresses
  See also Female Artists
Ad hoc groups, 58
  See also Groups, Ad hoc
Administrative Science Quarterly, 133, 139, 141
Aesthetic, 88
Aesthetic, Black, 171, 188
Affirmative action, 153, 156
Age, 26, 104
Androcentrism, 10, 31, 34, 42, 45, 53-54, 90, 92, 94-96, 100, 102-103, 136, 140-141, 145, 167, 172, 205, 243, 260-261
Androgyny, 221
Applied research, 133
Audience, 102, 110, 171, 209, 210, 217, 220
Autobiography, 264
Autonomy, 28
Bass, Charlotte Spears, 238
Behn, Aphra, 169
Bias:
  conservative, 28, 49

male, 66, 78-79, 101-102, 146, 172, 179, 187, 214, 216, 235
managerial, 126, 135, 138
Black aesthetic, 171, 188
  See also Aesthetic, black
Black Athena: The Afro Asian Roots of Classical Civilization, 188
Body, 92-93, 108-110
Bonding, 26-27, 259
Books in Print, 173, 175
Boxed In: Women and Television, 240
Brilliant Bylines, 236
Bourke-White, Margaret, 238
Canon:
  literary, 5, 177, 183
  performance, 5, 90-91, 183
  rhetorical, 5, 214
Case history, 66-67
  See also Research methodology, Case history
Change, 3, 7, 40-45
Characters, female, 167, 177-179, 232-233
Chicanas, 261
Class/Classism, 28, 32, 51, 54, 90, 96, 172, 222, 258, 269
Co-cultures, 258, 260
Collaborative knowing, 35, 69
Collaborative research, 30, 35, 64, 79-80
  See also Research methodology, Collaborative

Colonization, 262-263
Commedia dell arte, 168
Committee for Women of the Dramatists Guild, 176
Communication:
  interpersonal, 14, 19, 42, 59
  organizational, 15-16, 134-135, 139
  task-relevant, 61
Communication Monographs, 133, 139, 223
Communication Style, 59-60, 64, 66, 149, 153
Communication Yearbook, 133, 143
Community, feminist, 8-9, 12, 43
Comparative Drama, 173
Compensatory history, 179-180, 186
Competition, 63, 69, 74
Conference on Gender and Communication Research, 43
Conflict, 69
Connected knowing, 61, 71
Connection, 4, 5, 28, 35
Consciousness raising groups, 57, 63
  See also Group, Consciousness raising
Conservative Bias, 28-29, 44
  See also Bias, Conservative
Content Analysis, 231-236
  See also Research Methodology, Content Analysis
Contexts, social, 54-55
Conversational analysis, 71-72, 106
  See also Research Methodology, Conversational Analysis
Cooperation, 63, 69, 74
The Creative Woman, 176
Critical perspective, 142-145
Critical Studies in Mass Communication, 9

Critical theory, 96
Criticism:
  dramatic, 171-173
  dramatistic, 98-99, 215-216
  Marxist, 100, 171
  new Historical, 100
  reader response, 99-100
  rhetorical, 208, 215
Critique, feminist, 20, 27, 31, 35, 51, 57, 62, 70-71, 88, 104, 183, 213-218, 223
Cross gender performance, 94-96, 178
  See also Performances
Crossroads, 240
The Court of Last Resort: Mental Illness and the Law, 79
Cultivation Analysis, 234
  See also Research Methodology
Cultural:
  criticism, 256-258
  description, 255-256
  diversity, 251
  measurement, 253-255
  studies, 105, 239-242
  See also Research Methodology
Culture:
  monilithic, 251
  oral, 59
Culture and Interpersonal Communication, 254
Daily talk, 36
Decision making, 58-60, 64, 66-67
Decorum, 170
Developmental models, 25, 31
Deviance, 93
Dialectic, 207
Dialogic performance, 111
  See also Performance, Dialogic
Dialogic Theory, 112-113
  See also Theory, Dialogic
Diaries, 264
Discourse:

conversational, 60, 64, 71
propositional, 59, 63, 77
Discursive media, 251
Diversity, 26, 221
Dominance/Domination, 63, 70, 171, 214, 261
Double standard, 93
Drama critics, female, 173-174
Dramatic criticism, 171-173
  See also Criticism, Dramatic
Dramatic criticism, feminist, 184-185
Dramatic Theory, 170-171
  See also Theory, Dramatic
Dramatic Theory, feminist, 180-182, 185-186
Dramatism, 98-99, 215-216
  See also Criticism, Dramatistic
Economic theory, 54
Elderly, 26, 102
Ellman, Mary, 180
Embodiment, 91-94, 104
Empowerment, 35, 79, 88, 101, 132, 138, 250
Epistemology, 35, 130, 217
Ethic of care, 23
Ethic of rights, 24
Ethics, 5, 110
Ethnicity, 95, 104
Ethnocentrism, 10, 15, 140, 250, 257, 258, 268, 273
Ethnography, 106, 111, 255
Event talk, 36
Exchange theory, 21-23, 31
Fantasy theme analysis, 65, 139, 215
Feelings and Form, 171
Female:
  artists, 176
  characters, 167, 177-179, 232-233
  drama critics, 173-174
  playwrights, 168, 169, 172-173

Feminine interests, 22, 31
Feminism, 2-16, 20
  French, 109
  liberal, 11, 12, 13, 220, 235
  Marxist, 12, 13, 241
  progressive, 208, 220
  radical, 11, 12, 13, 15, 16, 220
  Socialist, 11, 12, 13, 214-215
Feminist:
  community, 9, 12, 43
  critique, 20, 27, 31, 35, 51, 57, 62, 70-71, 88, 104, 183, 213-218, 223
  cultural studies, 239, 241
  dramatic criticism, 184-185
  dramatic theory, 180-182, 185-186
  media, 240, 243
  pedagogy, 43
  perspective, 2-16, 125, 128, 131, 132, 250
  research methodology, 35, 154-156
  scholarship, 9, 32-37, 74-75, 96-105, 131, 146-148, 175, 182, 218-221, 258-266
  synalytics, 130-131, 137, 141
  theatre, 181-183
  theory, 125, 182
Feminist and Women Studies Division, SCA, 8
Ferraro, Geraldine, 222
Follett, Mary Parker, 153
Friendship, 27, 41
Functionalist theory, 57, 58-61, 134-138, 151
Funding, research, 53
Gabler, Hedda, 172
Gale, Zona, 169
Gay relationships, 26, 27, 41
Gender, 150-151, 30, 31, 33, 51, 92-96, 98, 107, 129, 136, 260
  parody, 113-114
  performance, 93, 113-114

politics, 92, 93
Gender-focused models, 33, 34, 42, 171
Generic pronouns, 213-214
Glaspell, Susan, 169
Glass-ceiling effect, 224
Great Women of the Press, 236
Group:
  consciousness, 65
  dynamics, 52-56, 68
  maintenance, 57, 61
Groups:
  ad hoc, 58
  consciousness raising, 57, 63
  social, 41
  support, 57
  task, 56
  therapy, 57
  volunteer, 41, 54, 78
  women's, 76-78
  work, 54
Gynandry, 13, 206, 221
Handicapped, 102
Hearth and Home, 232
Hegemony, 24, 158
Heterosexuality, 21, 27, 26, 32, 94, 177
Hierarchy, 25, 26, 30, 59-60, 75, 111-112, 250
Hildegard of Bingen, 168
Historical narrative, 236-239
History:
  compensatory, 179-180, 186, 236-239
  revisement, 179-180, 186
  theatre, 174
Homophobia, 95
Housework, 57, 265
Hrostwith of Gandersheim, 168, 180
Human Communication Research, 68
Identity, 107

Illiteracy, 91, 103
Inclusive scholarship, 38-40
International Communication Association, 8
International and Intercultural Communication Annual, 252
Interpersonal communication theory, 14, 19, 25, 59, 215
Interpretation theory
  See also performance theory
Interpretive perspective, 127, 138-142
Interruptions, 70-73
Intimacy, 22-27
Jane Eyre, 101
Journal of Broadcasting, 232
Journal of Communication, 8, 133, 232
Journal of Communication Inquiry, 76
Journal of Social and Personal Research, 19, 21
Katherine of Sutton, 168
Kernel stories, 66
Knowledge:
  probabilistic, 207
  scientific, 207
  subjective, 4, 130, 137
  women's, 130, 137
Labor:
  productive, 24, 54
  reproductive, 23, 54, 64, 78
Lacan, Jacques, 184
Ladies of the Press, 236
Language, 4, 149-150, 184, 207, 213, 260-262, 270
Language marked categories, 261
Leadership, 63, 66-68, 73, 74, 78-79, 147
League of Professional Theatre Women/New York, 176
Lesbian, 26, 27, 41, 100, 177, 221, 234, 222, 243

Liberal feminism, 11, 12, 220, 235, 241
Liberal humanism, 89, 91-94, 103, 115
Liberation, 30
Literary canon, 183
Literature in Performance, 88, 94, 96, 98-99
Logical Positivism, 29, 134, 135, 174
Lupino, Ida, 238
Male-as-norm
  See also androcentrism
Male bias, 66, 78-79, 101-102, 146, 172, 179, 187, 214, 216, 235
Malestream Scholarship
  See also Traditional Scholarship
Managerial bias126, 135, 138
Marginalization, 44, 88, 93, 105, 115
Marked categories, 261
Marxist criticism, 100, 144, 171, 239
Masculinist bias, 216
  See also male bias
Mein Kampf, 211
Men and Women of the Corporation, 150
Methodological integrity, 131, 137, 142
Mimes, 168
Misogyny, 33, 95
The Mod Donna, 173
Modern Drama, 173
Monolithic culture, 251, 254
Multicultural organizations, 151-154
Mystification, 143
Narrative, 66, 101, 143, 215
National Organization for Women, 232
Neo-Aristotelianism, 210
Neutrality
  See also objectivity

New Criticism, 97-99
New directions in scholarship, 37-45, 75-80, 105-114, 148-156, 182-188, 300 221-225, 266-273
New Historicist criticism, 100
Normal science, 130
Notable Women/The Modern Period, 238
Nuns, 167-168
Nuthead, Dinah, 236
Objectivity, 4, 5, 30, 93, 97, 130, 137, 174, 217, 218
O'Connor, Flannery, 111
Office of Naval Research, 53
Olsen, Tillie, 111
Oppositional categories, 112-113
Oppositional practice, 208, 218, 267
Oppression, 3, 28, 42, 90, 104, 111, 129, 235, 256, 266-267
Oppressive relationships, 41
Oral:
  culture, 59
  discourse
  See also Conversational discourse
  interpretation, 87, 98
  tradition, 91
Oresteia, 172
Organization for Research on Women and Communication (ORWAC), 8
Organization for the Study of Communication, Language and Gender (OSCLG), 8
Organizational:
  communication, 134-135, 139, 146, 215
  culture, 140, 141, 158
Ortega, Katherine Davalos, 222
Otherness, 110, 111
Outcomes, 27, 127
Patriarchy, 92, 93, 106, 111, 129,

132, 141, 144, 183, 223, 239, 243, 250, 268-269
Patterson, Alicia, 238
Pedagogy:
  feminist, 43
  rhetorical, 210
Performance:
  canon, 90-91, 183
  classroom, 89
  cross gender, 94-96
  gender, 93, 113-114, 178
  research, 106-107
  studies, 87, 105-110
  theory, 87-88, 107-110
Performing differences, 89
Perspective, situational or positional, 208-213
Phedre, 187
Phenomenlogy, 106
Playwrights, 168, 169,
  female, 172-173
Pluralism, 9, 10, 103-104, 151
The Poetics, 170
Political Change, 40, 45, 80, 104, 107-108, 132, 154-156, 242, 223, 250-251, 268-270
Pornography, 222
Porter, Katharine Anne
Portrayal of women, 167, 177-179, 183, 231-232
Positional rhetorical criticism, 209, 211-213
Postmodernism, 152
Poststructuralist Theory, 111
Power, 35, 51, 63, 78-79, 102, 111, 136, 138, 144, 158
Privilege, 24, 27, 28, 29, 32, 53, 102, 108, 129, 259
Probabilistic knowledge, 207
Problem solving, 58
Process, 5, 27
Productive labor, 25, 54
Progressive feminism, 208, 220

Project in the Status and Education of Women, 56
Propositional discourse, 59, 63, 77
Public sphere, 5, 25, 206, 214, 222, 265
Public vocabulary, 211- 213
Publication, 8, 44, 106, 146, 188, 223-224
Quarterly Journal of Speech, 8, 68, 133, 223, 224
Queen Elizabeth I, 205
Race/Racism, 26, 29, 32, 39-40, 51, 54, 90, 95, 100, 214, 258
Radical feminism, 11, 12, 15, 16
Rape, 35
Rationality, 90, 218, 253
Reader-response criticism, 99-100
Reading as a woman, 96-105
Reading the Romances, 240
Relational Evolution, 25, 26
Relationships:
  abusive, 35, 41
  autonomy, 28
  caretaking, 23
  connection, 28, 35, 215
  gay, 26, 27, 41
  heterosexual, 21, 26-27, 32
  intimate, 22, 27
  lesbian, 26, 27, 41
  oppressive, 41
  violent, 41
Representation, 108-110, 177-179
Reproductive labor, 23, 54, 64, 78
Reproductive technologies, 222
The Republic, 170
Research funding, 53-54
Research methodology, 5, 10, 28, 29, 30, 217-218
Research methodology:
  case history, 66-67
  collaborative, 30, 64, 79-80
  content analysis, 231-236
  conversational analysis, 71-72

cultivation analysis, 234
cultural description, 255-256
cultural measurement, 253-255
cultural criticism, 256-258
feminist, 34, 35, 266
internal validity, 29
performance, 106-107
qualitative 218
variable-analytic, 29-32, 73
Resistance, 108, 152, 259
Revalorizing communication
research, 34-36
Revisionist history, 179-180, 186
Revolutionary Pragmatism, 132-
133, 137, 138, 142, 145
Rhetoric:
gynandrous, 221
western, 206, 214
Rhetoric of Inquiry, 217
Rhetorical:
analysis, 98
canon, 13, 214, 215
pedagogy, 210
perspective, 206-207
Rhetorical criticism, 13, 208
positional, 209, 211-213
situational, 208-209, 210-211
Rich, Adrienne, 101, 111
Rockwell, Norman, 211
Scholarship: 32-37, 74-75
feminist, 96-105, 131, 146-
148,175-182, 218-221, 258-266
inclusive, 38-40
new directions, 37-45, 75-80,
105-114, 148-156, 182-188,
221-225, 266-273
traditional, 20-32, 58-68, 89-96,
126-128, 133-145, 169-175,
206-218, 251-257
Scholarship Interest Group, ICA, 8
Scientific knowledge, 207
Self/Self Concept, 41, 107
Sexism, 30, 31, 33, 44, 56, 62, 64,

66, 77, 89, 93, 99, 188, 213, 222,
235, 239
Sexual orientation, 26, 27, 41, 100,
177, 221, 222, 234
Showalter, Elaine, 180
Silence, silencing, 35, 88, 102,
129, 212, 256, 260-261
Simultaneous talk
See also Interruptions
Situational Rhetorical Criticism,
208-209, 210-211, 217
Social Exchange Theory, 21, 31,
134
Socialist feminism, 11, 12, 214-215
The Southern Speech Communication
Journal, 9, 257
Speech Communication Association,
8, 43
Stanton, Elizabeth Cady, 211
Stereotypes, 70, 178, 233-234
Storytelling, 34, 66
Structuralist Theory, 61-65
Studies in Symbolic Interaction, 55
Subject relations, 106, 110-112
Subjectivity, 5, 30, 110-111, 130
Subordination, 10, 11, 28, 52, 80,
132, 186, 239, 251
Support groups, 57
Syllabus Sourcebook on Media and
Women, 237
Symbolic annihilation, 235
Symbolic Convergence Theory, 65-
67
Symbolic order, 42
Synalytics, 130-131, 137, 141
Systems perspective, 127
Talk:
daily, 36
event, 36
topics of, 37
women's, 36
Task groups, 54, 56
Task-relevant communication, 61, 57

Text and Performance Quarterly, 88
Theatre history, 167, 174-175, 179-182, 186-188
Theatre Research International, 175
Theatrical theory, 185, 186-188
Theories of the Theatre, 171
Theory:
  developmental models, 25, 31
  dialogic, 112-113
  dramatic, 170-171
  economic, 54
  feminist, 2-16, 125, 182
  functionalist, 57, 58-61
  gender-focused models, 33-34
  interpersonal communication, 19, 25
  logical positivism, 29
  performance, 87-88, 107-110
  post-structuralist, 111
  relationship evolution, 25
  rhetorical, 208
  social exchange, 21, 31, 134
  structuation, 61-65
  symbolic convergence, 65-67
  theatrical, 185, 186-188
Traditional scholarship, 7, 20-32, 58-68, 89-96, 126-128, 133-145, 169-175, 206-218, 251-257
Therapy groups, 57
Tokens, 137-138
Tuskegee Syphilis Project, 217
Universality, 91, 97, 102
Up from the Footnote: A History of Women Journalists, 236
Variable analytic research, 29 - 32, 73, 135-136, 253-255, 266
Victimization, 259
Violence, 41
Voice, 93, 101, 108, 113, 132
Volunteer groups, 41, 54, 78
Waller, Judith Carey, 238

Walters, Barbara, 238
Wells, Ida B., 238
Western Journal of Speech Communication, 139
Western rhetoric, 214
Western society, 32, 34, 259
Window Dressing on the Set: Women and Minorities in Television, 232, 233, 237
Women and Language, 8
Women Communicating: Studies of Women's Talk, 74
Women in American Theatre, 178
Women and Media: A Documentary Source Book, 236, 237
Women in Television News, 236
Women of color, 101, 177, 222, 237, 269
Womens Caucus, SCA, 8, 43
Women, communication of, 36, 68-73, 256, 262
Women's diaries, 264
Women's autobiographies, 264
Women's groups, 76-78
Women's Institute for the Freedom of the Press, 237
Women's knowledge, 3, 129-130, 137
Women's performance, 91
Women's problematics, 128-129, 136, 141, 146-147
The Women's Program of the American Theatre Association, 176
Women's Project of the American Place Theatre, 176
Women's Studies, 263
Women's Studies in Communication, 8, 43, 74, 76, 223
Women's texts, 90-91
Women's voices, 92-93, 130, 144, 147
Women's work, 54, 243